As a Reincarnated ARISTOCRAT, I'll Use My Appraisal Skill to Rise in the World

8

[Story] **Miraijin A**
[Art] **Natsumi Inoue**
[Character Design] **jimmy**

CONTENTS

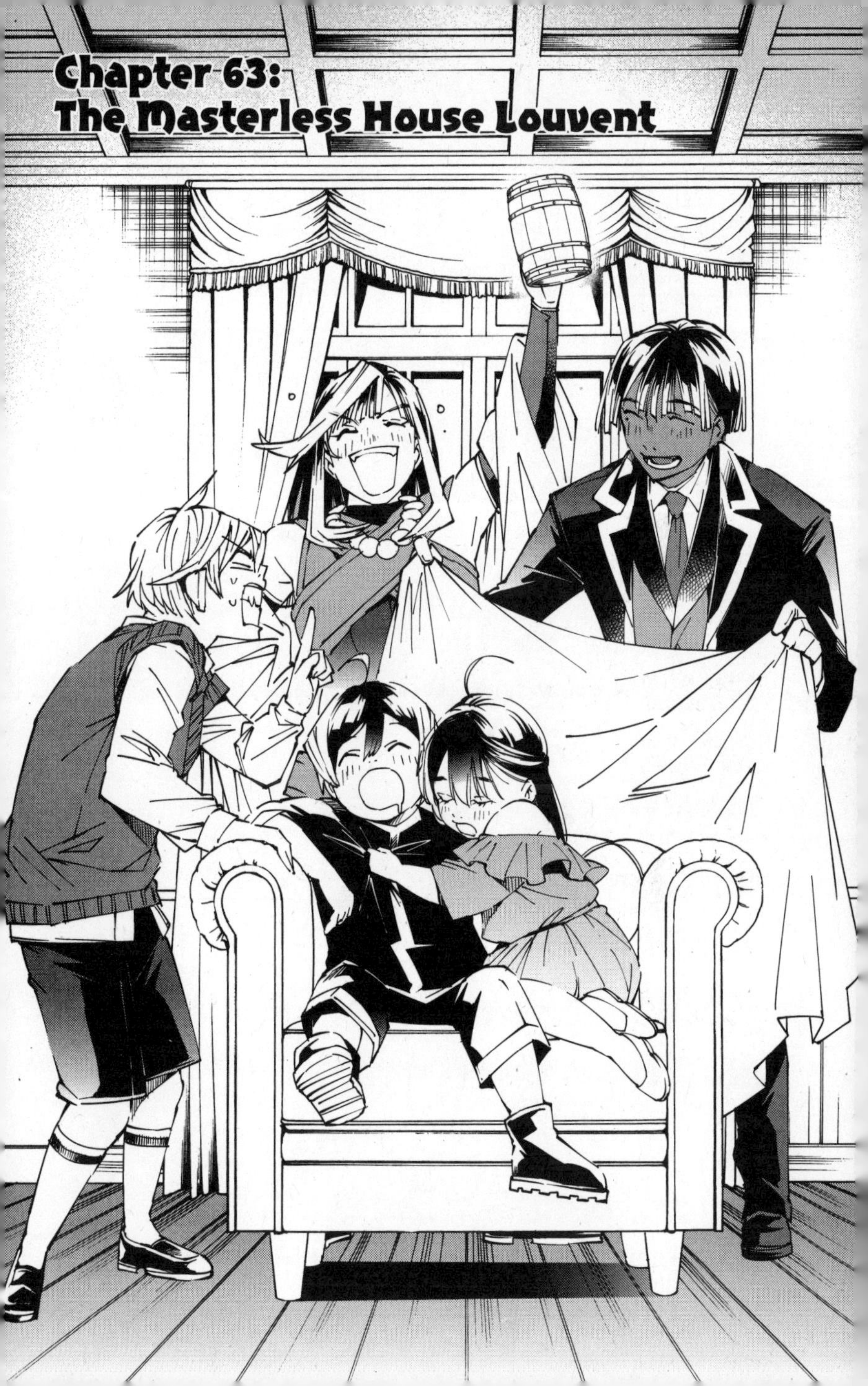
Chapter 63:
The Masterless House Louvent

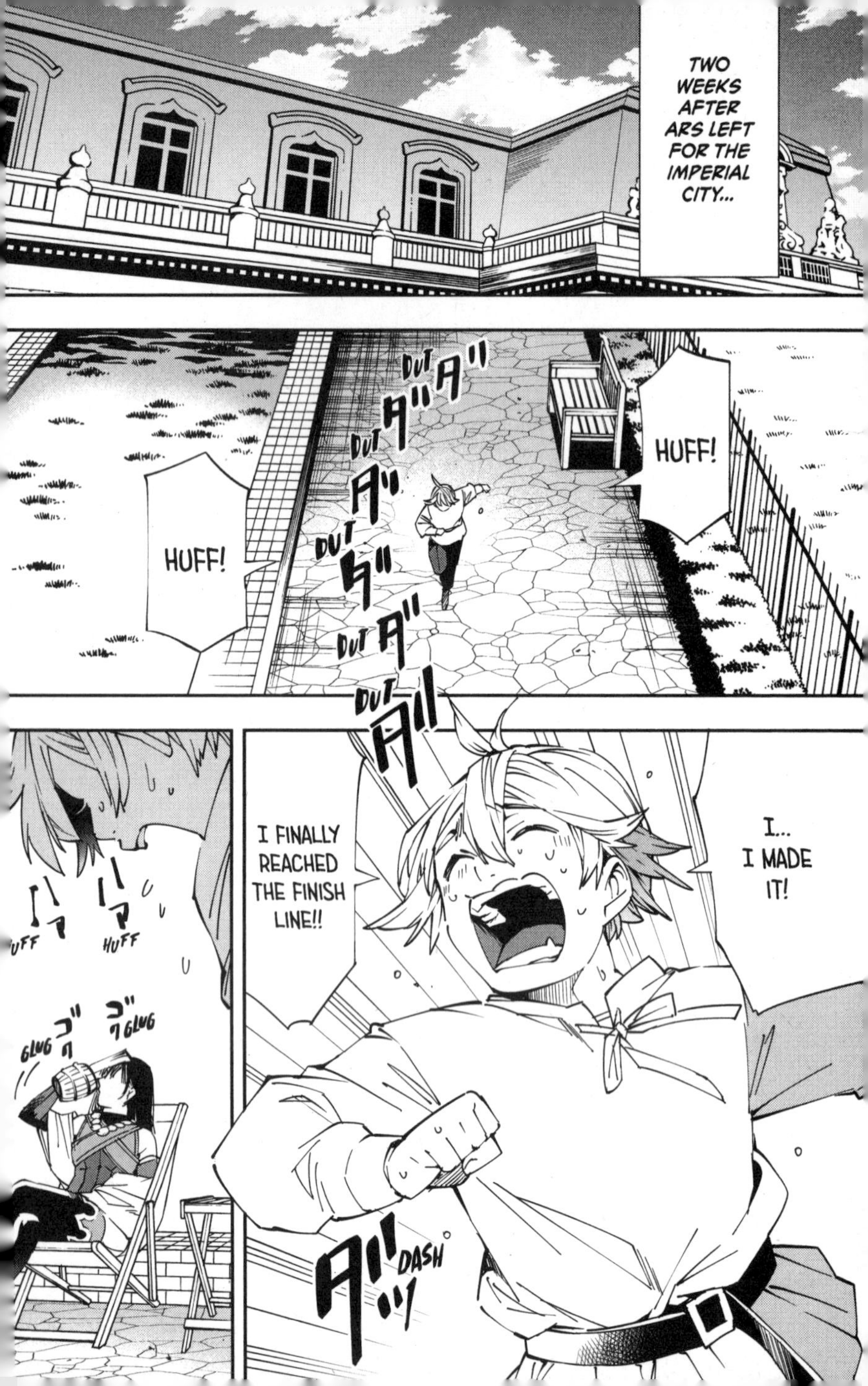
TWO WEEKS AFTER ARS LEFT FOR THE IMPERIAL CITY...
HUFF!
HUFF!
DUT
DUT
DUT
DUT
DUT
I... I MADE IT!
I FINALLY REACHED THE FINISH LINE!!
DASH
HUFF
HUFF
GLUG
GLUG

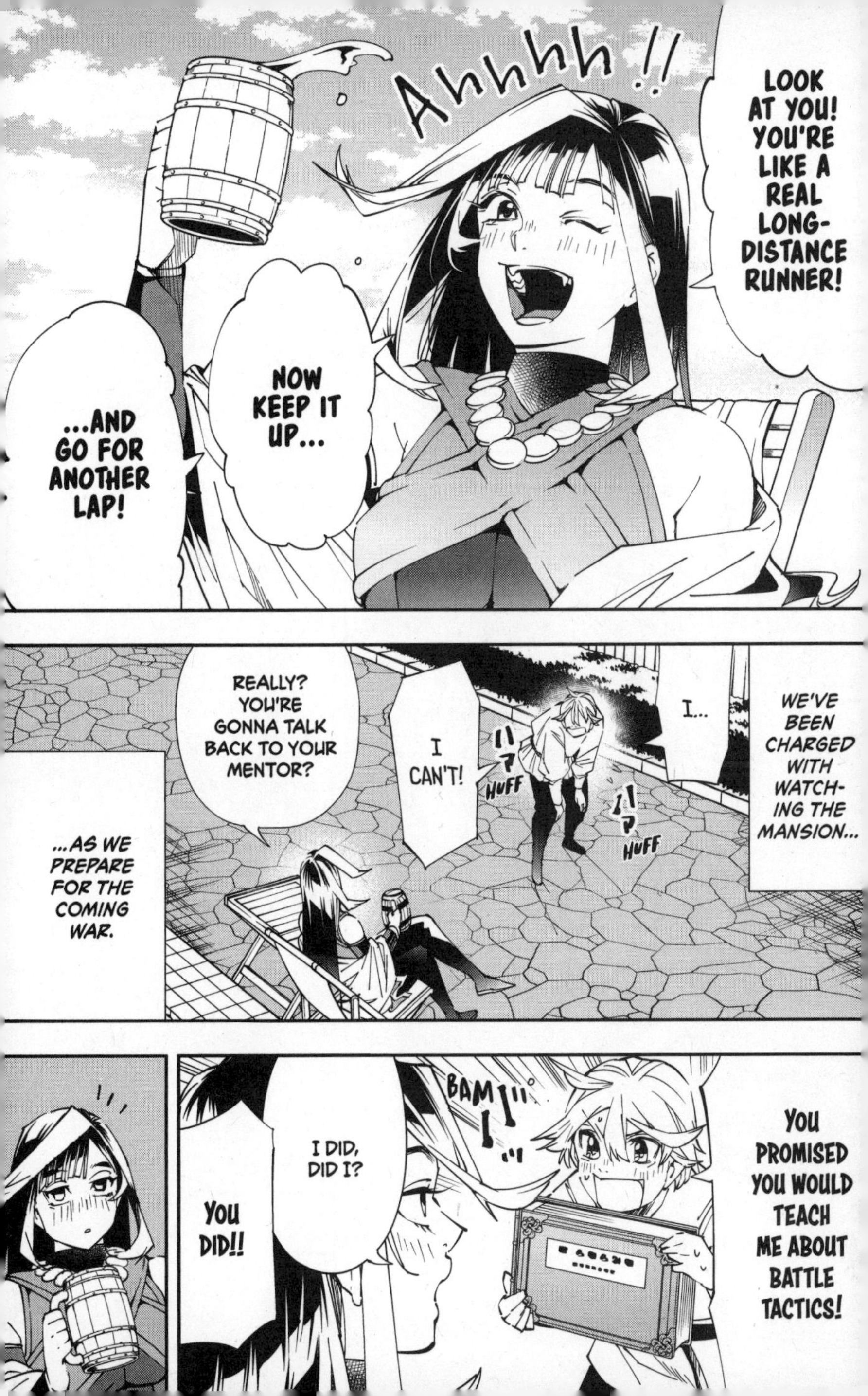
Ahhhh!!
LOOK AT YOU! YOU'RE LIKE A REAL LONG-DISTANCE RUNNER!
NOW KEEP IT UP...
...AND GO FOR ANOTHER LAP!
WE'VE BEEN CHARGED WITH WATCHING THE MANSION...
I...
HUFF
HUFF
I CAN'T!
REALLY? YOU'RE GONNA TALK BACK TO YOUR MENTOR?
...AS WE PREPARE FOR THE COMING WAR.
YOU PROMISED YOU WOULD TEACH ME ABOUT BATTLE TACTICS!
BAM
I DID, DID I?
YOU DID!!

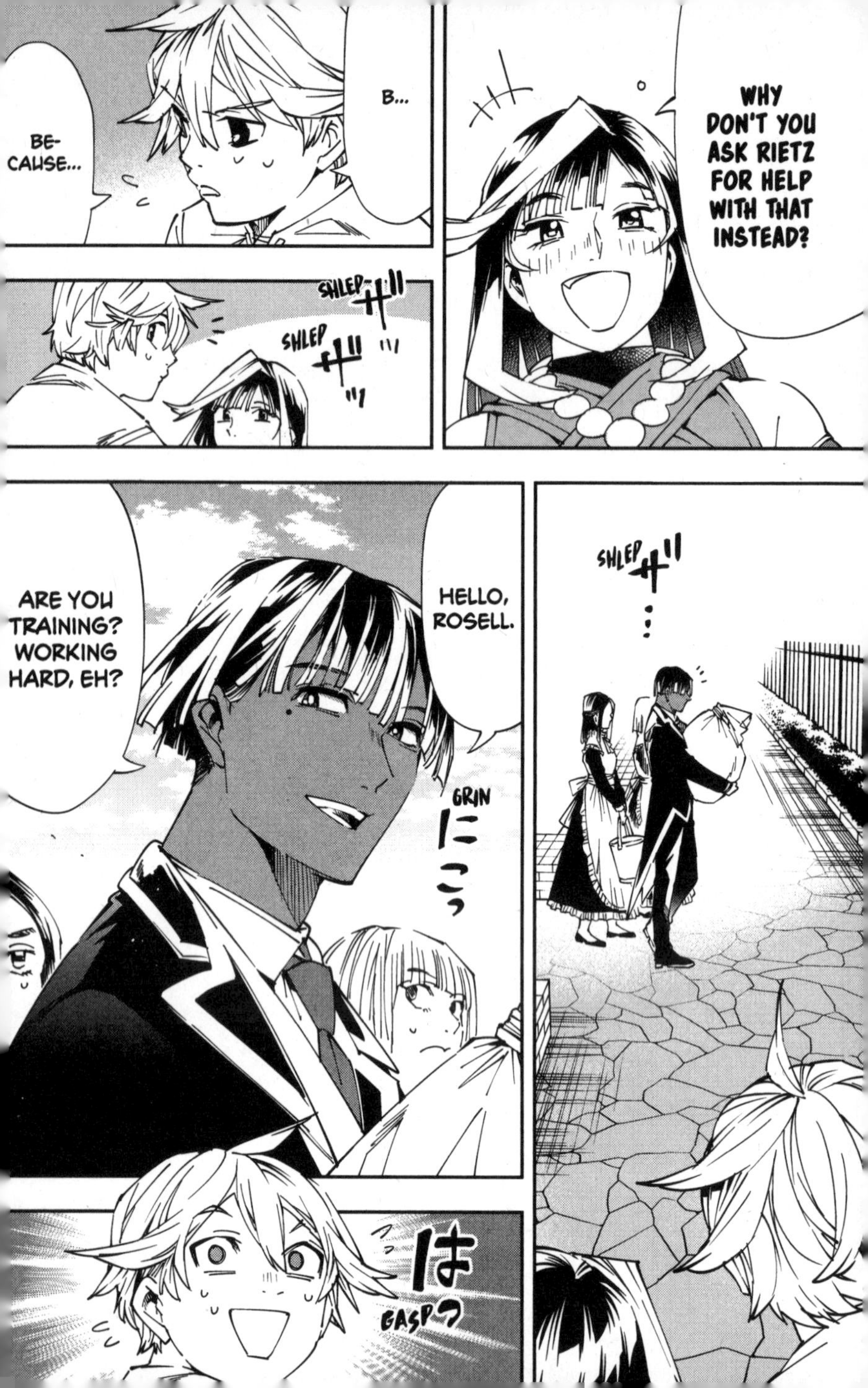
WHY DON'T YOU ASK RIETZ FOR HELP WITH THAT INSTEAD?
B...
BE-CAUSE...
SHLEP
SHLEP
SHLEP
...
HELLO, ROSELL.
ARE YOU TRAINING? WORKING HARD, EH?
GRIN
にこっ
はっ
GASP

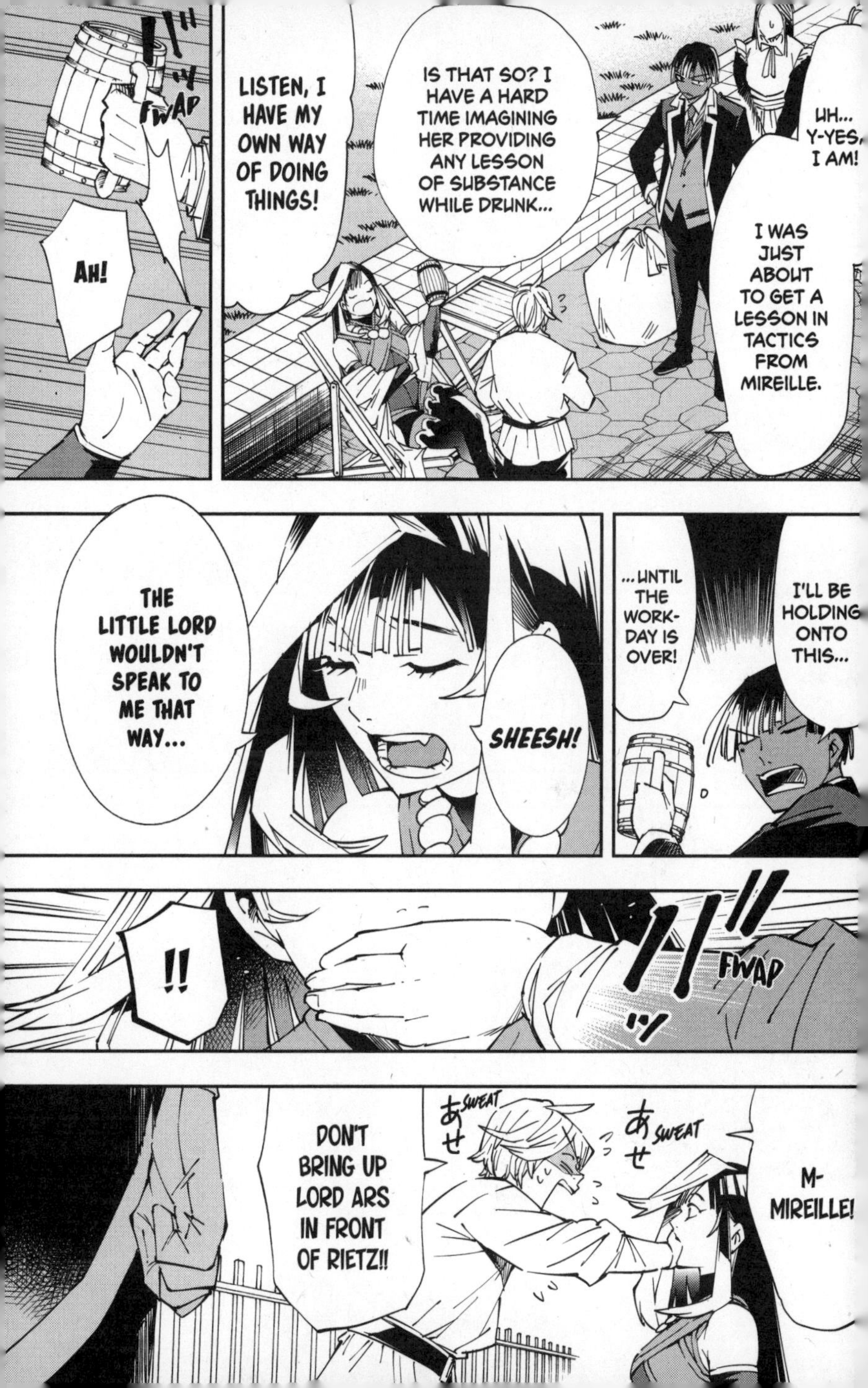
UH... Y-YES, I AM!
I WAS JUST ABOUT TO GET A LESSON IN TACTICS FROM MIREILLE.
IS THAT SO? I HAVE A HARD TIME IMAGINING HER PROVIDING ANY LESSON OF SUBSTANCE WHILE DRUNK...
LISTEN, I HAVE MY OWN WAY OF DOING THINGS!
FWAP
AH!
I'LL BE HOLDING ONTO THIS...
...UNTIL THE WORK-DAY IS OVER!
SHEESH!
THE LITTLE LORD WOULDN'T SPEAK TO ME THAT WAY...
FWAP
!!
M-MIREILLE!
あせ SWEAT
あせ SWEAT
DON'T BRING UP LORD ARS IN FRONT OF RIETZ!!

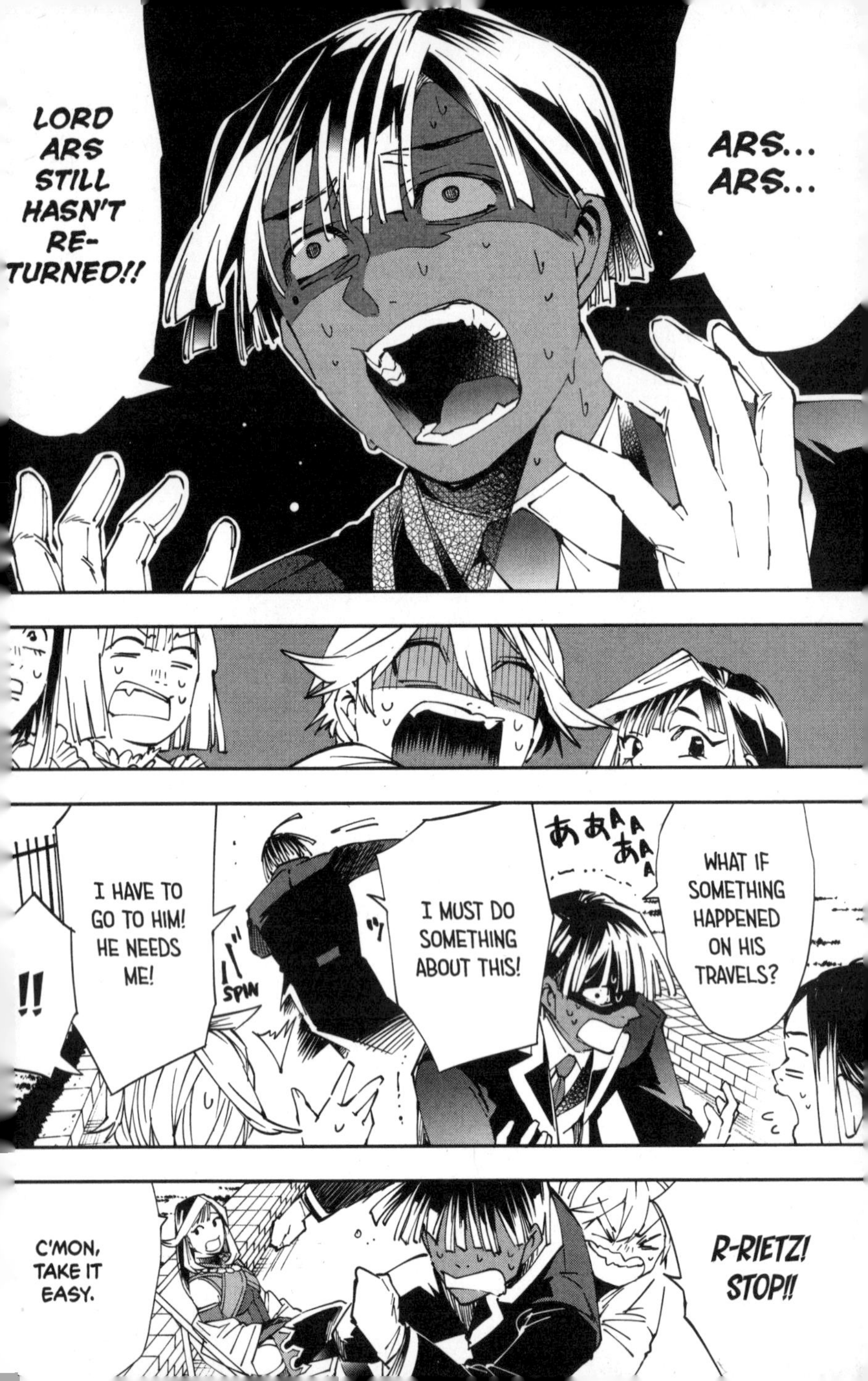
ARS... ARS...
LORD ARS STILL HASN'T RE-TURNED!!
WHAT IF SOMETHING HAPPENED ON HIS TRAVELS?
ああAAあAA
I MUST DO SOMETHING ABOUT THIS!
ッ
SPIN
I HAVE TO GO TO HIM! HE NEEDS ME!
!!
R-RIETZ! STOP!!
C'MON, TAKE IT EASY.

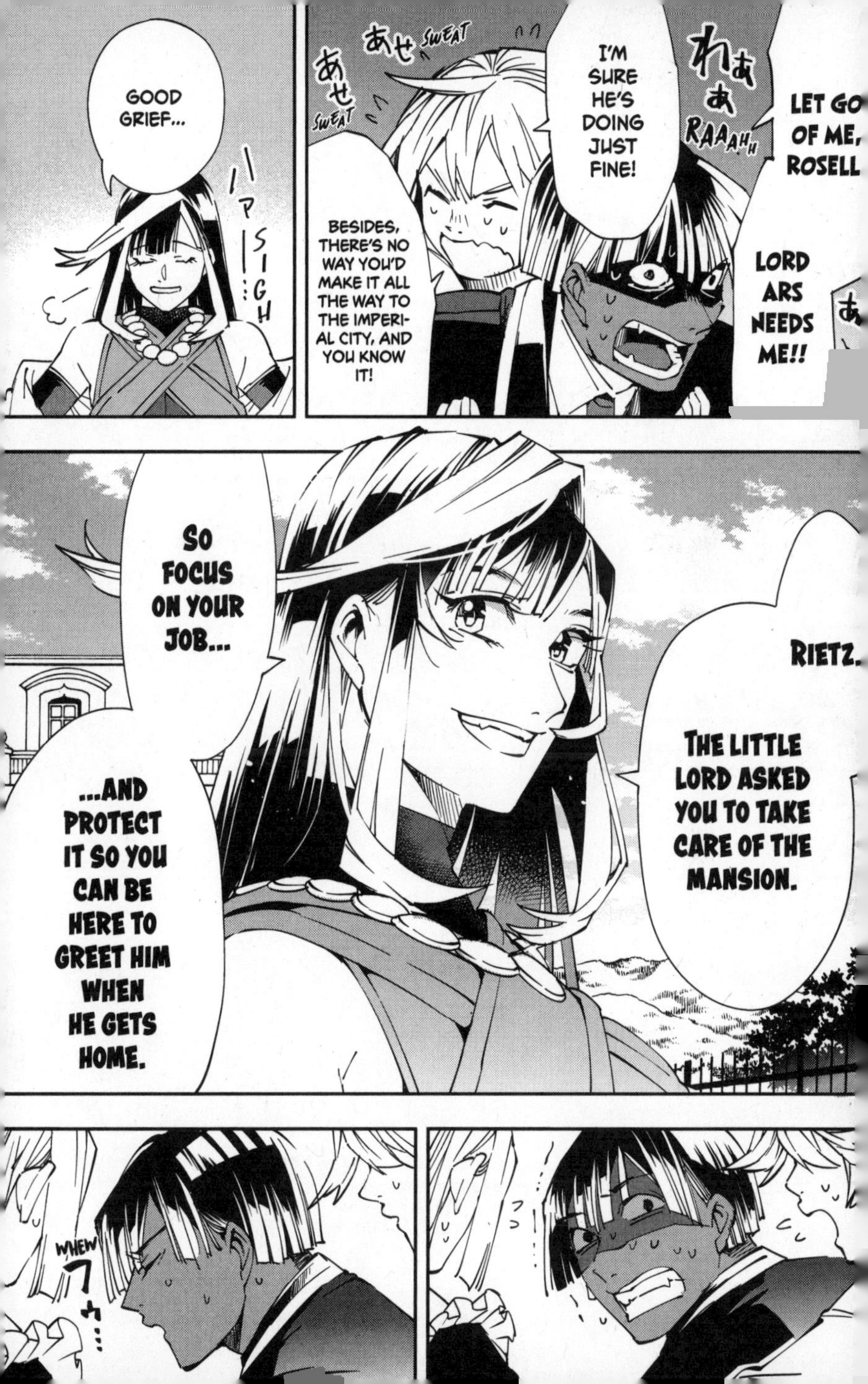
LET GO OF ME, ROSELL
わぁぁ RAAAAHH
I'M SURE HE'S DOING JUST FINE!
LORD ARS NEEDS ME!!
あせ SWEAT
あせ SWEAT
BESIDES, THERE'S NO WAY YOU'D MAKE IT ALL THE WAY TO THE IMPERIAL CITY, AND YOU KNOW IT!
GOOD GRIEF...
ハァー… SIGH
RIETZ.
THE LITTLE LORD ASKED YOU TO TAKE CARE OF THE MANSION.
SO FOCUS ON YOUR JOB...
...AND PROTECT IT SO YOU CAN BE HERE TO GREET HIM WHEN HE GETS HOME.
WHEW

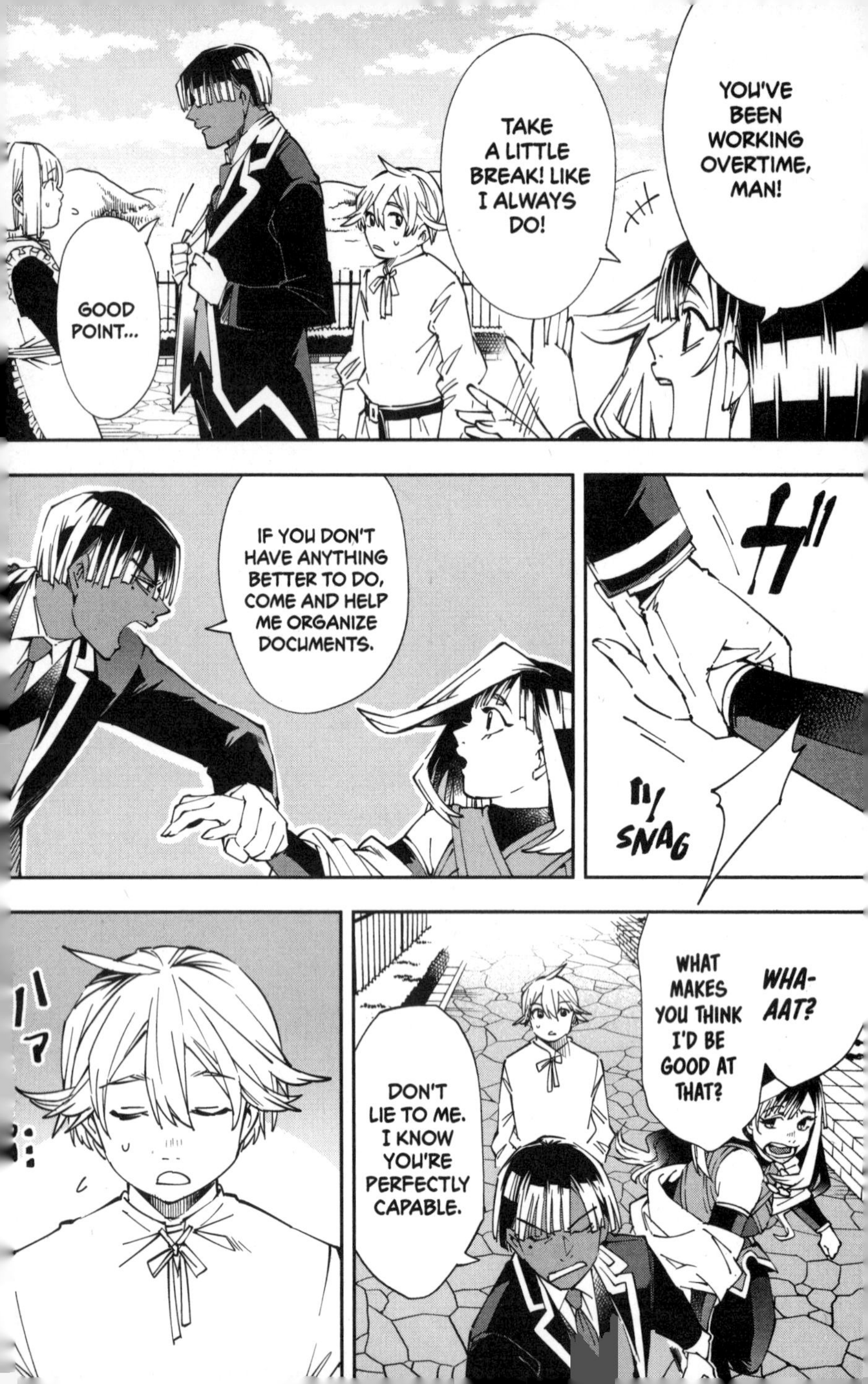
YOU'VE BEEN WORKING OVERTIME, MAN!
TAKE A LITTLE BREAK! LIKE I ALWAYS DO!
GOOD POINT...
SNAG
IF YOU DON'T HAVE ANYTHING BETTER TO DO, COME AND HELP ME ORGANIZE DOCUMENTS.
WHA-AAT?
WHAT MAKES YOU THINK I'D BE GOOD AT THAT?
DON'T LIE TO ME. I KNOW YOU'RE PERFECTLY CAPABLE.

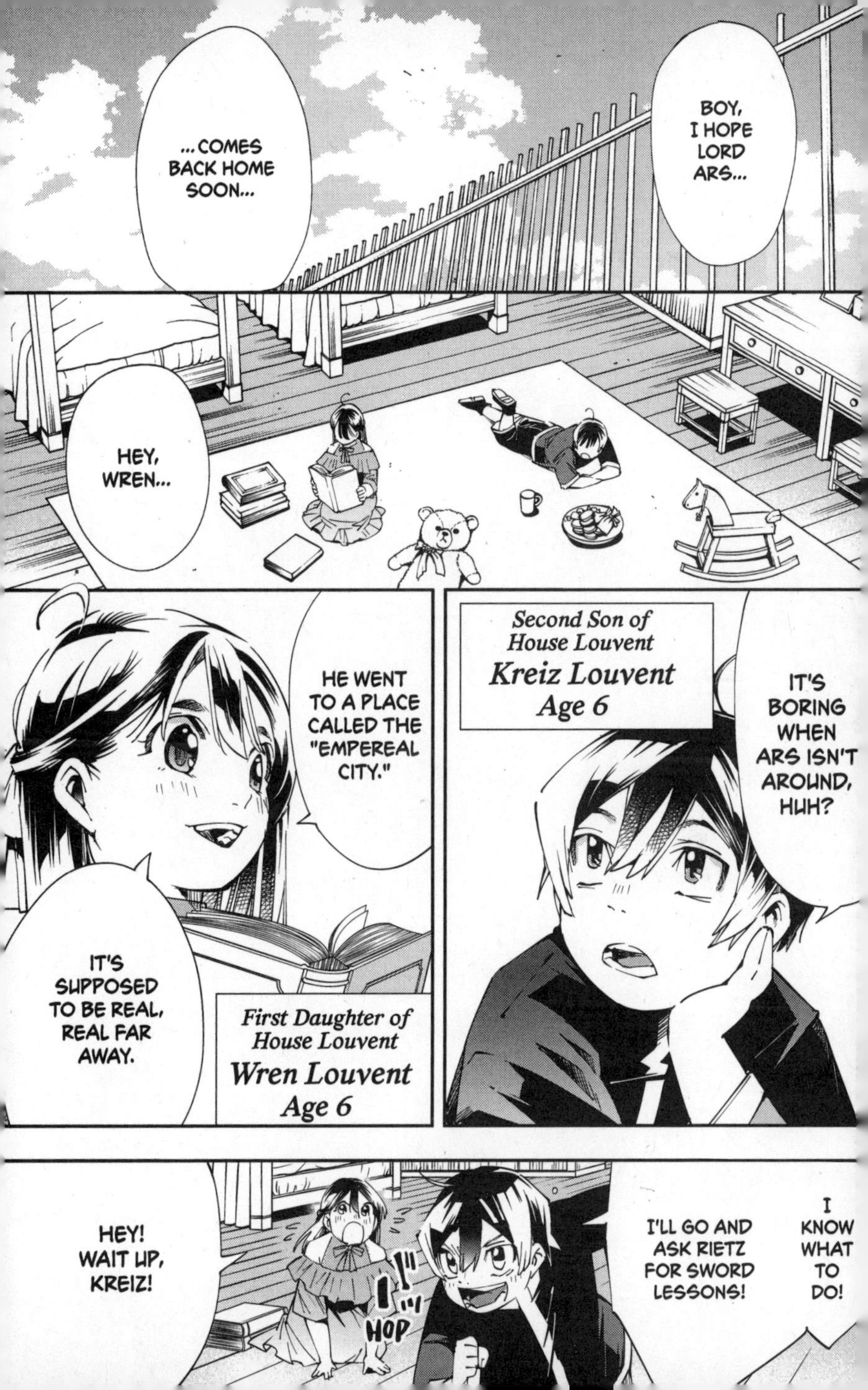
BOY, I HOPE LORD ARS...
...COMES BACK HOME SOON...
HEY, WREN...
Second Son of House Louvent Kreiz Louvent Age 6
IT'S BORING WHEN ARS ISN'T AROUND, HUH?
HE WENT TO A PLACE CALLED THE "EMPEREAL CITY."
IT'S SUPPOSED TO BE REAL, REAL FAR AWAY.
First Daughter of House Louvent Wren Louvent Age 6
I KNOW WHAT TO DO!
I'LL GO AND ASK RIETZ FOR SWORD LESSONS!
HOP
HEY! WAIT UP, KREIZ!

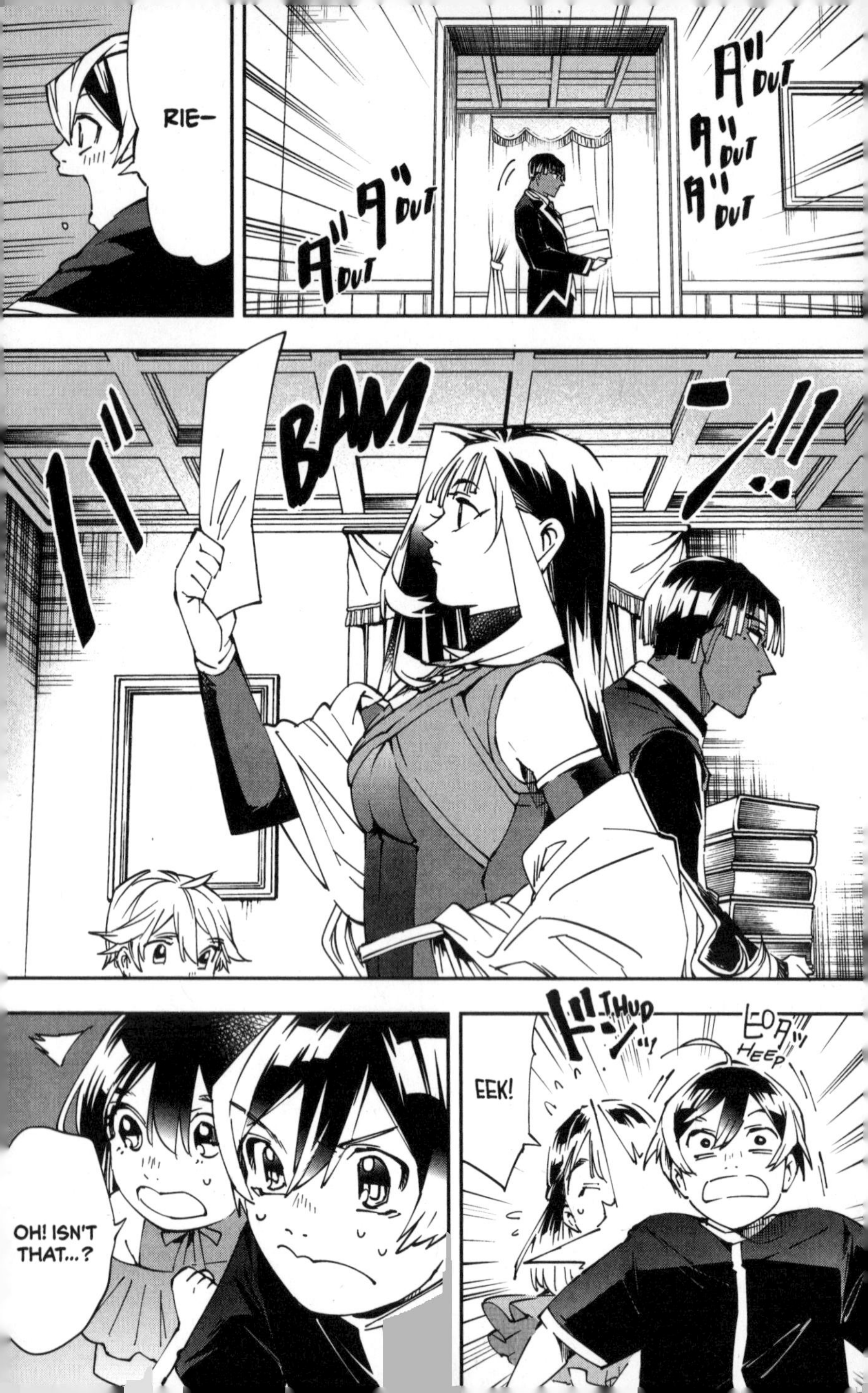

DUT
DUT
DUT
DUT
DUT
RIE-
BAM
THUD
HEEP
EEK!
OH! ISN'T THAT...?

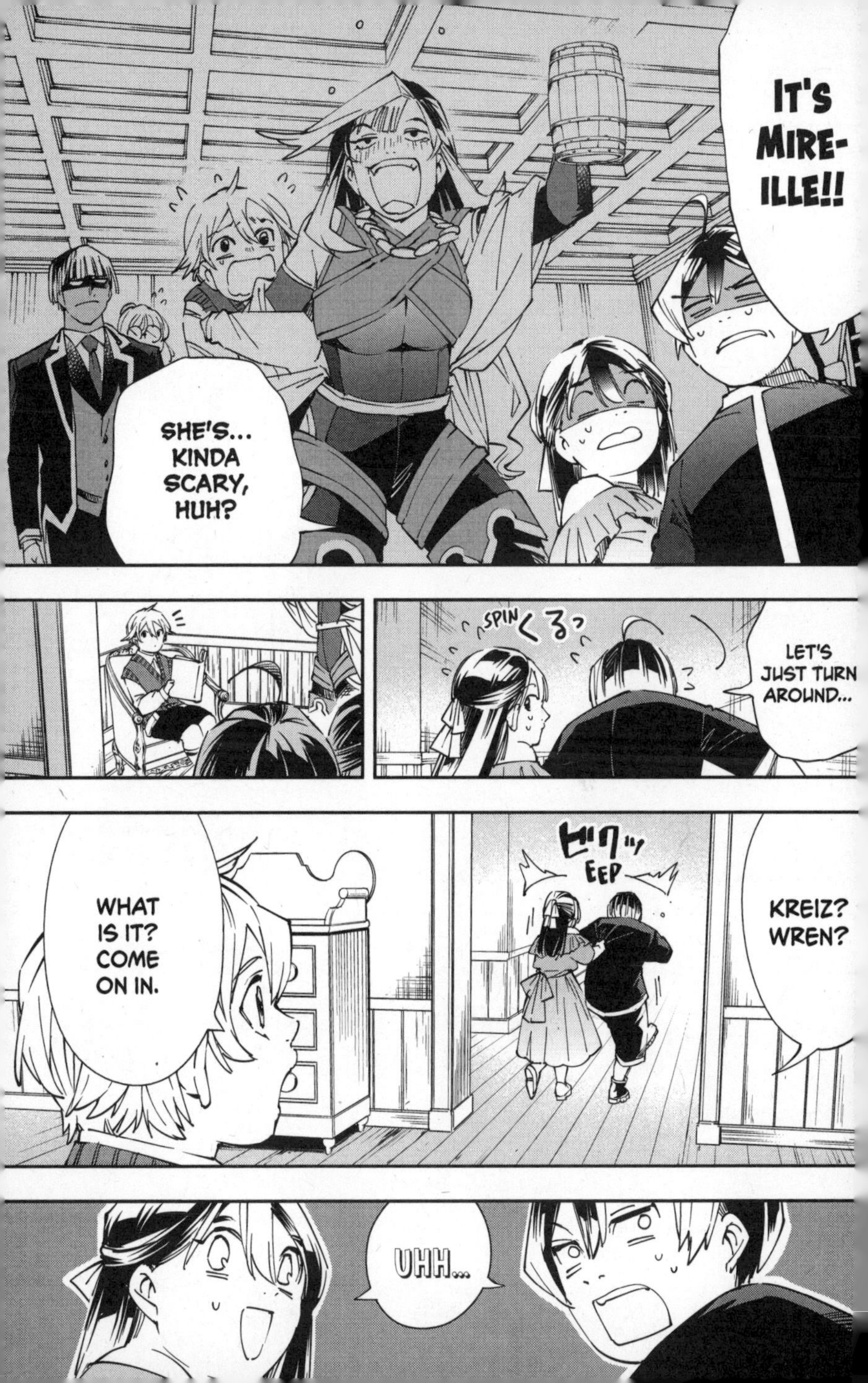
IT'S MIRE-ILLE!!
SHE'S... KINDA SCARY, HUH?
LET'S JUST TURN AROUND...
SPIN くるっ
KREIZ? WREN?
ビクッ EEP
WHAT IS IT? COME ON IN.
UHH...

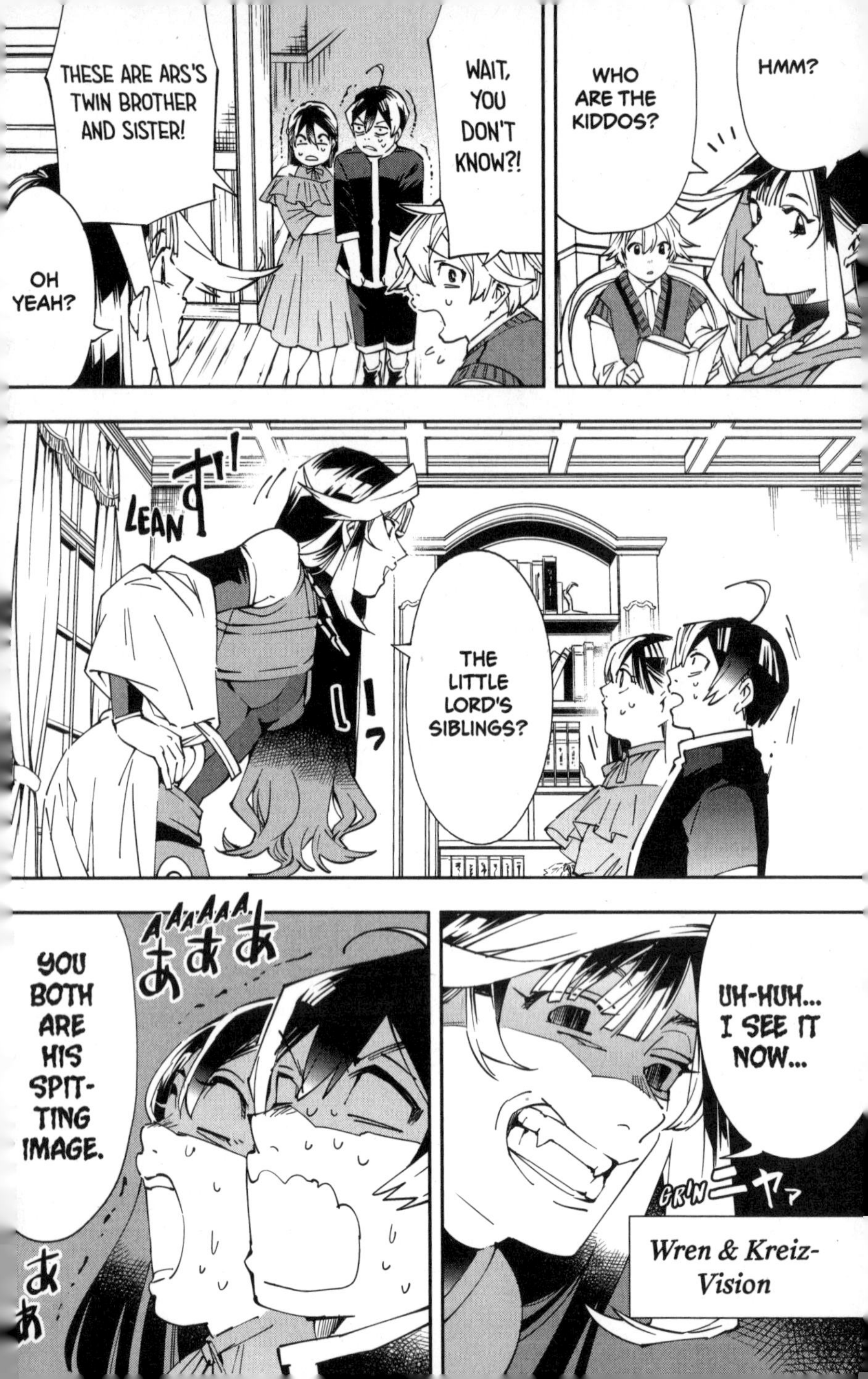
HMM?
WHO ARE THE KIDDOS?
WAIT, YOU DON'T KNOW?!
THESE ARE ARS'S TWIN BROTHER AND SISTER!
OH YEAH?
すっ! LEAN
THE LITTLE LORD'S SIBLINGS?
UH-HUH... I SEE IT NOW...
GRIN ニヤァ
Wren & Kreiz-Vision
AAAAAA あああ
YOU BOTH ARE HIS SPIT-TING IMAGE.
ああ

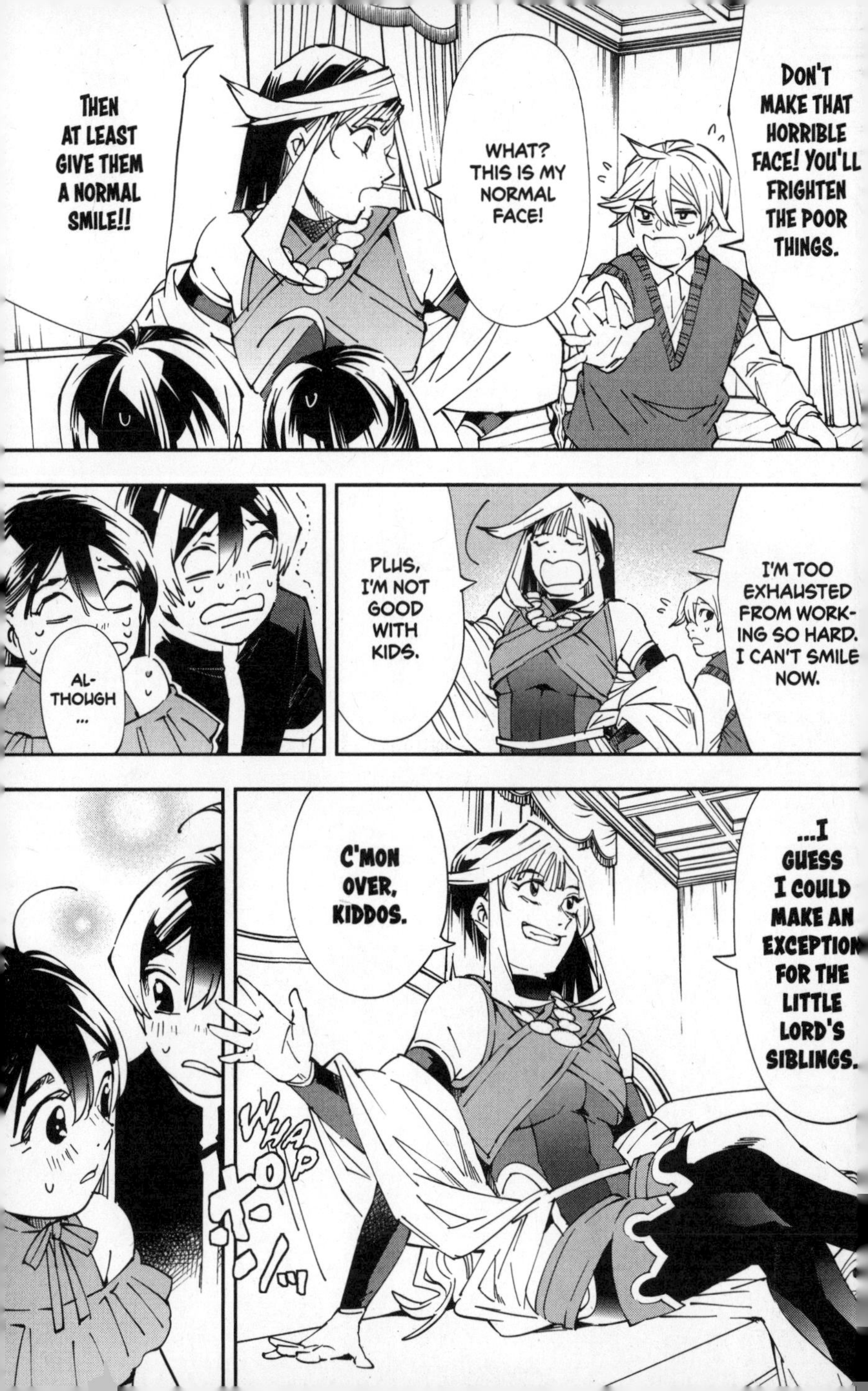
DON'T MAKE THAT HORRIBLE FACE! YOU'LL FRIGHTEN THE POOR THINGS.
WHAT? THIS IS MY NORMAL FACE!
THEN AT LEAST GIVE THEM A NORMAL SMILE!!
I'M TOO EXHAUSTED FROM WORK-ING SO HARD. I CAN'T SMILE NOW.
PLUS, I'M NOT GOOD WITH KIDS.
AL-THOUGH...
...I GUESS I COULD MAKE AN EXCEPTION FOR THE LITTLE LORD'S SIBLINGS.
C'MON OVER, KIDDOS.
WHAP

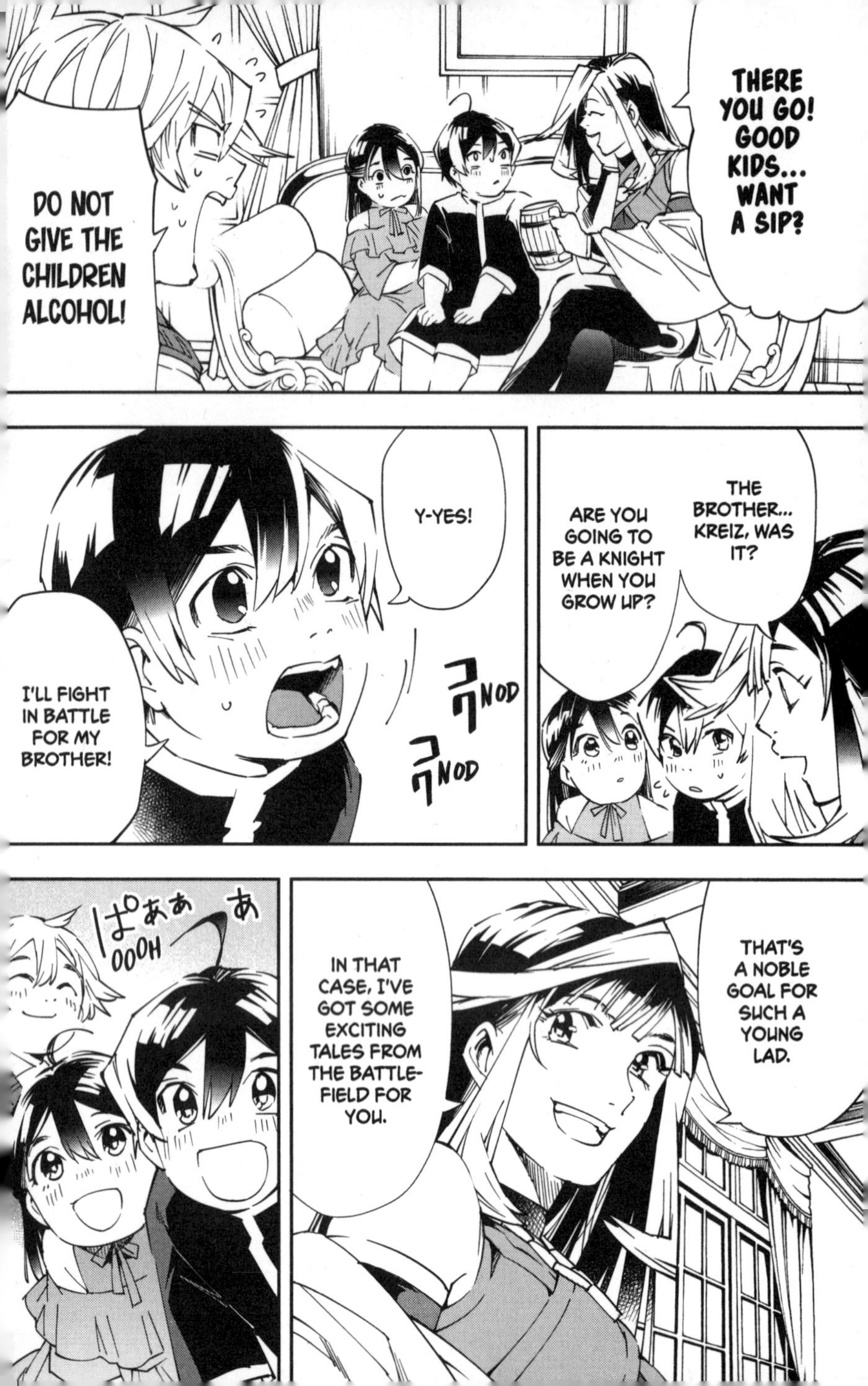
THERE YOU GO! GOOD KIDS... WANT A SIP?
DO NOT GIVE THE CHILDREN ALCOHOL!
THE BROTHER... KREIZ, WAS IT?
ARE YOU GOING TO BE A KNIGHT WHEN YOU GROW UP?
Y-YES!
コク NOD
コク NOD
I'LL FIGHT IN BATTLE FOR MY BROTHER!
THAT'S A NOBLE GOAL FOR SUCH A YOUNG LAD.
IN THAT CASE, I'VE GOT SOME EXCITING TALES FROM THE BATTLE-FIELD FOR YOU.
ぱあああ OOOH

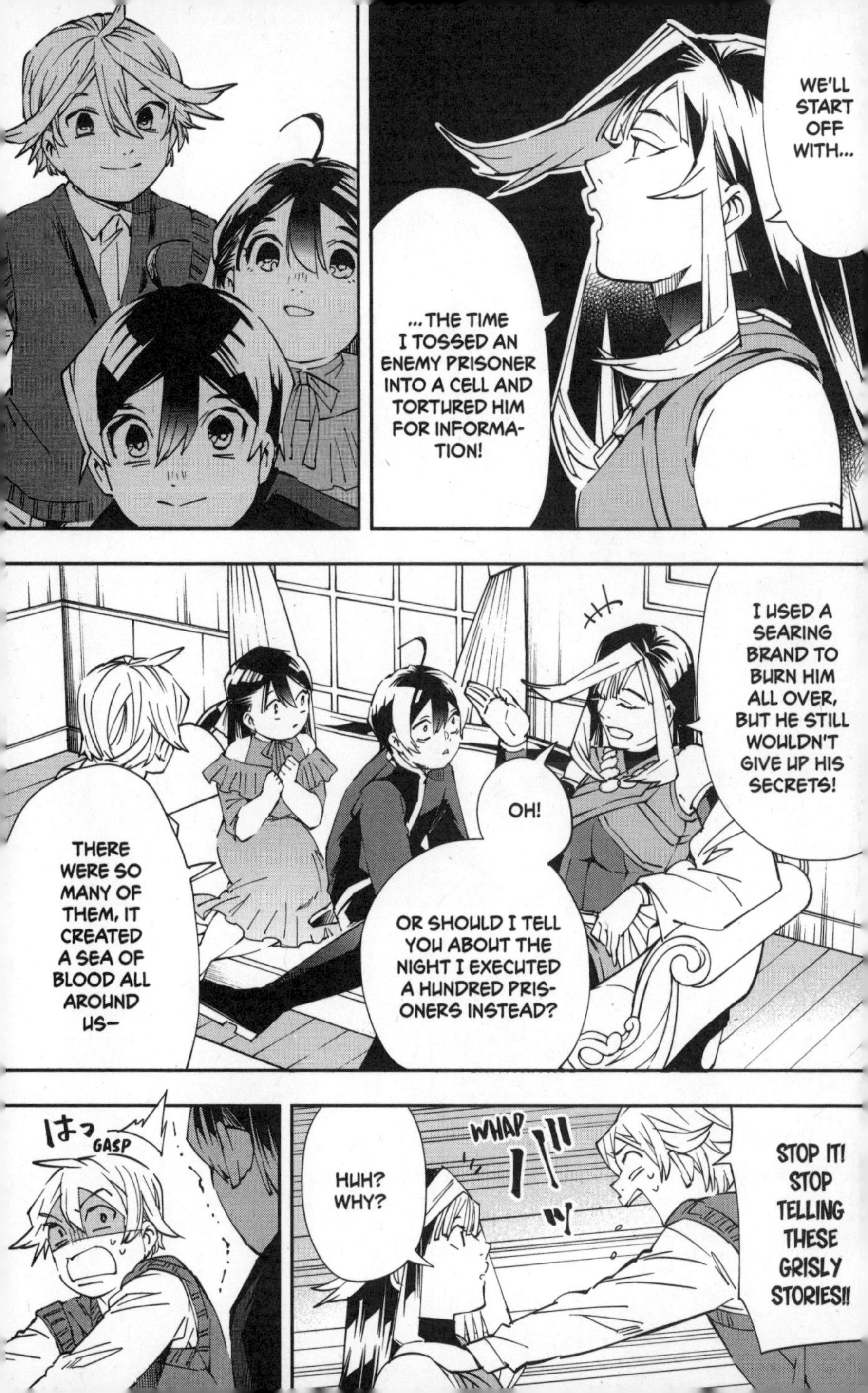
WE'LL START OFF WITH...
...THE TIME I TOSSED AN ENEMY PRISONER INTO A CELL AND TORTURED HIM FOR INFORMATION!
I USED A SEARING BRAND TO BURN HIM ALL OVER, BUT HE STILL WOULDN'T GIVE UP HIS SECRETS!
OH!
OR SHOULD I TELL YOU ABOUT THE NIGHT I EXECUTED A HUNDRED PRISONERS INSTEAD?
THERE WERE SO MANY OF THEM, IT CREATED A SEA OF BLOOD ALL AROUND US—
STOP IT! STOP TELLING THESE GRISLY STORIES!!
WHAP
HUH? WHY?
はっ
GASP

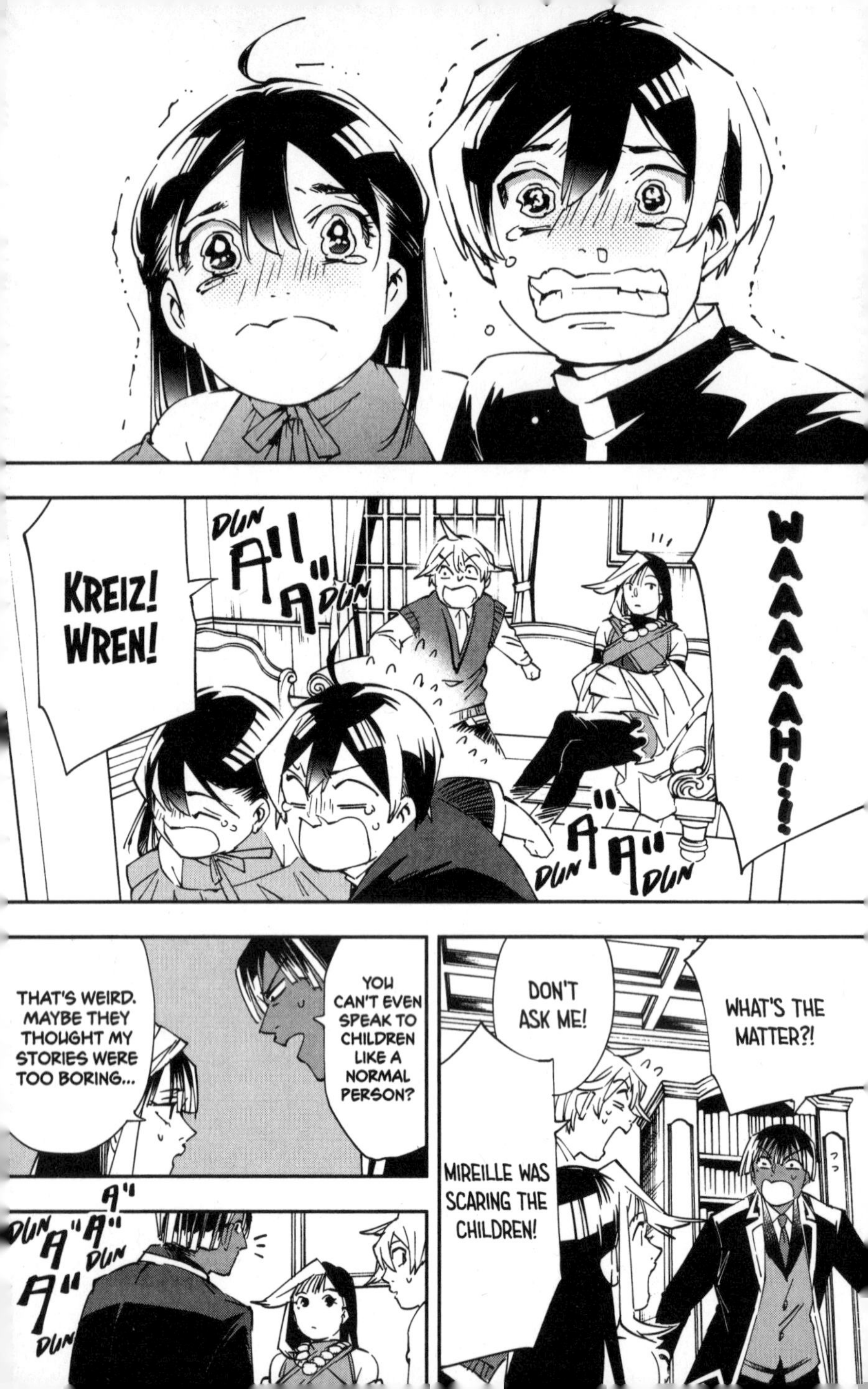
WAAAAAAH!!!
KREIZ! WREN!
DUN A" A" DUN
DUN A" A" DUN
WHAT'S THE MATTER?!
DON'T ASK ME!
MIREILLE WAS SCARING THE CHILDREN!
YOU CAN'T EVEN SPEAK TO CHILDREN LIKE A NORMAL PERSON?
THAT'S WEIRD. MAYBE THEY THOUGHT MY STORIES WERE TOO BORING...
DUN A" A" A" A" DUN DUN

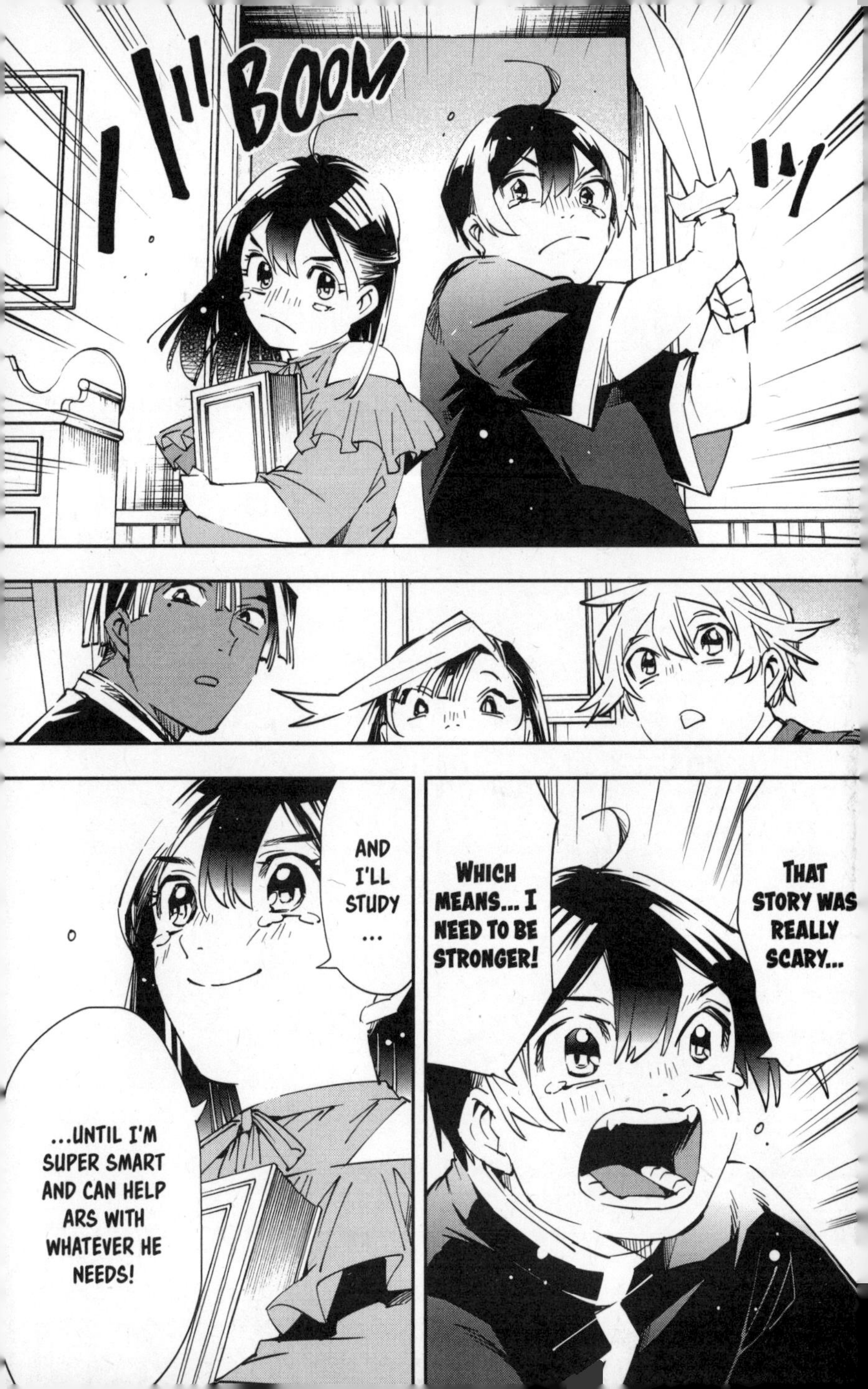
BOOM
THAT STORY WAS REALLY SCARY...
WHICH MEANS... I NEED TO BE STRONGER!
AND I'LL STUDY ...
...UNTIL I'M SUPER SMART AND CAN HELP ARS WITH WHATEVER HE NEEDS!

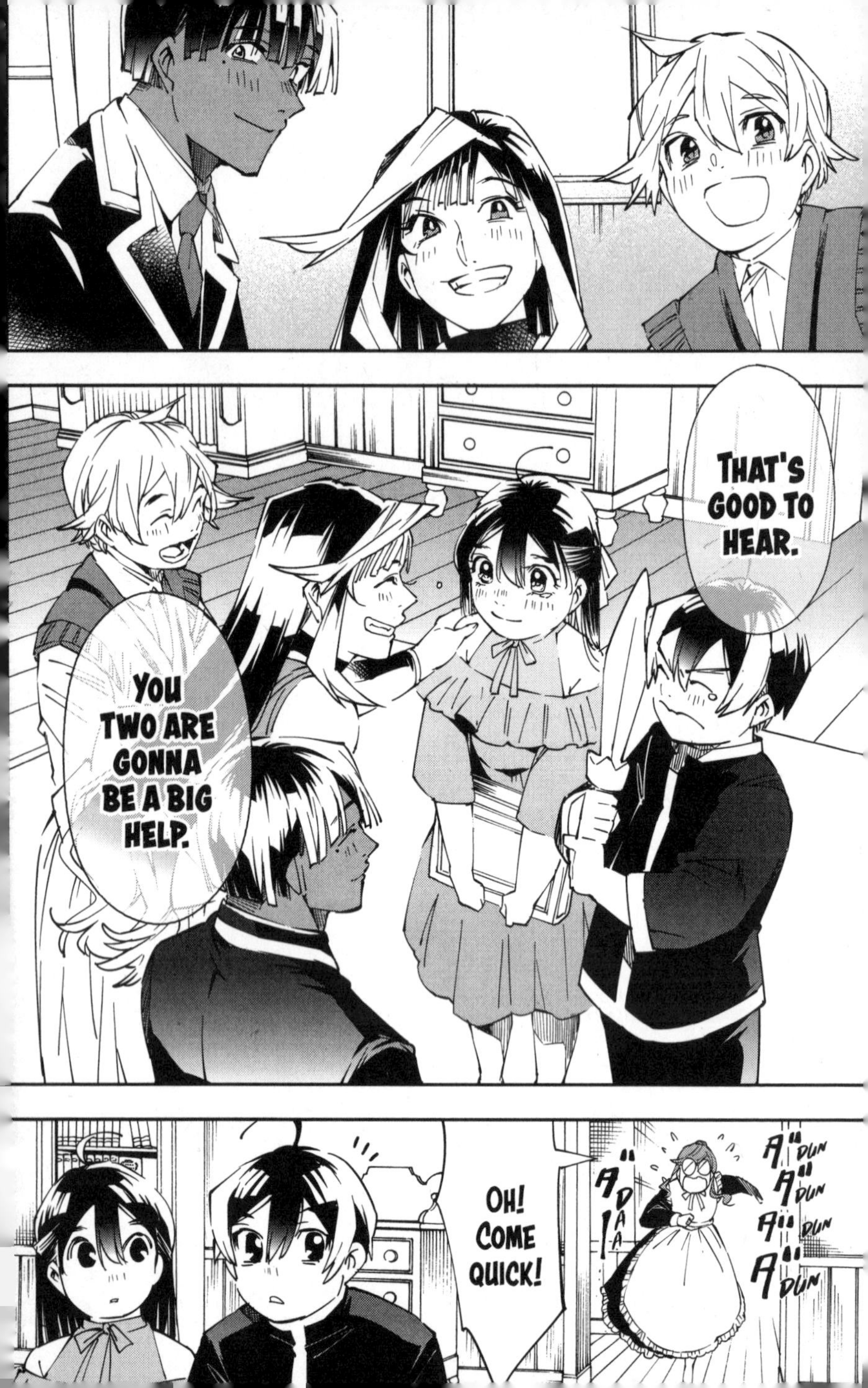
THAT'S GOOD TO HEAR.
YOU TWO ARE GONNA BE A BIG HELP.
ダ DUN ダ DUN ダ DUN ダ DUN
ダ! DAAA
OH! COME QUICK!

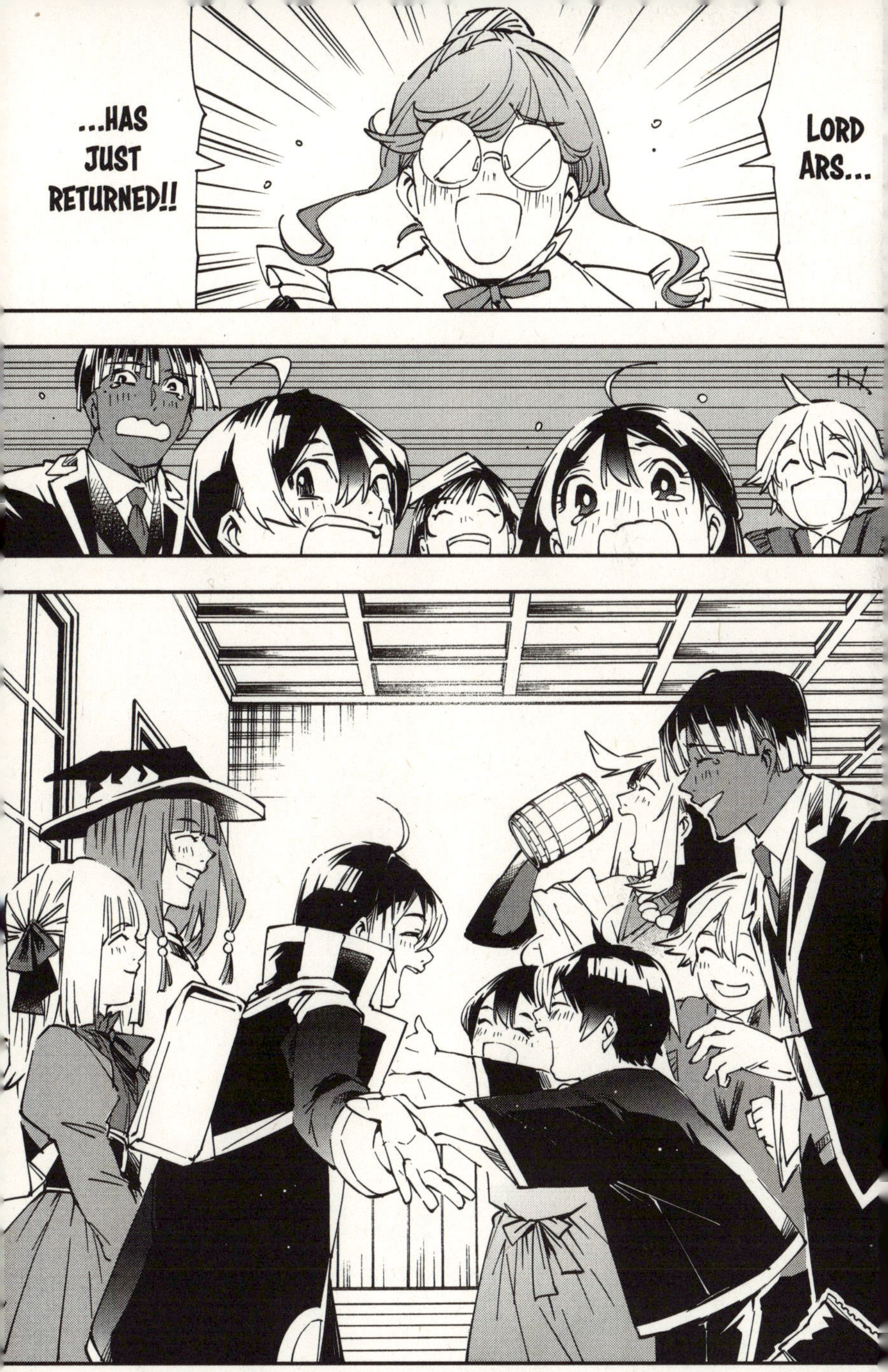
LORD ARS...
...HAS JUST RETURNED!!

As a Reincarnated ARISTOCRAT, I'll Use My Appraisal Skill to Rise in the World

Chapter 64: Homecoming and Departure

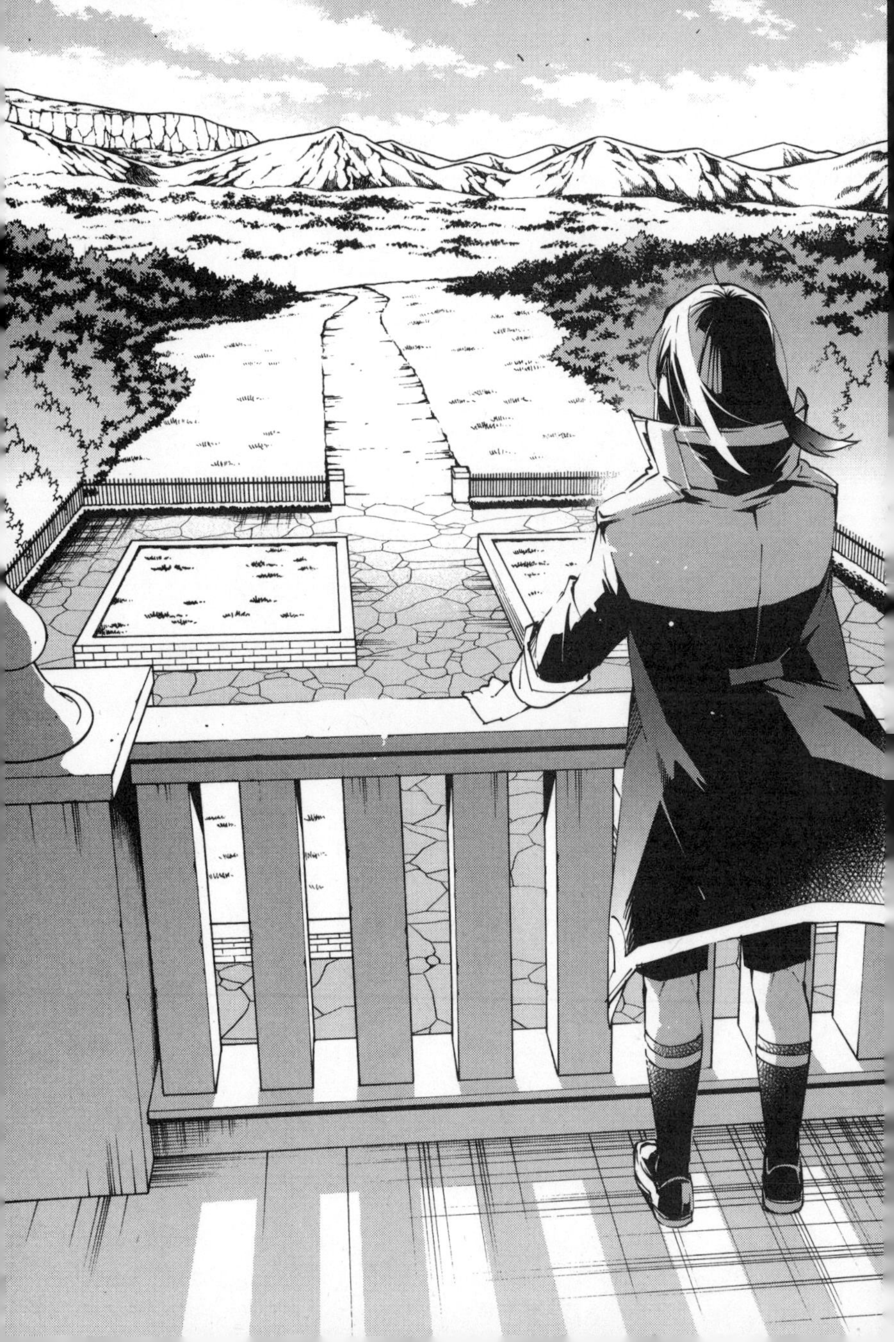

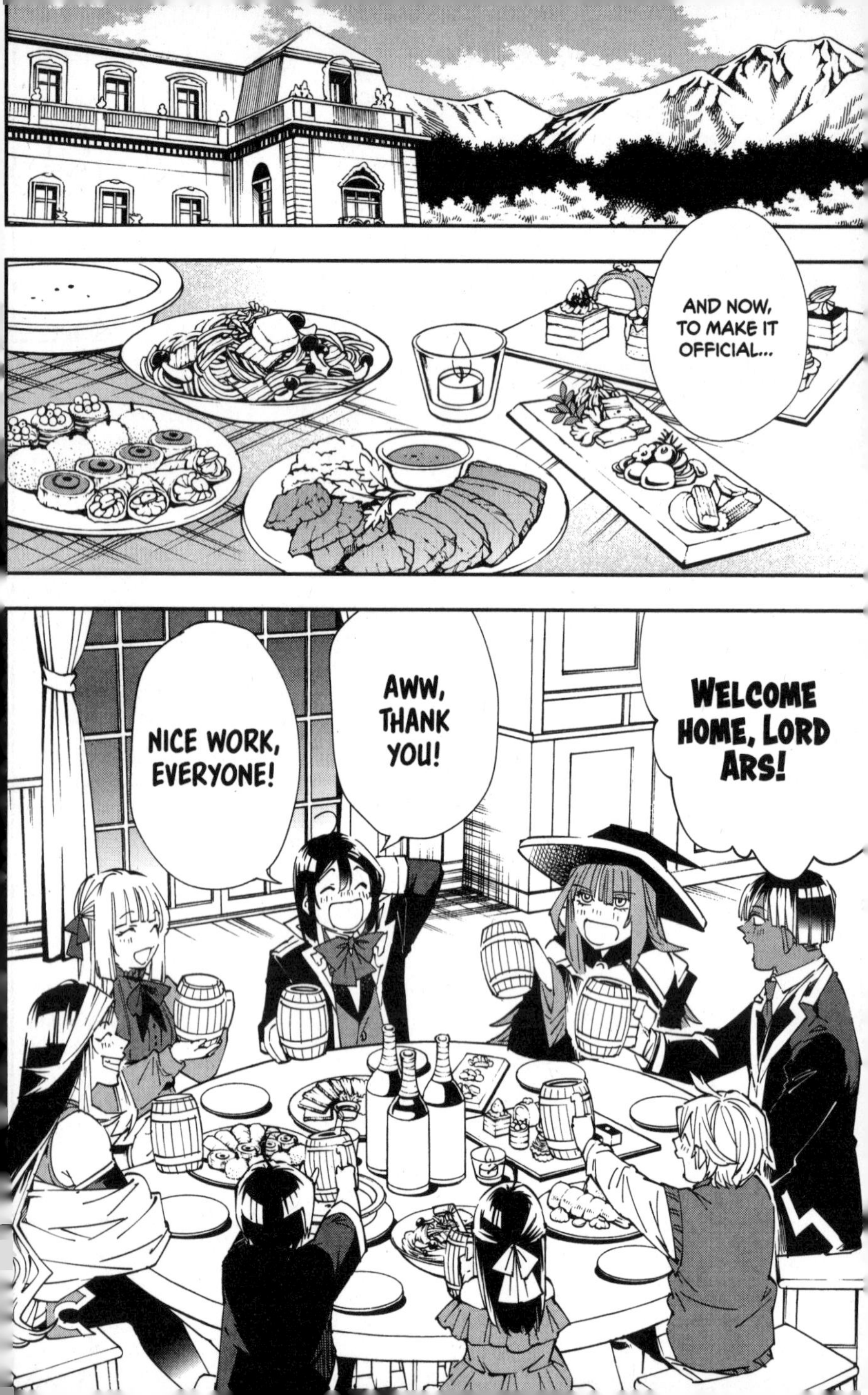
AND NOW, TO MAKE IT OFFICIAL...
WELCOME HOME, LORD ARS!
AWW, THANK YOU!
NICE WORK, EVERYONE!

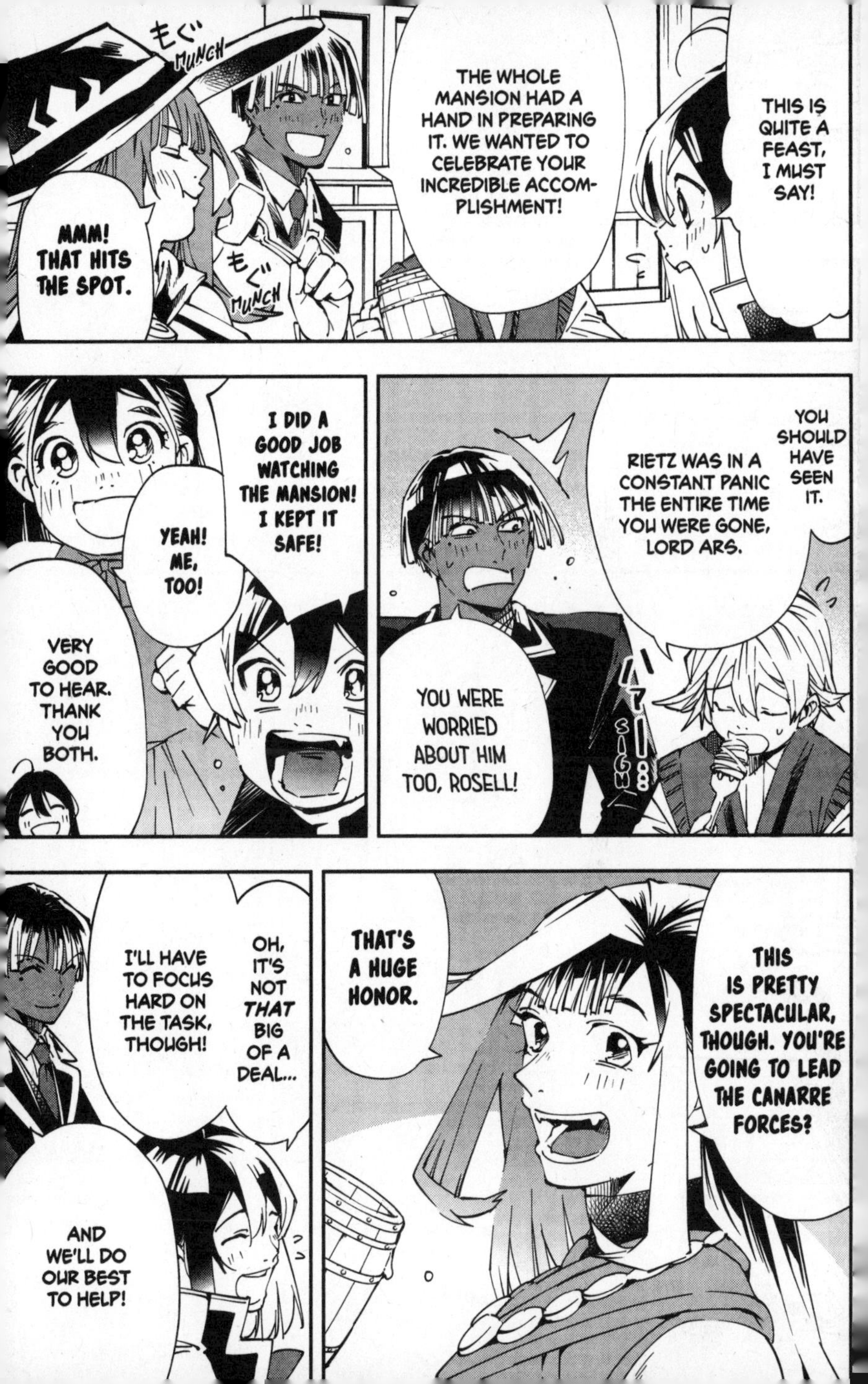
THIS IS QUITE A FEAST, I MUST SAY!
THE WHOLE MANSION HAD A HAND IN PREPARING IT. WE WANTED TO CELEBRATE YOUR INCREDIBLE ACCOM-PLISHMENT!
もぐ MUNCH
MMM! THAT HITS THE SPOT.
もぐ MUNCH
YOU SHOULD HAVE SEEN IT.
RIETZ WAS IN A CONSTANT PANIC THE ENTIRE TIME YOU WERE GONE, LORD ARS.
SIGH
YOU WERE WORRIED ABOUT HIM TOO, ROSELL!
I DID A GOOD JOB WATCHING THE MANSION! I KEPT IT SAFE!
YEAH! ME, TOO!
VERY GOOD TO HEAR. THANK YOU BOTH.
THIS IS PRETTY SPECTACULAR, THOUGH. YOU'RE GOING TO LEAD THE CANARRE FORCES?
THAT'S A HUGE HONOR.
OH, IT'S NOT *THAT* BIG OF A DEAL...
I'LL HAVE TO FOCUS HARD ON THE TASK, THOUGH!
AND WE'LL DO OUR BEST TO HELP!

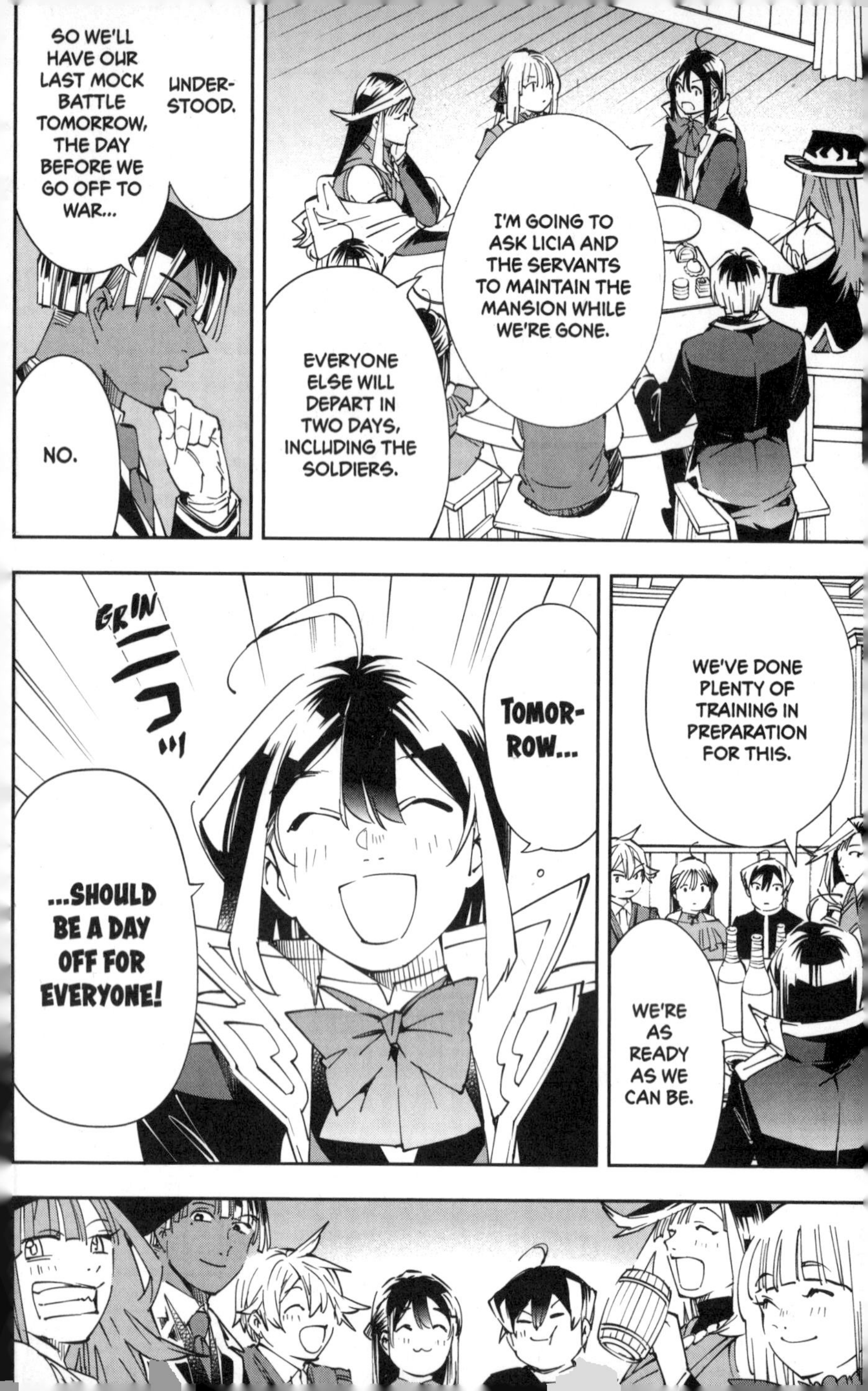
I'M GOING TO ASK LICIA AND THE SERVANTS TO MAINTAIN THE MANSION WHILE WE'RE GONE.
EVERYONE ELSE WILL DEPART IN TWO DAYS, INCLUDING THE SOLDIERS.
UNDER-STOOD.
SO WE'LL HAVE OUR LAST MOCK BATTLE TOMORROW, THE DAY BEFORE WE GO OFF TO WAR...
NO.
WE'VE DONE PLENTY OF TRAINING IN PREPARATION FOR THIS.
WE'RE AS READY AS WE CAN BE.
TOMOR-ROW...
GRIN
...SHOULD BE A DAY OFF FOR EVERYONE!

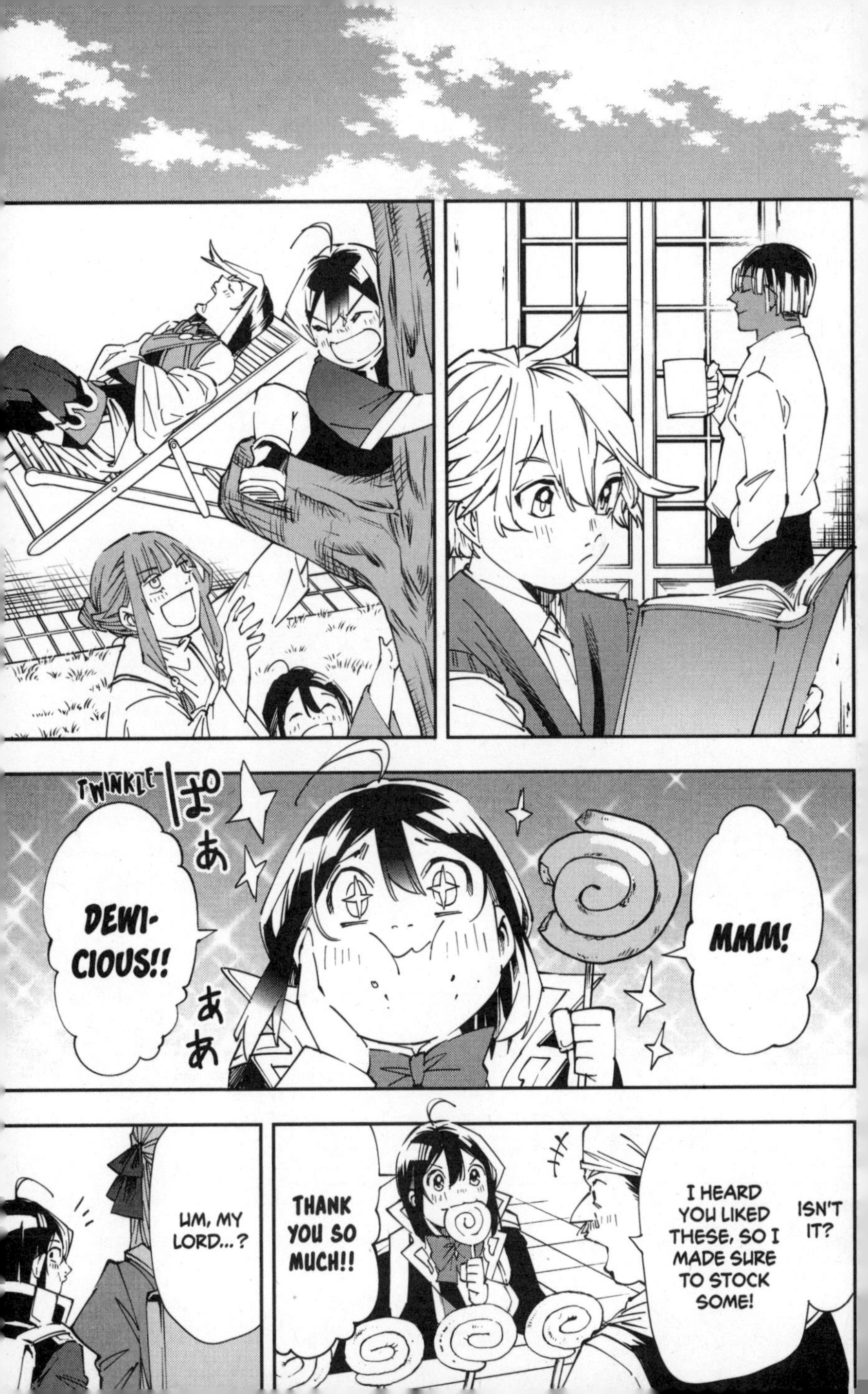
MMM!
TWINKLE
ぱあああ
DEWI-CIOUS!!
ISN'T IT?
I HEARD YOU LIKED THESE, SO I MADE SURE TO STOCK SOME!
THANK YOU SO MUCH!!
UM, MY LORD...?

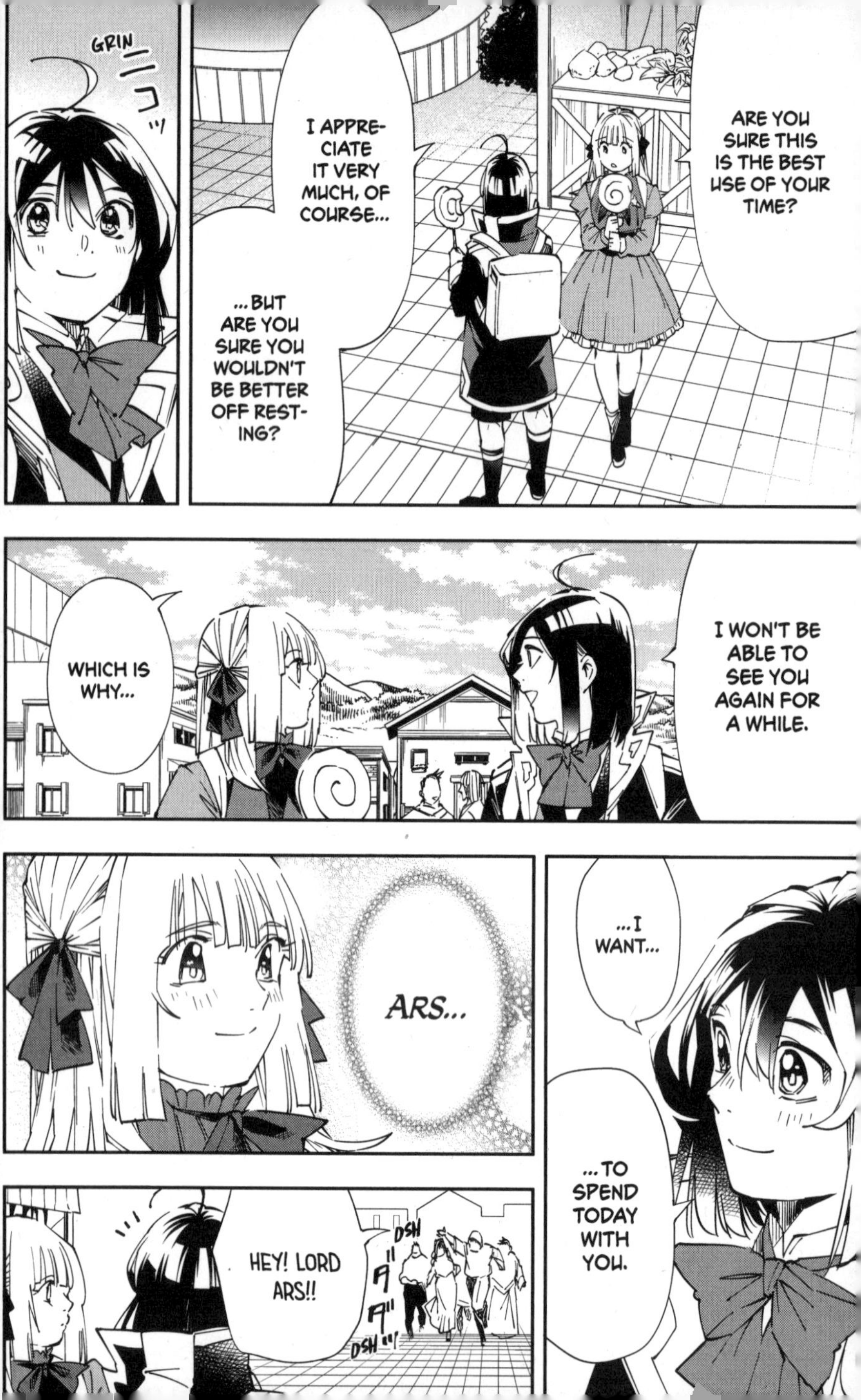
ARE YOU SURE THIS IS THE BEST USE OF YOUR TIME?
I APPRECIATE IT VERY MUCH, OF COURSE...
...BUT ARE YOU SURE YOU WOULDN'T BE BETTER OFF RESTING?
GRIN
I WON'T BE ABLE TO SEE YOU AGAIN FOR A WHILE.
WHICH IS WHY...
...I WANT...
...TO SPEND TODAY WITH YOU.
ARS...
HEY! LORD ARS!!
DSH
DSH

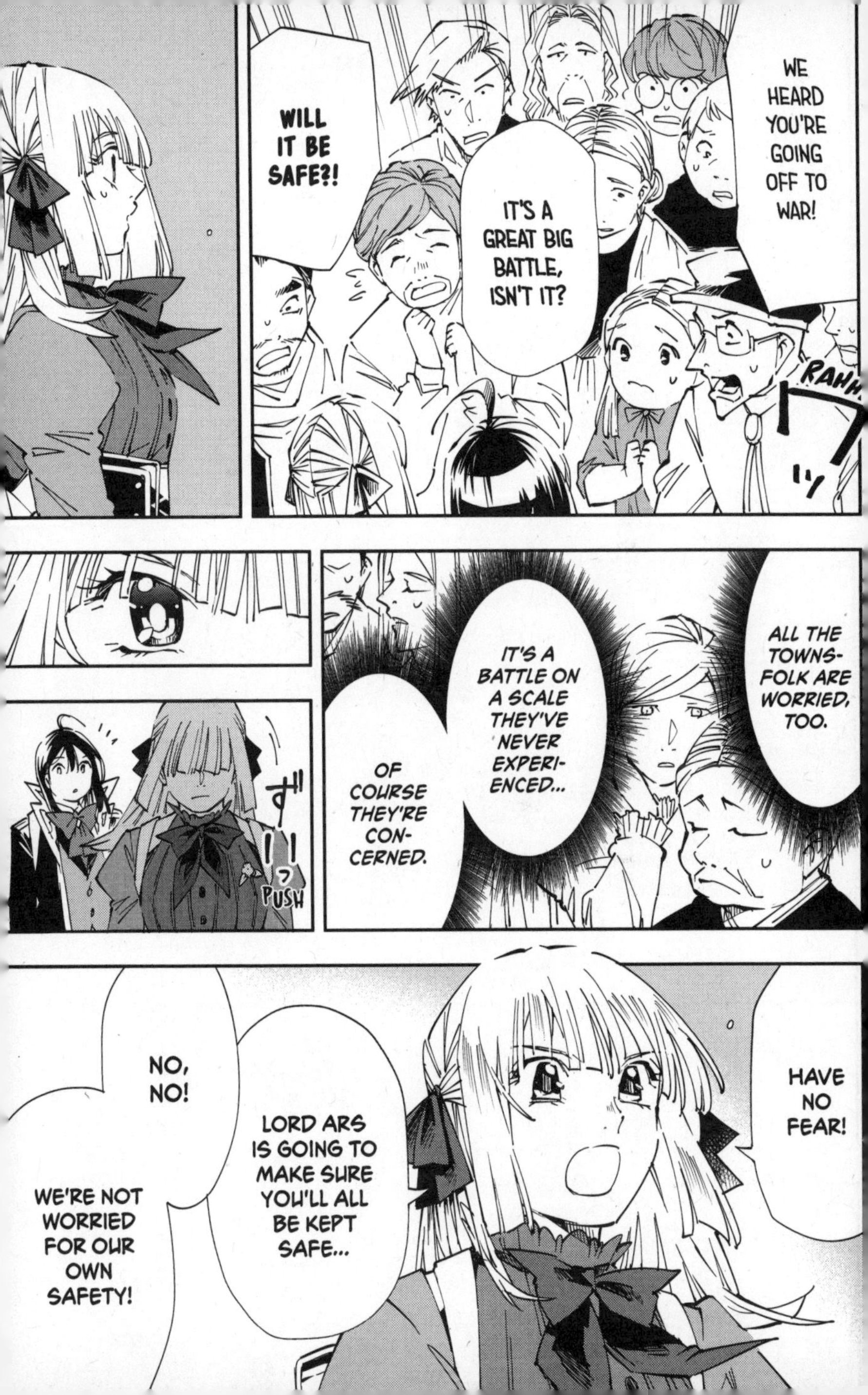
WE HEARD YOU'RE GOING OFF TO WAR!
IT'S A GREAT BIG BATTLE, ISN'T IT?
WILL IT BE SAFE?!
RAHH
ALL THE TOWNS-FOLK ARE WORRIED, TOO.
IT'S A BATTLE ON A SCALE THEY'VE NEVER EXPERI-ENCED...
OF COURSE THEY'RE CON-CERNED.
PUSH
HAVE NO FEAR!
LORD ARS IS GOING TO MAKE SURE YOU'LL ALL BE KEPT SAFE...
NO, NO!
WE'RE NOT WORRIED FOR OUR OWN SAFETY!

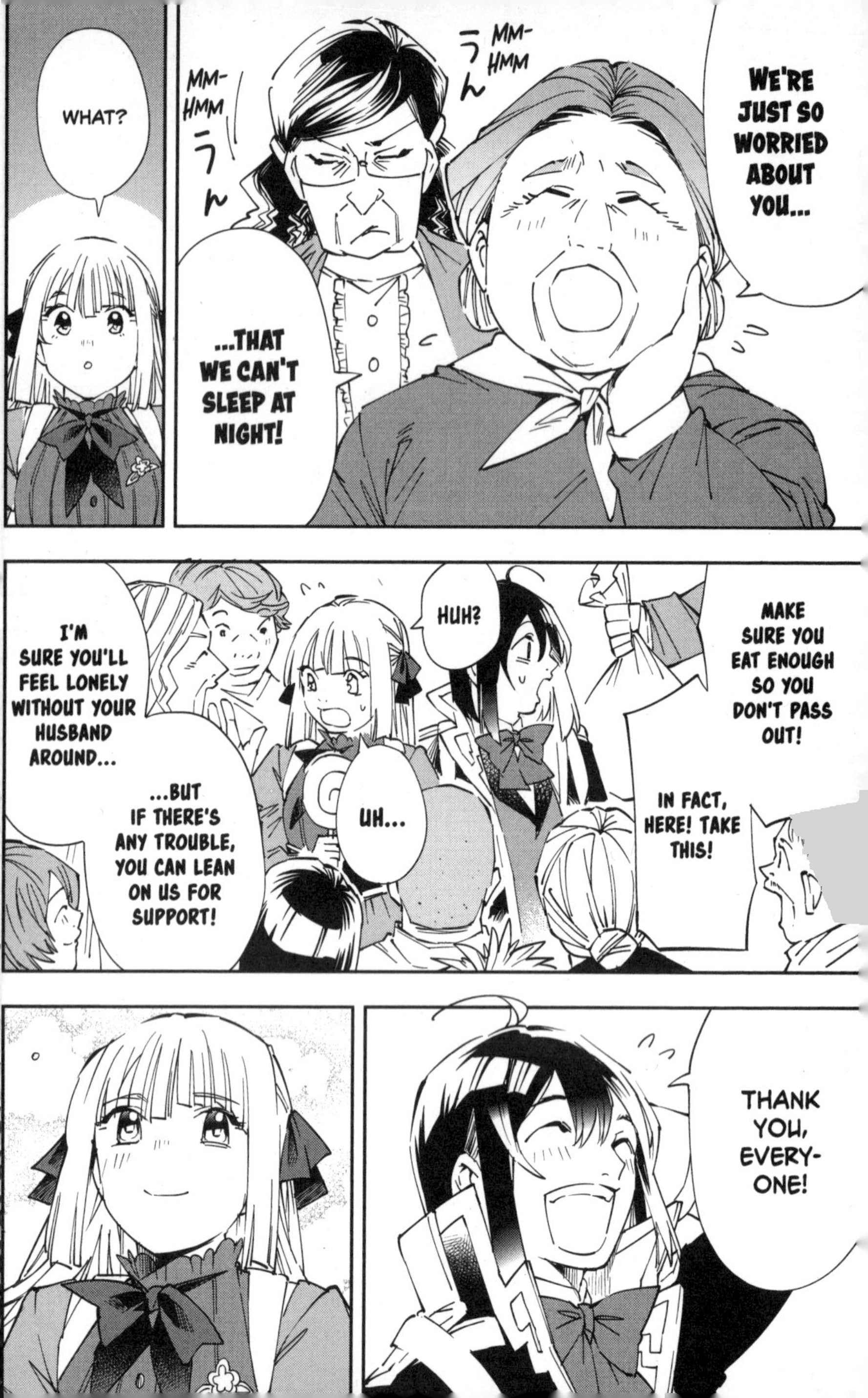
MM-HMM
WE'RE JUST SO WORRIED ABOUT YOU...
MM-HMM
...THAT WE CAN'T SLEEP AT NIGHT!
WHAT?
MAKE SURE YOU EAT ENOUGH SO YOU DON'T PASS OUT!
IN FACT, HERE! TAKE THIS!
HUH?
UH...
I'M SURE YOU'LL FEEL LONELY WITHOUT YOUR HUSBAND AROUND...
...BUT IF THERE'S ANY TROUBLE, YOU CAN LEAN ON US FOR SUPPORT!
THANK YOU, EVERYONE!

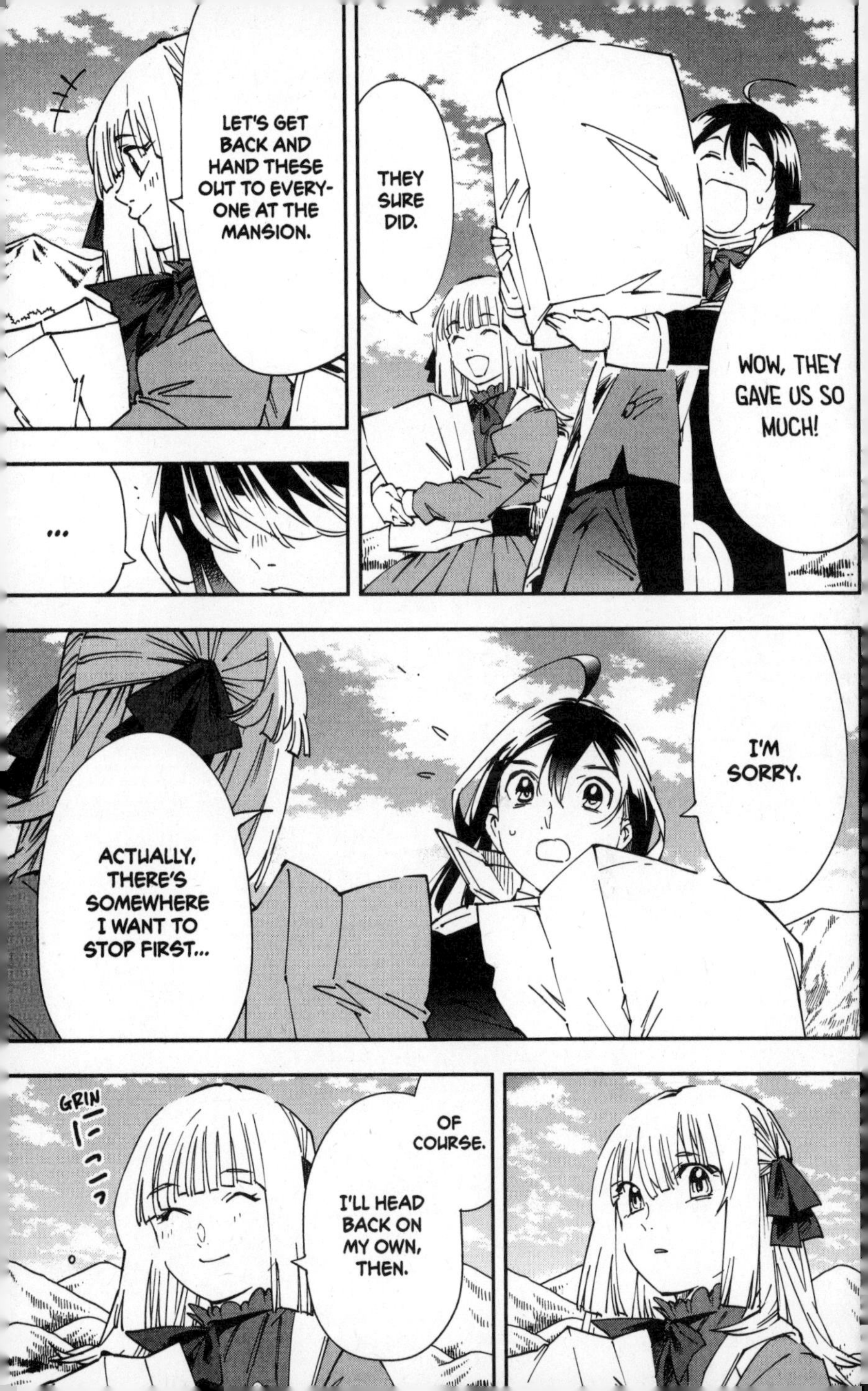
WOW, THEY GAVE US SO MUCH!
THEY SURE DID.
LET'S GET BACK AND HAND THESE OUT TO EVERYONE AT THE MANSION.
...
I'M SORRY.
ACTUALLY, THERE'S SOMEWHERE I WANT TO STOP FIRST...
OF COURSE.
I'LL HEAD BACK ON MY OWN, THEN.
GRIN

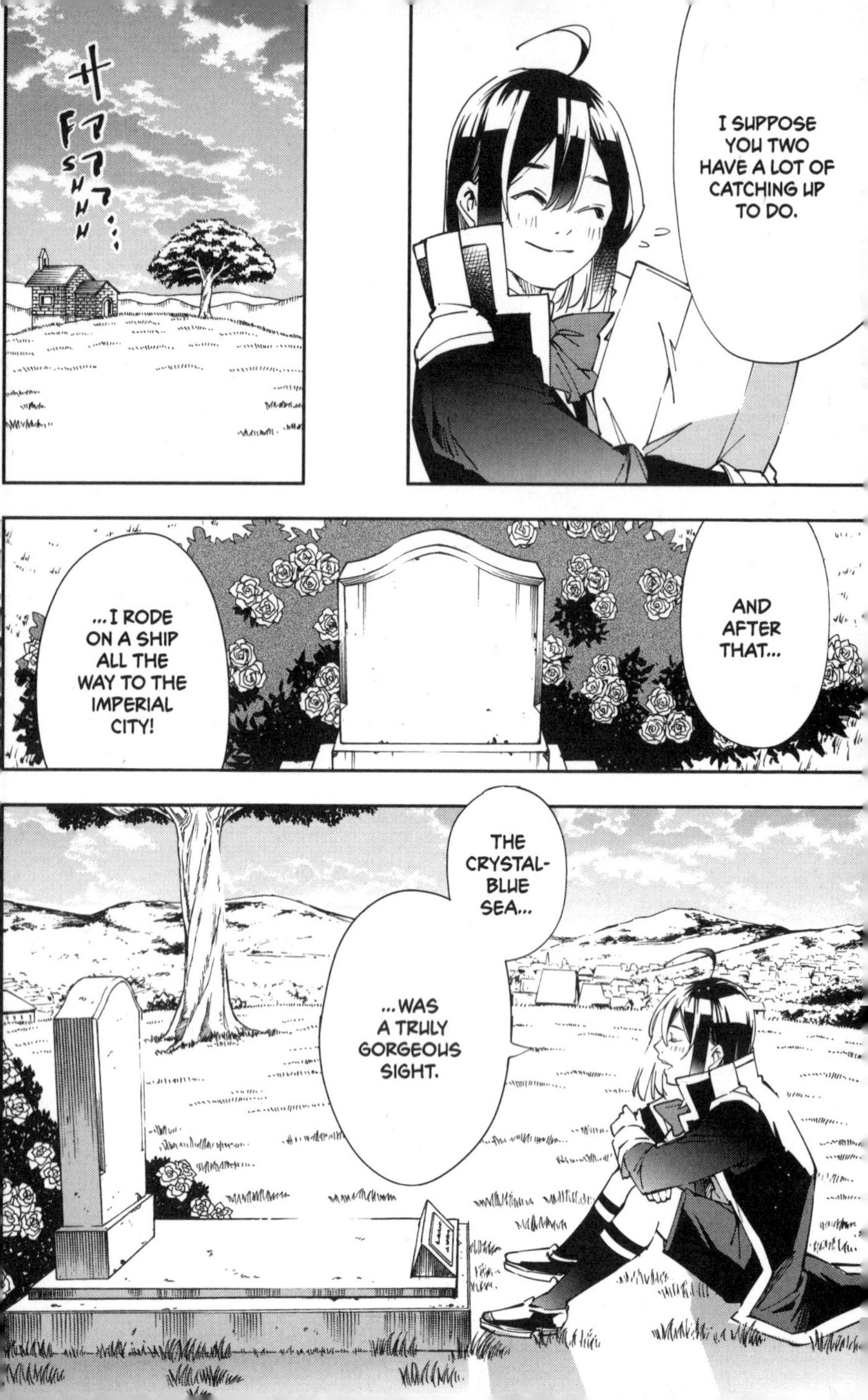
I SUPPOSE YOU TWO HAVE A LOT OF CATCHING UP TO DO.
FSHHH
AND AFTER THAT...
...I RODE ON A SHIP ALL THE WAY TO THE IMPERIAL CITY!
THE CRYSTAL-BLUE SEA...
...WAS A TRULY GORGEOUS SIGHT.

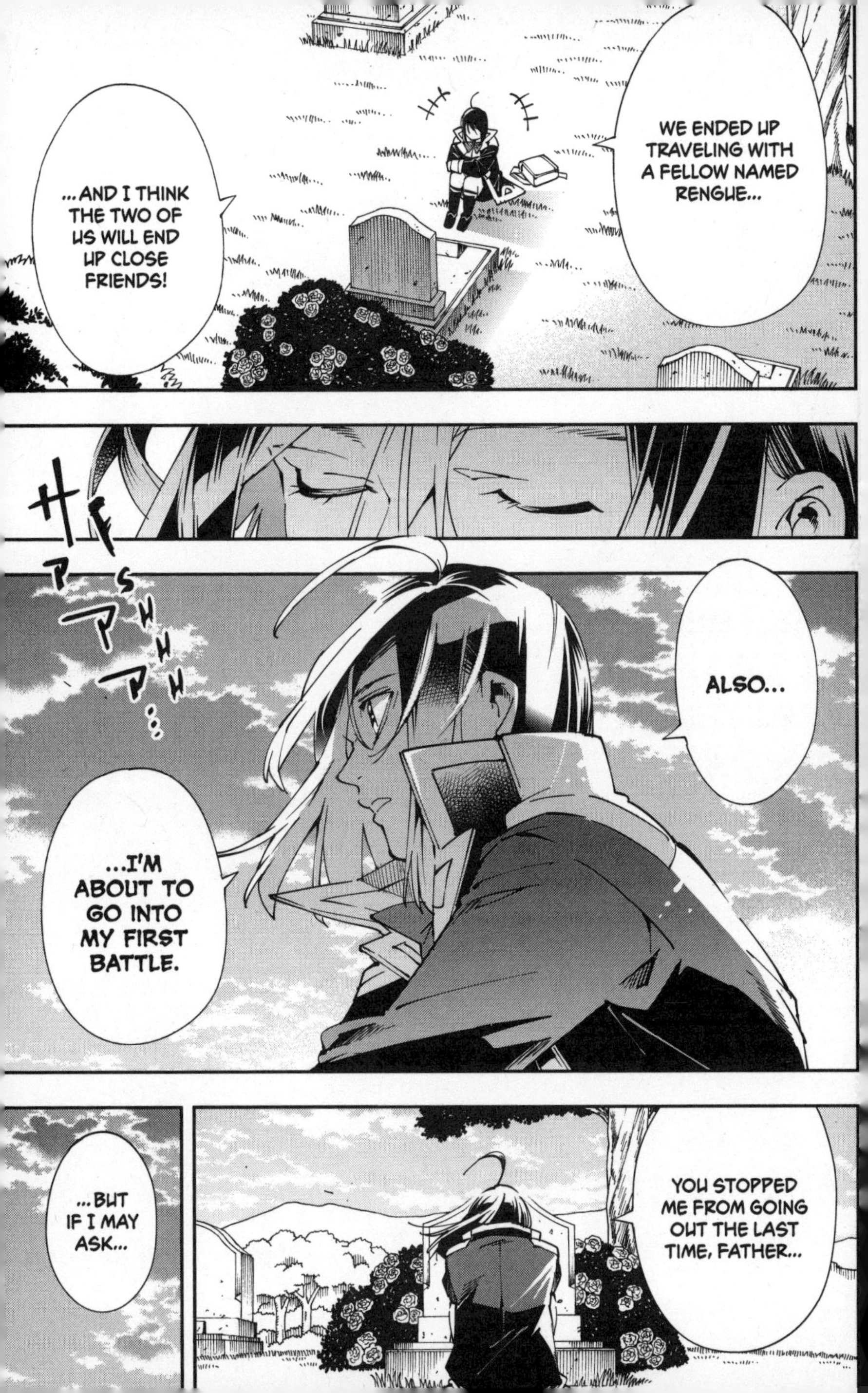
WE ENDED UP TRAVELING WITH A FELLOW NAMED RENGUE...
...AND I THINK THE TWO OF US WILL END UP CLOSE FRIENDS!
FSHHHH...
ALSO...
...I'M ABOUT TO GO INTO MY FIRST BATTLE.
YOU STOPPED ME FROM GOING OUT THE LAST TIME, FATHER...
...BUT IF I MAY ASK...

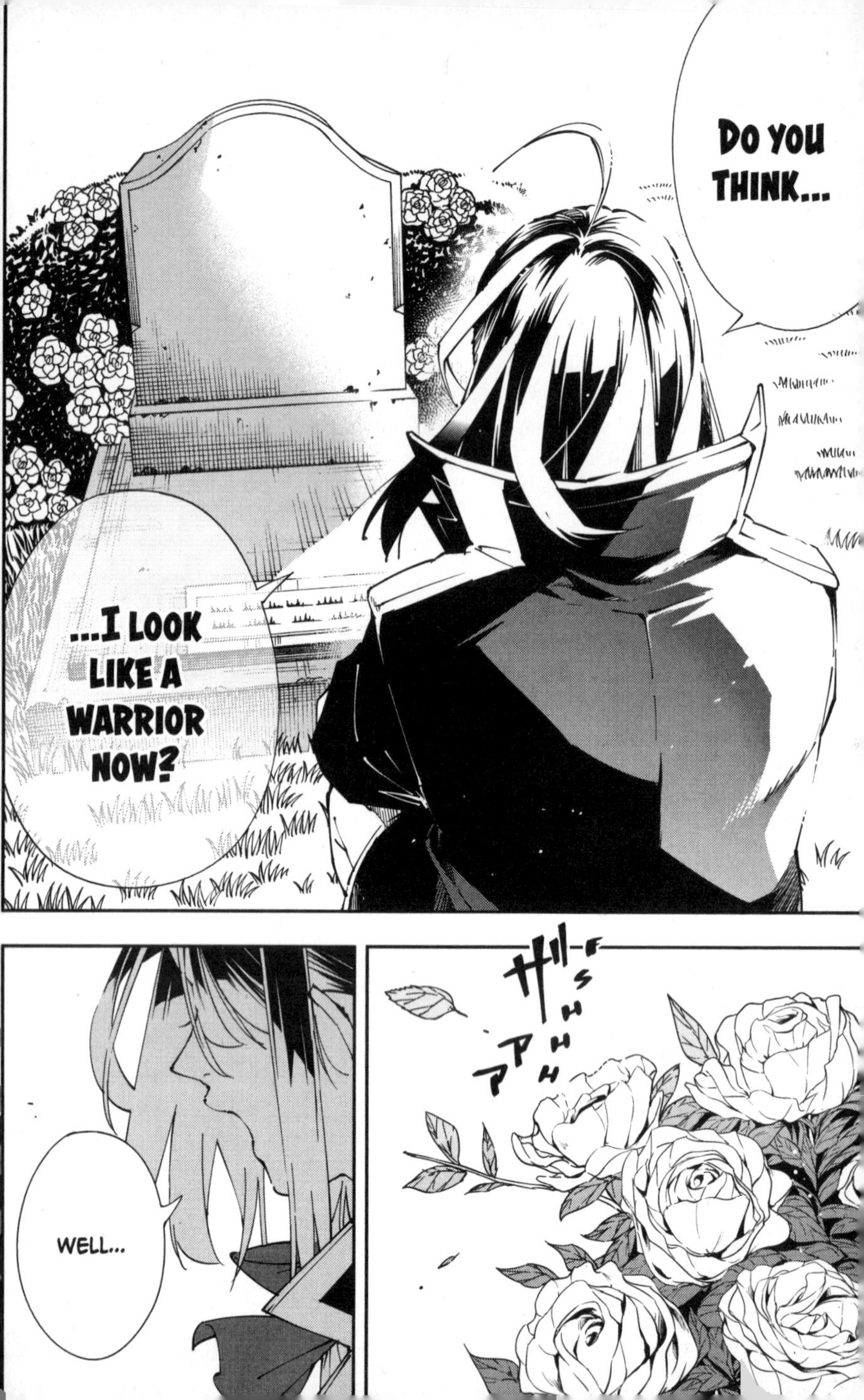
DO YOU THINK...
...I LOOK LIKE A WARRIOR NOW?
FSHHHH
WELL...

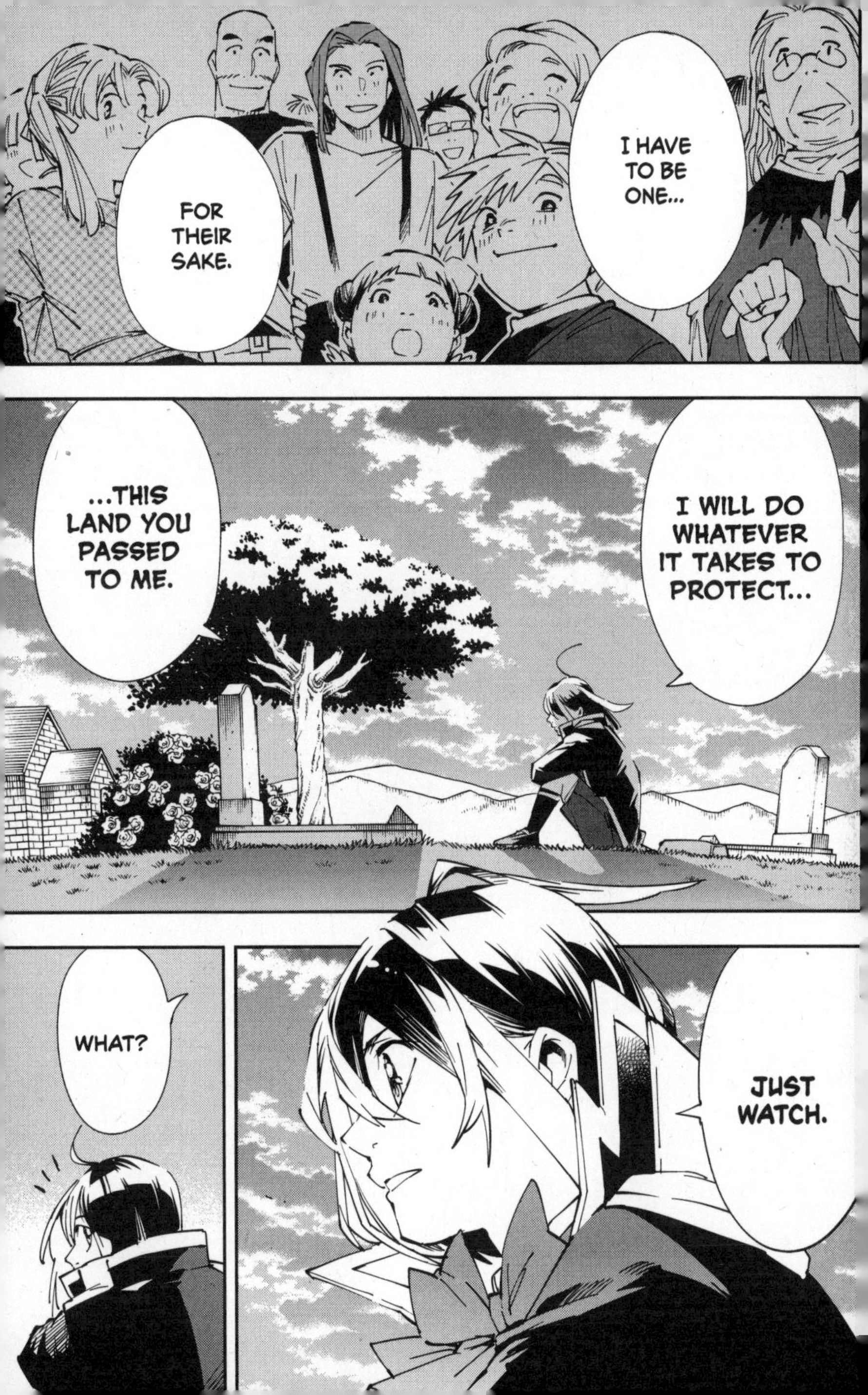
I HAVE TO BE ONE...
FOR THEIR SAKE.
I WILL DO WHATEVER IT TAKES TO PROTECT...
...THIS LAND YOU PASSED TO ME.
JUST WATCH.
WHAT?

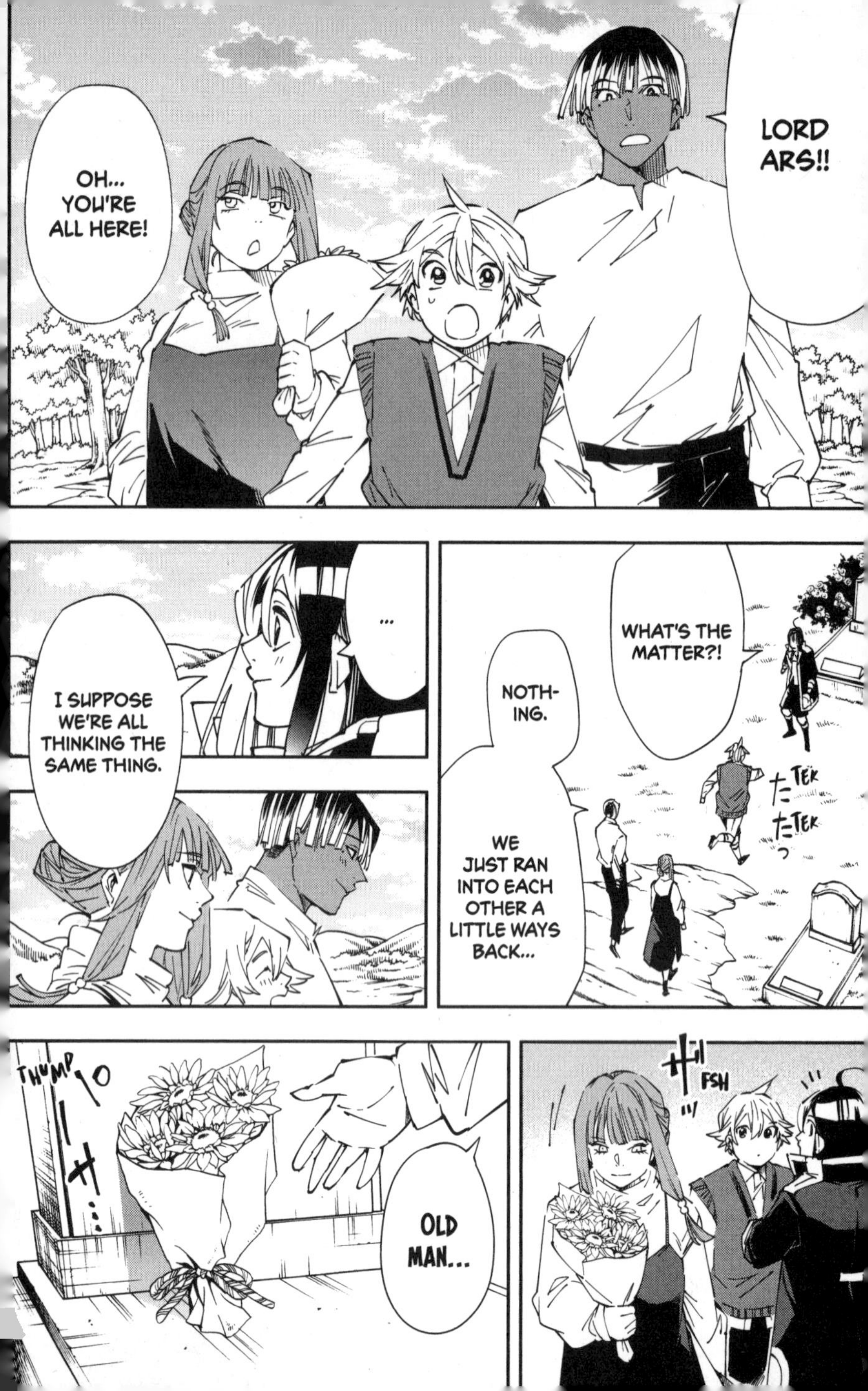
LORD ARS!!
OH... YOU'RE ALL HERE!
WHAT'S THE MATTER?!
NOTH-ING.
WE JUST RAN INTO EACH OTHER A LITTLE WAYS BACK...
TEK TEK
...
I SUPPOSE WE'RE ALL THINKING THE SAME THING.
FSH
OLD MAN...
THUMP

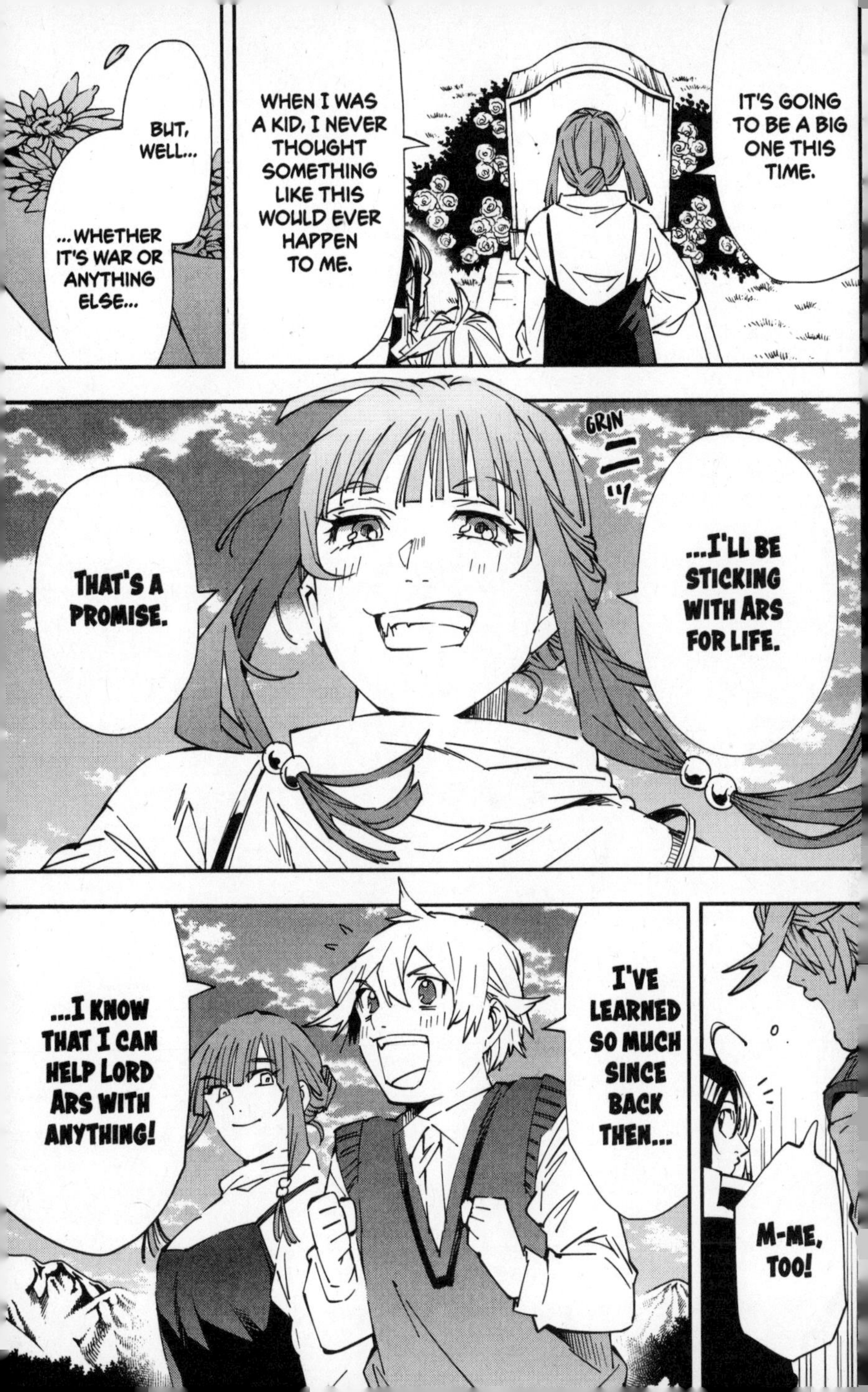
IT'S GOING TO BE A BIG ONE THIS TIME.
WHEN I WAS A KID, I NEVER THOUGHT SOMETHING LIKE THIS WOULD EVER HAPPEN TO ME.
BUT, WELL...
...WHETHER IT'S WAR OR ANYTHING ELSE...
GRIN
...I'LL BE STICKING WITH ARS FOR LIFE.
THAT'S A PROMISE.
M-ME, TOO!
I'VE LEARNED SO MUCH SINCE BACK THEN...
...I KNOW THAT I CAN HELP LORD ARS WITH ANYTHING!

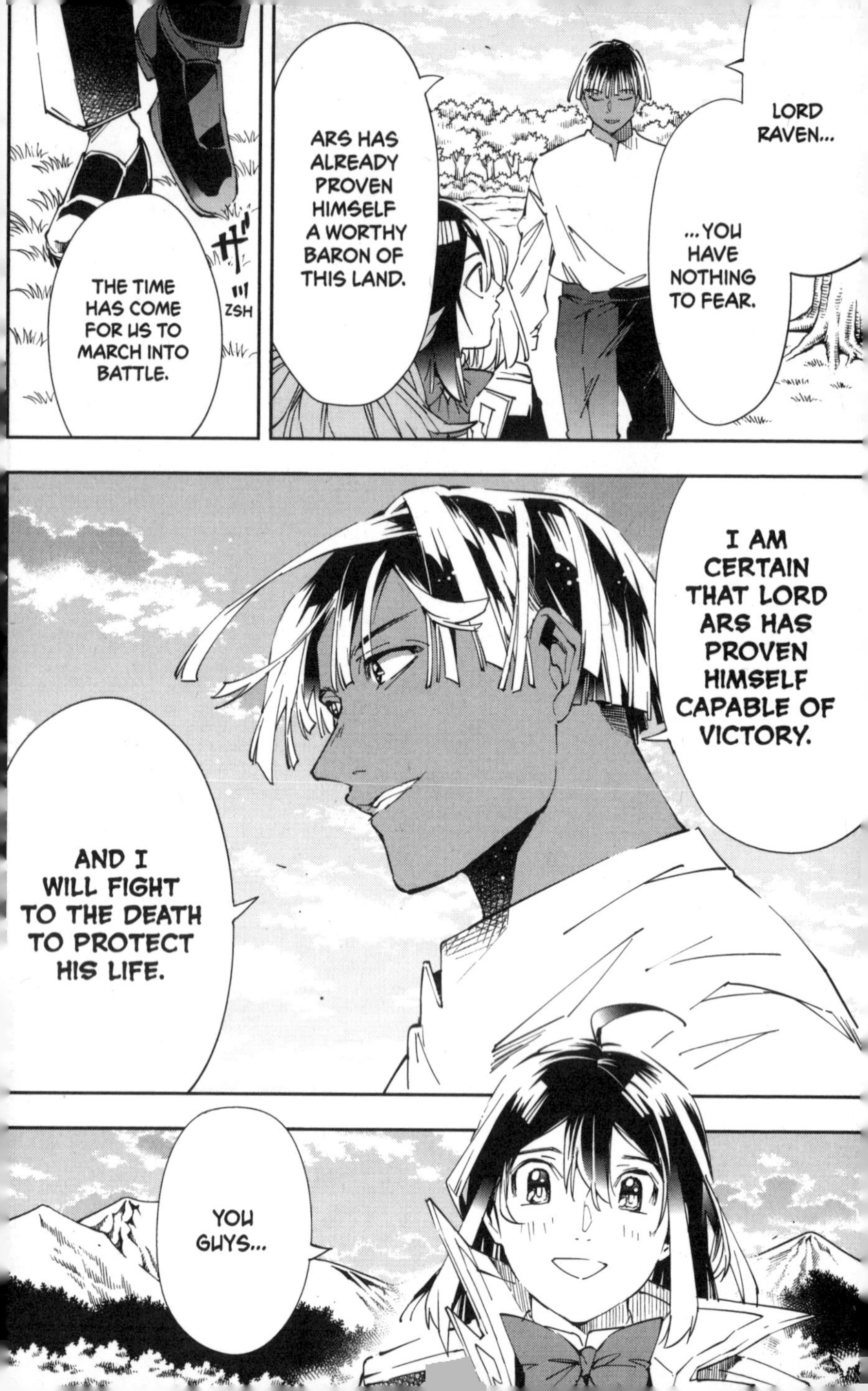
LORD RAVEN...
...YOU HAVE NOTHING TO FEAR.
ARS HAS ALREADY PROVEN HIMSELF A WORTHY BARON OF THIS LAND.
ZSH
THE TIME HAS COME FOR US TO MARCH INTO BATTLE.
I AM CERTAIN THAT LORD ARS HAS PROVEN HIMSELF CAPABLE OF VICTORY.
AND I WILL FIGHT TO THE DEATH TO PROTECT HIS LIFE.
YOU GUYS...

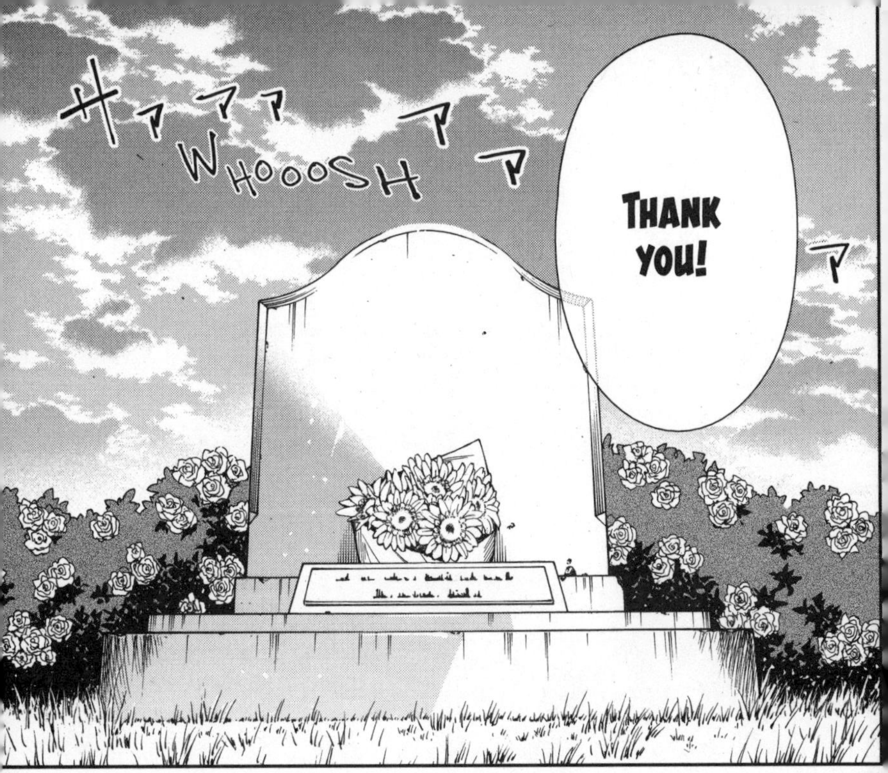
WHOOOSH
THANK YOU!
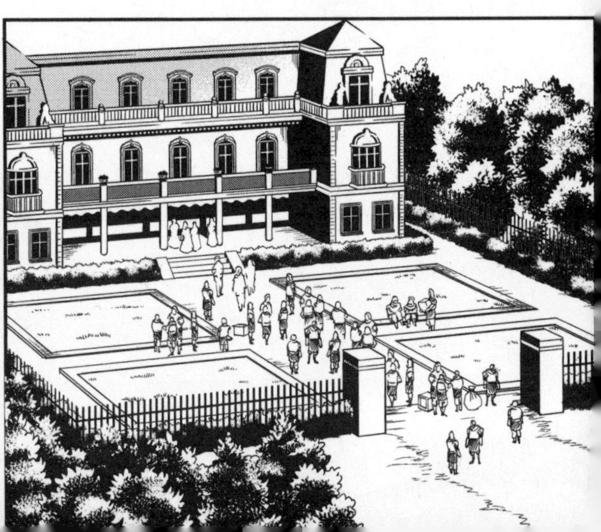
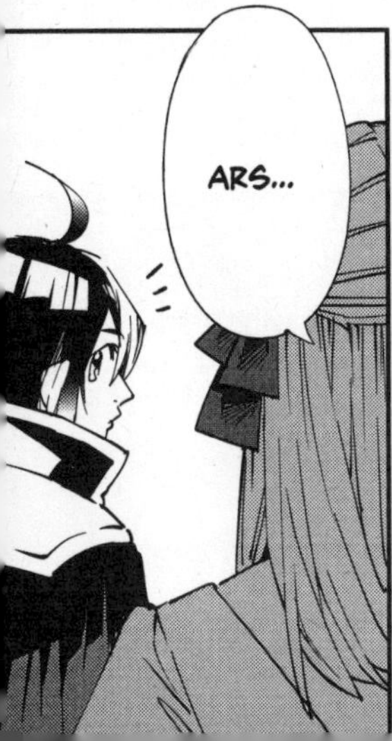
ARS...

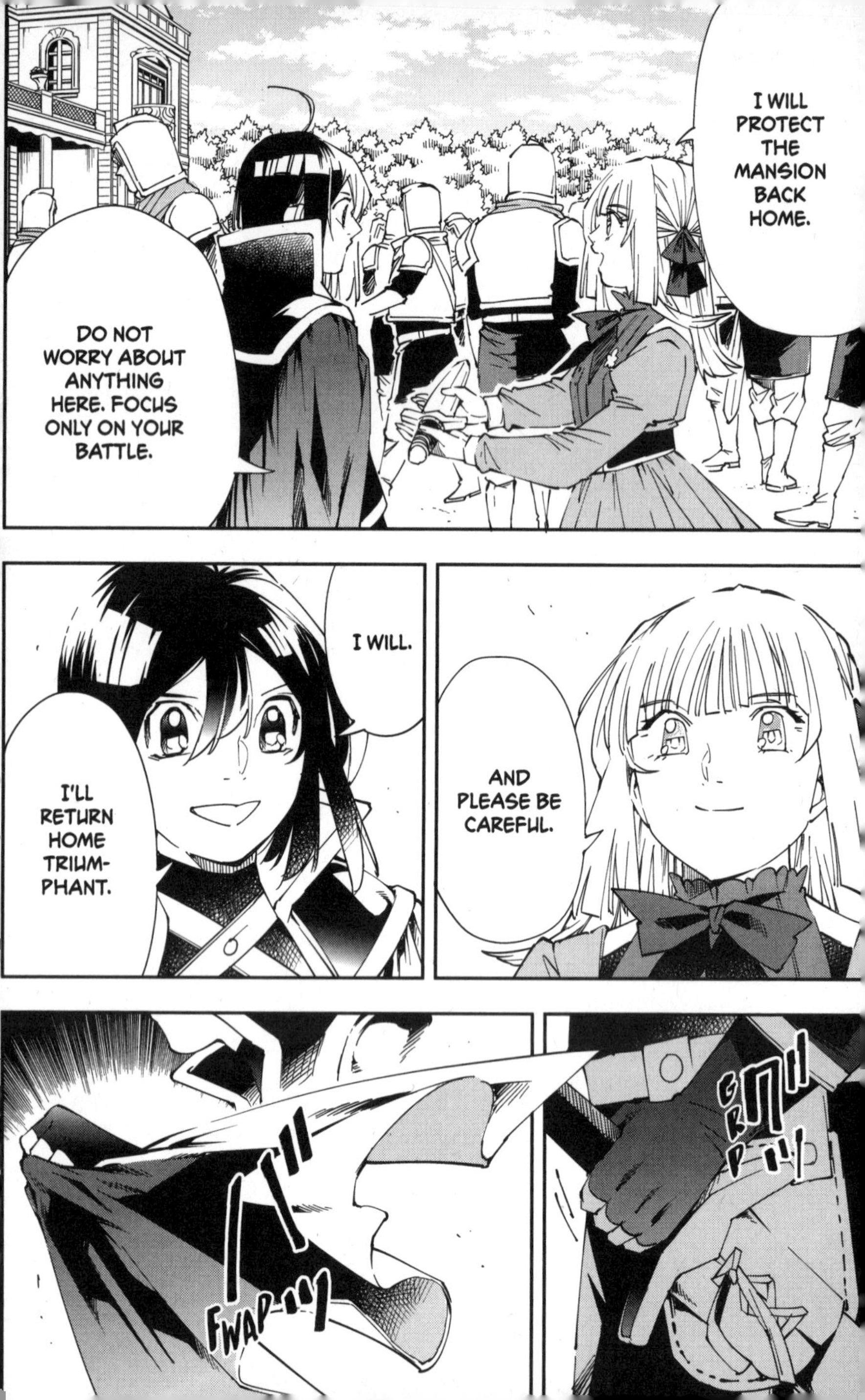
I WILL PROTECT THE MANSION BACK HOME.
DO NOT WORRY ABOUT ANYTHING HERE. FOCUS ONLY ON YOUR BATTLE.
AND PLEASE BE CAREFUL.
I WILL.
I'LL RETURN HOME TRIUMPHANT.
FWAP!!

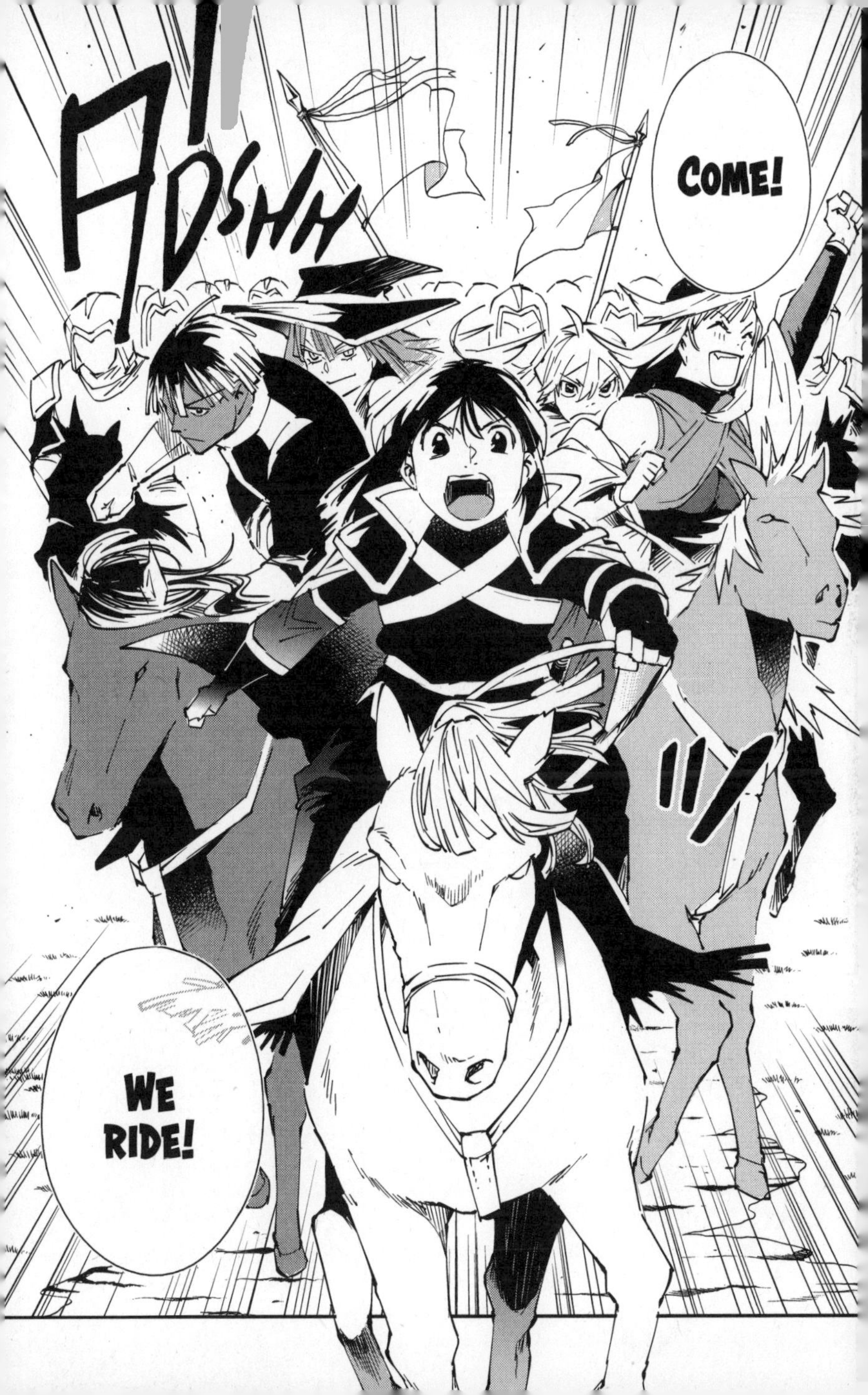
COME!
WE RIDE!

As a Reincarnated
ARISTOCRAT,
I'll Use My Appraisal Skill to
Rise in the World

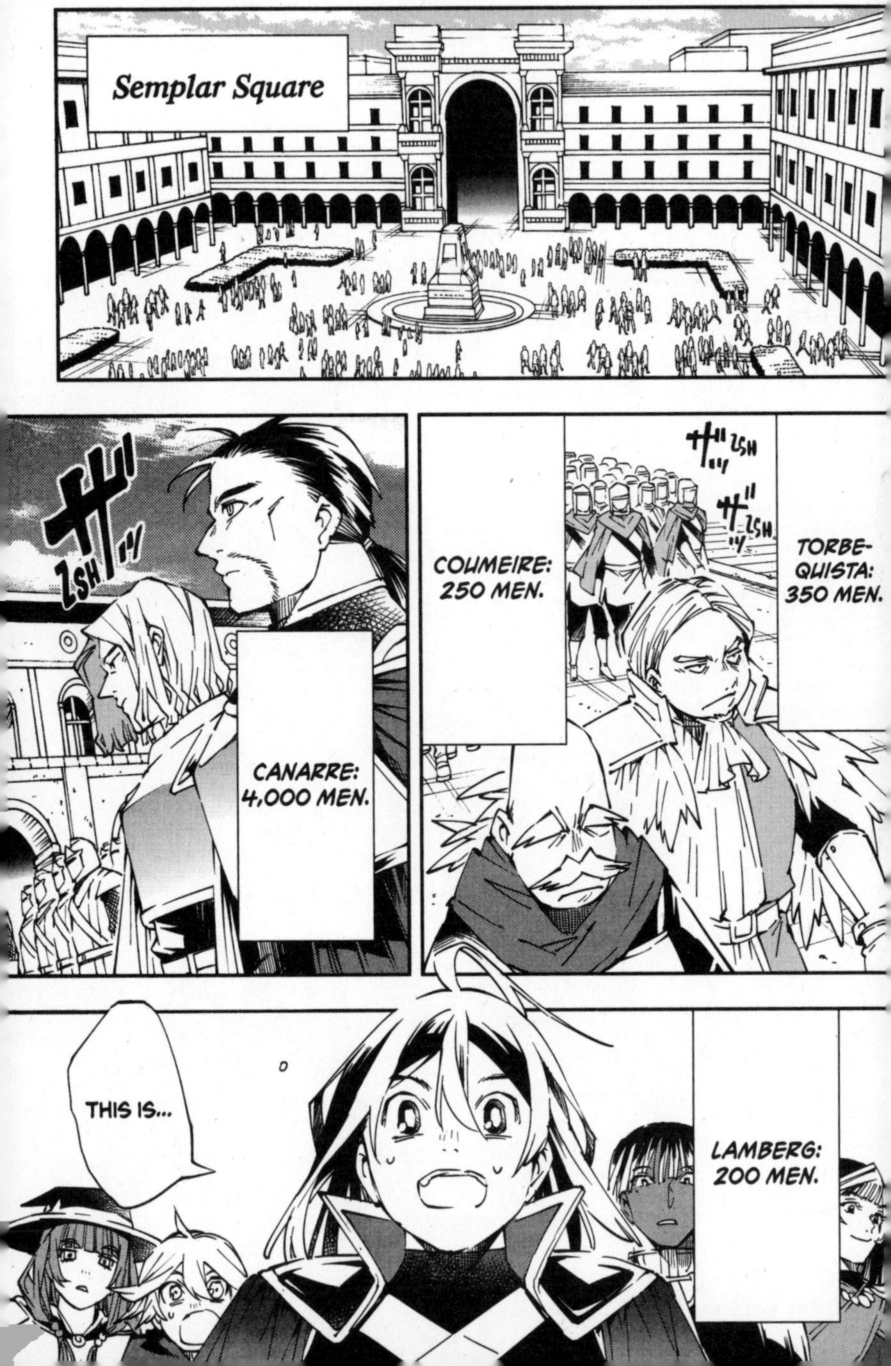
Semplar Square
ZSH
ZSH
TORBE-
QUISTA:
350 MEN.
COUMEIRE:
250 MEN.
ZSH
CANARRE:
4,000 MEN.
LAMBERG:
200 MEN.
THIS IS...

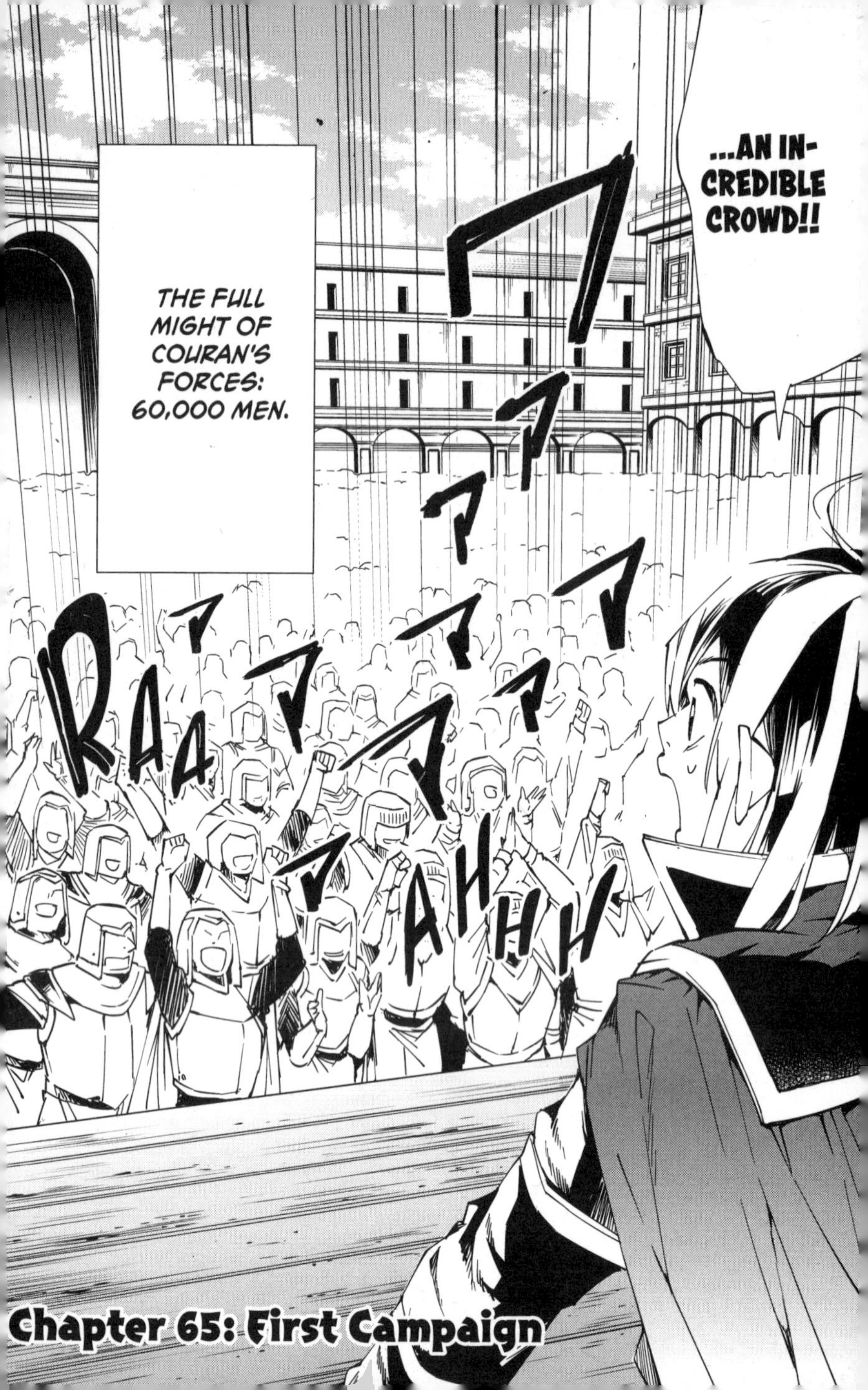
...AN INCREDIBLE CROWD!!
THE FULL MIGHT OF COURAN'S FORCES: 60,000 MEN.
RAA AHHH

Chapter 65: First Campaign

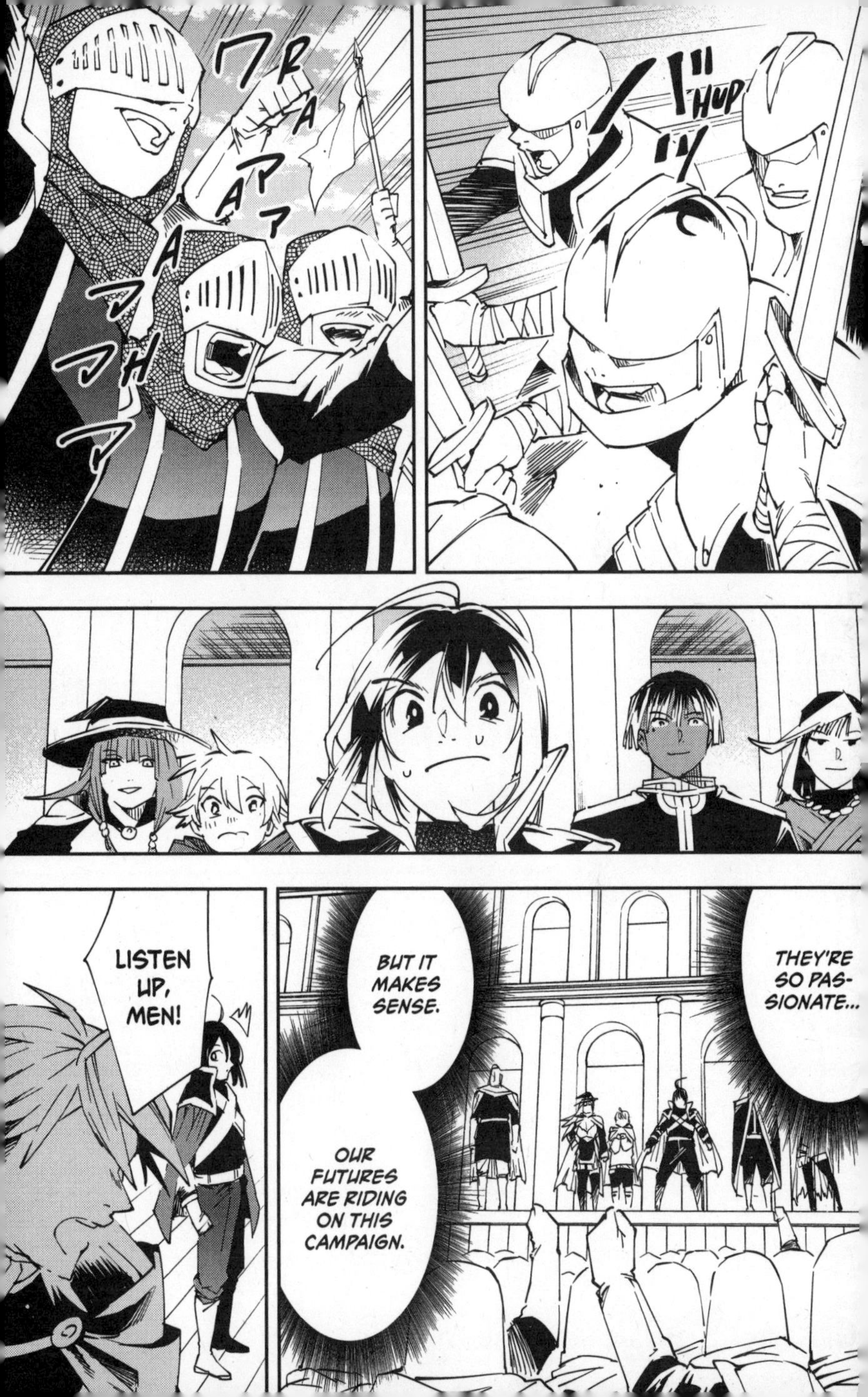

HUP
RAAAAH
THEY'RE SO PAS-SIONATE...
BUT IT MAKES SENSE.
OUR FUTURES ARE RIDING ON THIS CAMPAIGN.
LISTEN UP, MEN!

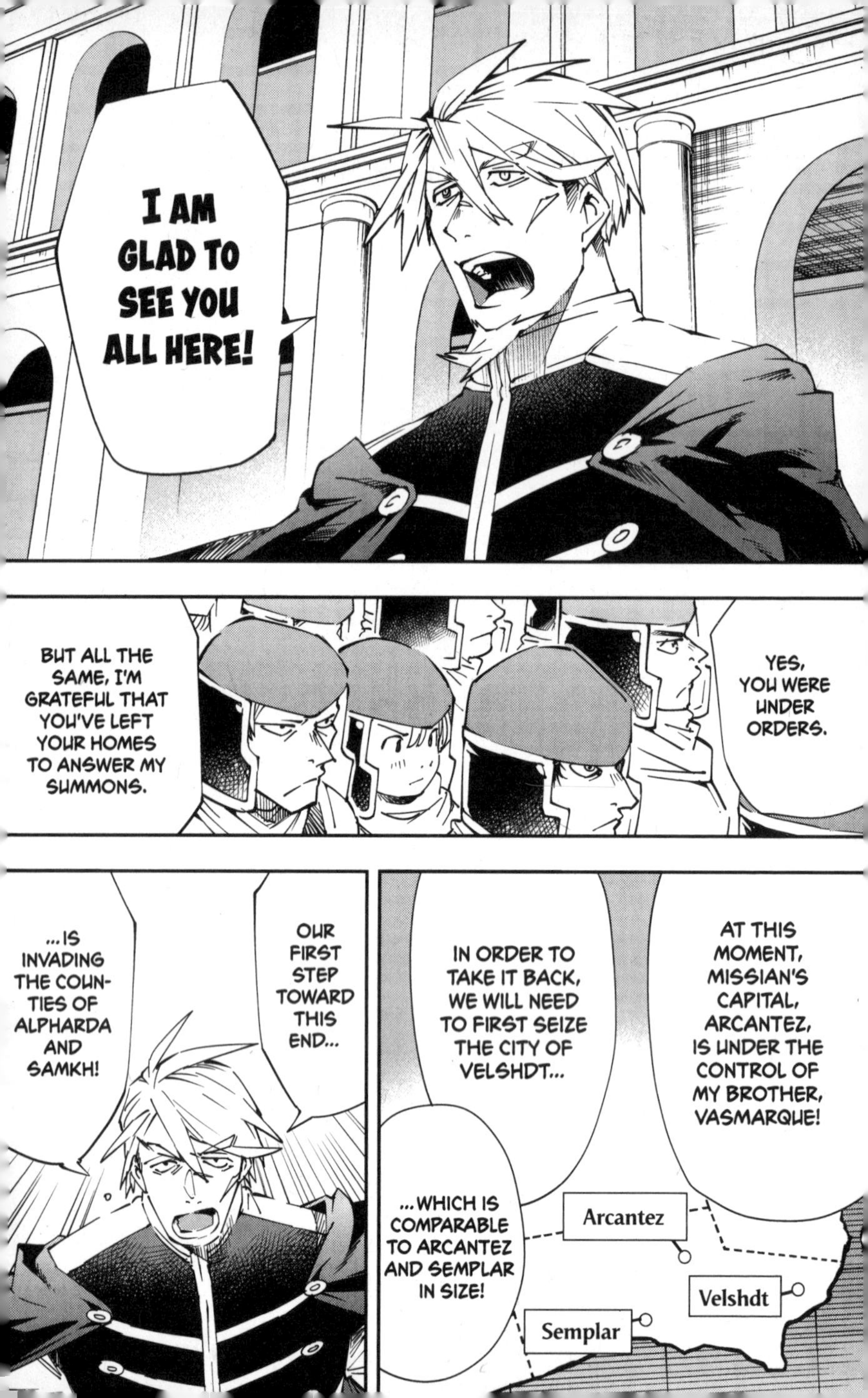
I AM GLAD TO SEE YOU ALL HERE!
YES, YOU WERE UNDER ORDERS.
BUT ALL THE SAME, I'M GRATEFUL THAT YOU'VE LEFT YOUR HOMES TO ANSWER MY SUMMONS.
AT THIS MOMENT, MISSIAN'S CAPITAL, ARCANTEZ, IS UNDER THE CONTROL OF MY BROTHER, VASMARQUE!
IN ORDER TO TAKE IT BACK, WE WILL NEED TO FIRST SEIZE THE CITY OF VELSHDT...
...WHICH IS COMPARABLE TO ARCANTEZ AND SEMPLAR IN SIZE!
Arcantez
Velshdt
Semplar
OUR FIRST STEP TOWARD THIS END...
...IS INVADING THE COUN-TIES OF ALPHARDA AND SAMKH!

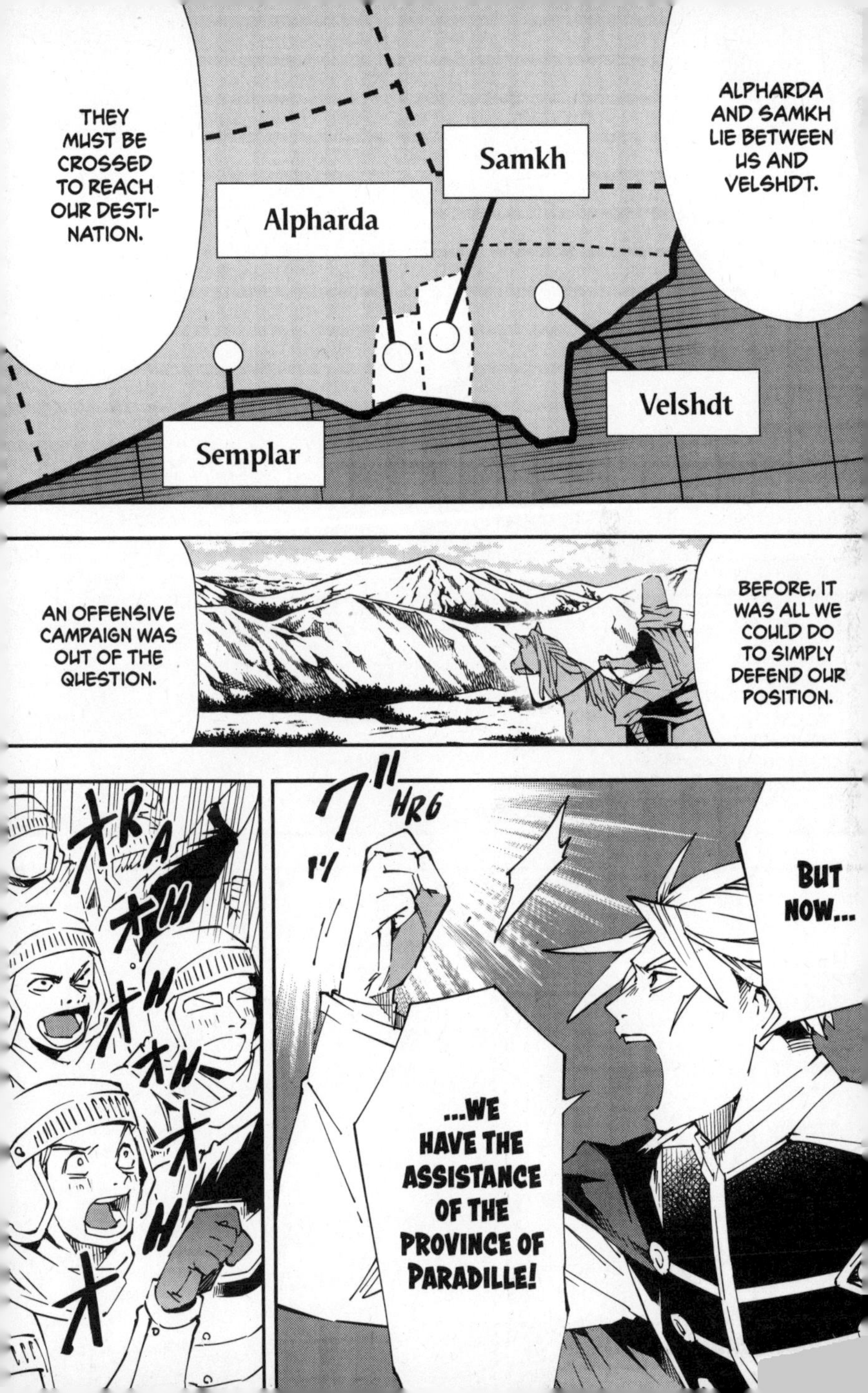
ALPHARDA AND SAMKH LIE BETWEEN US AND VELSHDT.
Samkh
Alpharda
Velshdt
Semplar
THEY MUST BE CROSSED TO REACH OUR DESTINATION.
BEFORE, IT WAS ALL WE COULD DO TO SIMPLY DEFEND OUR POSITION.
AN OFFENSIVE CAMPAIGN WAS OUT OF THE QUESTION.
BUT NOW...
HRG
...WE HAVE THE ASSISTANCE OF THE PROVINCE OF PARADILLE!
RAHHHH

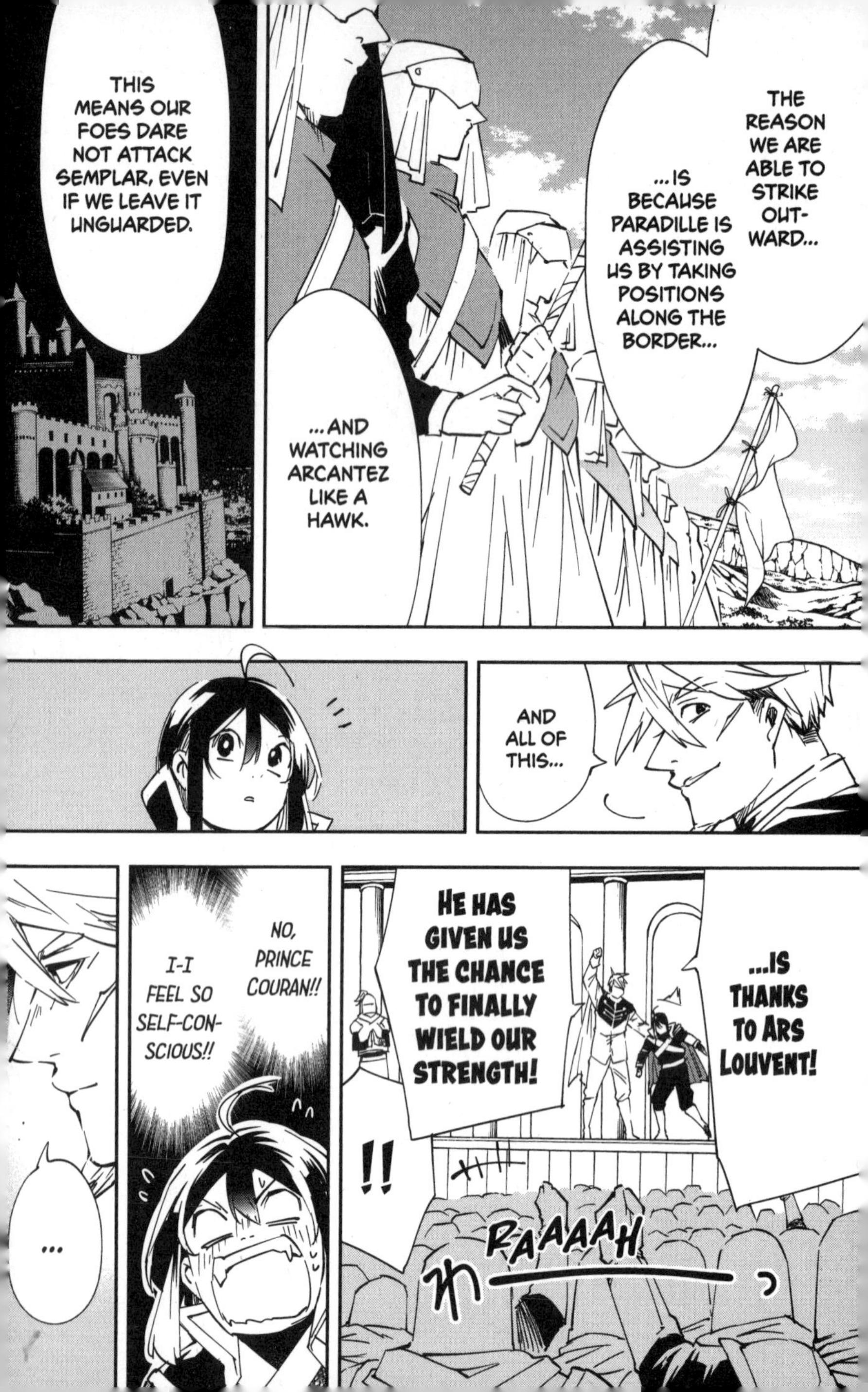
THE REASON WE ARE ABLE TO STRIKE OUTWARD...
...IS BECAUSE PARADILLE IS ASSISTING US BY TAKING POSITIONS ALONG THE BORDER...
...AND WATCHING ARCANTEZ LIKE A HAWK.
THIS MEANS OUR FOES DARE NOT ATTACK SEMPLAR, EVEN IF WE LEAVE IT UNGUARDED.
AND ALL OF THIS...
...IS THANKS TO ARS LOUVENT!
HE HAS GIVEN US THE CHANCE TO FINALLY WIELD OUR STRENGTH!
!!
RAAAAH
NO, PRINCE COURAN!!
I-I FEEL SO SELF-CONSCIOUS!!
...

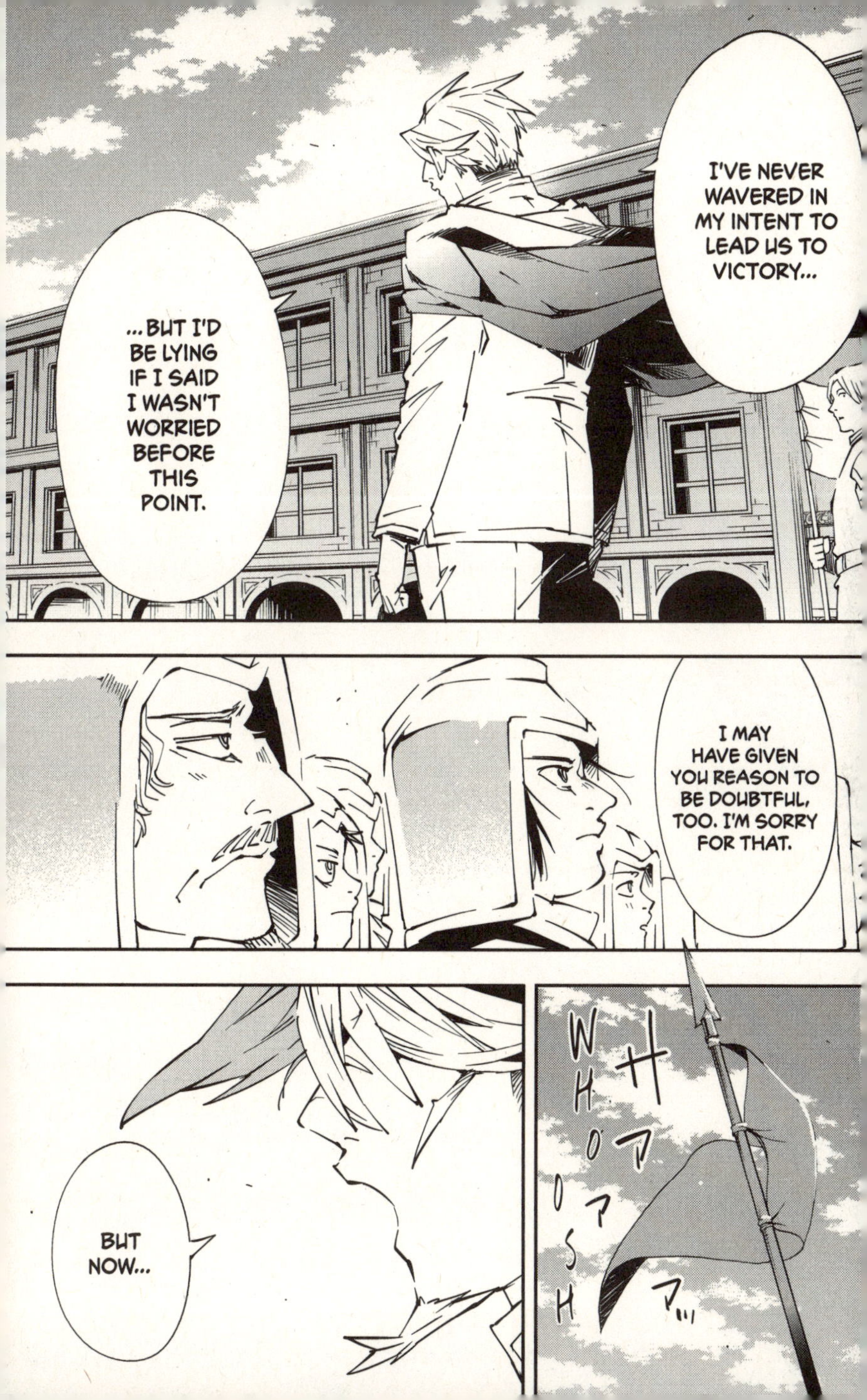
I'VE NEVER WAVERED IN MY INTENT TO LEAD US TO VICTORY...
...BUT I'D BE LYING IF I SAID I WASN'T WORRIED BEFORE THIS POINT.
I MAY HAVE GIVEN YOU REASON TO BE DOUBTFUL, TOO. I'M SORRY FOR THAT.
WHOOSH
BUT NOW...

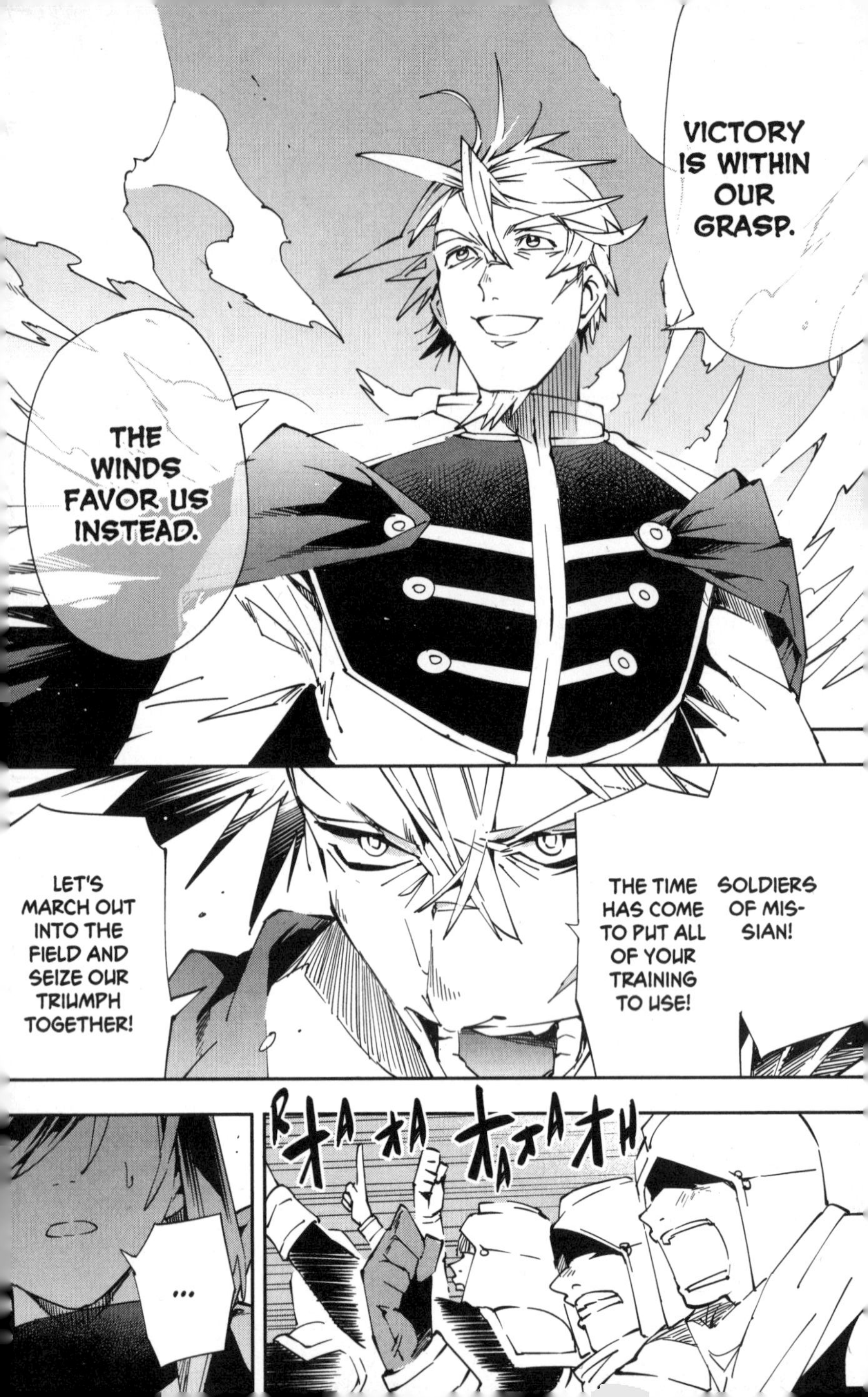
VICTORY IS WITHIN OUR GRASP.
THE WINDS FAVOR US INSTEAD.
SOLDIERS OF MIS-SIAN!
THE TIME HAS COME TO PUT ALL OF YOUR TRAINING TO USE!
LET'S MARCH OUT INTO THE FIELD AND SEIZE OUR TRIUMPH TOGETHER!
RAAAAAAH
...

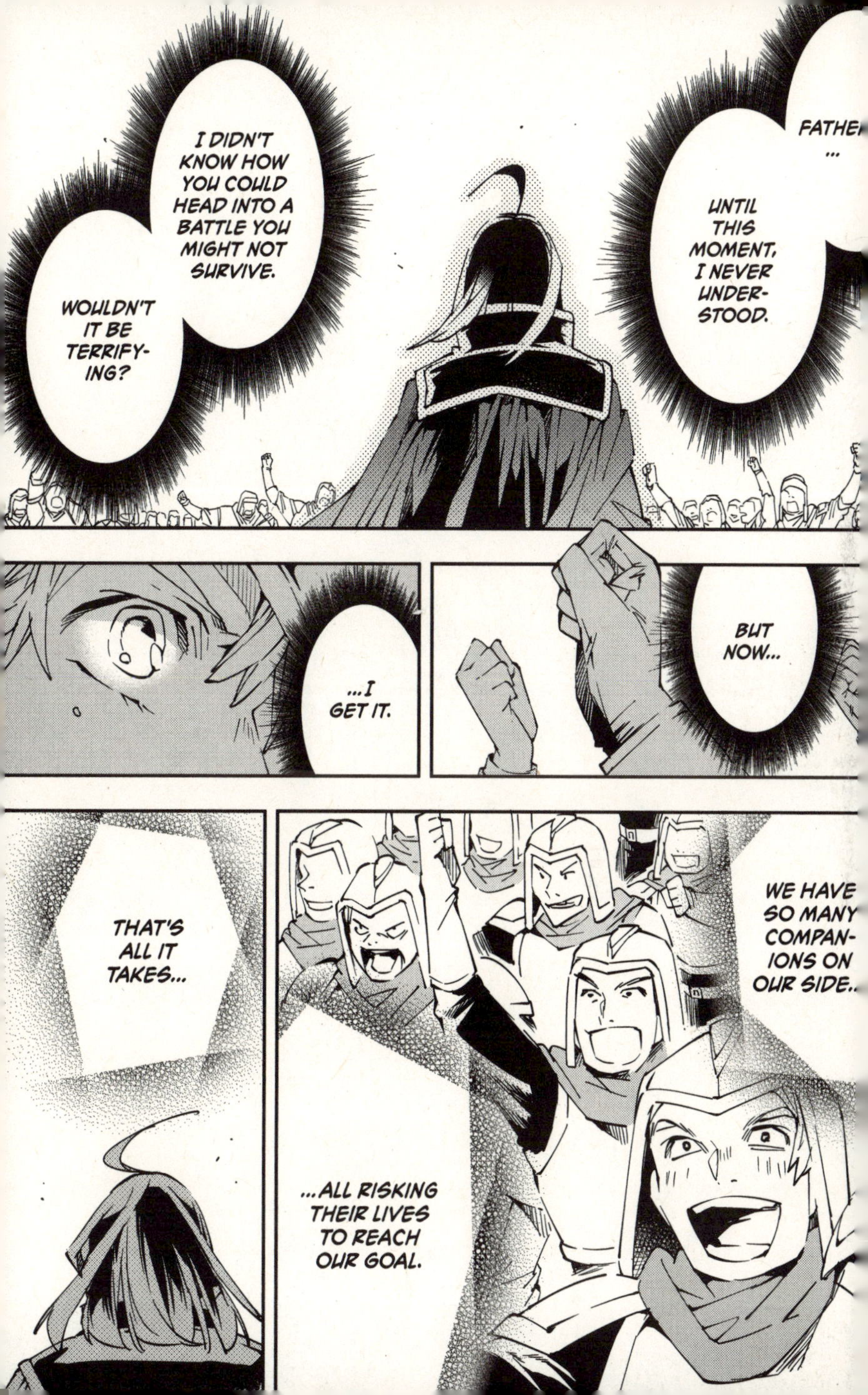
FATHE ...
UNTIL THIS MOMENT, I NEVER UNDERSTOOD.
I DIDN'T KNOW HOW YOU COULD HEAD INTO A BATTLE YOU MIGHT NOT SURVIVE.
WOULDN'T IT BE TERRIFYING?
BUT NOW...
...I GET IT.
WE HAVE SO MANY COMPANIONS ON OUR SIDE...
...ALL RISKING THEIR LIVES TO REACH OUR GOAL.
THAT'S ALL IT TAKES...

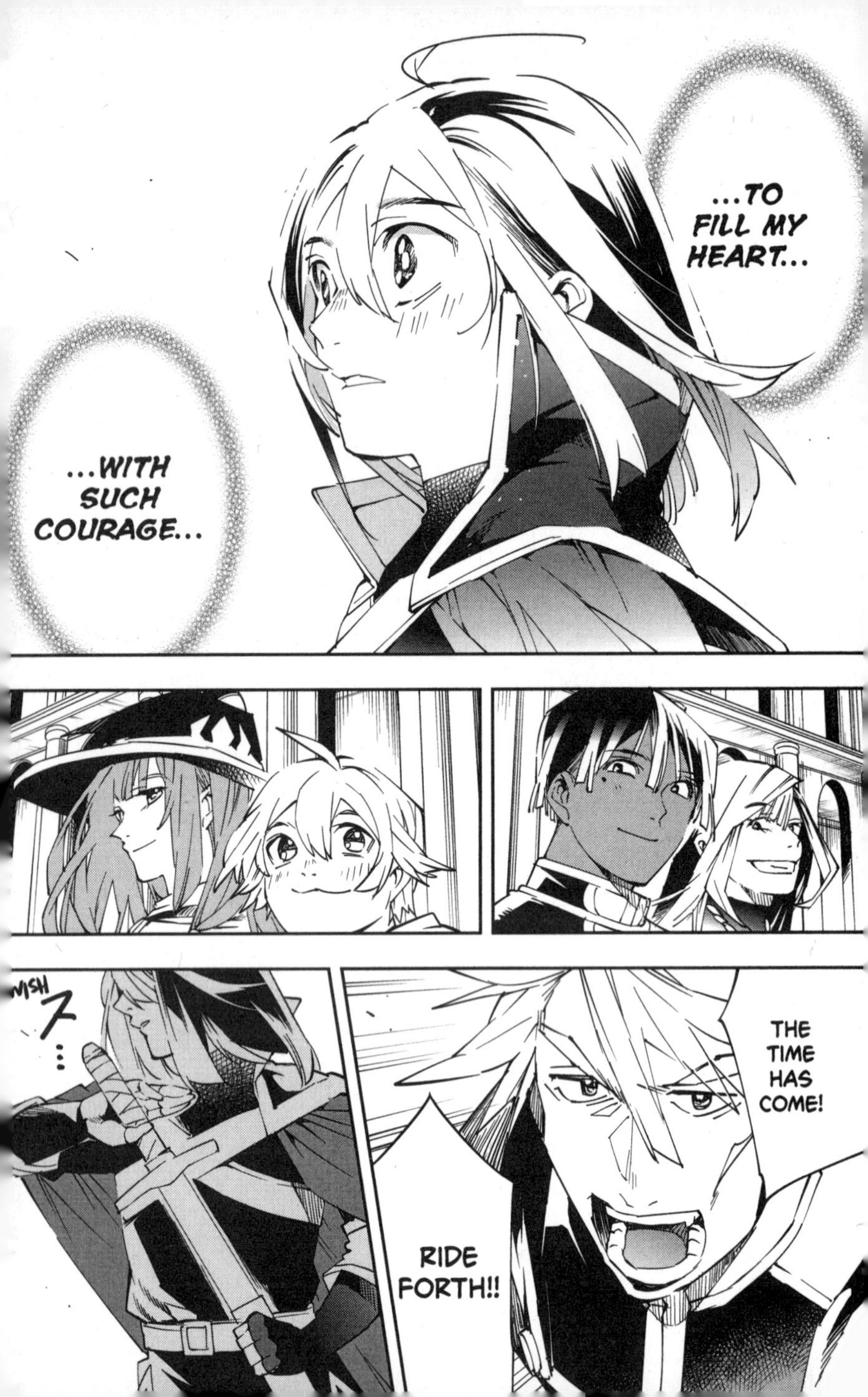
...TO FILL MY HEART...
...WITH SUCH COURAGE...
THE TIME HAS COME!
RIDE FORTH!!
...

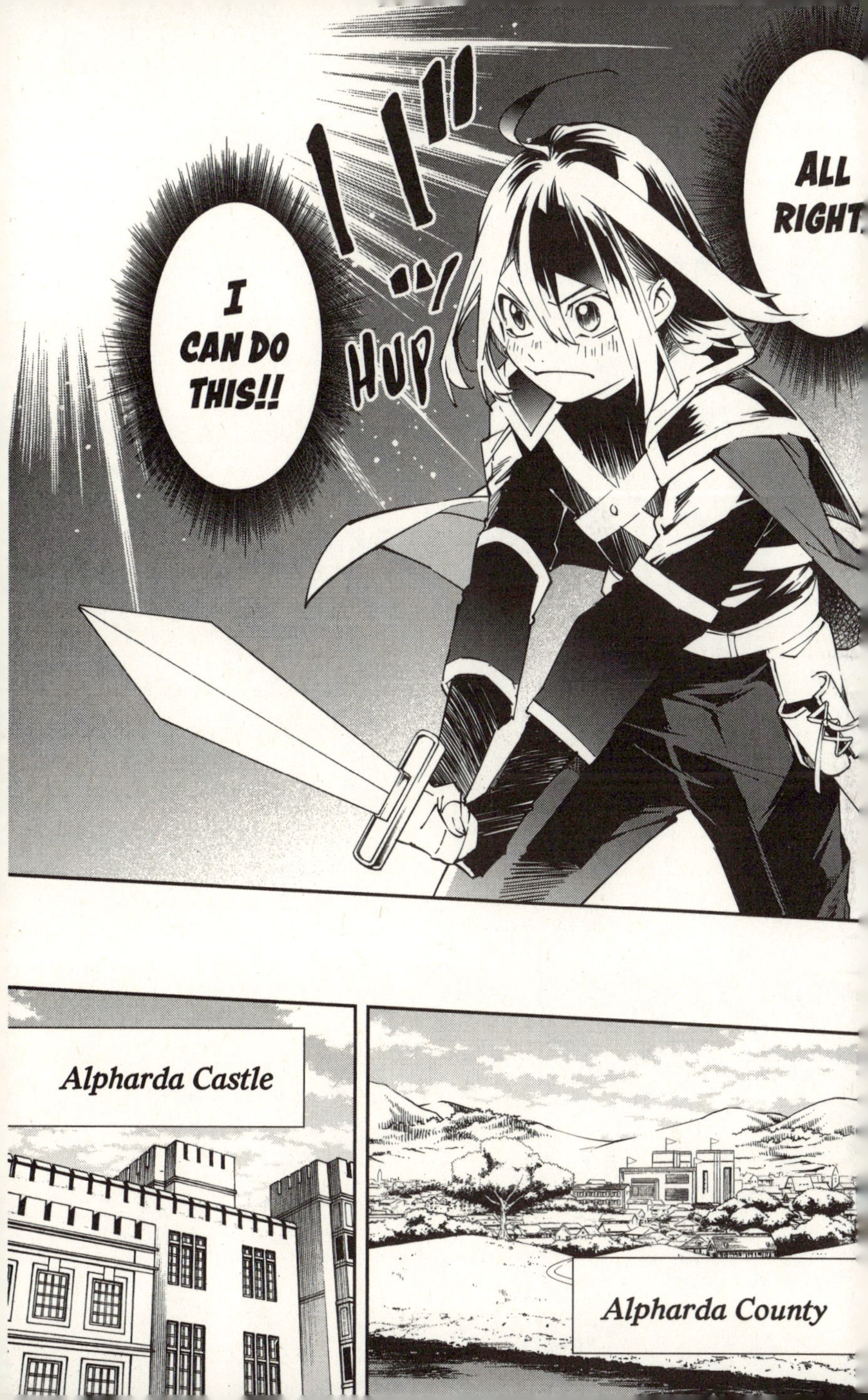
ALL RIGHT.
HUP
I CAN DO THIS!!
Alpharda County
Alpharda Castle

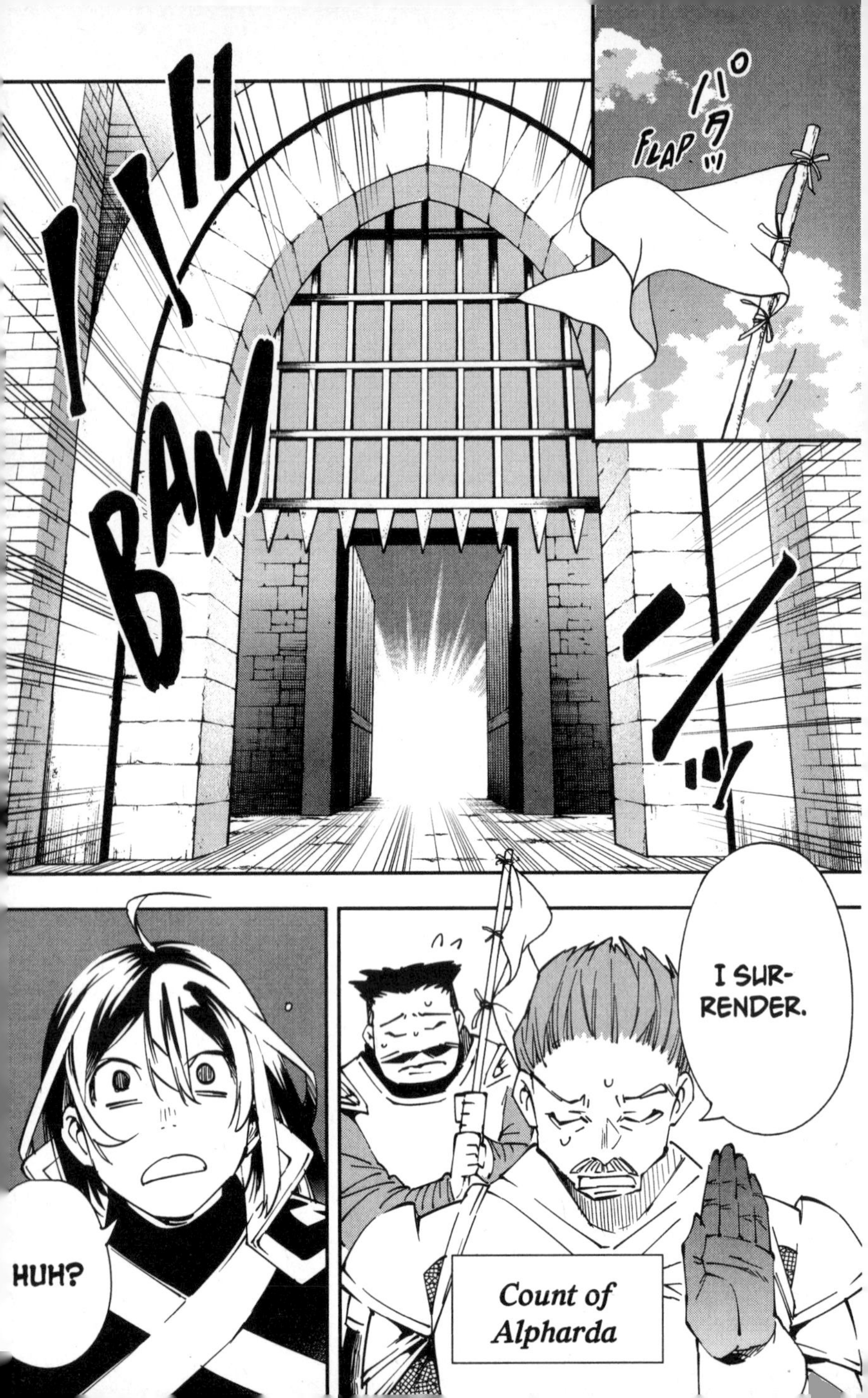
パタッ
FLAP
BAM
I SUR-RENDER.
Count of Alpharda
HUH?

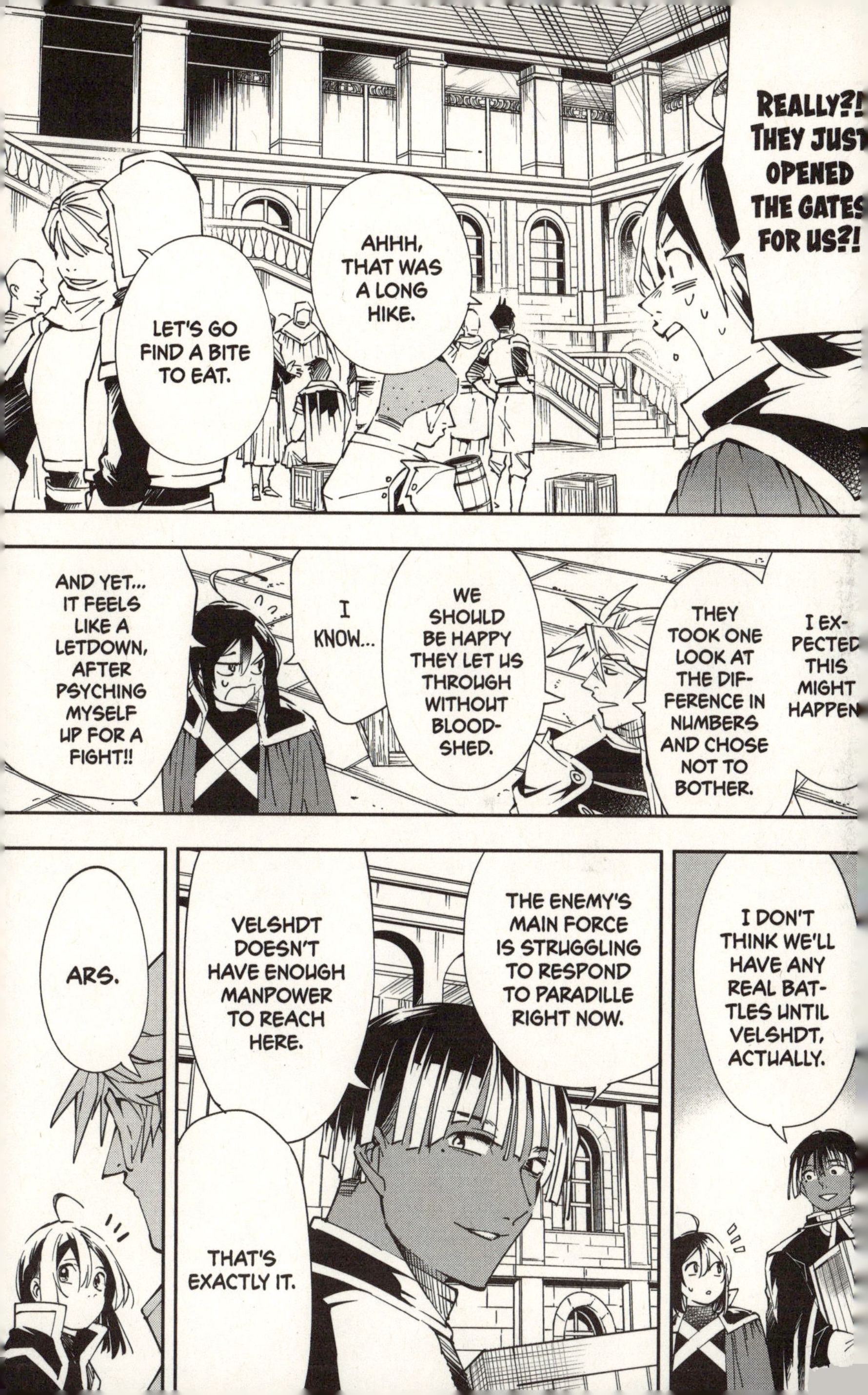
REALLY?! THEY JUST OPENED THE GATES FOR US?!
AHHH, THAT WAS A LONG HIKE.
LET'S GO FIND A BITE TO EAT.
I EXPECTED THIS MIGHT HAPPEN
THEY TOOK ONE LOOK AT THE DIFFERENCE IN NUMBERS AND CHOSE NOT TO BOTHER.
WE SHOULD BE HAPPY THEY LET US THROUGH WITHOUT BLOODSHED.
I KNOW...
AND YET... IT FEELS LIKE A LETDOWN, AFTER PSYCHING MYSELF UP FOR A FIGHT!!
I DON'T THINK WE'LL HAVE ANY REAL BATTLES UNTIL VELSHDT, ACTUALLY.
THE ENEMY'S MAIN FORCE IS STRUGGLING TO RESPOND TO PARADILLE RIGHT NOW.
VELSHDT DOESN'T HAVE ENOUGH MANPOWER TO REACH HERE.
THAT'S EXACTLY IT.
ARS.

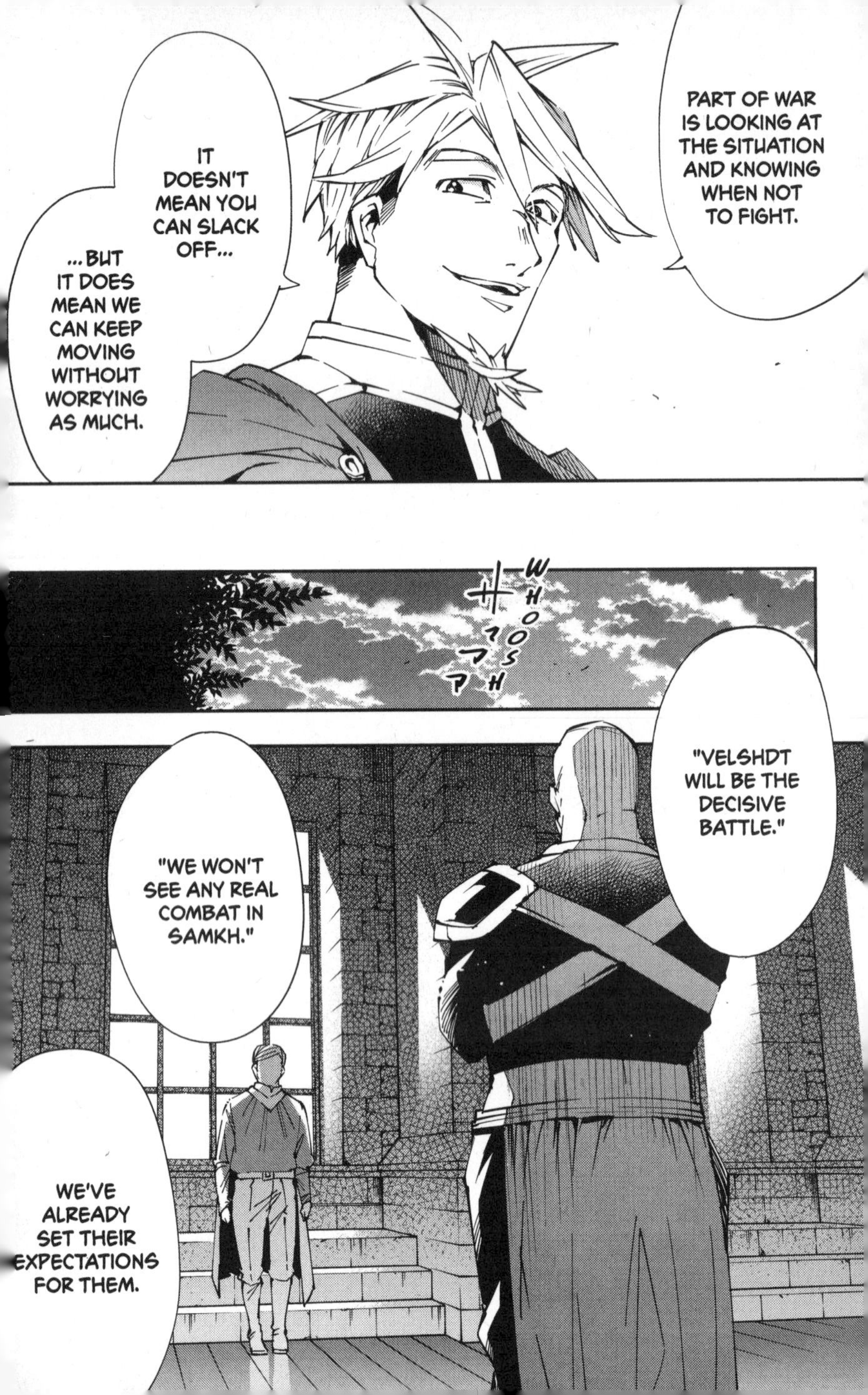
PART OF WAR IS LOOKING AT THE SITUATION AND KNOWING WHEN NOT TO FIGHT.
IT DOESN'T MEAN YOU CAN SLACK OFF...
...BUT IT DOES MEAN WE CAN KEEP MOVING WITHOUT WORRYING AS MUCH.
WHOOSH
"VELSHDT WILL BE THE DECISIVE BATTLE."
"WE WON'T SEE ANY REAL COMBAT IN SAMKH."
WE'VE ALREADY SET THEIR EXPECTATIONS FOR THEM.

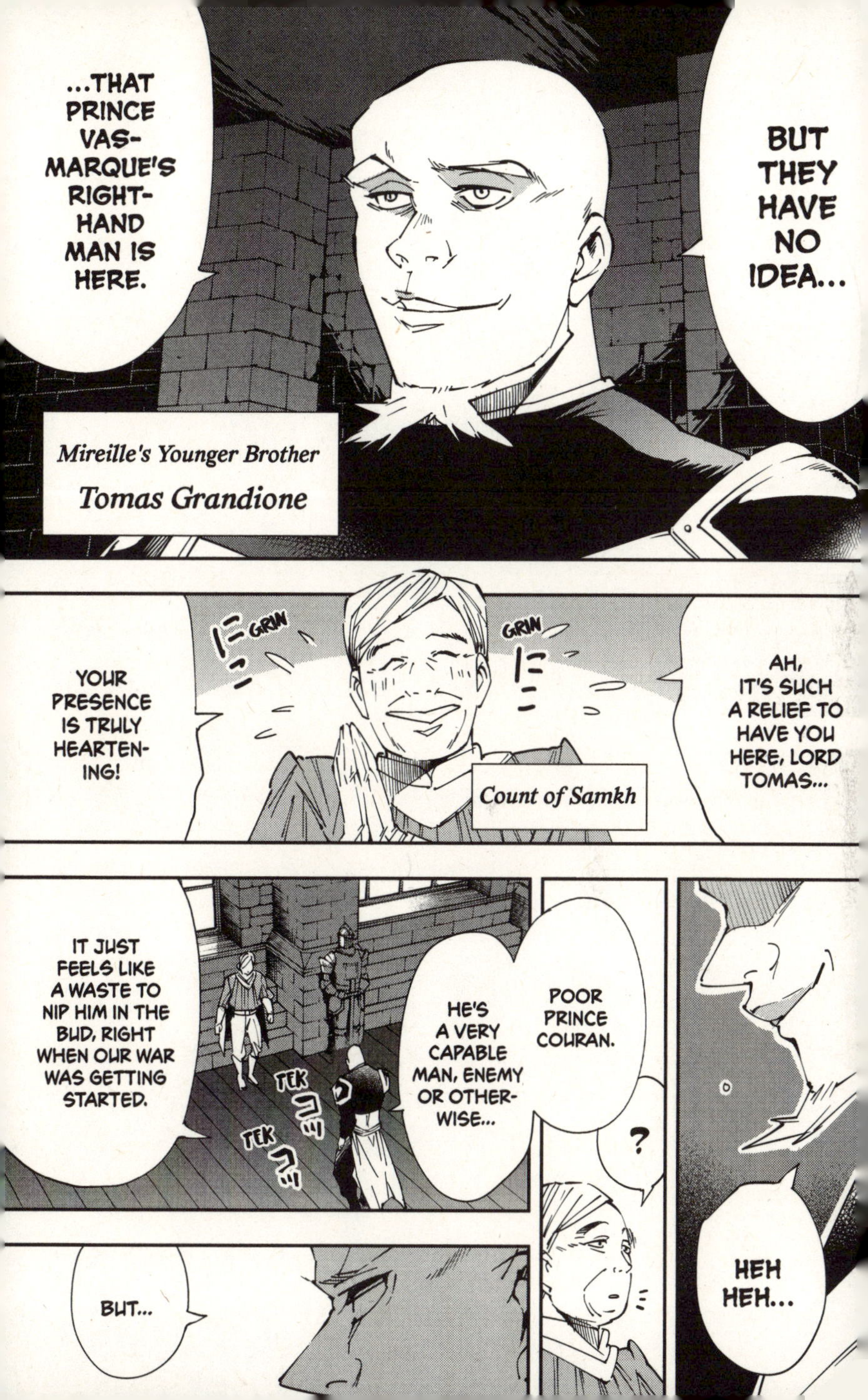
BUT THEY HAVE NO IDEA...
...THAT PRINCE VAS-MARQUE'S RIGHT-HAND MAN IS HERE.
Mireille's Younger Brother
Tomas Grandione
AH, IT'S SUCH A RELIEF TO HAVE YOU HERE, LORD TOMAS...
GRIN
GRIN
YOUR PRESENCE IS TRULY HEARTEN-ING!
Count of Samkh
HEH HEH...
POOR PRINCE COURAN.
?
HE'S A VERY CAPABLE MAN, ENEMY OR OTHER-WISE...
IT JUST FEELS LIKE A WASTE TO NIP HIM IN THE BUD, RIGHT WHEN OUR WAR WAS GETTING STARTED.
TEK
TEK
BUT...

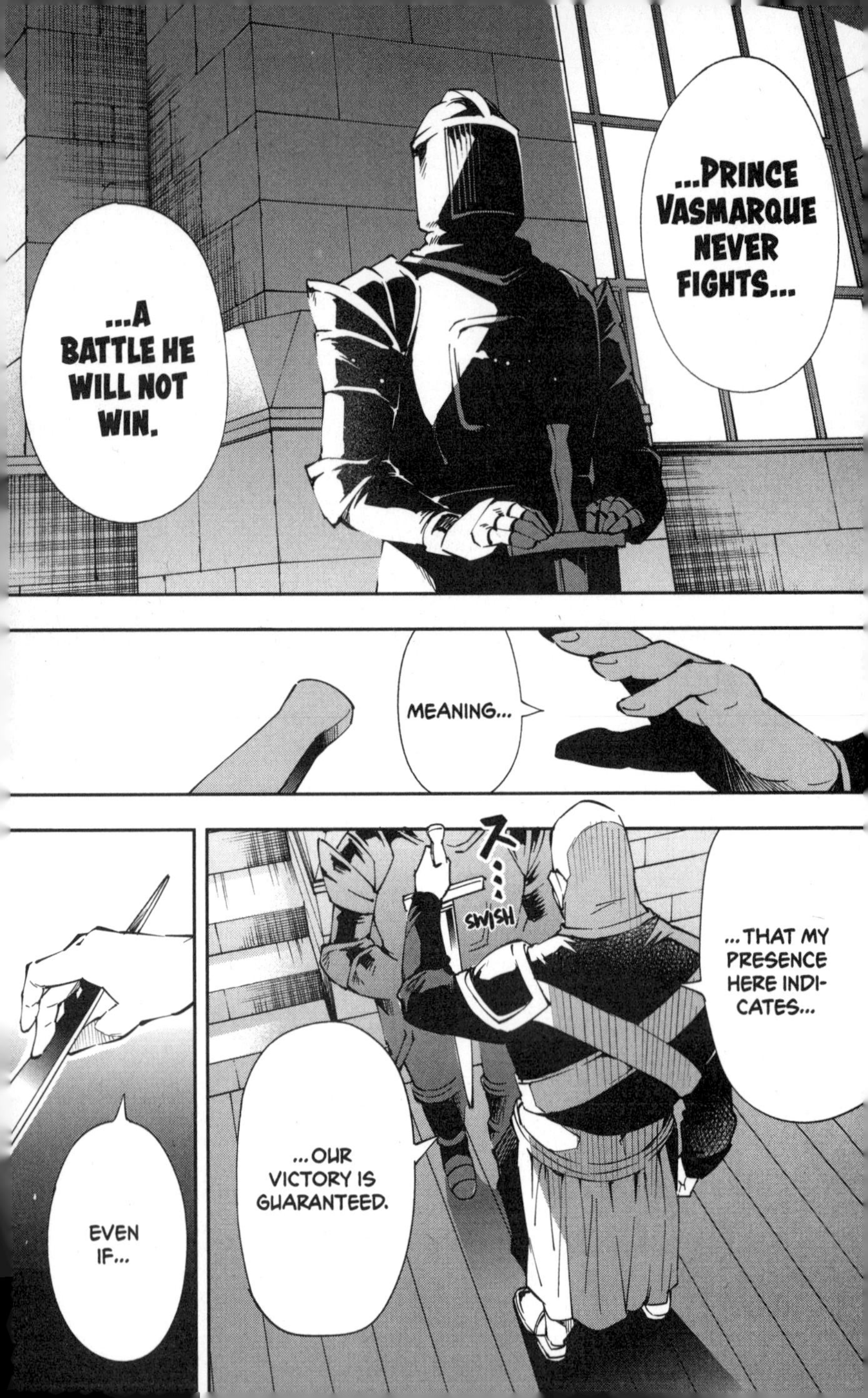
...PRINCE VASMARQUE NEVER FIGHTS...
...A BATTLE HE WILL NOT WIN.
MEANING...
...THAT MY PRESENCE HERE INDI-CATES...
SWISH
...OUR VICTORY IS GUARANTEED.
EVEN IF...

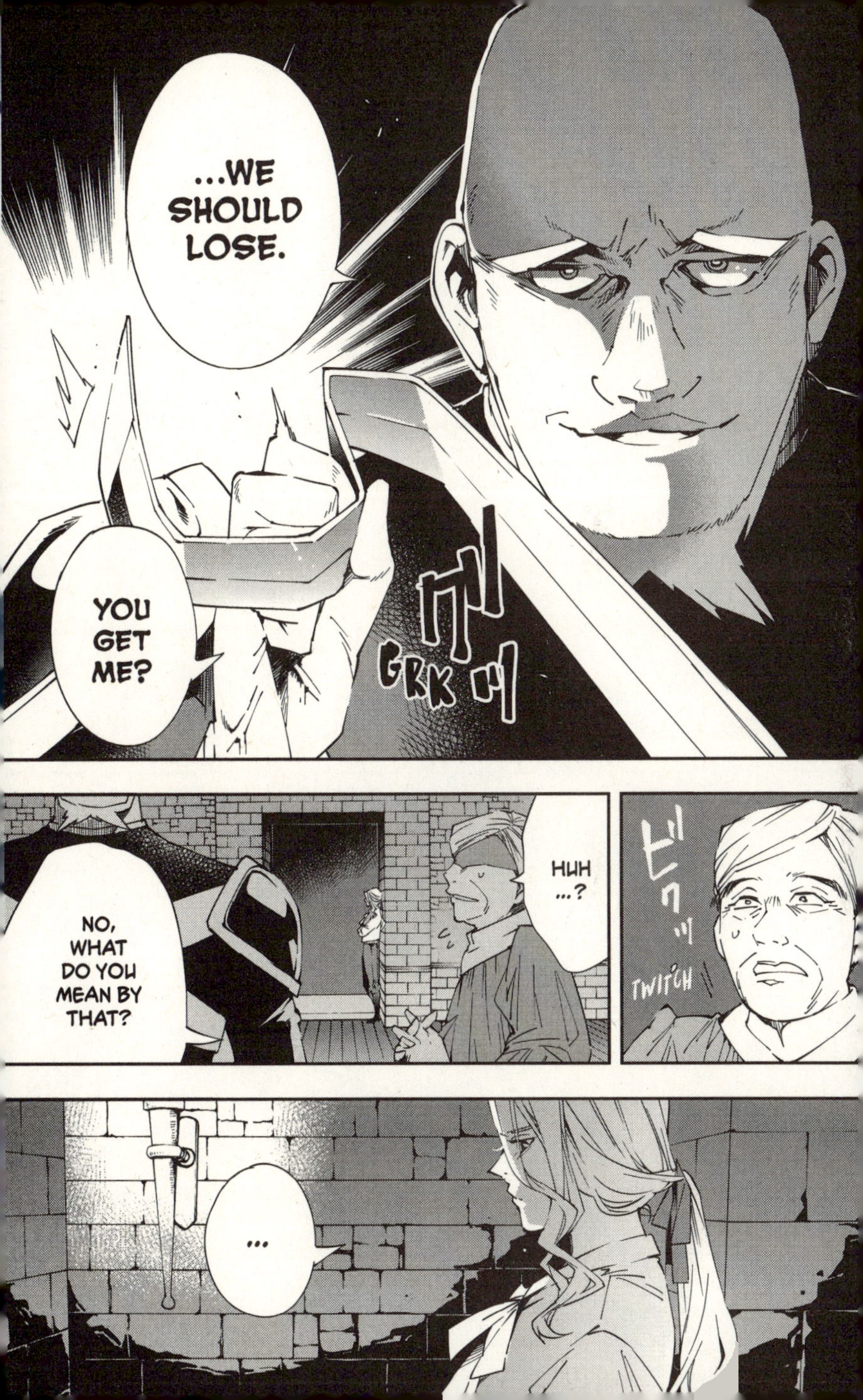
...WE SHOULD LOSE.
YOU GET ME?
GRK
ビクッ
TWITCH
HUH ...?
NO, WHAT DO YOU MEAN BY THAT?
...

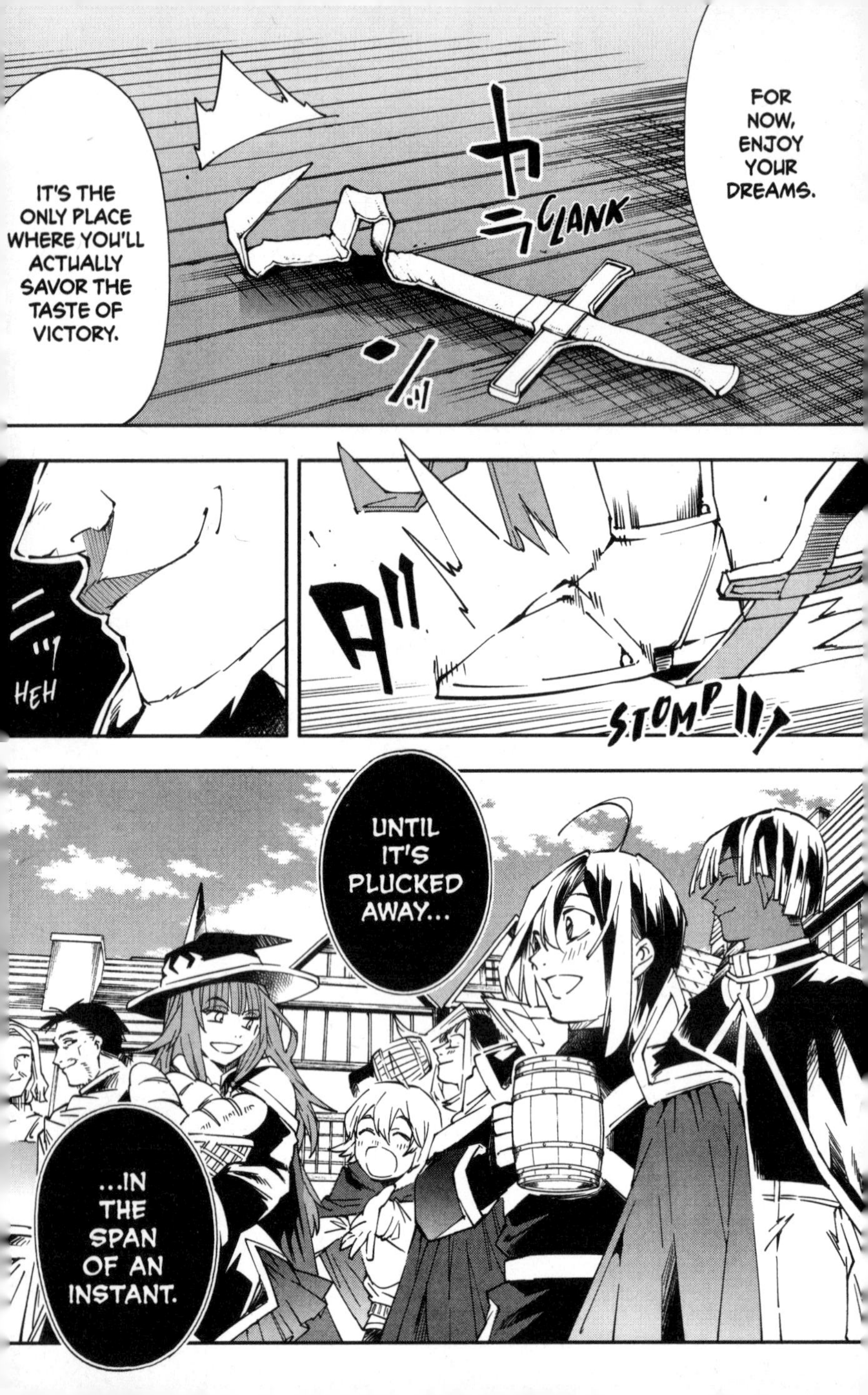
FOR NOW, ENJOY YOUR DREAMS.
CLANK
IT'S THE ONLY PLACE WHERE YOU'LL ACTUALLY SAVOR THE TASTE OF VICTORY.
STOMP
HEH
UNTIL IT'S PLUCKED AWAY...
...IN THE SPAN OF AN INSTANT.

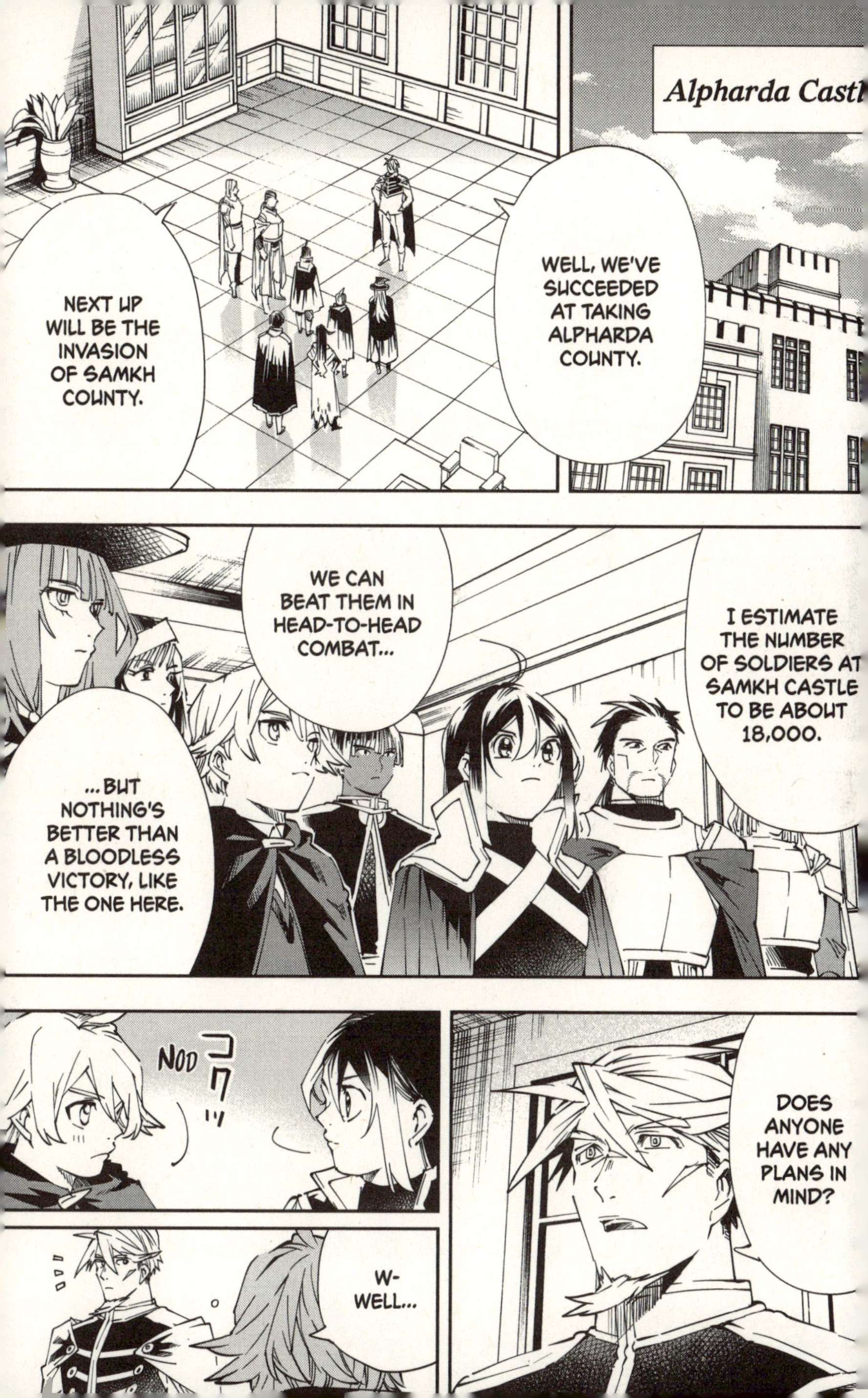
Alpharda Castl
WELL, WE'VE SUCCEEDED AT TAKING ALPHARDA COUNTY.
NEXT UP WILL BE THE INVASION OF SAMKH COUNTY.
I ESTIMATE THE NUMBER OF SOLDIERS AT SAMKH CASTLE TO BE ABOUT 18,000.
WE CAN BEAT THEM IN HEAD-TO-HEAD COMBAT...
...BUT NOTHING'S BETTER THAN A BLOODLESS VICTORY, LIKE THE ONE HERE.
DOES ANYONE HAVE ANY PLANS IN MIND?
NOD
W- WELL...

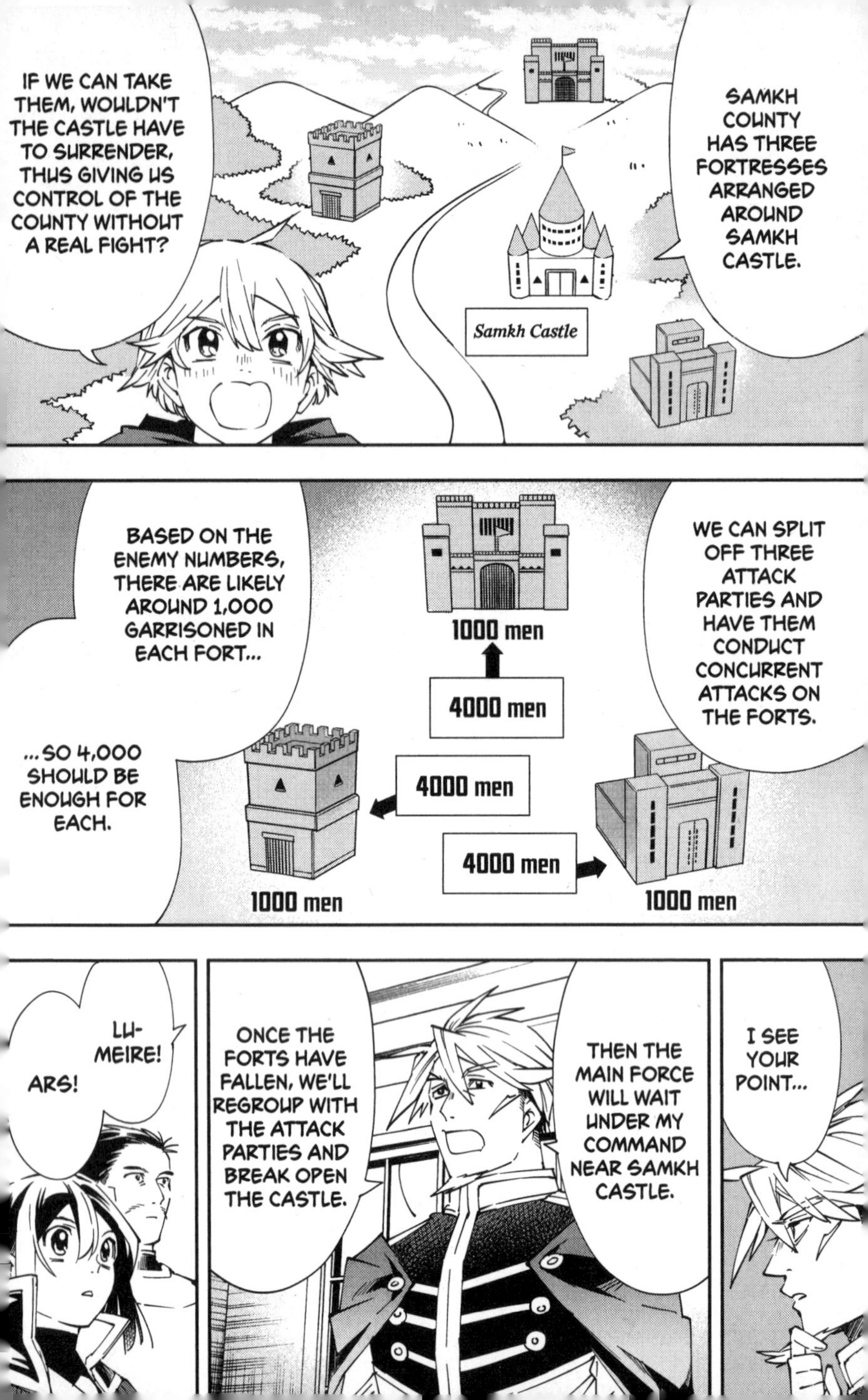
SAMKH COUNTY HAS THREE FORTRESSES ARRANGED AROUND SAMKH CASTLE.
Samkh Castle
IF WE CAN TAKE THEM, WOULDN'T THE CASTLE HAVE TO SURRENDER, THUS GIVING US CONTROL OF THE COUNTY WITHOUT A REAL FIGHT?
WE CAN SPLIT OFF THREE ATTACK PARTIES AND HAVE THEM CONDUCT CONCURRENT ATTACKS ON THE FORTS.
BASED ON THE ENEMY NUMBERS, THERE ARE LIKELY AROUND 1,000 GARRISONED IN EACH FORT...
1000 men
4000 men
4000 men
4000 men
1000 men
1000 men
...SO 4,000 SHOULD BE ENOUGH FOR EACH.
I SEE YOUR POINT...
THEN THE MAIN FORCE WILL WAIT UNDER MY COMMAND NEAR SAMKH CASTLE.
ONCE THE FORTS HAVE FALLEN, WE'LL REGROUP WITH THE ATTACK PARTIES AND BREAK OPEN THE CASTLE.
LU-MEIRE!
ARS!

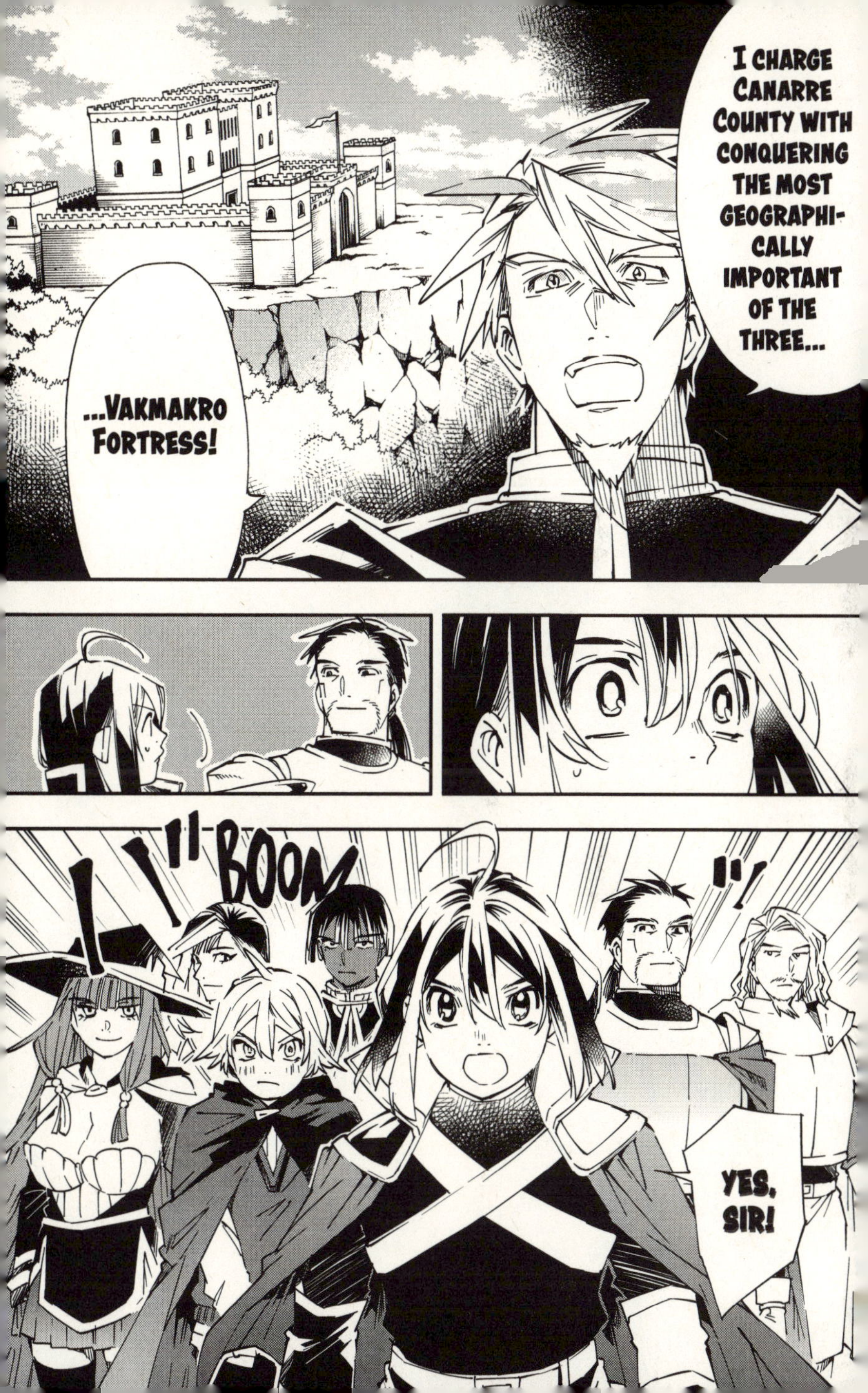
I CHARGE CANARRE COUNTY WITH CONQUERING THE MOST GEOGRAPHI-CALLY IMPORTANT OF THE THREE...
...VAKMAKRO FORTRESS!
BOOM
YES, SIR!

Chapter 66: Master and Apprentice

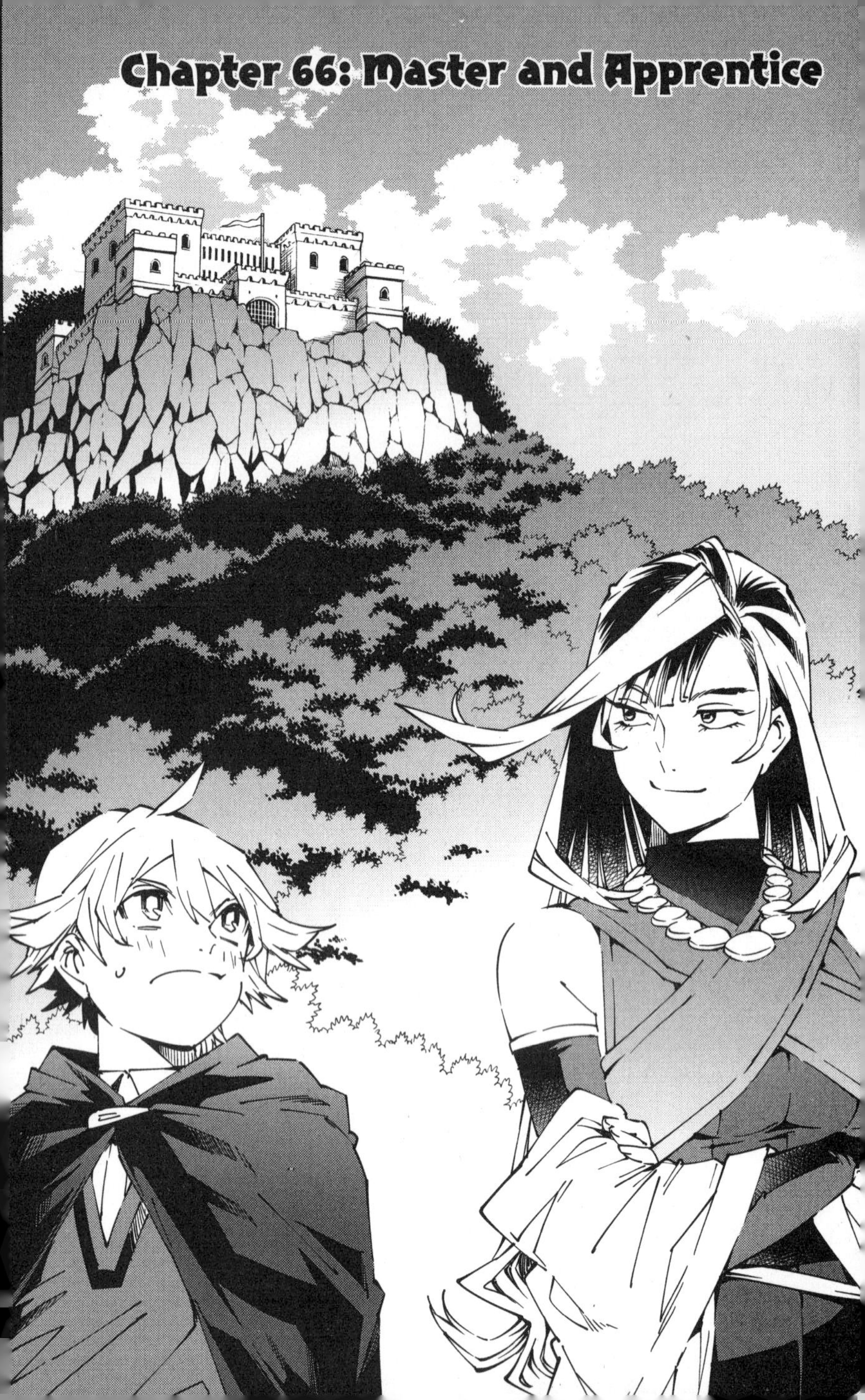

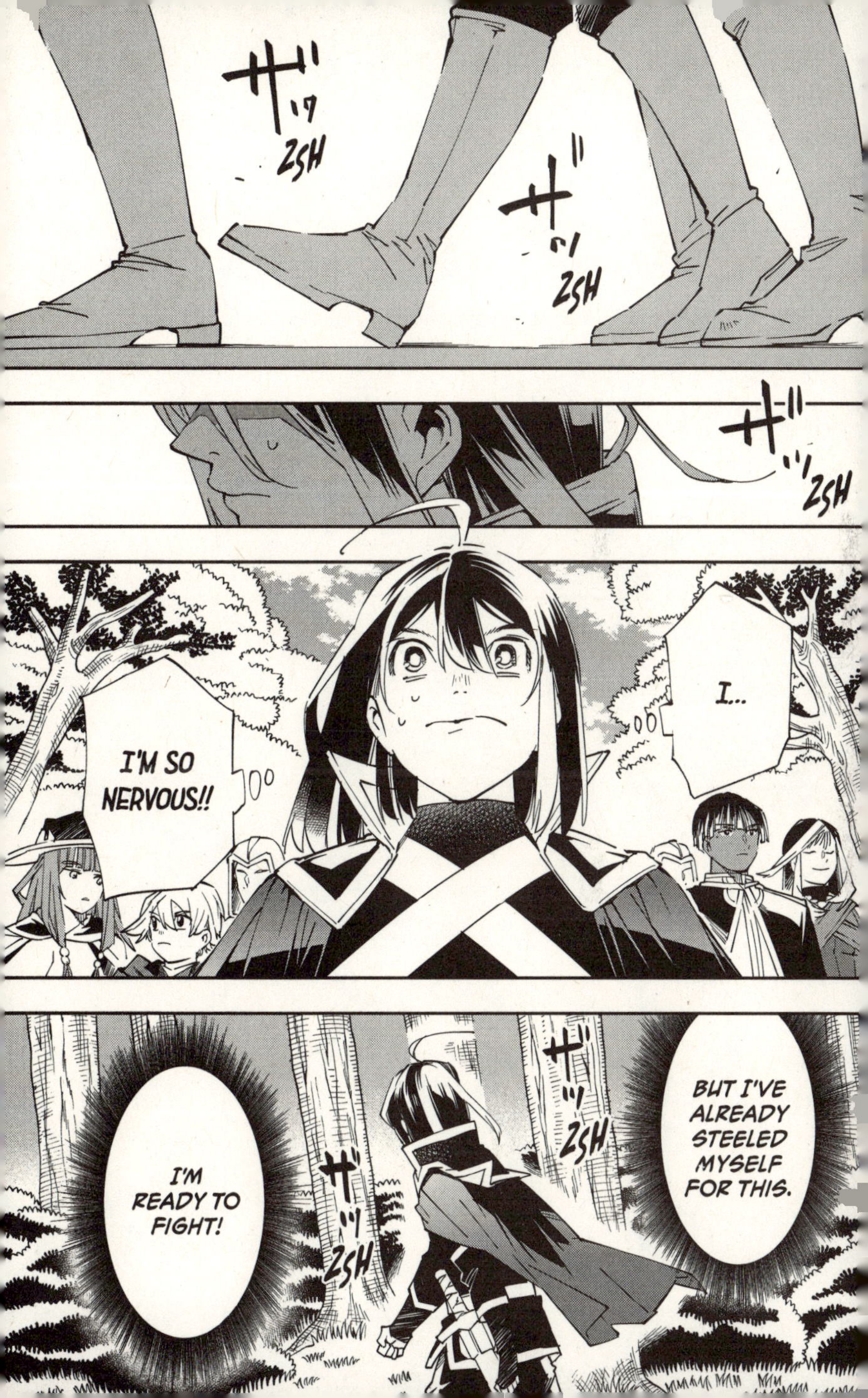

ザッ
ZSH
ザッ
ZSH
ザッ
ZSH
I...
I'M SO NERVOUS!!
BUT I'VE ALREADY STEELED MYSELF FOR THIS.
ザッ
ZSH
ザッ
ZSH
I'M READY TO FIGHT!

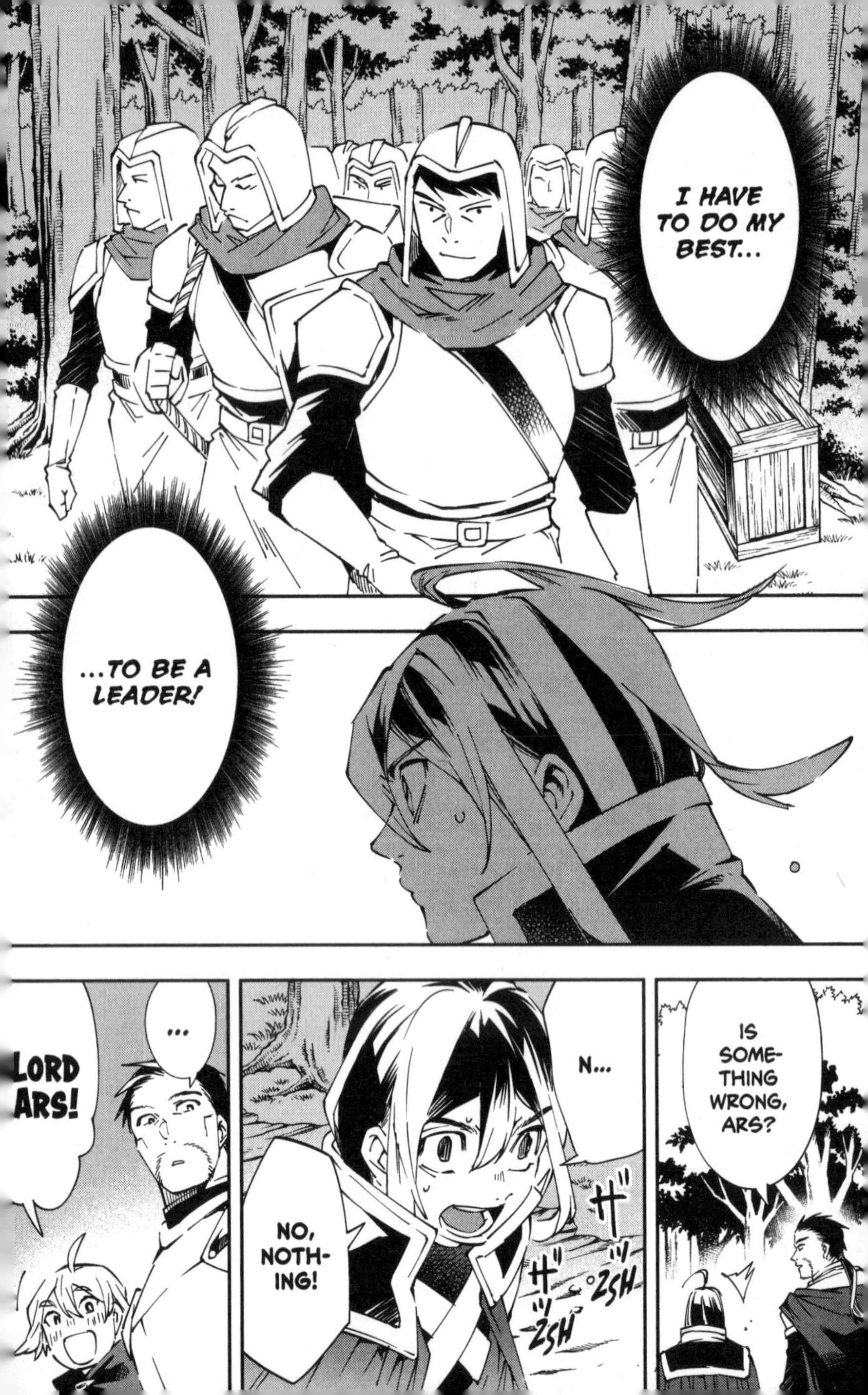
I HAVE TO DO MY BEST...
...TO BE A LEADER!
IS SOMETHING WRONG, ARS?
N...
ザッ ZSH
ザッ ZSH
NO, NOTHING!
...
LORD ARS!

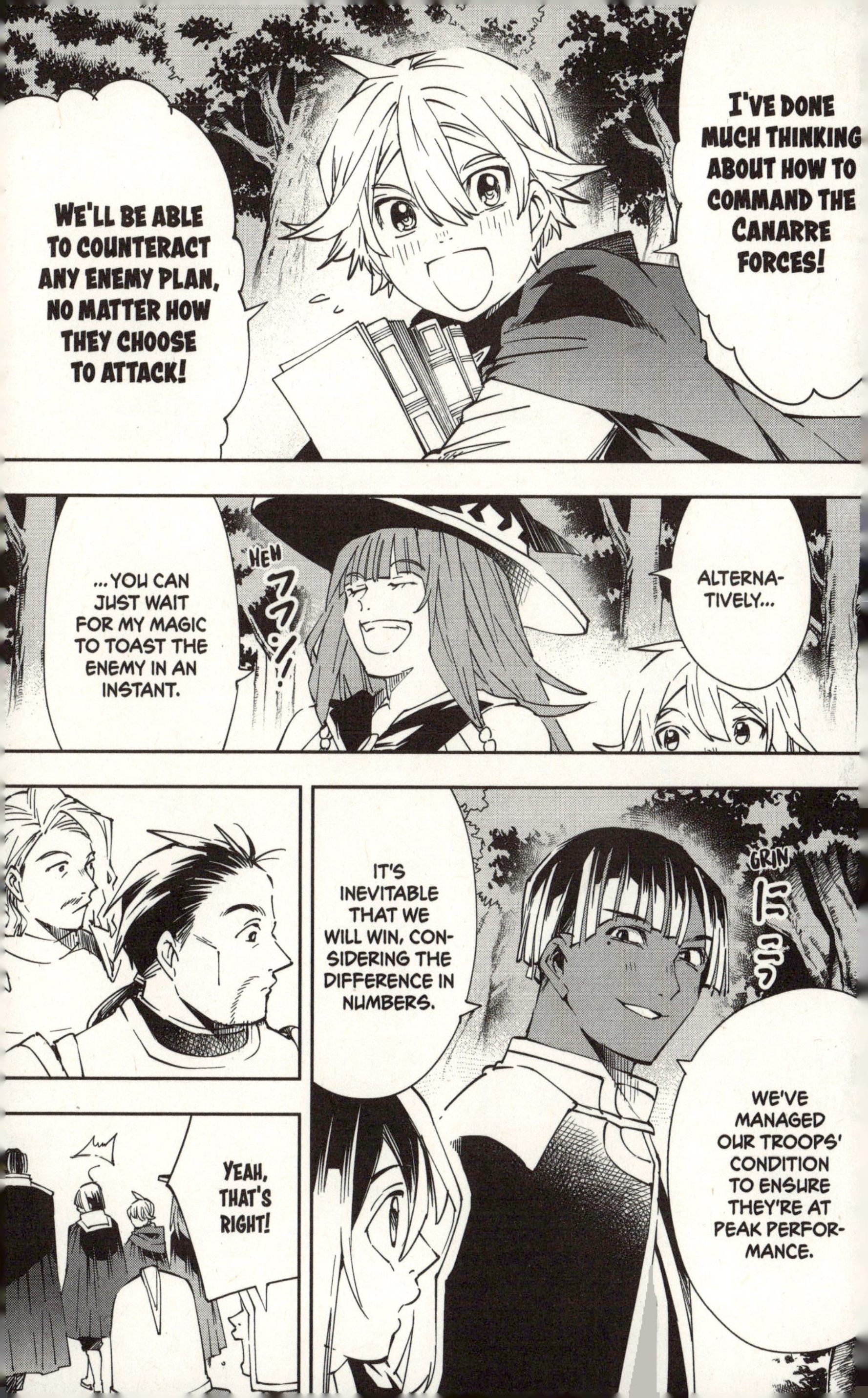

I'VE DONE MUCH THINKING ABOUT HOW TO COMMAND THE CANARRE FORCES!
WE'LL BE ABLE TO COUNTERACT ANY ENEMY PLAN, NO MATTER HOW THEY CHOOSE TO ATTACK!
ALTERNATIVELY...
HEM
...YOU CAN JUST WAIT FOR MY MAGIC TO TOAST THE ENEMY IN AN INSTANT.
GRIN
IT'S INEVITABLE THAT WE WILL WIN, CONSIDERING THE DIFFERENCE IN NUMBERS.
WE'VE MANAGED OUR TROOPS' CONDITION TO ENSURE THEY'RE AT PEAK PERFORMANCE.
YEAH, THAT'S RIGHT!

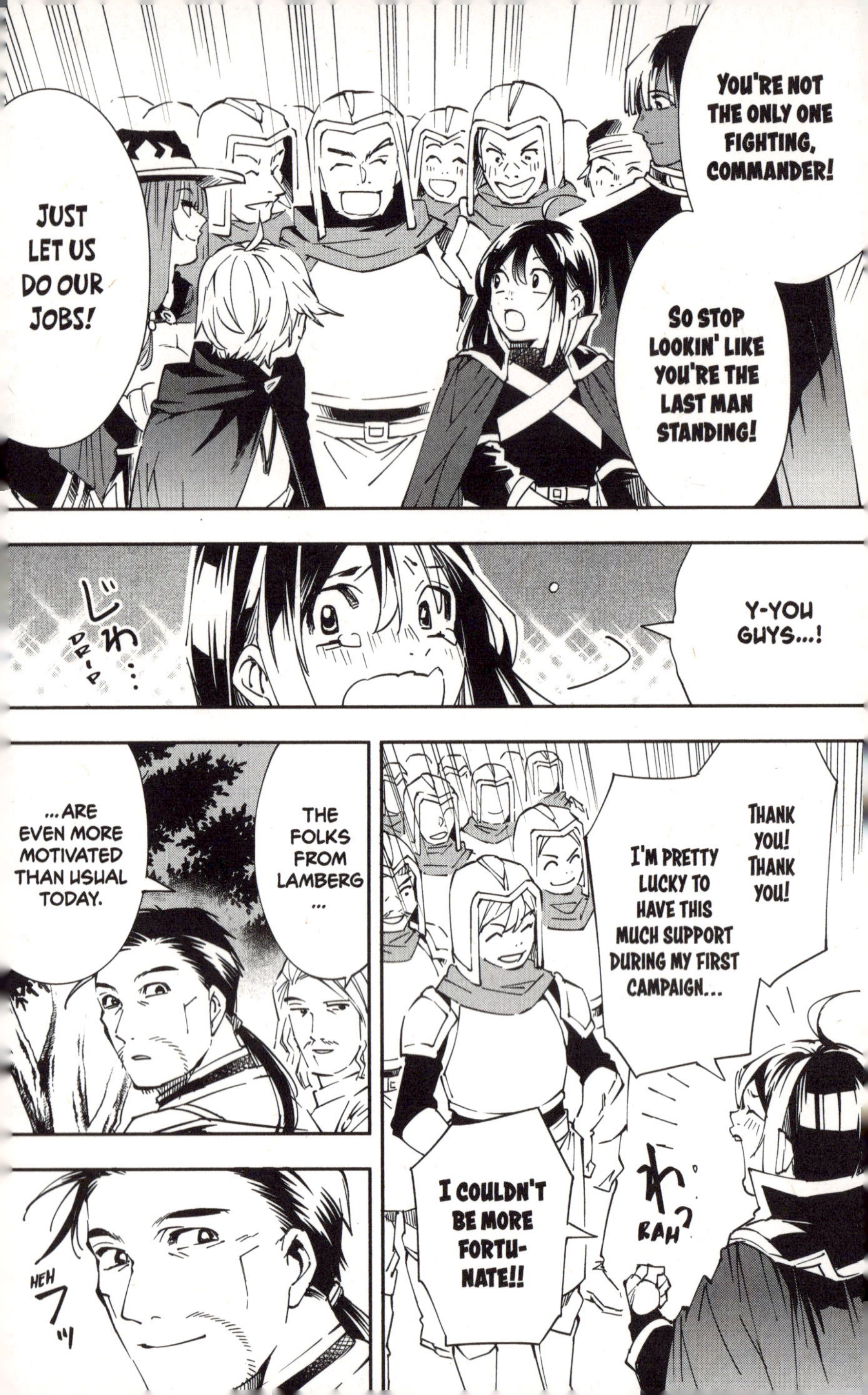
YOU'RE NOT THE ONLY ONE FIGHTING, COMMANDER!
SO STOP LOOKIN' LIKE YOU'RE THE LAST MAN STANDING!
JUST LET US DO OUR JOBS!
Y-YOU GUYS...!
じわ...
DRIP
THANK YOU! THANK YOU!
I'M PRETTY LUCKY TO HAVE THIS MUCH SUPPORT DURING MY FIRST CAMPAIGN...
わ
RAH?
I COULDN'T BE MORE FORTU-NATE!!
THE FOLKS FROM LAMBERG ...
...ARE EVEN MORE MOTIVATED THAN USUAL TODAY.
フッ
HEH

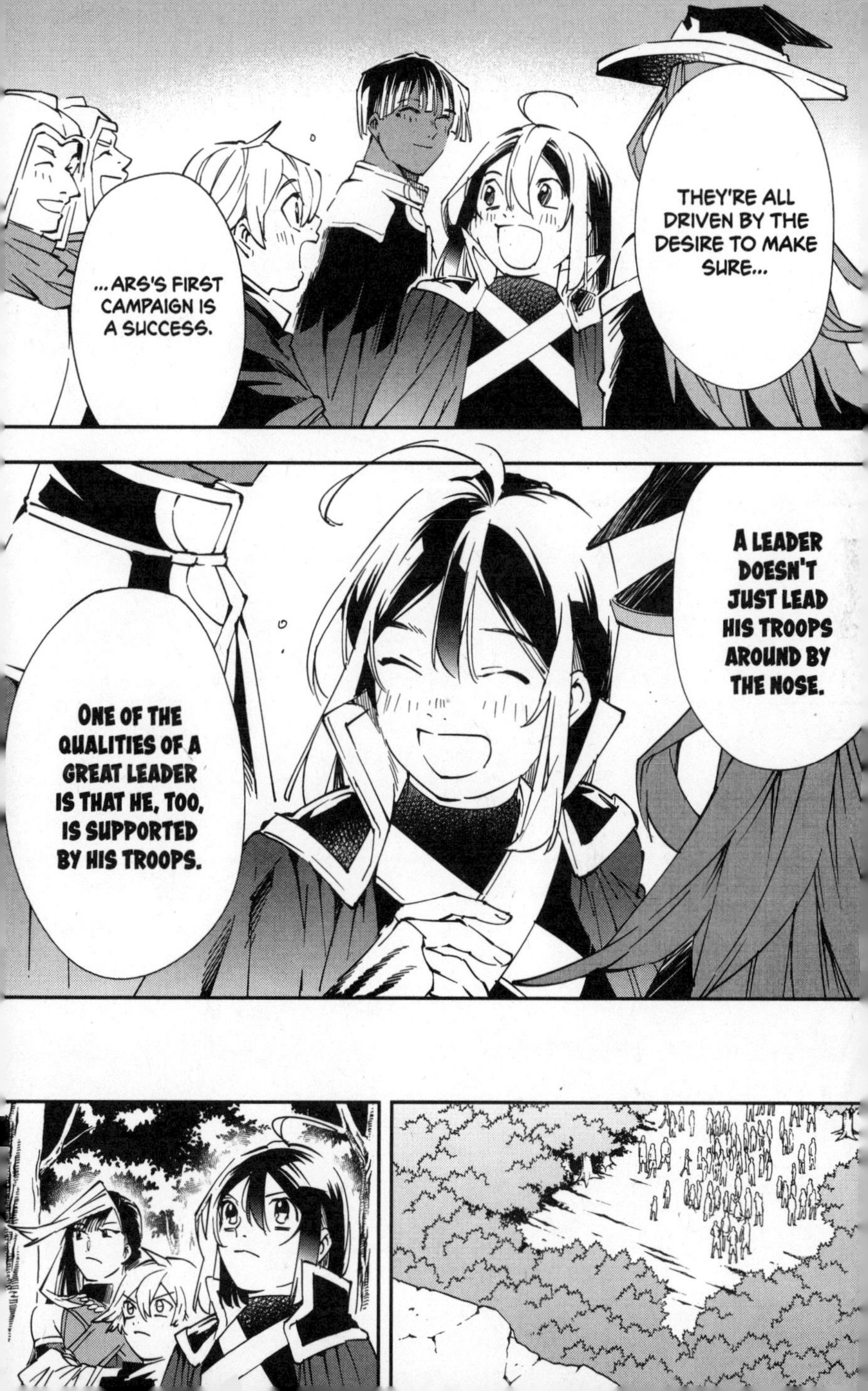
THEY'RE ALL DRIVEN BY THE DESIRE TO MAKE SURE...
...ARS'S FIRST CAMPAIGN IS A SUCCESS.
A LEADER DOESN'T JUST LEAD HIS TROOPS AROUND BY THE NOSE.
ONE OF THE QUALITIES OF A GREAT LEADER IS THAT HE, TOO, IS SUPPORTED BY HIS TROOPS.

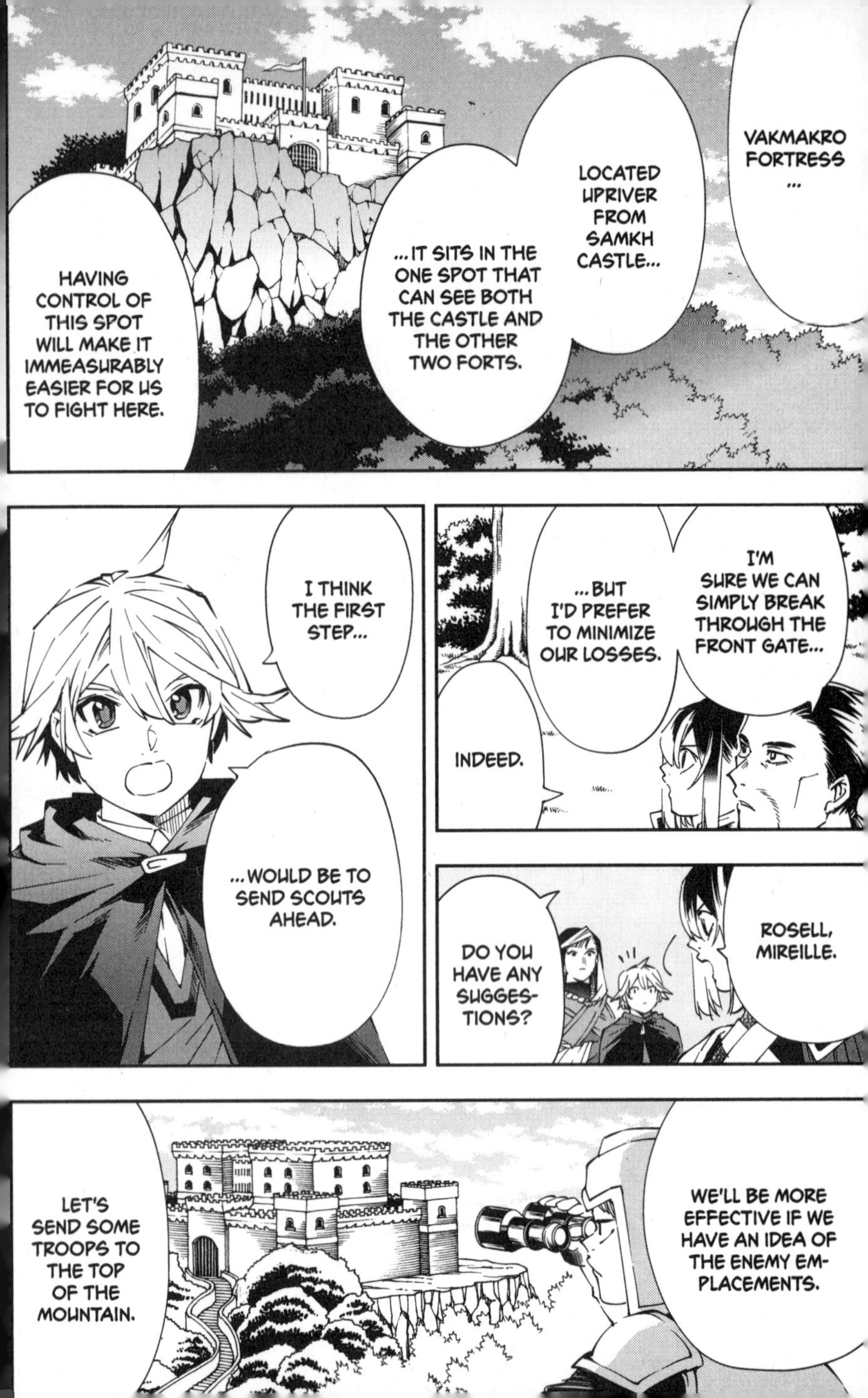
VAKMAKRO FORTRESS...
LOCATED UPRIVER FROM SAMKH CASTLE...
...IT SITS IN THE ONE SPOT THAT CAN SEE BOTH THE CASTLE AND THE OTHER TWO FORTS.
HAVING CONTROL OF THIS SPOT WILL MAKE IT IMMEASURABLY EASIER FOR US TO FIGHT HERE.
I'M SURE WE CAN SIMPLY BREAK THROUGH THE FRONT GATE...
...BUT I'D PREFER TO MINIMIZE OUR LOSSES.
INDEED.
ROSELL, MIREILLE.
DO YOU HAVE ANY SUGGES-TIONS?
I THINK THE FIRST STEP...
...WOULD BE TO SEND SCOUTS AHEAD.
WE'LL BE MORE EFFECTIVE IF WE HAVE AN IDEA OF THE ENEMY EM-PLACEMENTS.
LET'S SEND SOME TROOPS TO THE TOP OF THE MOUNTAIN.

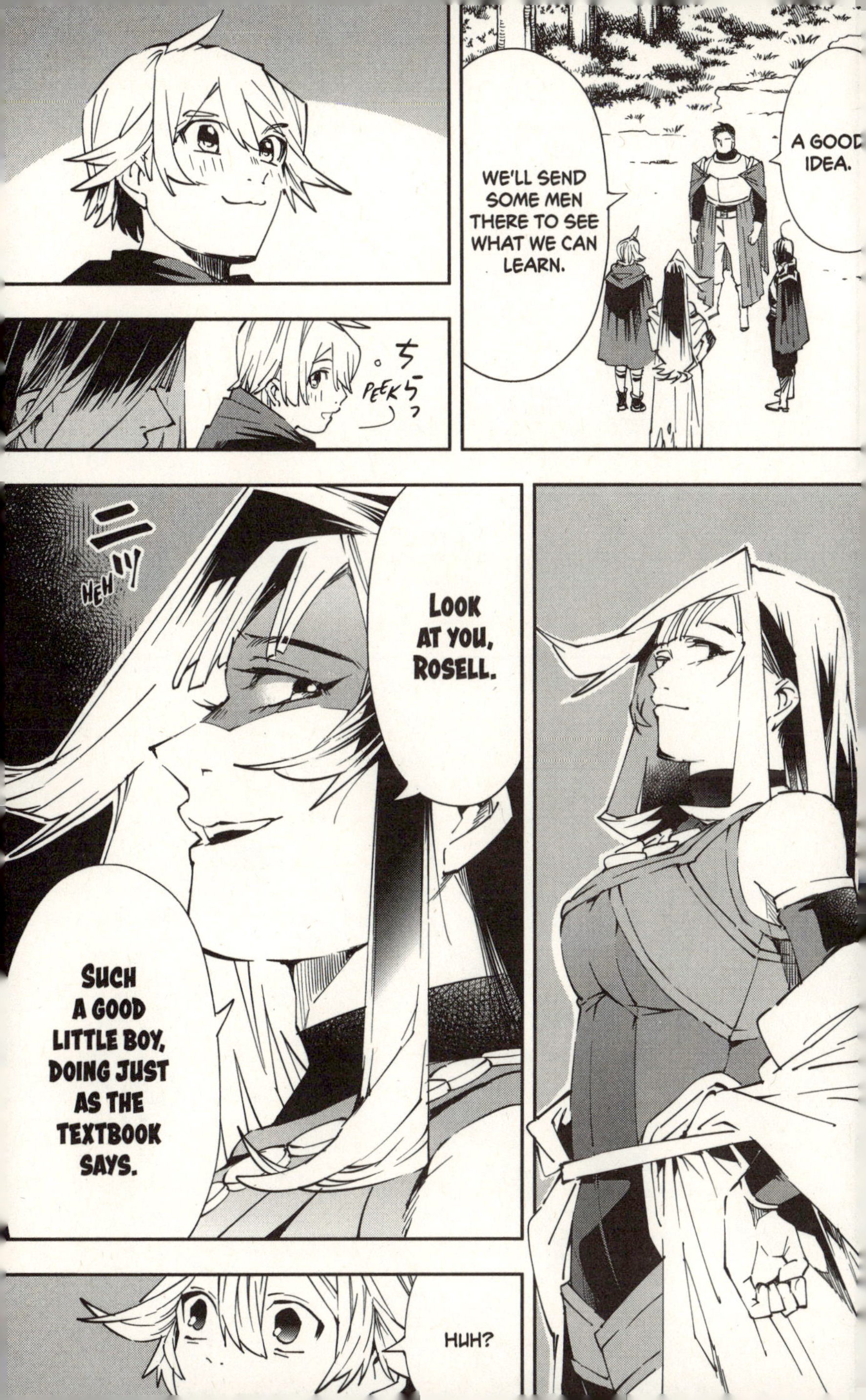
A GOOD IDEA.
WE'LL SEND SOME MEN THERE TO SEE WHAT WE CAN LEARN.
PEEK
HEH
LOOK AT YOU, ROSELL.
SUCH A GOOD LITTLE BOY, DOING JUST AS THE TEXTBOOK SAYS.
HUH?

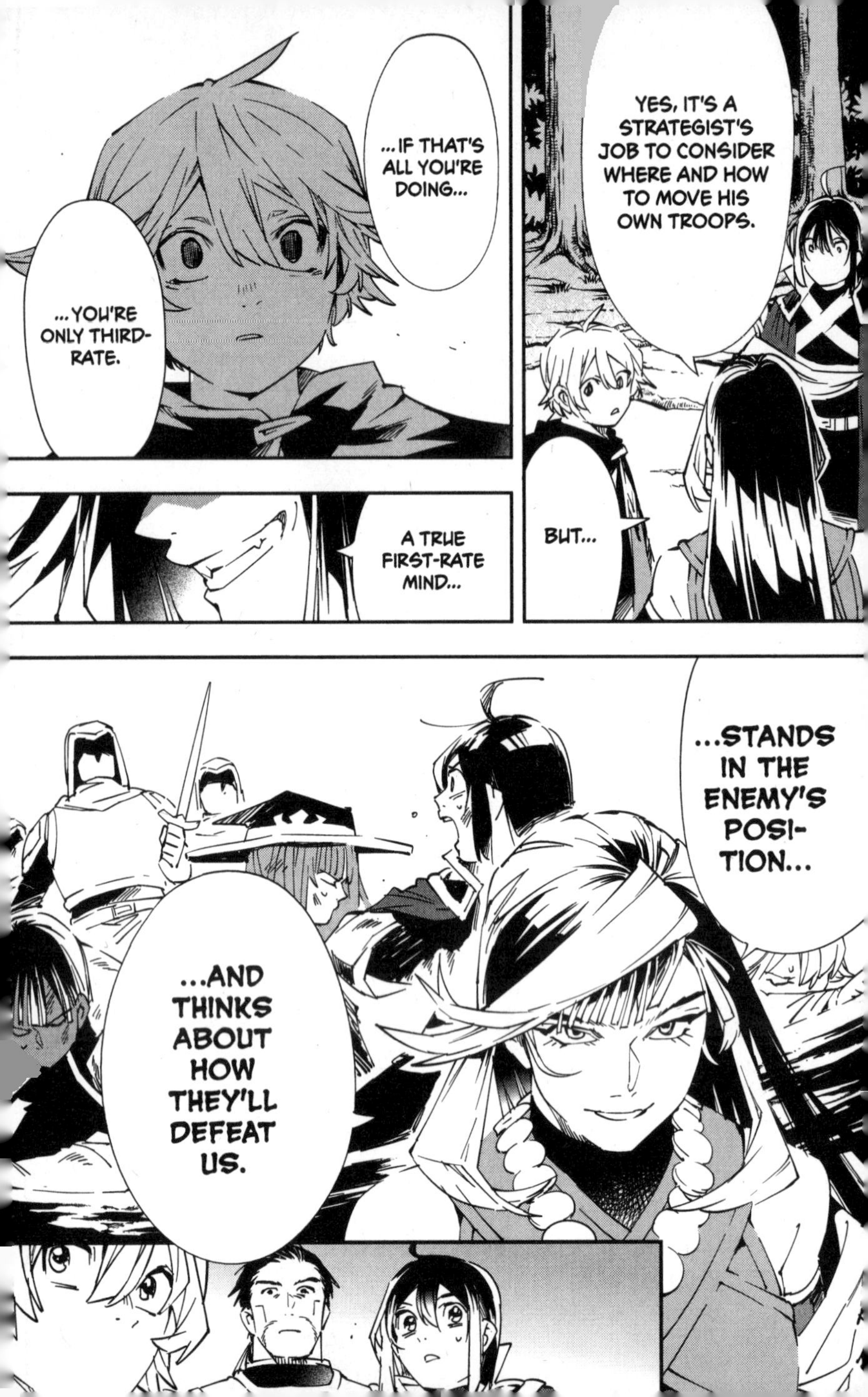
YES, IT'S A STRATEGIST'S JOB TO CONSIDER WHERE AND HOW TO MOVE HIS OWN TROOPS.
BUT...
...IF THAT'S ALL YOU'RE DOING...
...YOU'RE ONLY THIRD-RATE.
A TRUE FIRST-RATE MIND...
...STANDS IN THE ENEMY'S POSI-TION...
...AND THINKS ABOUT HOW THEY'LL DEFEAT US.

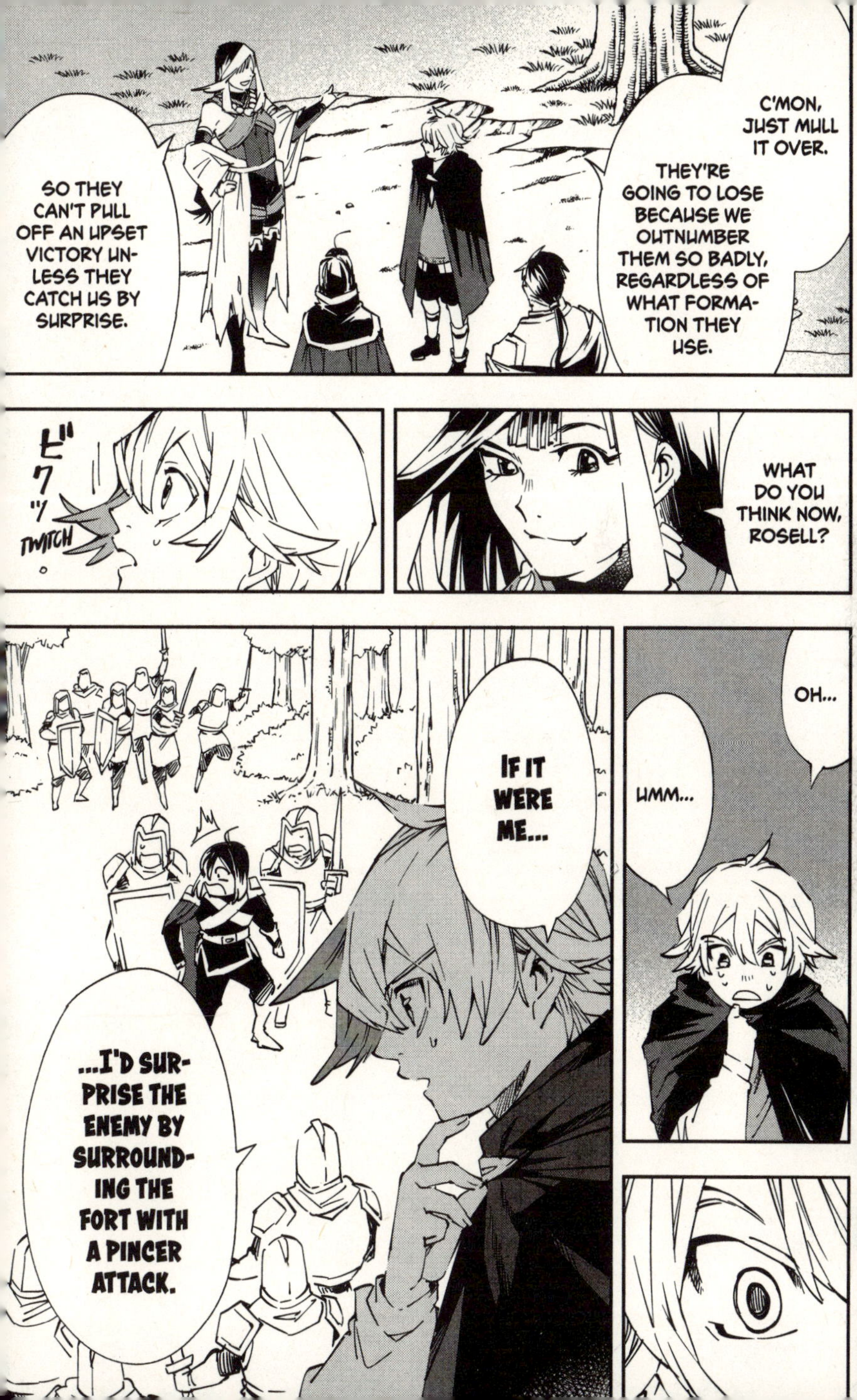
C'MON, JUST MULL IT OVER.
THEY'RE GOING TO LOSE BECAUSE WE OUTNUMBER THEM SO BADLY, REGARDLESS OF WHAT FORMATION THEY USE.
SO THEY CAN'T PULL OFF AN UPSET VICTORY UNLESS THEY CATCH US BY SURPRISE.
WHAT DO YOU THINK NOW, ROSELL?
ビクッ
TWITCH
OH...
UMM...
IF IT WERE ME...
...I'D SURPRISE THE ENEMY BY SURROUNDING THE FORT WITH A PINCER ATTACK.

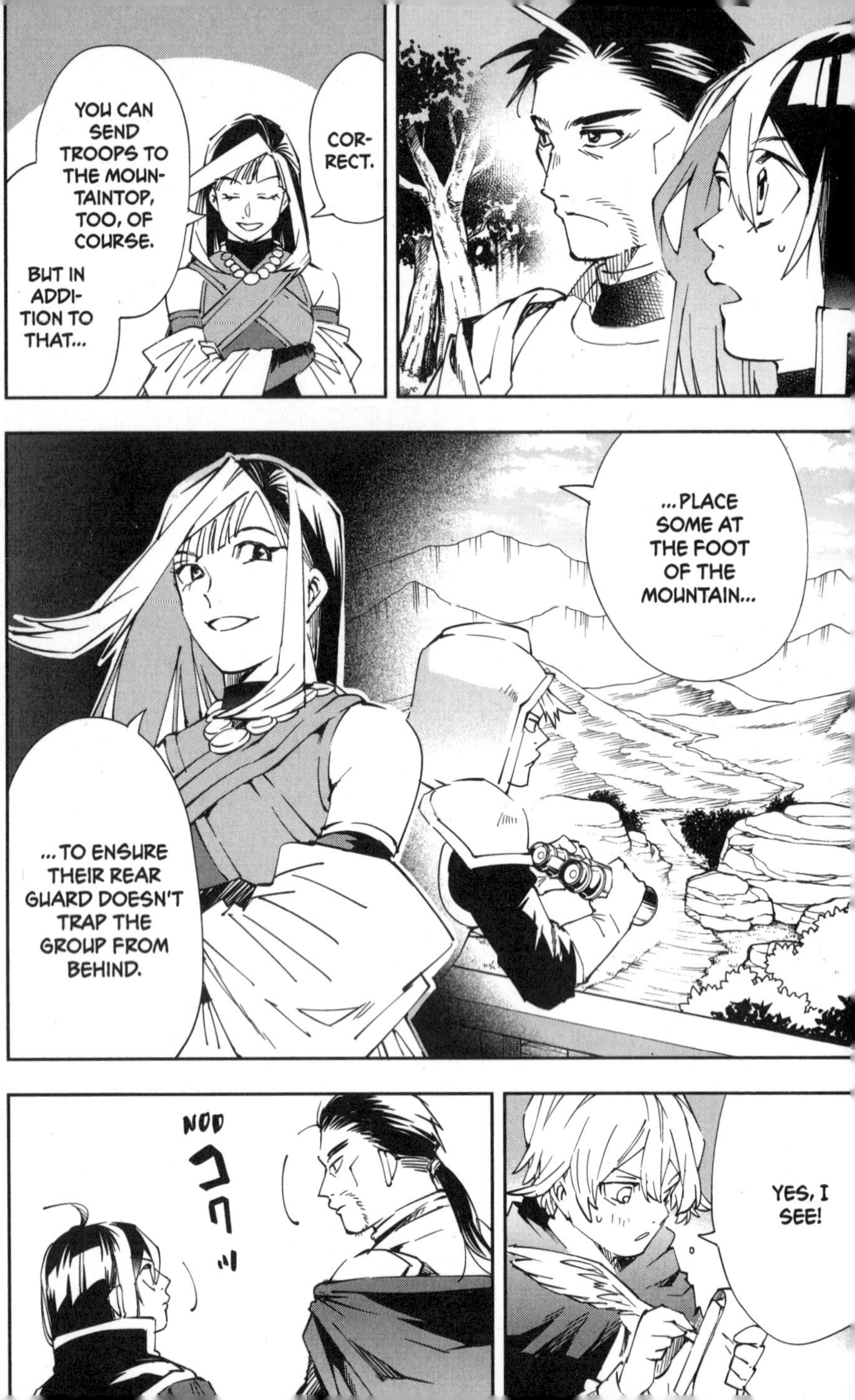
CORRECT.
YOU CAN SEND TROOPS TO THE MOUNTAINTOP, TOO, OF COURSE.
BUT IN ADDITION TO THAT...
...PLACE SOME AT THE FOOT OF THE MOUNTAIN...
...TO ENSURE THEIR REAR GUARD DOESN'T TRAP THE GROUP FROM BEHIND.
YES, I SEE!
NOD

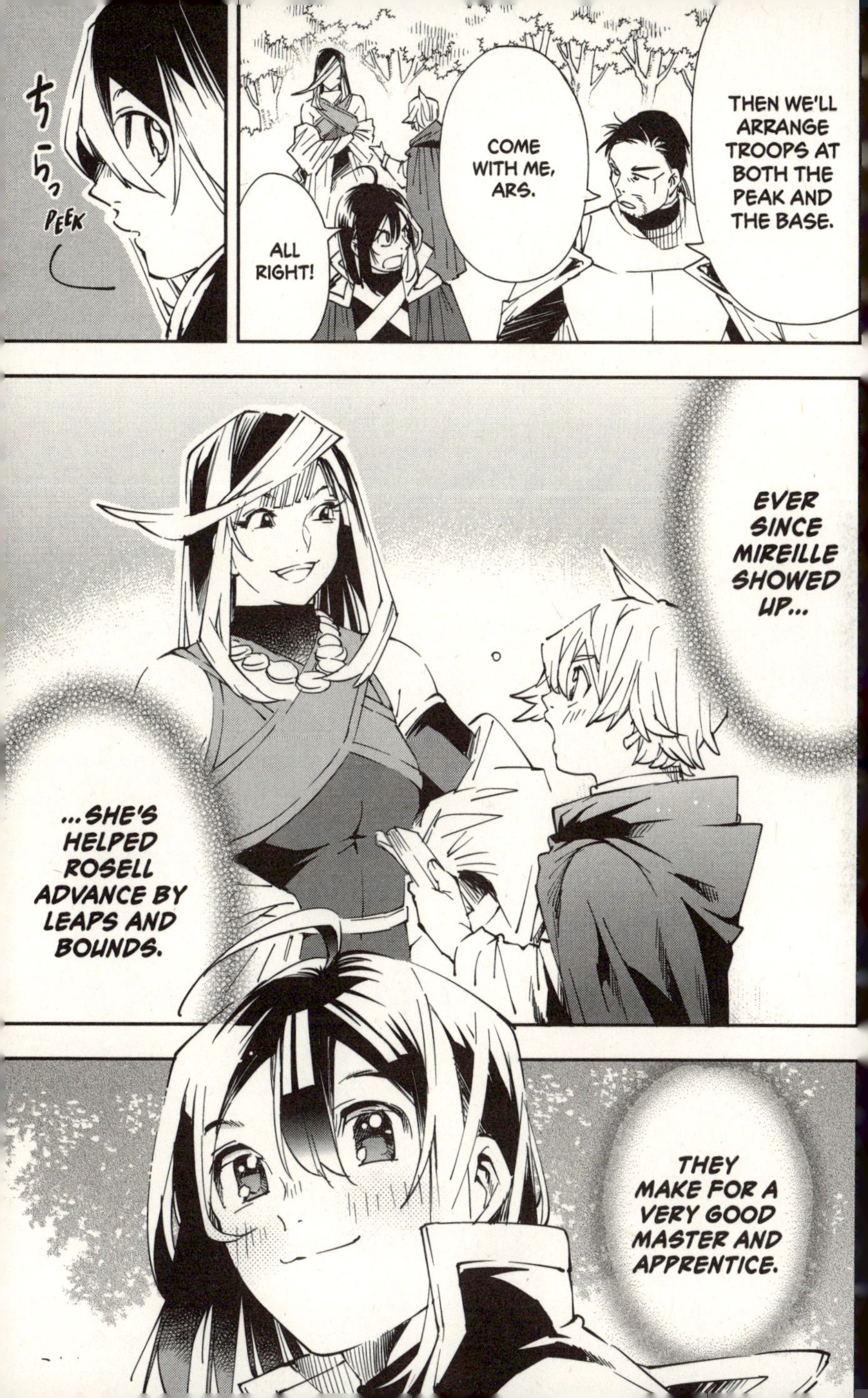
THEN WE'LL ARRANGE TROOPS AT BOTH THE PEAK AND THE BASE.
COME WITH ME, ARS.
ALL RIGHT!
ちらっ
PEEK
EVER SINCE MIREILLE SHOWED UP...
...SHE'S HELPED ROSELL ADVANCE BY LEAPS AND BOUNDS.
THEY MAKE FOR A VERY GOOD MASTER AND APPRENTICE.

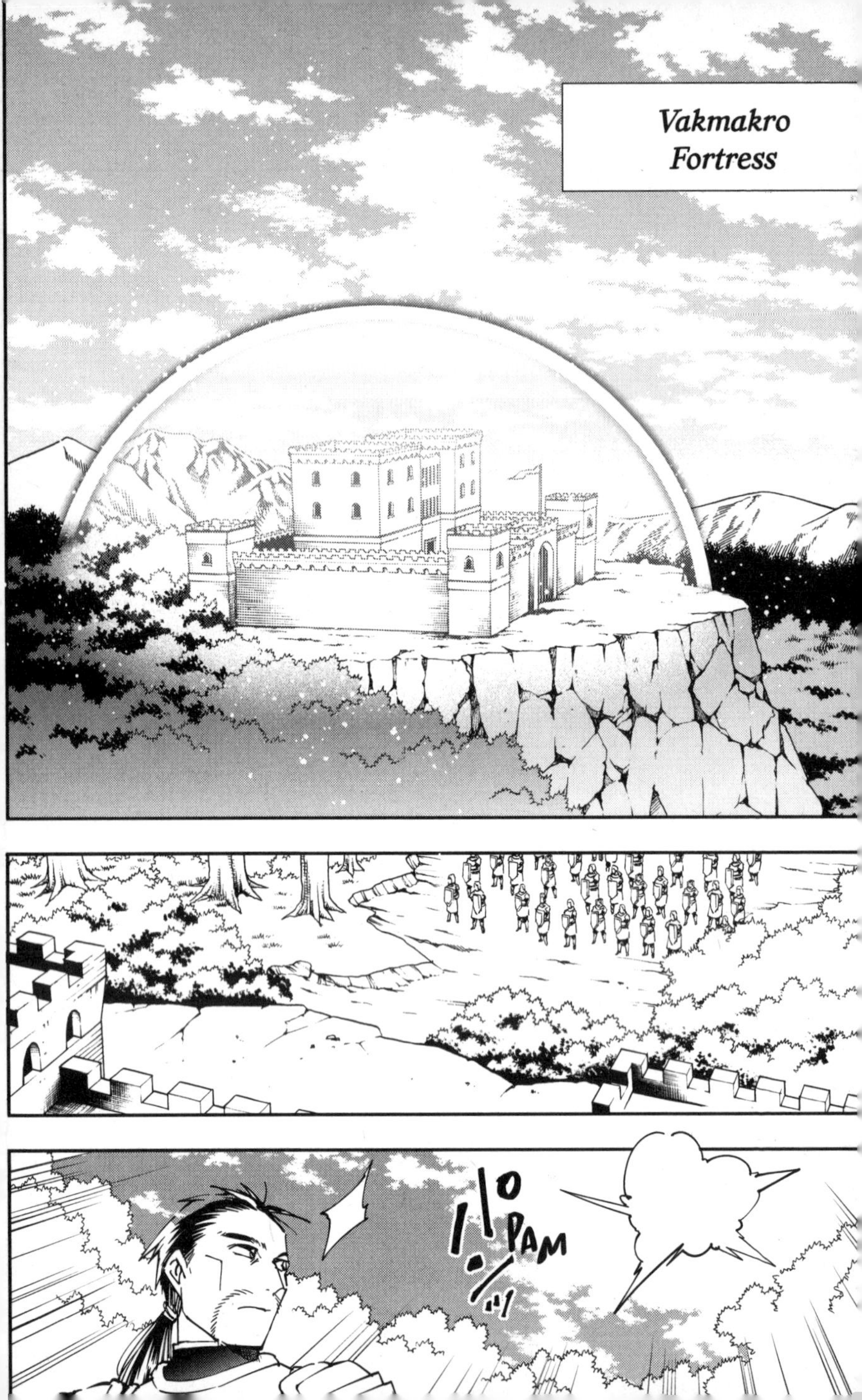
Vakmakro Fortress
PAM

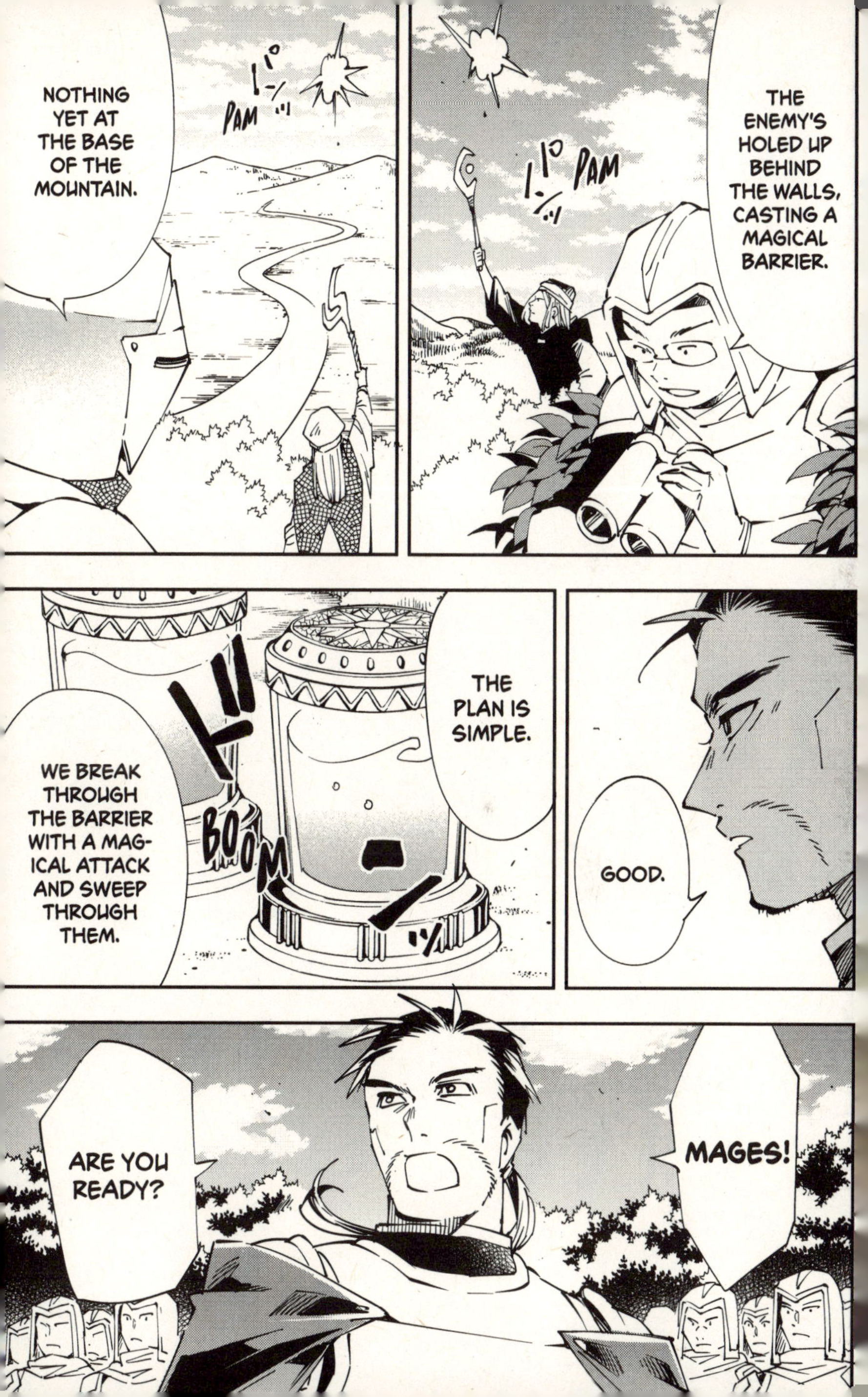
PAM
THE ENEMY'S HOLED UP BEHIND THE WALLS, CASTING A MAGICAL BARRIER.
PAM
NOTHING YET AT THE BASE OF THE MOUNTAIN.
GOOD.
THE PLAN IS SIMPLE.
BOOM
WE BREAK THROUGH THE BARRIER WITH A MAG-ICAL ATTACK AND SWEEP THROUGH THEM.
MAGES!
ARE YOU READY?

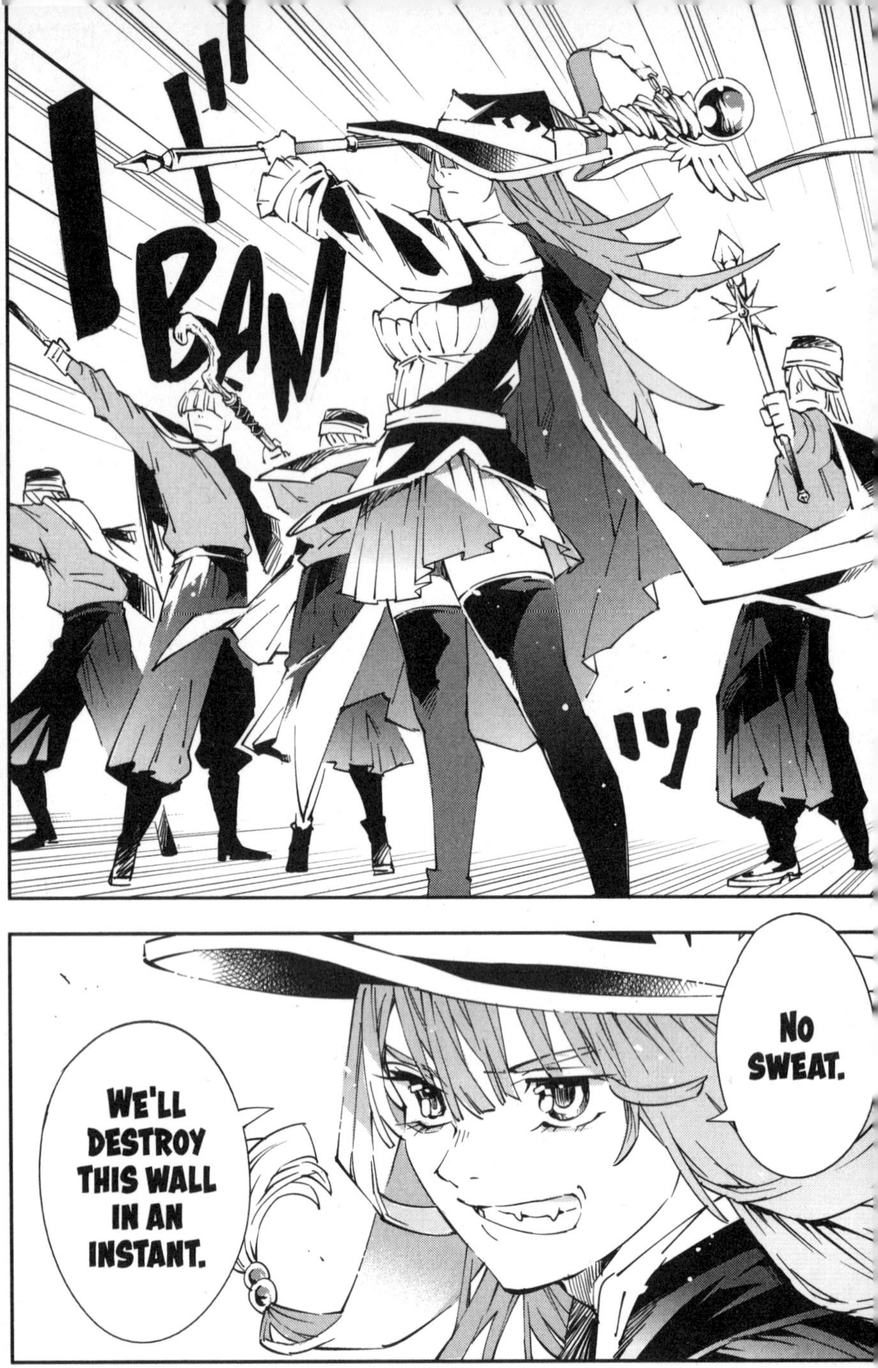
BAM
ッ
NO SWEAT.
WE'LL DESTROY THIS WALL IN AN INSTANT.

Chapter 67: Vakmakro Fortress

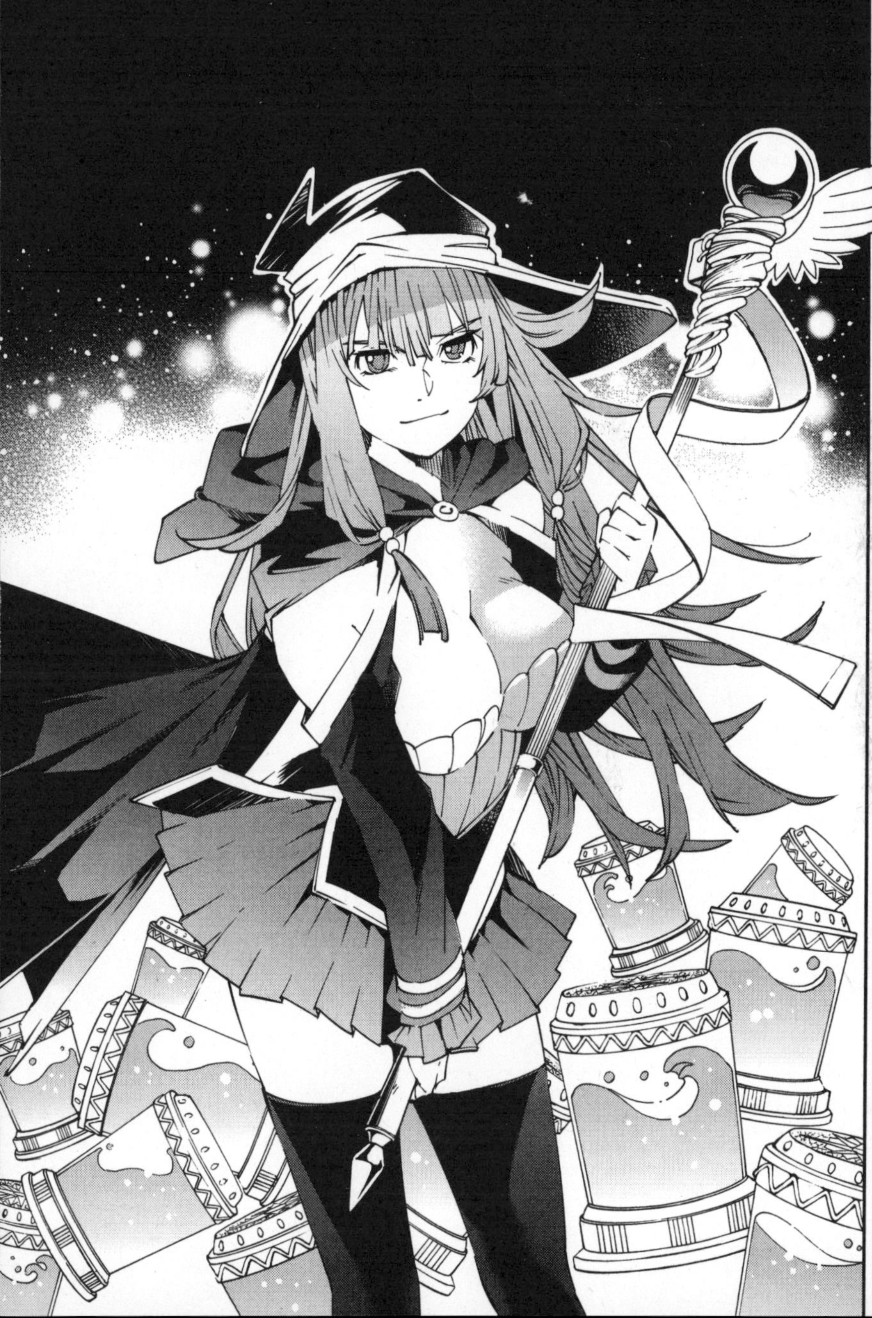

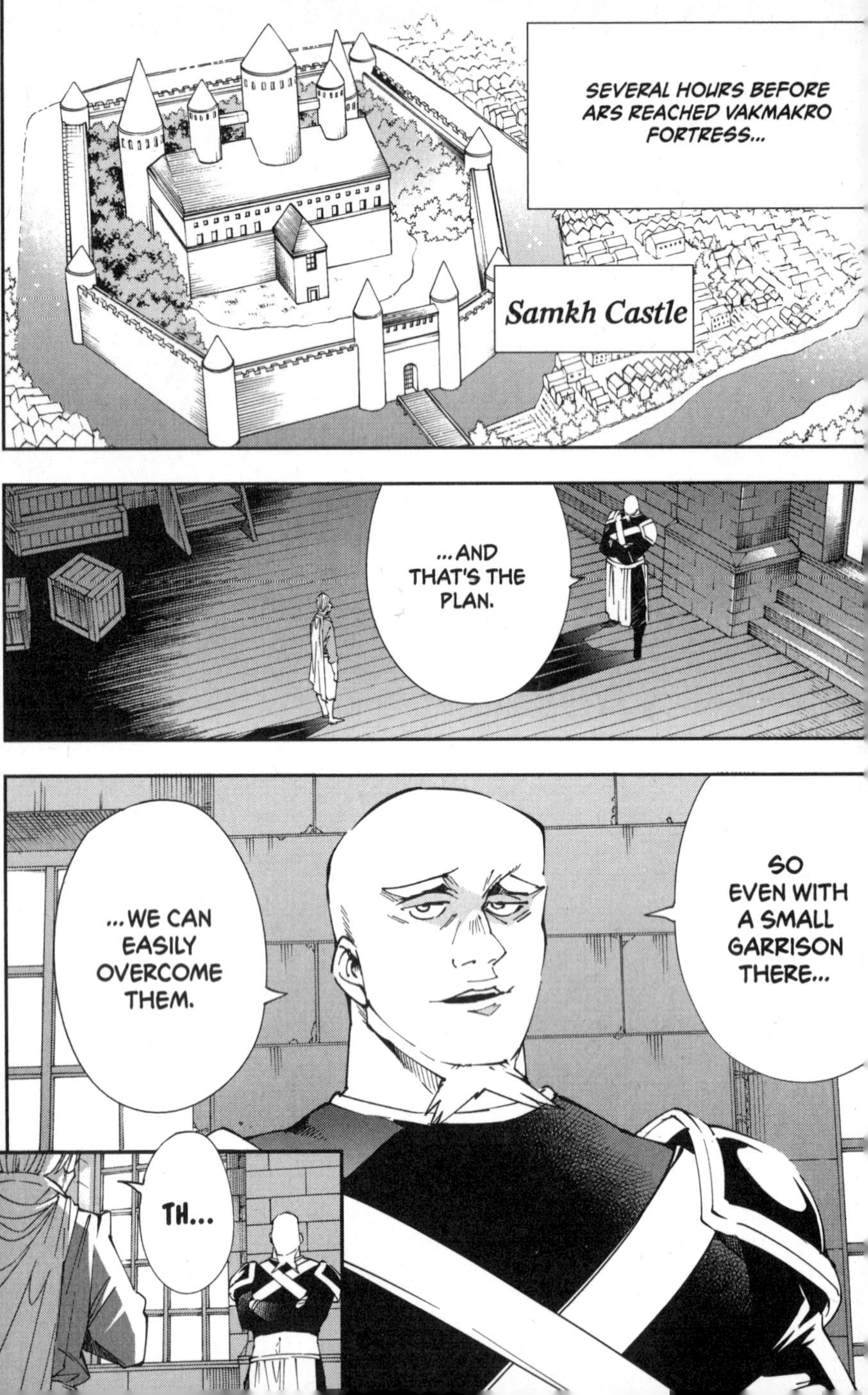
SEVERAL HOURS BEFORE ARS REACHED VAKMAKRO FORTRESS...
Samkh Castle
...AND THAT'S THE PLAN.
SO EVEN WITH A SMALL GARRISON THERE...
...WE CAN EASILY OVERCOME THEM.
TH...

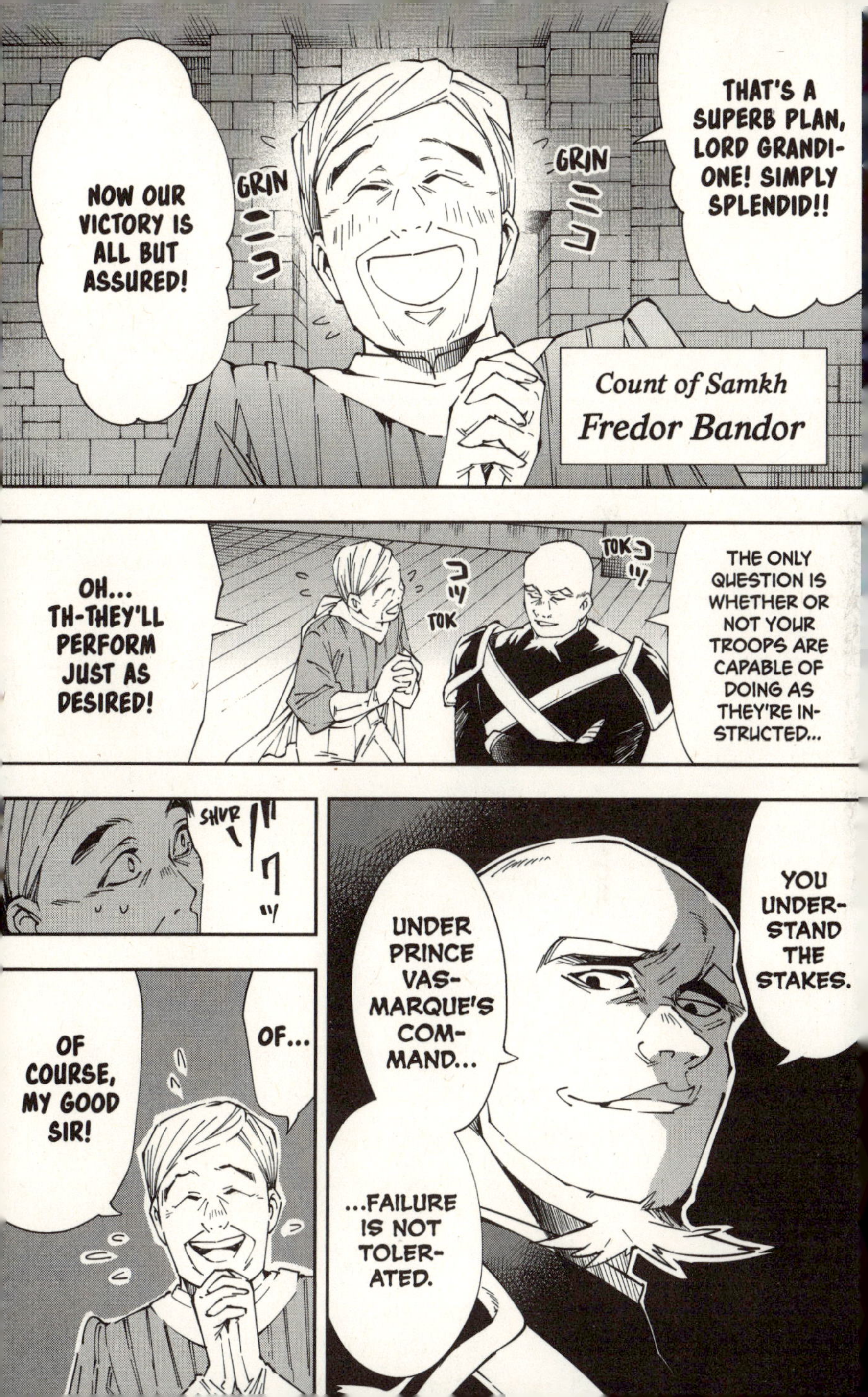
THAT'S A SUPERB PLAN, LORD GRANDIONE! SIMPLY SPLENDID!!
GRIN
GRIN
NOW OUR VICTORY IS ALL BUT ASSURED!
Count of Samkh
Fredor Bandor
THE ONLY QUESTION IS WHETHER OR NOT YOUR TROOPS ARE CAPABLE OF DOING AS THEY'RE INSTRUCTED...
TOK
TOK
OH... TH-THEY'LL PERFORM JUST AS DESIRED!
YOU UNDERSTAND THE STAKES.
UNDER PRINCE VASMARQUE'S COMMAND...
...FAILURE IS NOT TOLERATED.
SHVR
OF...
OF COURSE, MY GOOD SIR!

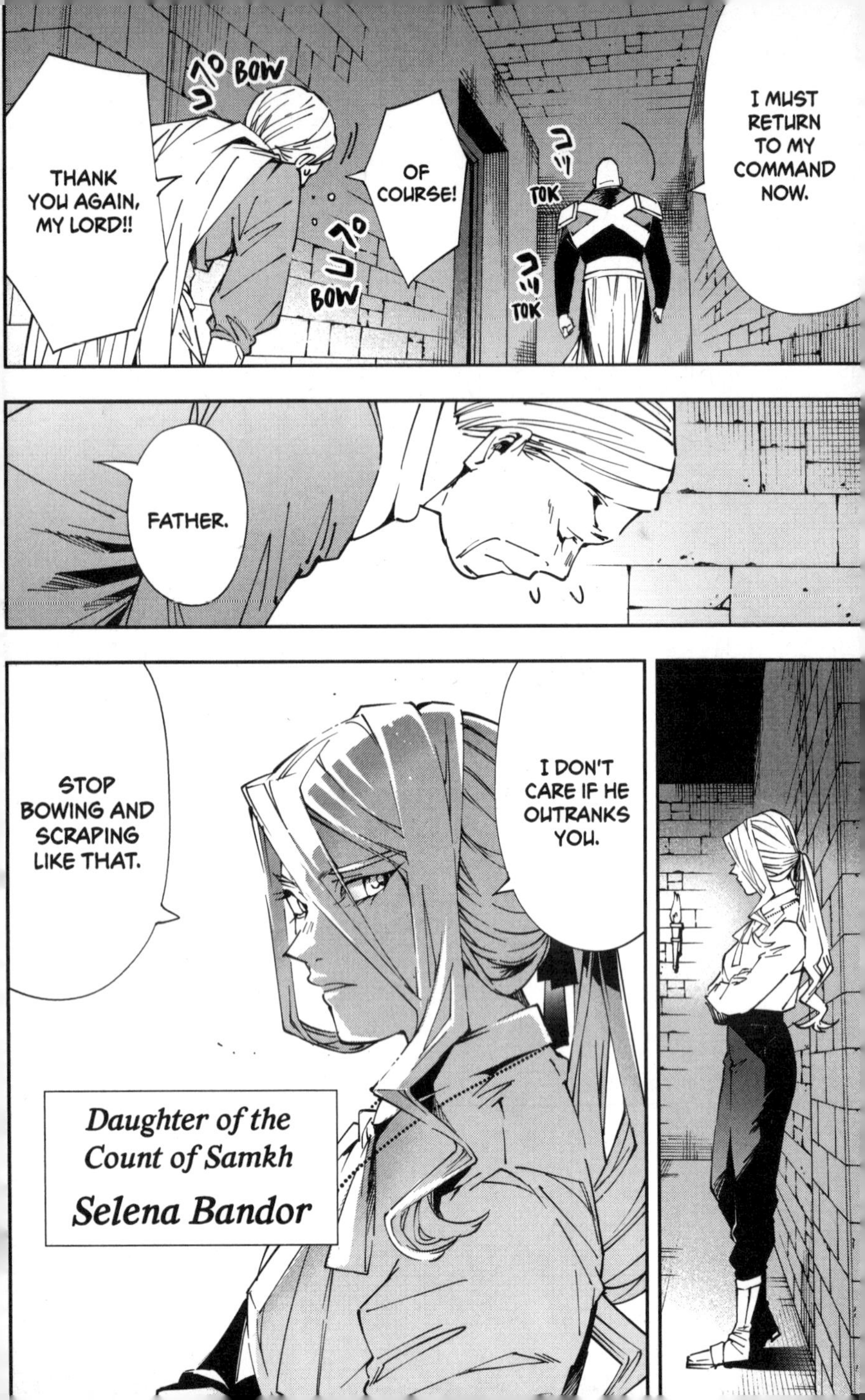
I MUST RETURN TO MY COMMAND NOW.
コツ TOK
コツ TOK
OF COURSE!
ペコ BOW
ペコ BOW
THANK YOU AGAIN, MY LORD!!
FATHER.
I DON'T CARE IF HE OUTRANKS YOU.
STOP BOWING AND SCRAPING LIKE THAT.
Daughter of the Count of Samkh
Selena Bandor

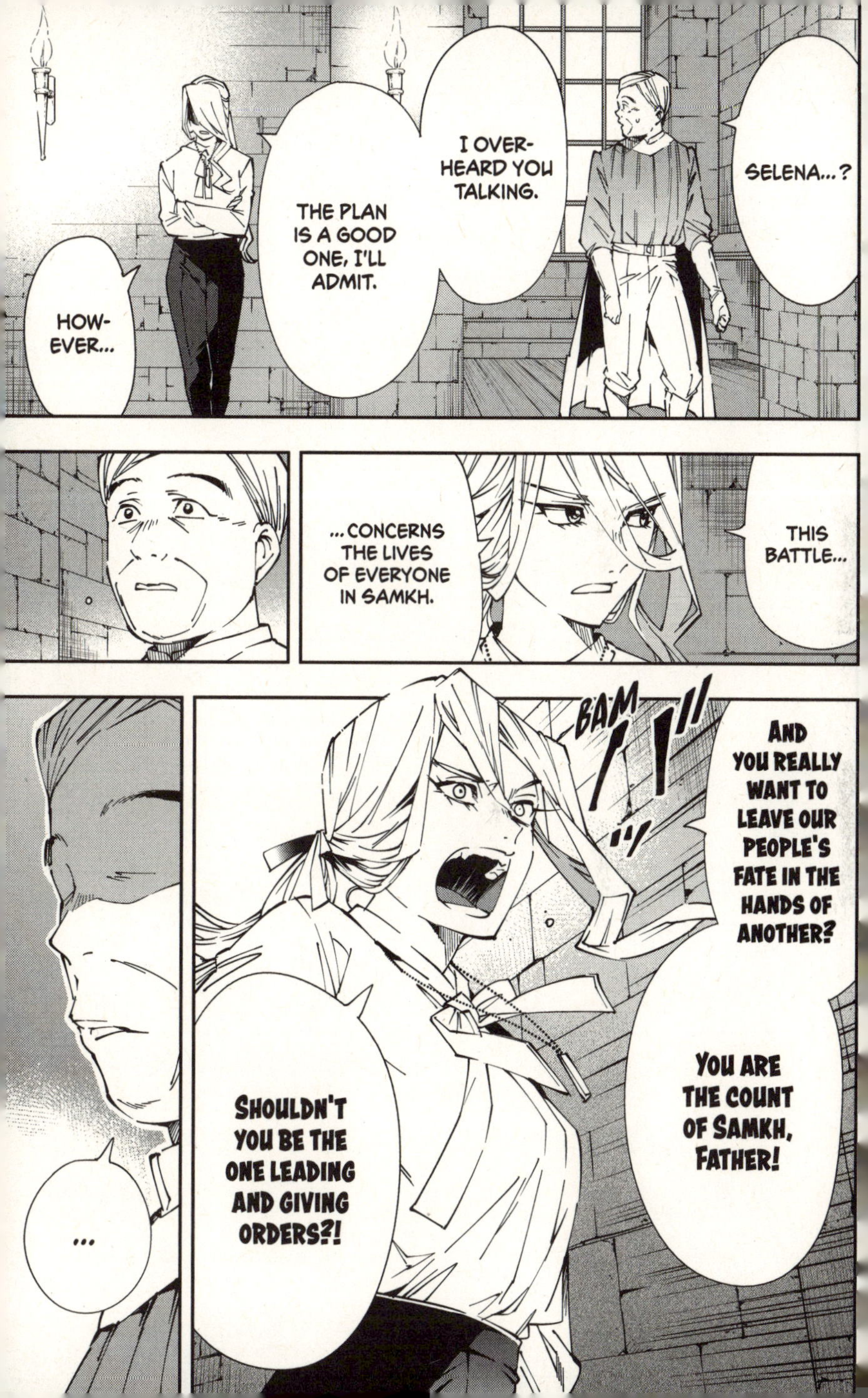
SELENA...?
I OVER-HEARD YOU TALKING.
THE PLAN IS A GOOD ONE, I'LL ADMIT.
HOW-EVER...
THIS BATTLE...
...CONCERNS THE LIVES OF EVERYONE IN SAMKH.
BAM
AND YOU REALLY WANT TO LEAVE OUR PEOPLE'S FATE IN THE HANDS OF ANOTHER?
YOU ARE THE COUNT OF SAMKH, FATHER!
SHOULDN'T YOU BE THE ONE LEADING AND GIVING ORDERS?!
...

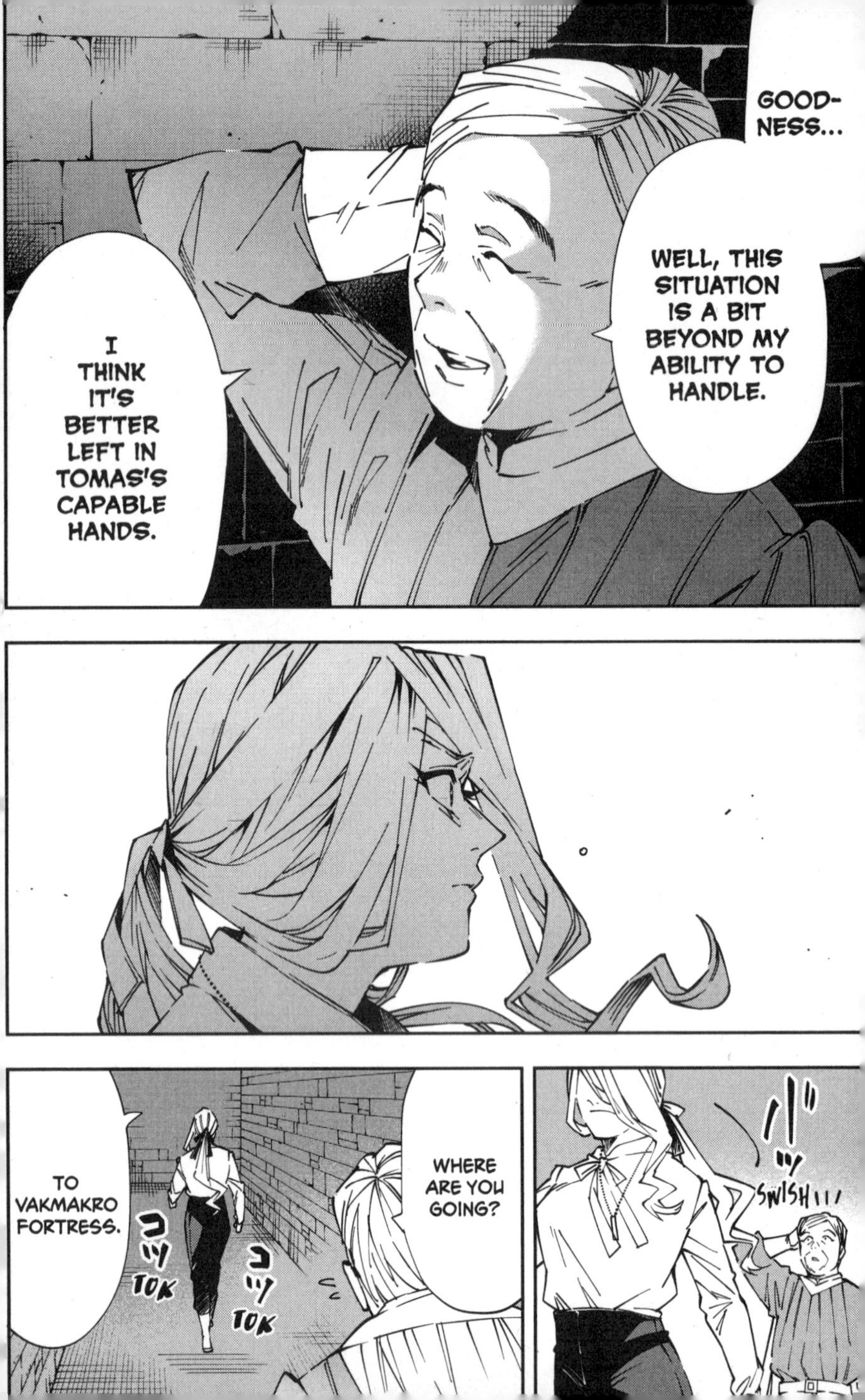
GOOD-NESS...
WELL, THIS SITUATION IS A BIT BEYOND MY ABILITY TO HANDLE.
I THINK IT'S BETTER LEFT IN TOMAS'S CAPABLE HANDS.
バッ
SWISH
WHERE ARE YOU GOING?
TO VAKMAKRO FORTRESS.
コツ
TOK
コツ
TOK

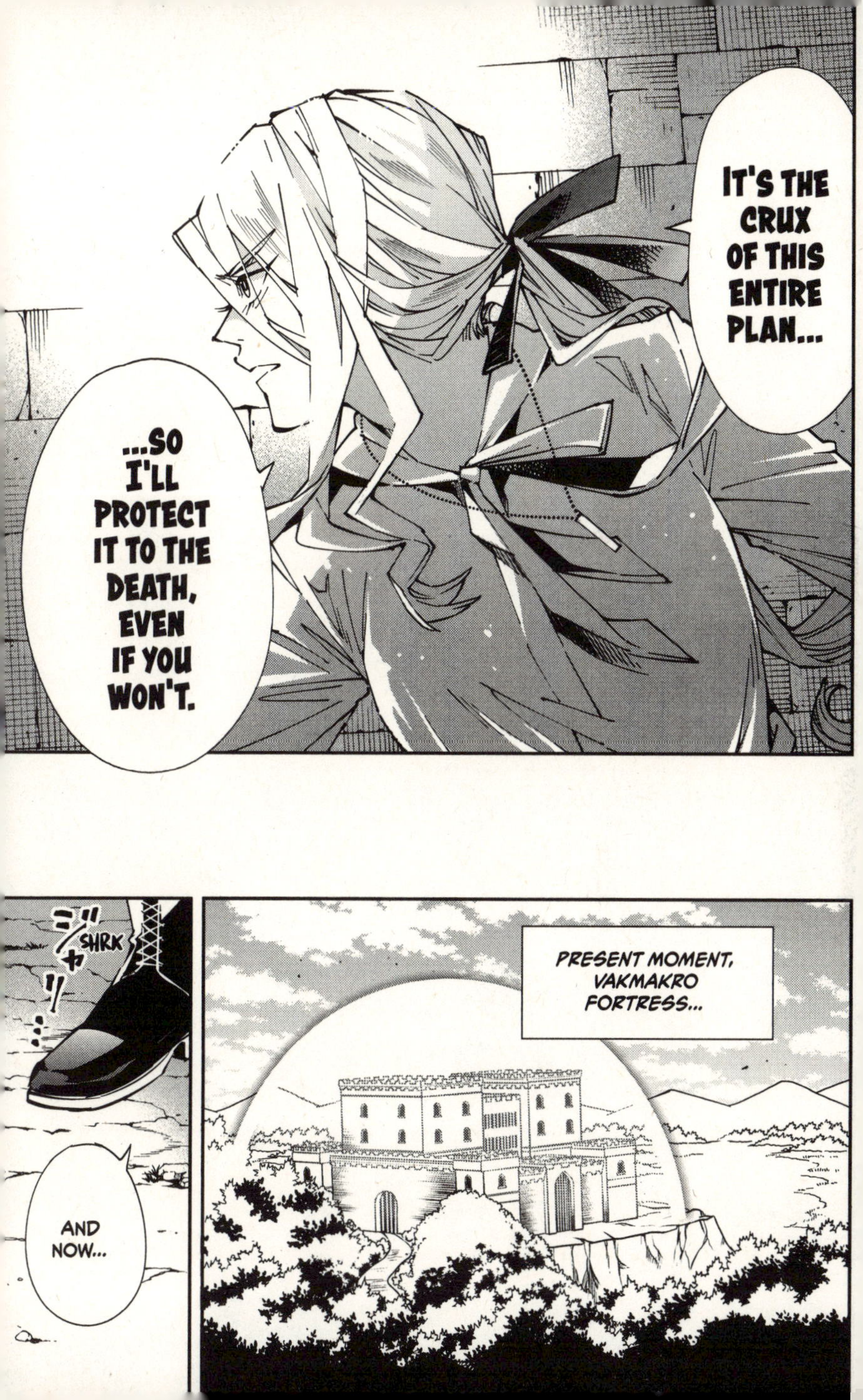
IT'S THE CRUX OF THIS ENTIRE PLAN...
...SO I'LL PROTECT IT TO THE DEATH, EVEN IF YOU WON'T.
PRESENT MOMENT, VAKMAKRO FORTRESS...
ジャリ…
SHRK
AND NOW...

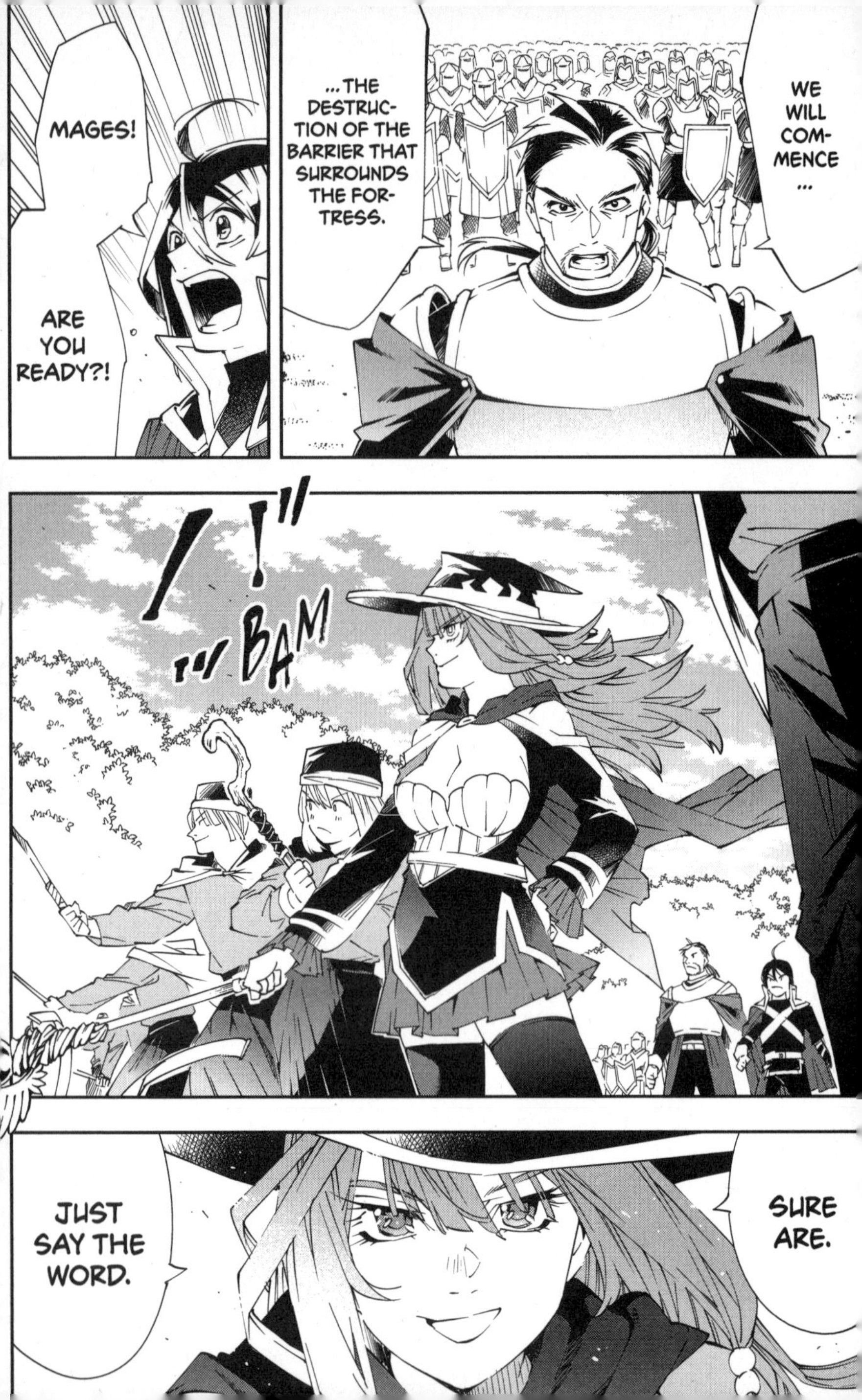
WE WILL COM-MENCE ...
...THE DESTRUC-TION OF THE BARRIER THAT SURROUNDS THE FOR-TRESS.
MAGES!
ARE YOU READY?!
BAM
SURE ARE.
JUST SAY THE WORD.

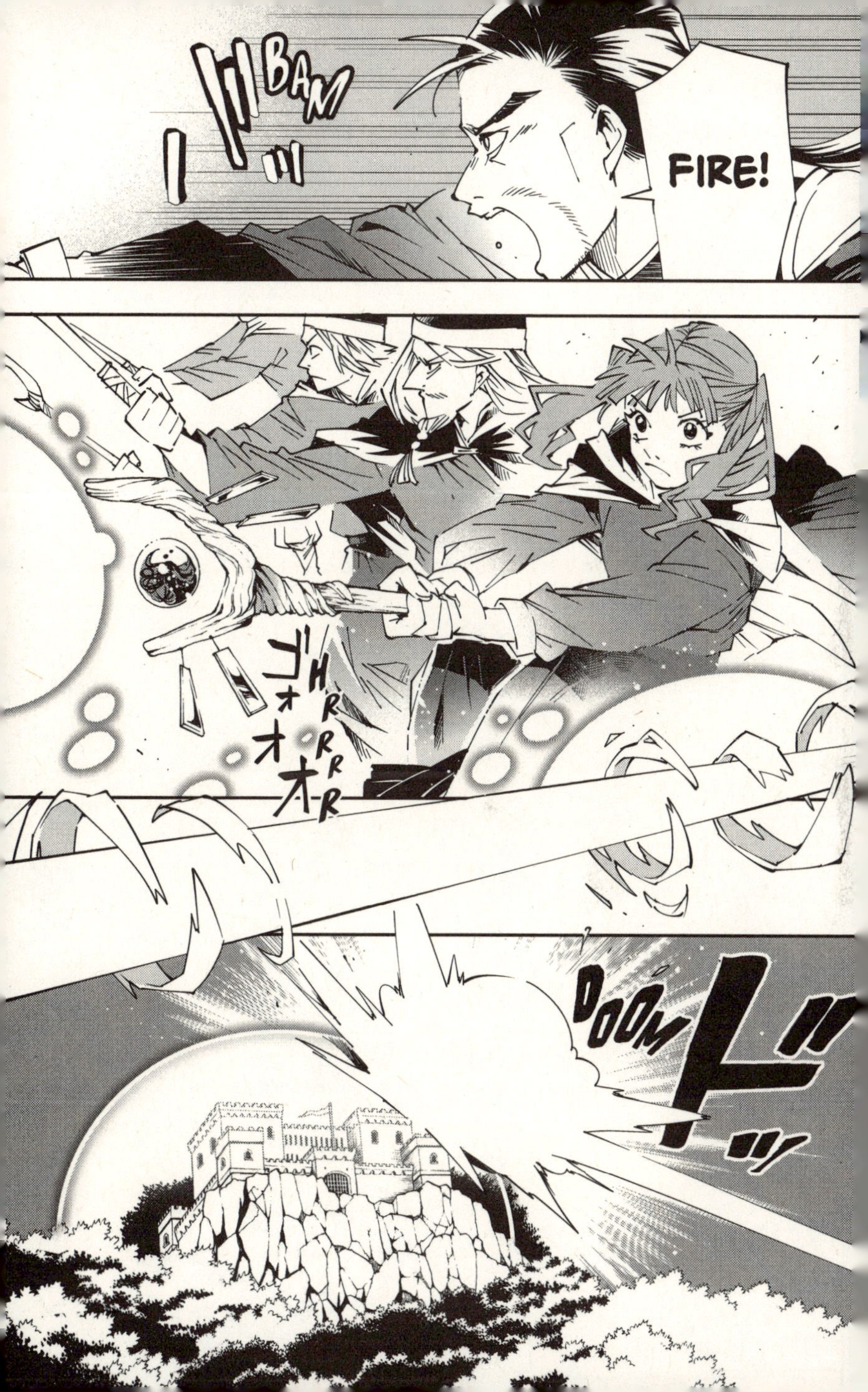
FIRE!
BAM
ゴォオオ
HRRRRR
DOOM
ドッ

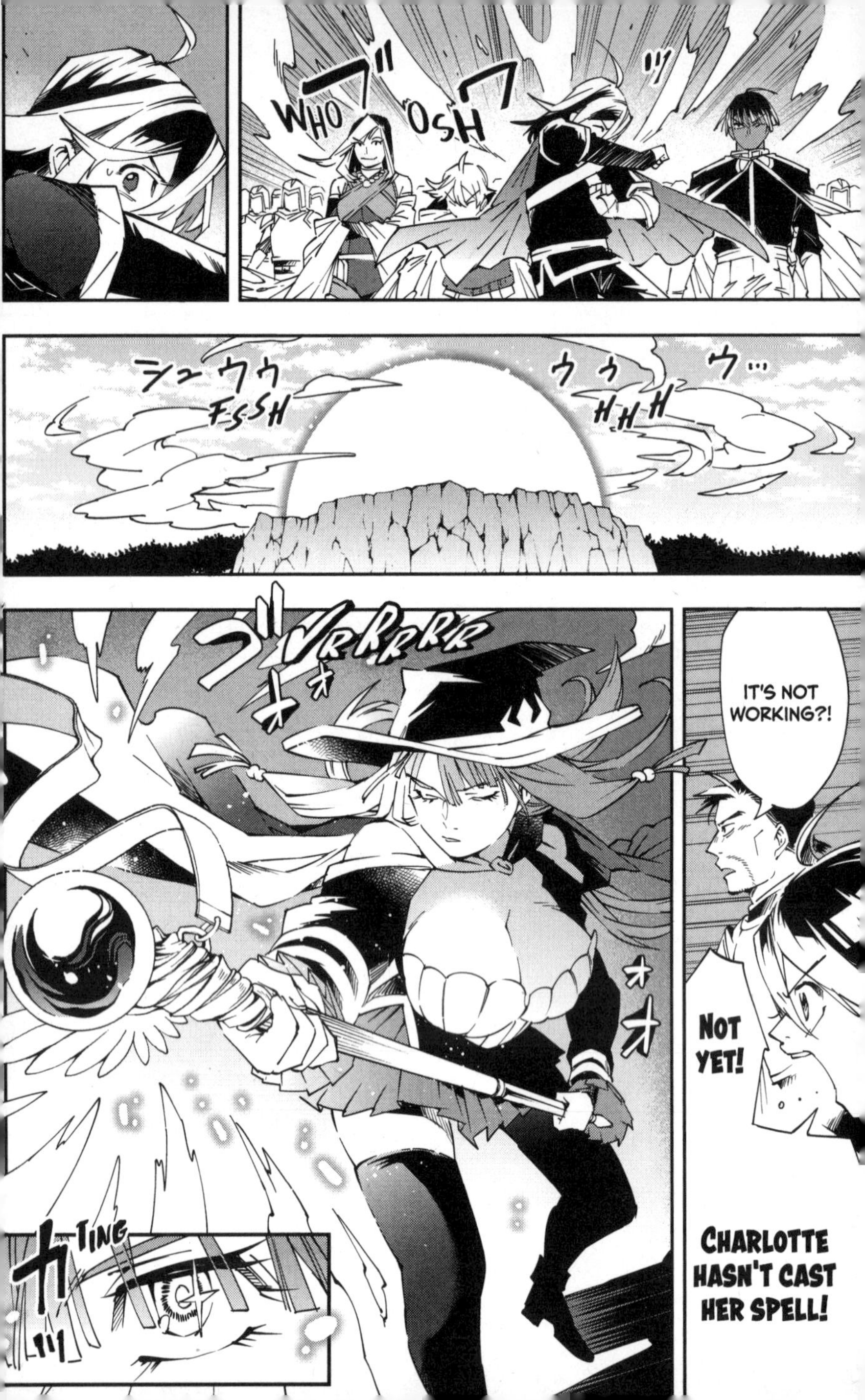
WHOOSH
シュウウ
FSSH
HHH
IT'S NOT WORKING?!
NOT YET!
CHARLOTTE HASN'T CAST HER SPELL!
VRRRRRR
TING

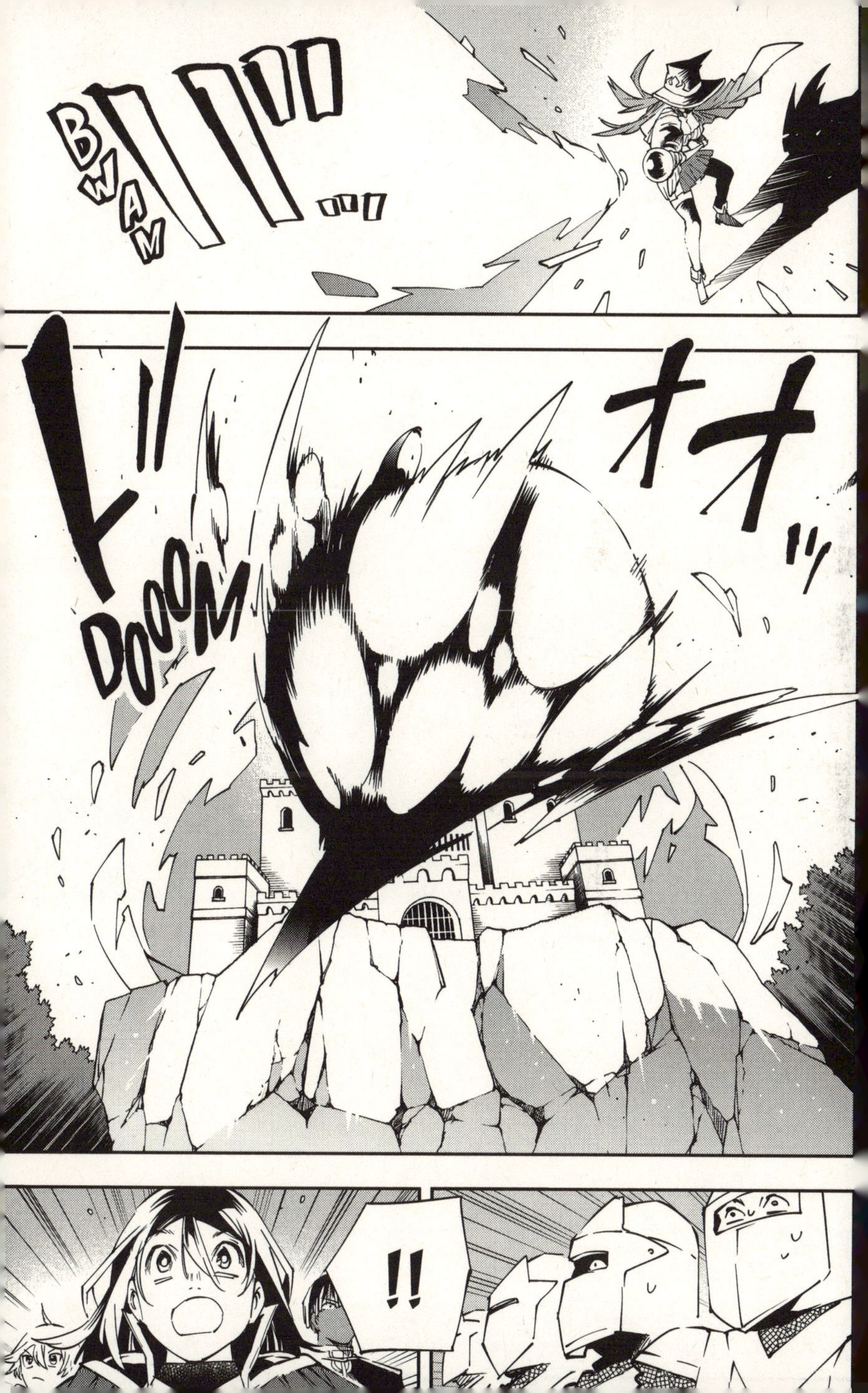
BWAM
ドオオッ
DOOOM
!!

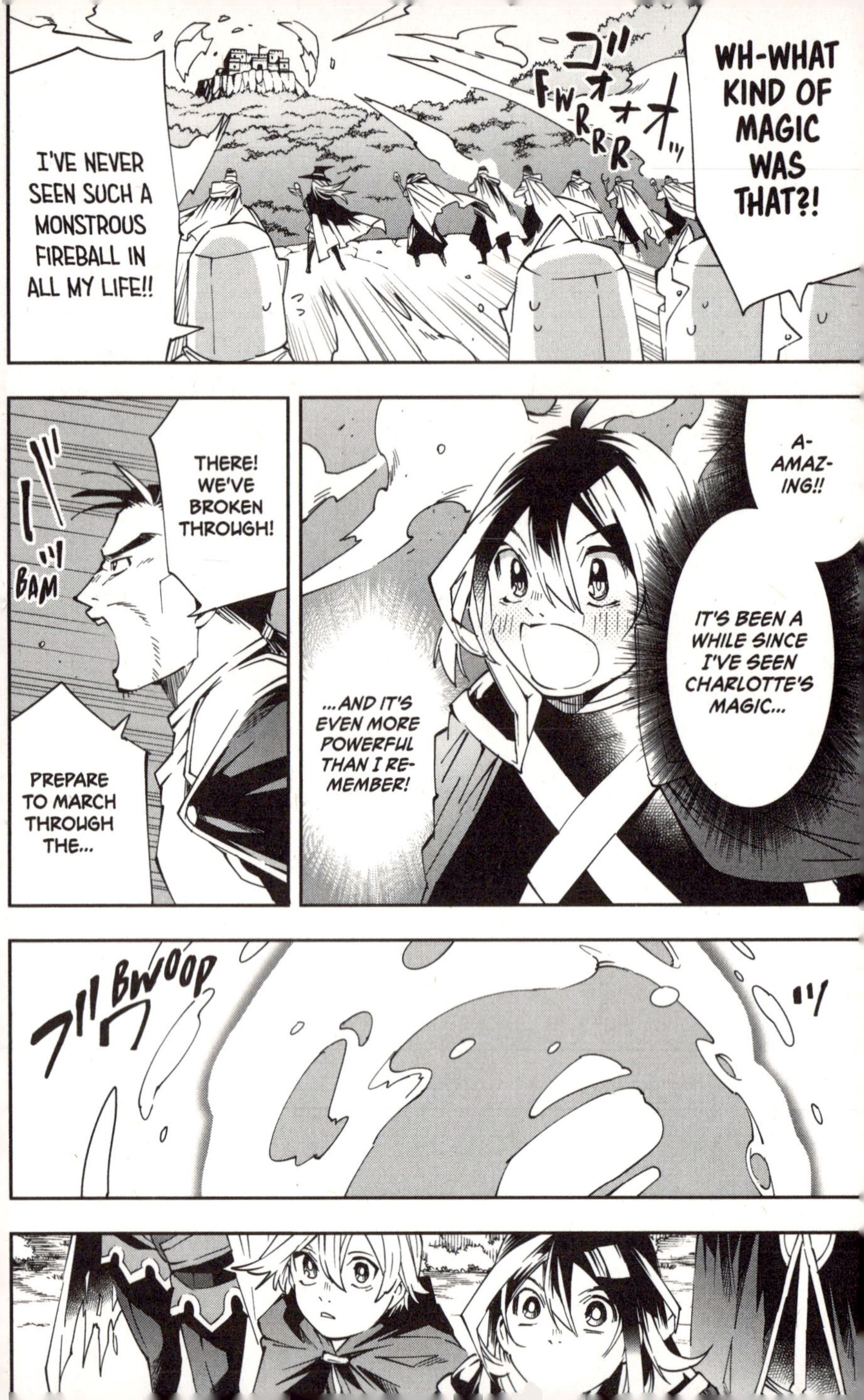
WH-WHAT KIND OF MAGIC WAS THAT?!
FWRRRR
I'VE NEVER SEEN SUCH A MONSTROUS FIREBALL IN ALL MY LIFE!!
A-AMAZING!!
IT'S BEEN A WHILE SINCE I'VE SEEN CHARLOTTE'S MAGIC...
...AND IT'S EVEN MORE POWERFUL THAN I RE-MEMBER!
BAM
THERE! WE'VE BROKEN THROUGH!
PREPARE TO MARCH THROUGH THE...
BWOOP

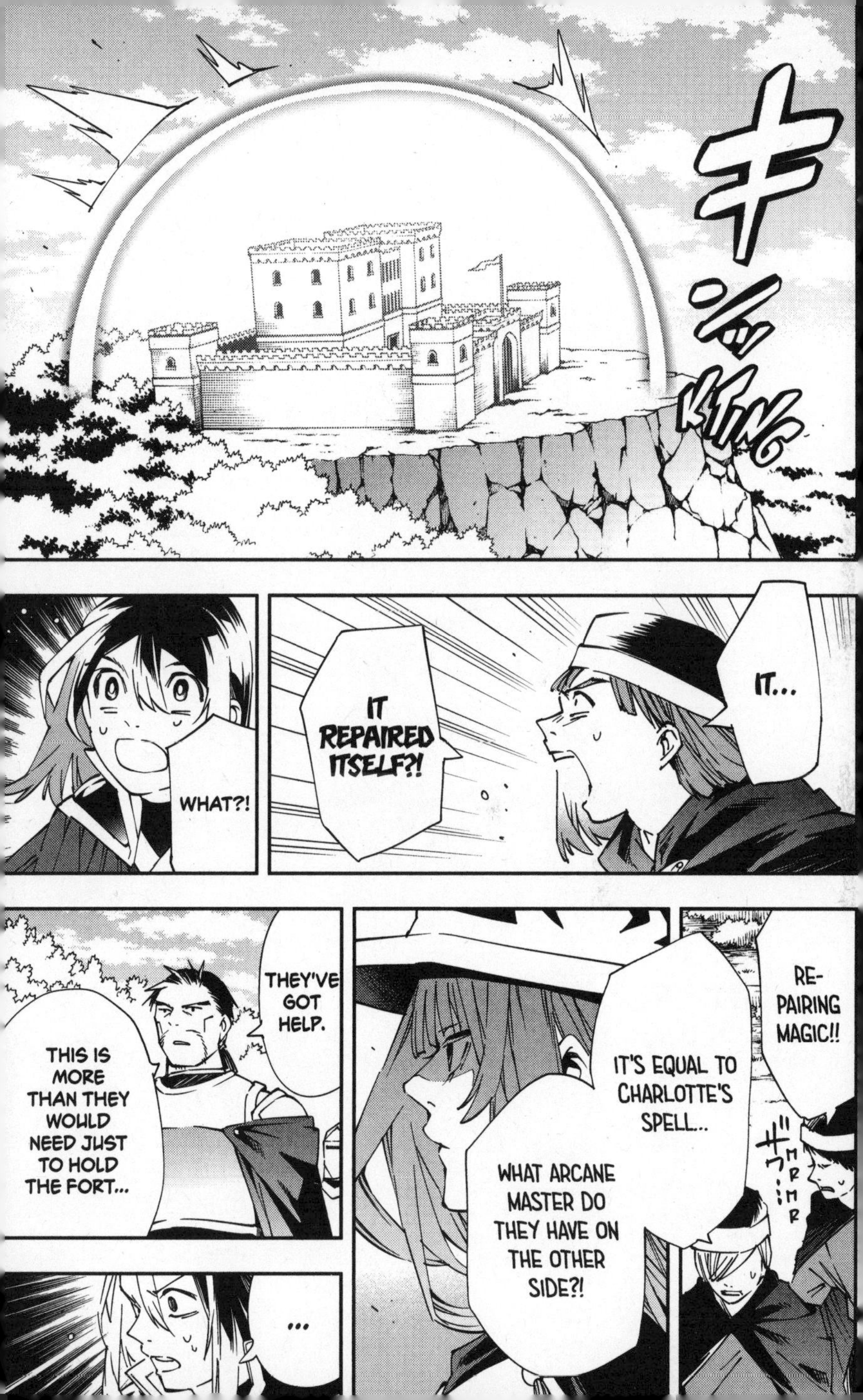
KTING
IT...
IT REPAIRED ITSELF?!
WHAT?!
RE-PAIRING MAGIC!!
MRMR
IT'S EQUAL TO CHARLOTTE'S SPELL...
WHAT ARCANE MASTER DO THEY HAVE ON THE OTHER SIDE?!
THEY'VE GOT HELP.
THIS IS MORE THAN THEY WOULD NEED JUST TO HOLD THE FORT...
...

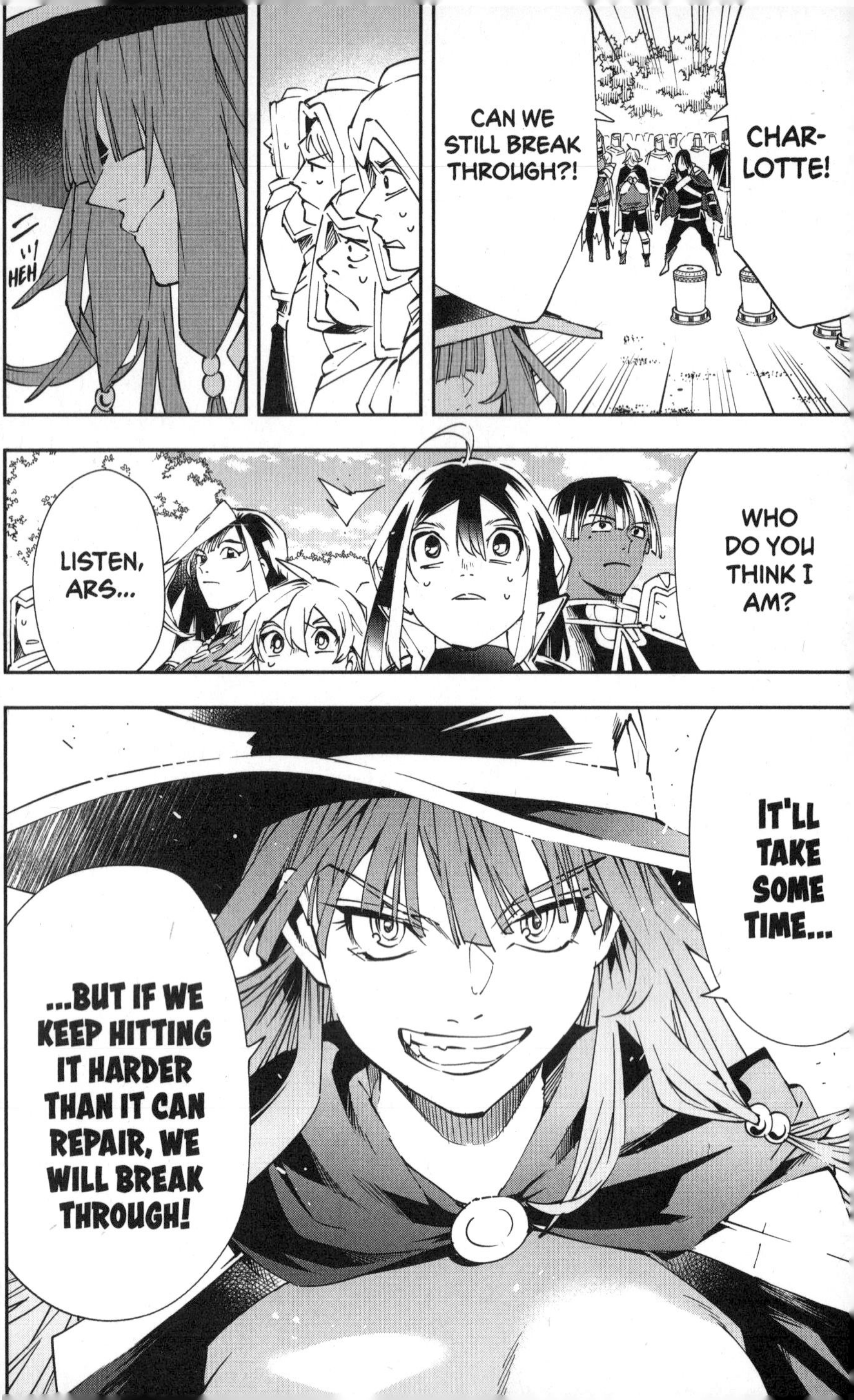
CHAR-LOTTE!
CAN WE STILL BREAK THROUGH?!
HEH
WHO DO YOU THINK I AM?
LISTEN, ARS...
IT'LL TAKE SOME TIME...
...BUT IF WE KEEP HITTING IT HARDER THAN IT CAN REPAIR, WE WILL BREAK THROUGH!

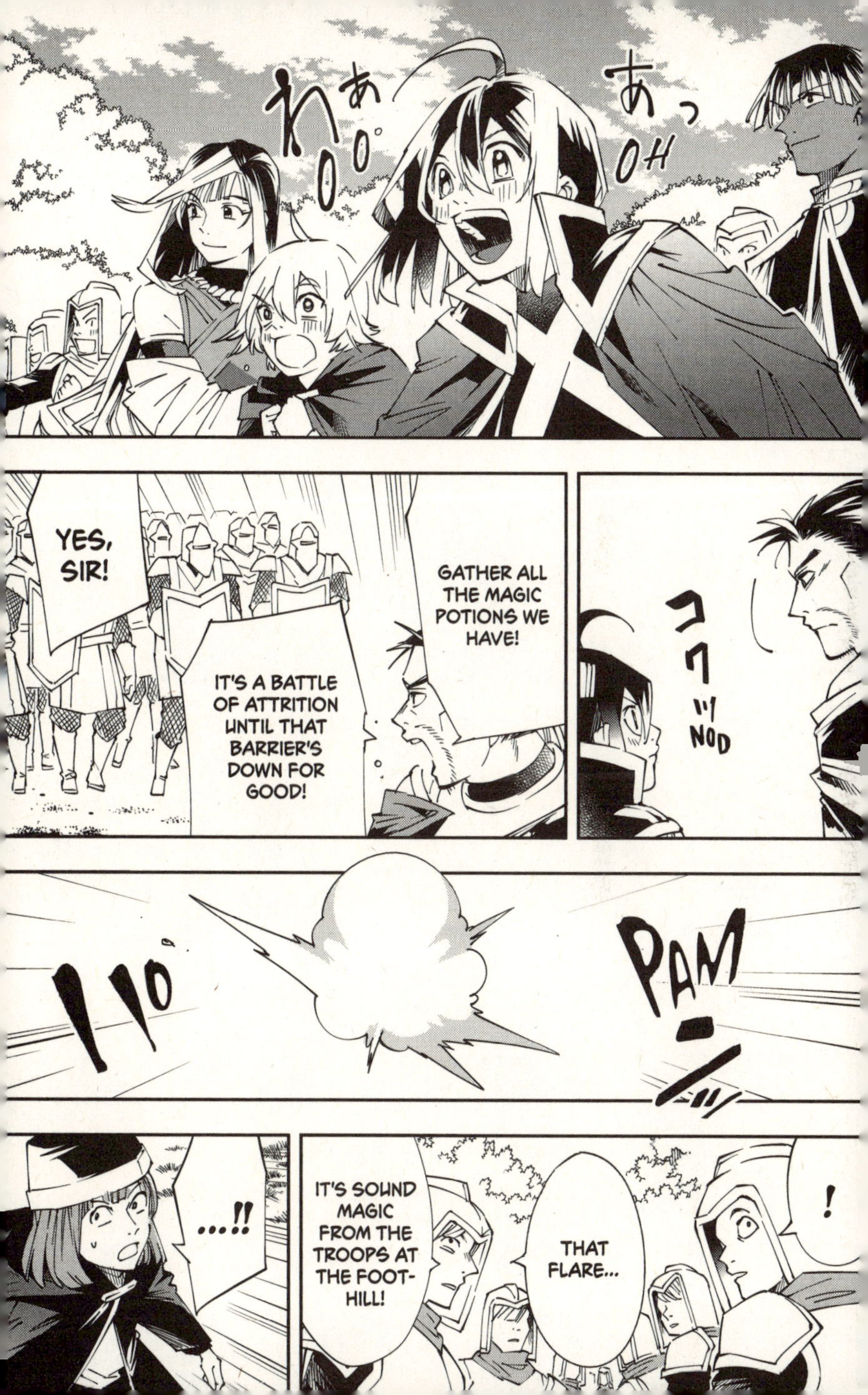
あっ
OH
わあ
コクッ
NOD
GATHER ALL THE MAGIC POTIONS WE HAVE!
IT'S A BATTLE OF ATTRITION UNTIL THAT BARRIER'S DOWN FOR GOOD!
YES, SIR!
PAM
!
THAT FLARE...
IT'S SOUND MAGIC FROM THE TROOPS AT THE FOOT-HILL!
...!!

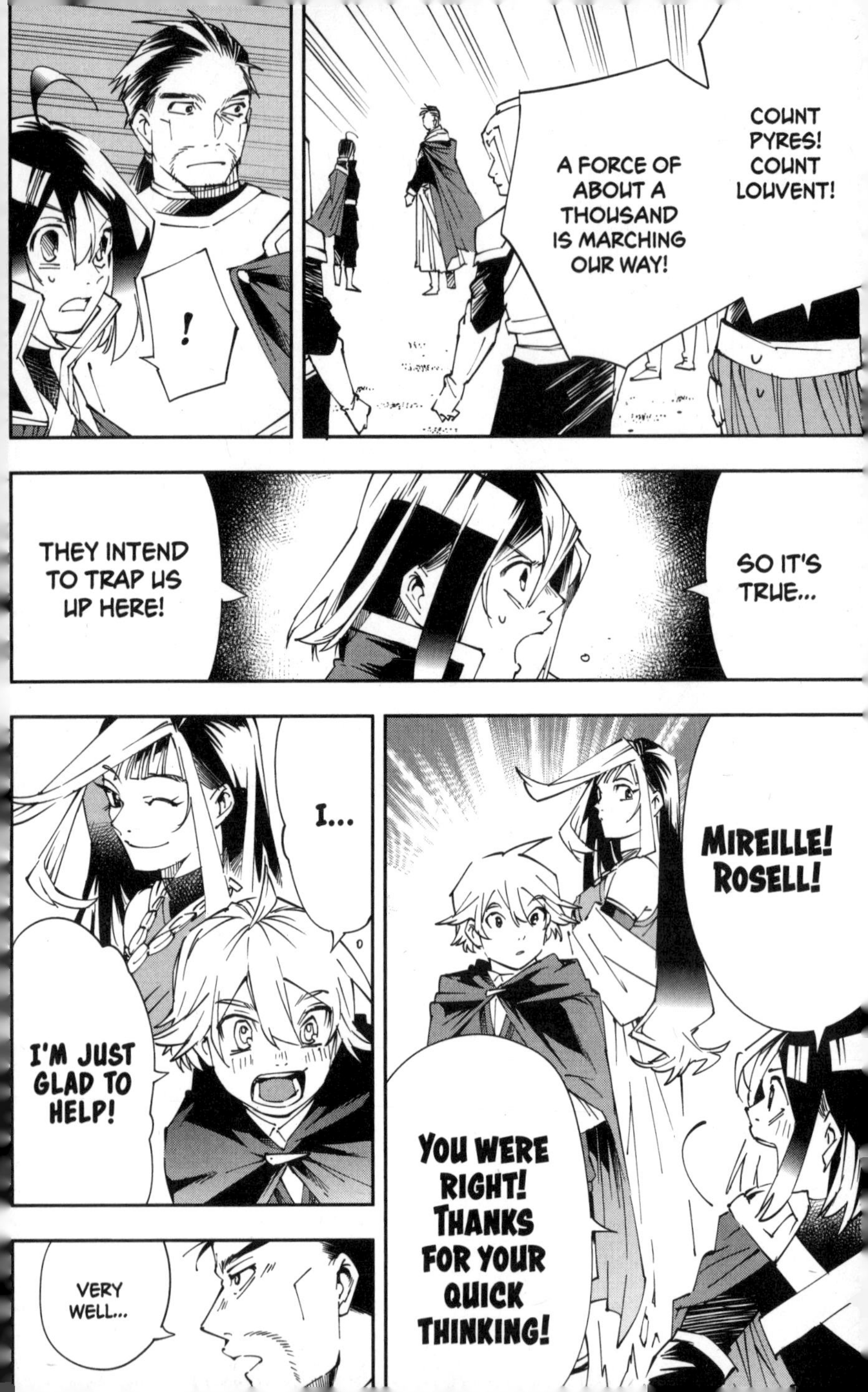
COUNT PYRES! COUNT LOUVENT!
A FORCE OF ABOUT A THOUSAND IS MARCHING OUR WAY!
!
SO IT'S TRUE...
THEY INTEND TO TRAP US UP HERE!
MIREILLE! ROSELL!
YOU WERE RIGHT! THANKS FOR YOUR QUICK THINKING!
I...
I'M JUST GLAD TO HELP!
VERY WELL...

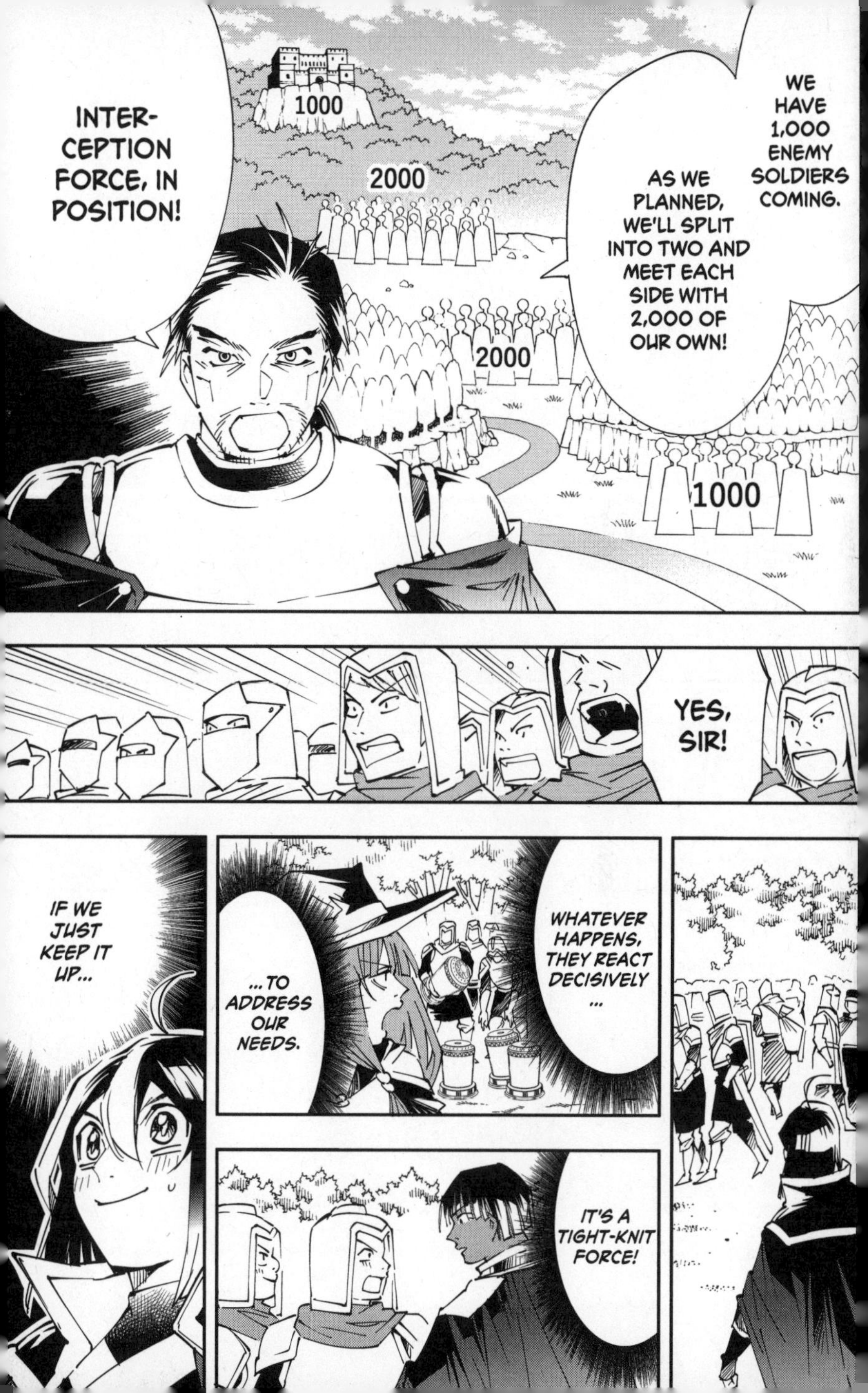
WE HAVE 1,000 ENEMY SOLDIERS COMING.
AS WE PLANNED, WE'LL SPLIT INTO TWO AND MEET EACH SIDE WITH 2,000 OF OUR OWN!
1000
2000
2000
1000
INTER-CEPTION FORCE, IN POSITION!
YES, SIR!
WHATEVER HAPPENS, THEY REACT DECISIVELY...
...TO ADDRESS OUR NEEDS.
IT'S A TIGHT-KNIT FORCE!
IF WE JUST KEEP IT UP...

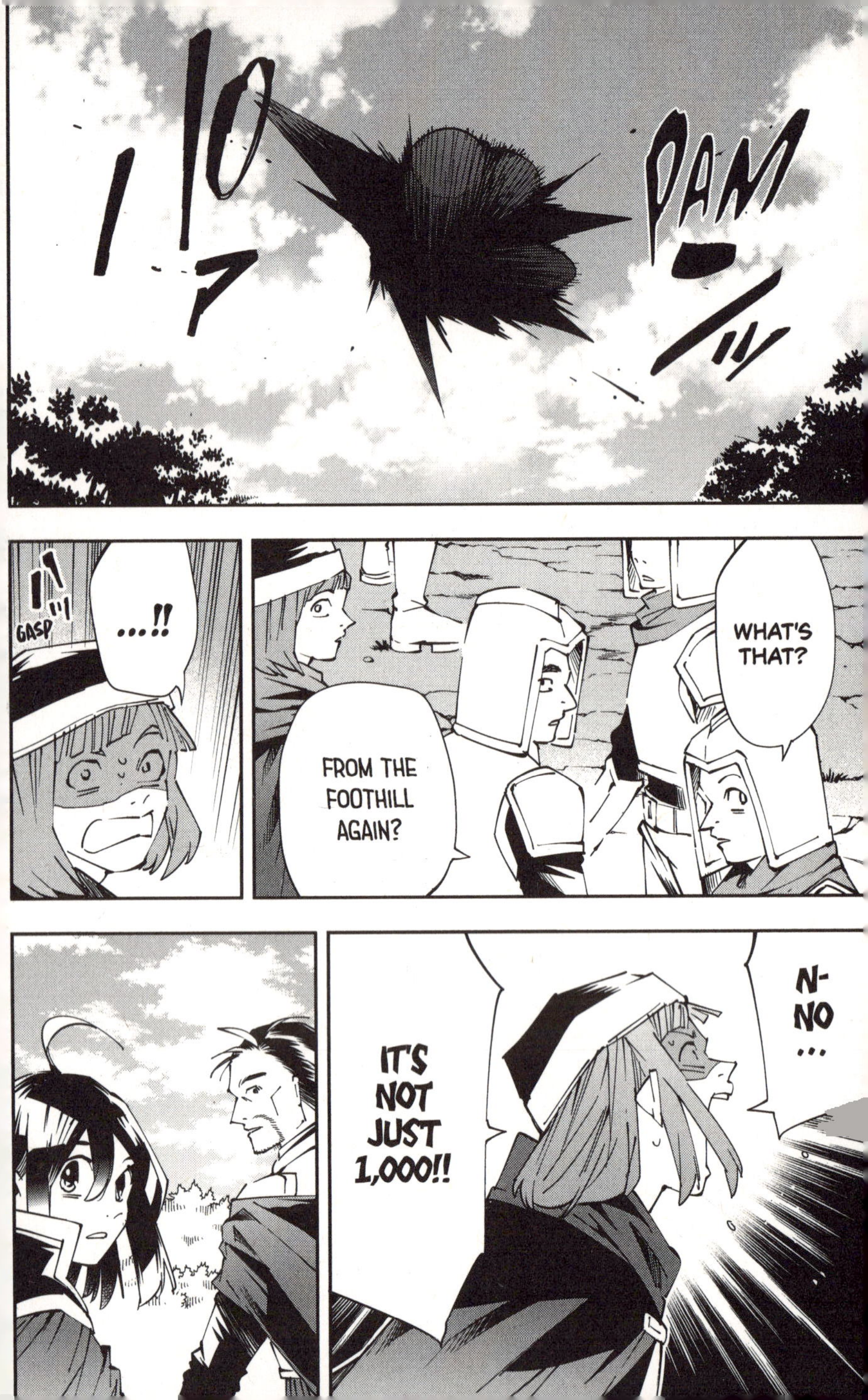
PAM
WHAT'S THAT?
FROM THE FOOTHILL AGAIN?
GASP
...!!
N-NO...
IT'S NOT JUST 1,000!!

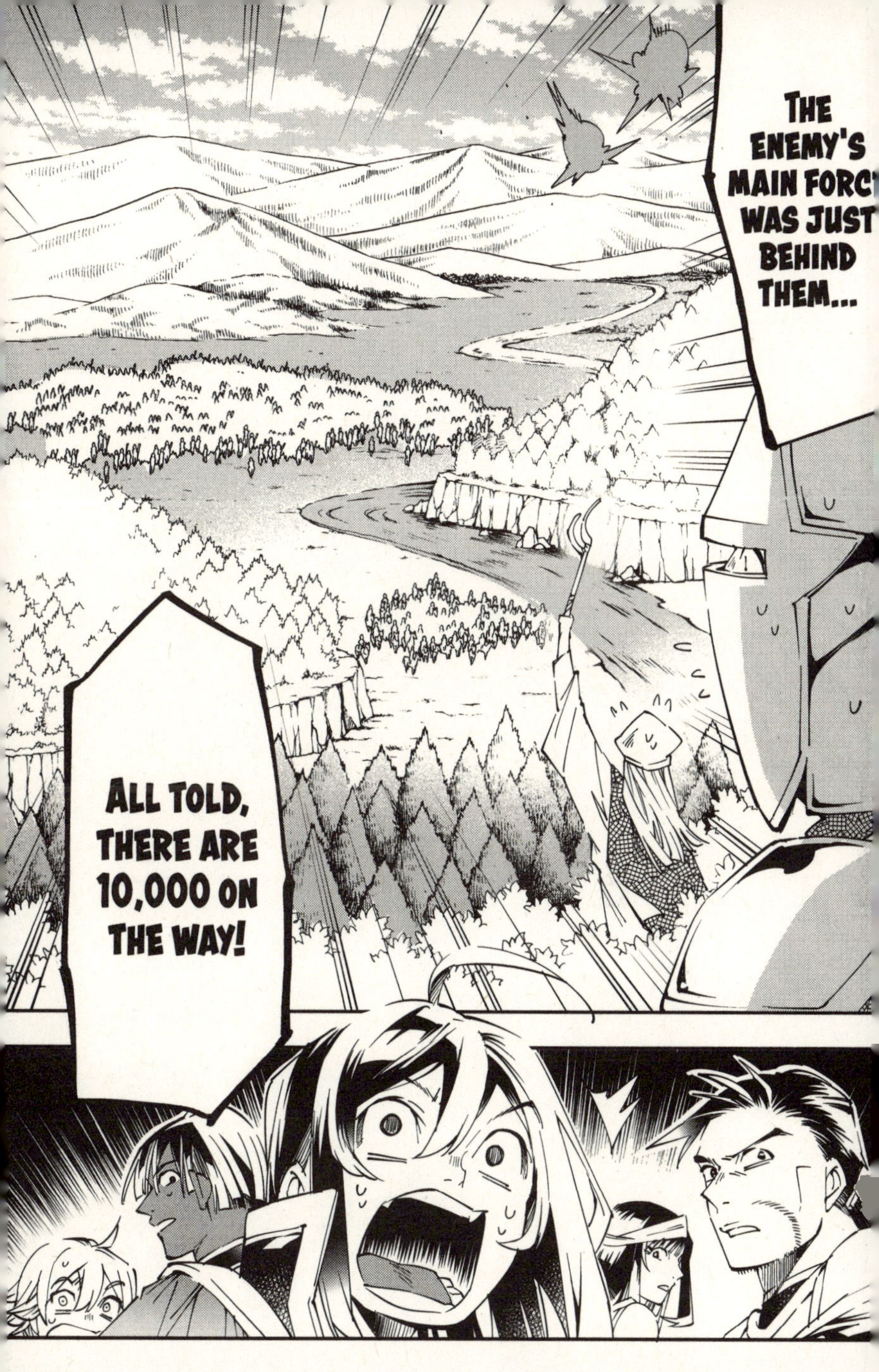
THE ENEMY'S MAIN FORC WAS JUST BEHIND THEM...
ALL TOLD, THERE ARE 10,000 ON THE WAY!

As a Reincarnated ARISTOCRAT, I'll Use My Appraisal Skill to Rise in the World

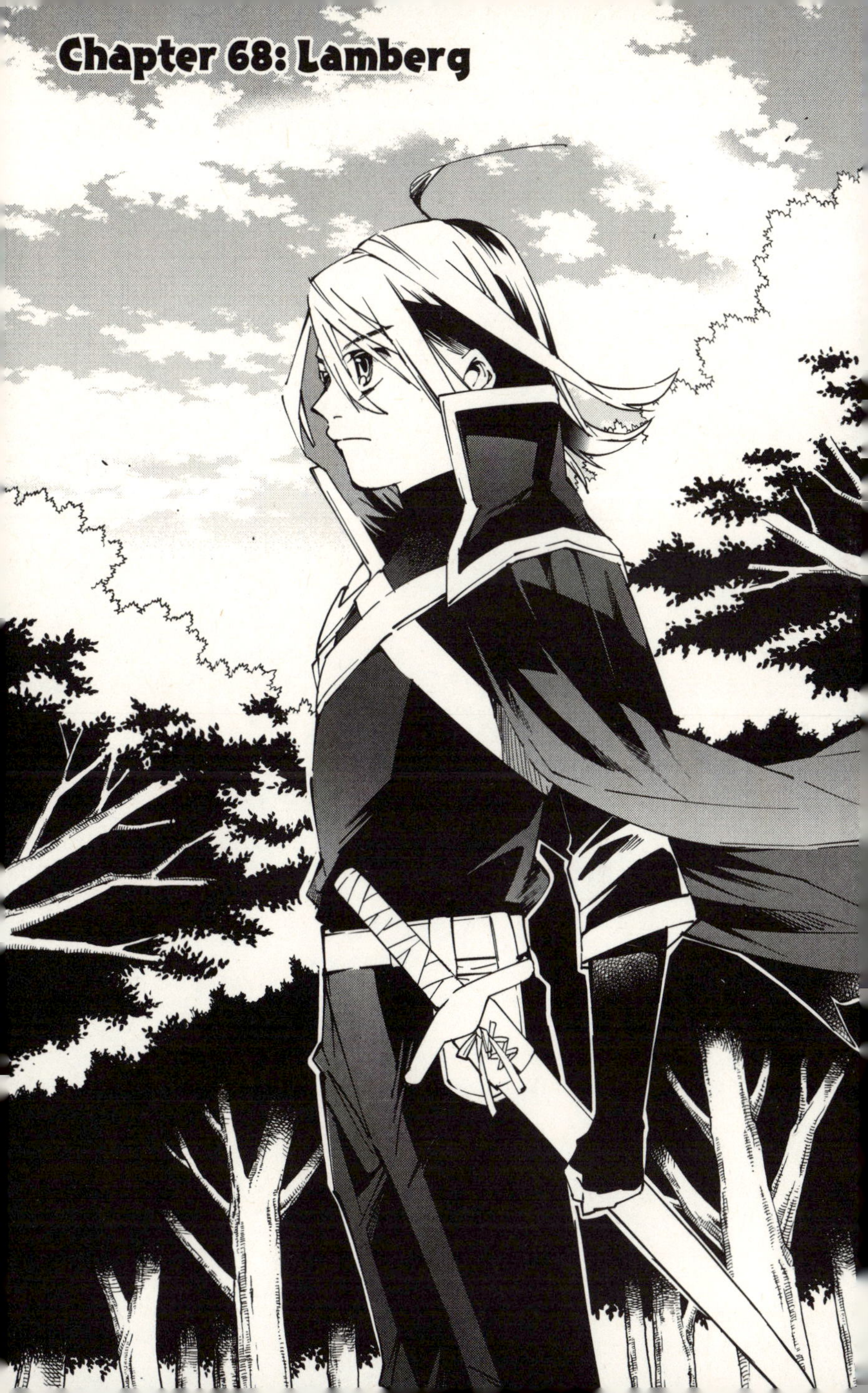
Chapter 68: Lamberg

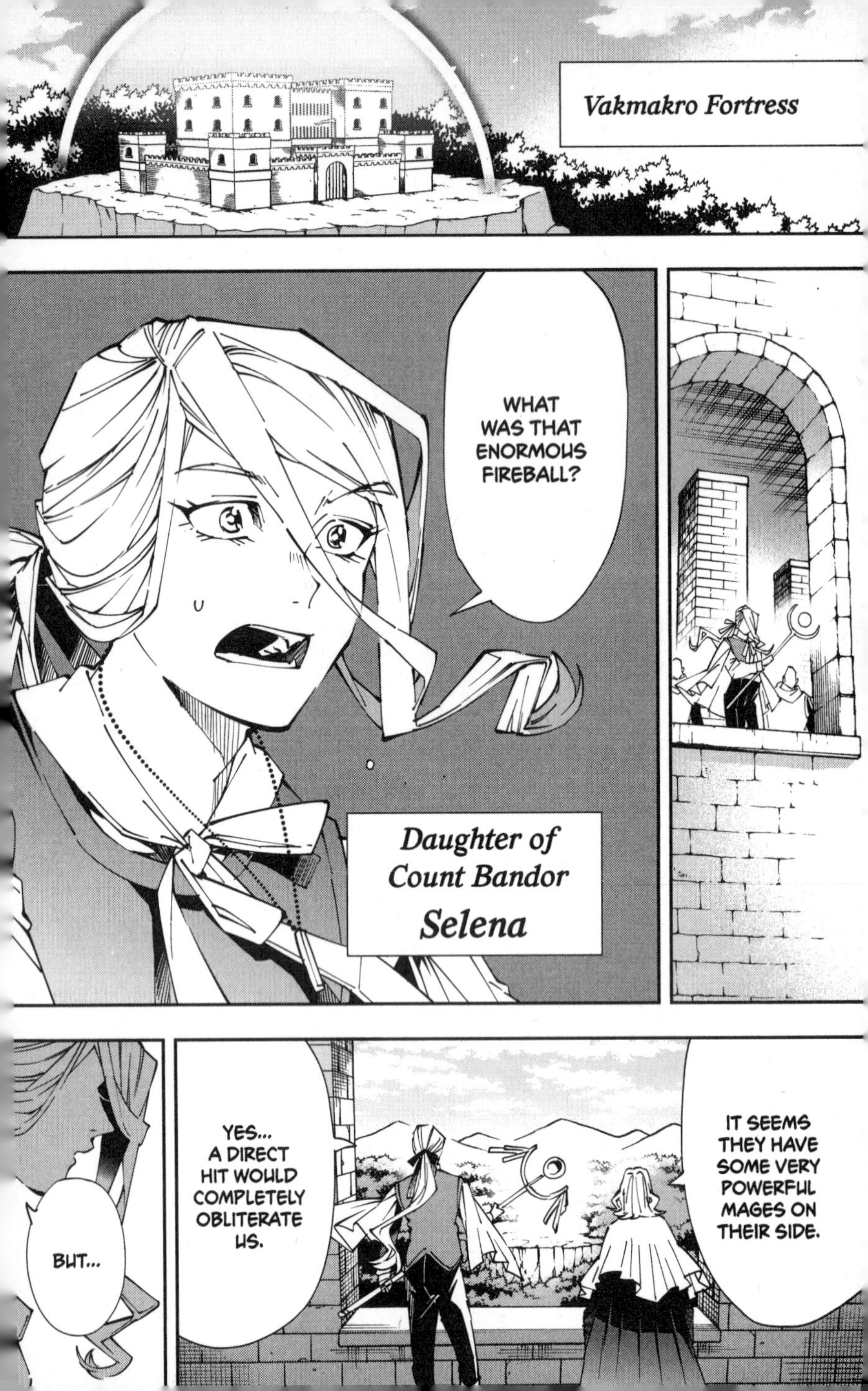
Vakmakro Fortress
WHAT WAS THAT ENORMOUS FIREBALL?
Daughter of Count Bandor Selena
IT SEEMS THEY HAVE SOME VERY POWERFUL MAGES ON THEIR SIDE.
YES... A DIRECT HIT WOULD COMPLETELY OBLITERATE US.
BUT...

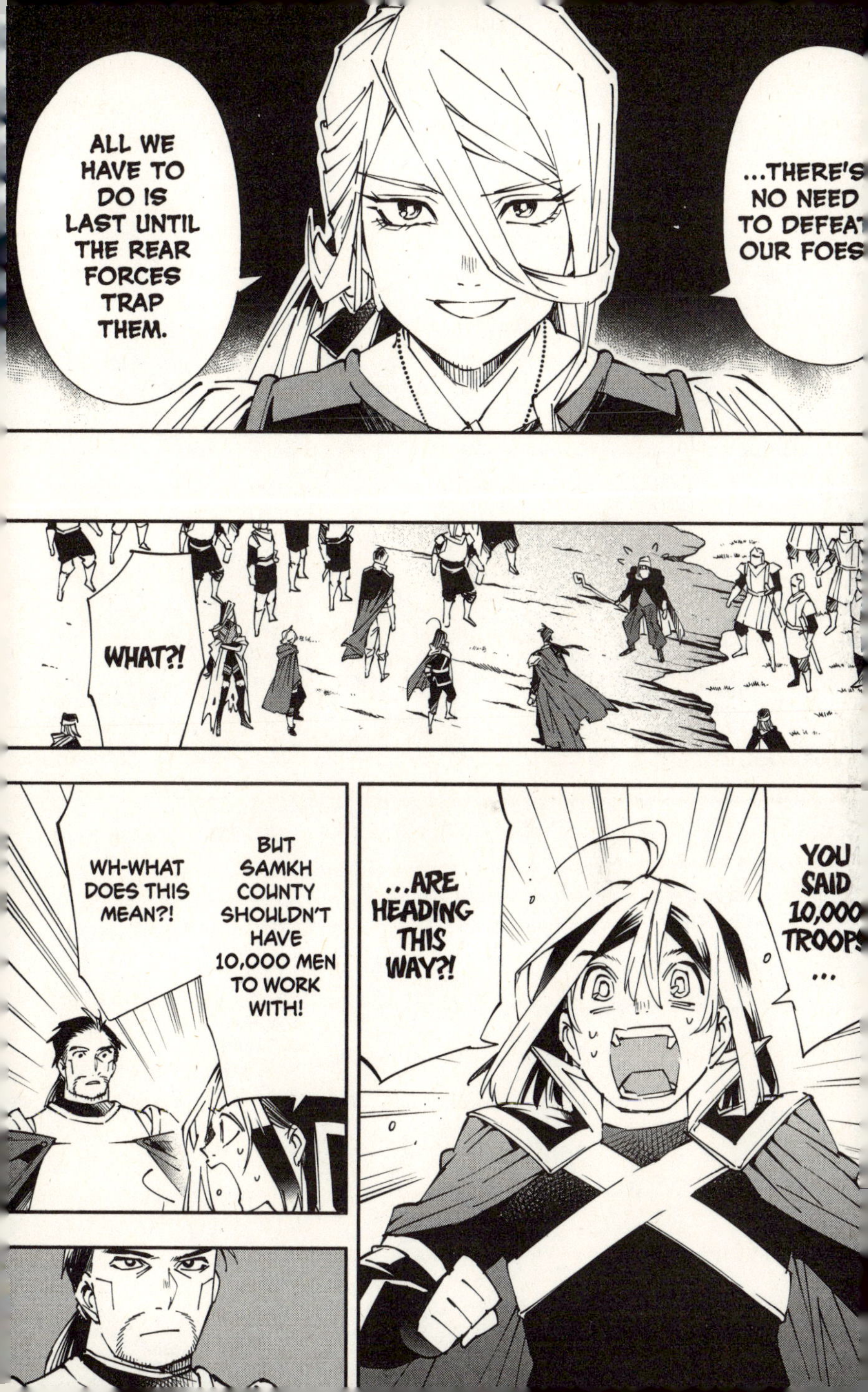
...THERE'S NO NEED TO DEFEAT OUR FOES
ALL WE HAVE TO DO IS LAST UNTIL THE REAR FORCES TRAP THEM.
WHAT?!
YOU SAID 10,000 TROOPS...
...ARE HEADING THIS WAY?!
BUT SAMKH COUNTY SHOULDN'T HAVE 10,000 MEN TO WORK WITH!
WH-WHAT DOES THIS MEAN?!

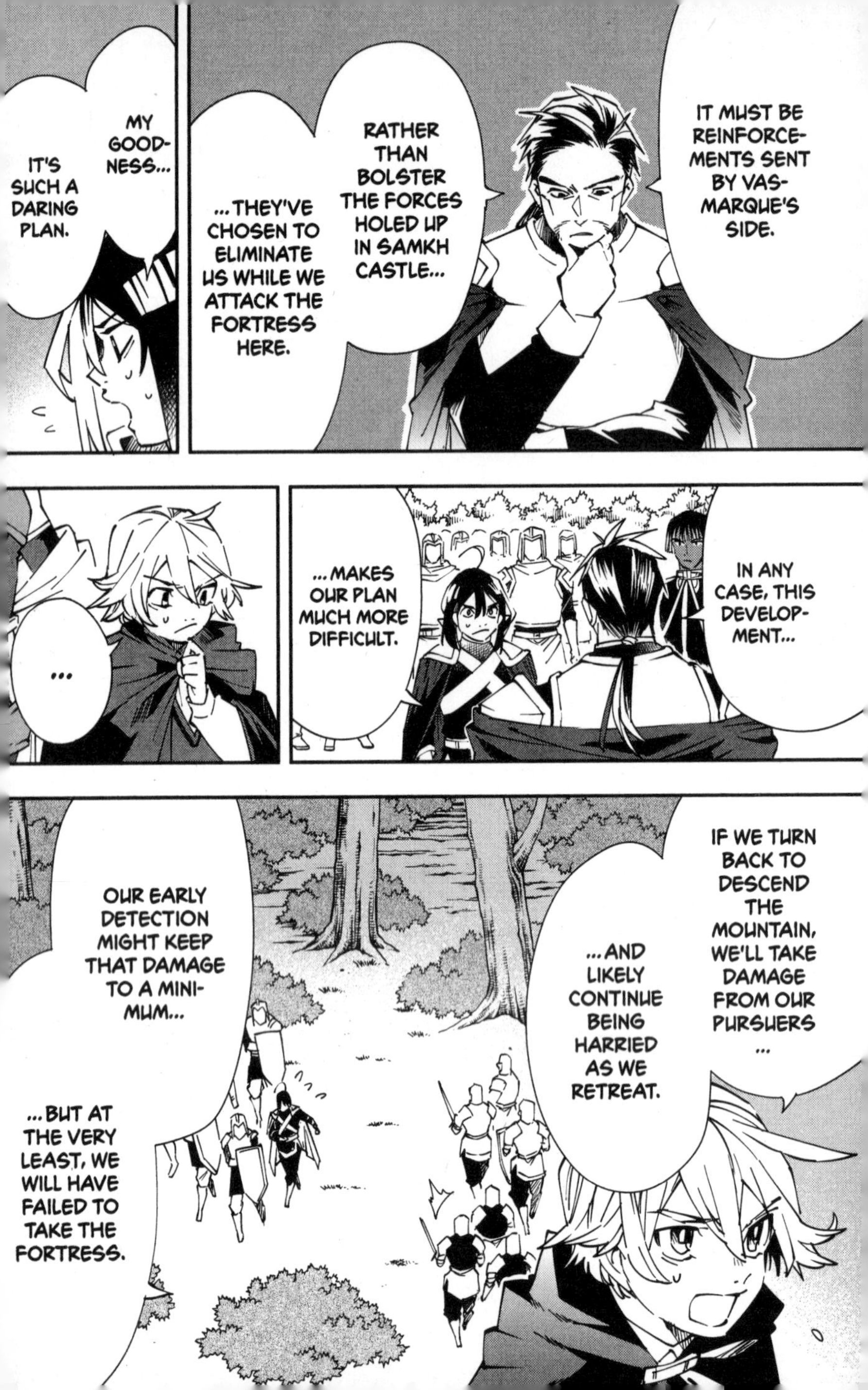

IT MUST BE REINFORCEMENTS SENT BY VAS-MARQUE'S SIDE.
RATHER THAN BOLSTER THE FORCES HOLED UP IN SAMKH CASTLE...
...THEY'VE CHOSEN TO ELIMINATE US WHILE WE ATTACK THE FORTRESS HERE.
MY GOODNESS...
IT'S SUCH A DARING PLAN.
IN ANY CASE, THIS DEVELOPMENT...
...MAKES OUR PLAN MUCH MORE DIFFICULT.
...
IF WE TURN BACK TO DESCEND THE MOUNTAIN, WE'LL TAKE DAMAGE FROM OUR PURSUERS...
...AND LIKELY CONTINUE BEING HARRIED AS WE RETREAT.
OUR EARLY DETECTION MIGHT KEEP THAT DAMAGE TO A MINIMUM...
...BUT AT THE VERY LEAST, WE WILL HAVE FAILED TO TAKE THE FORTRESS.

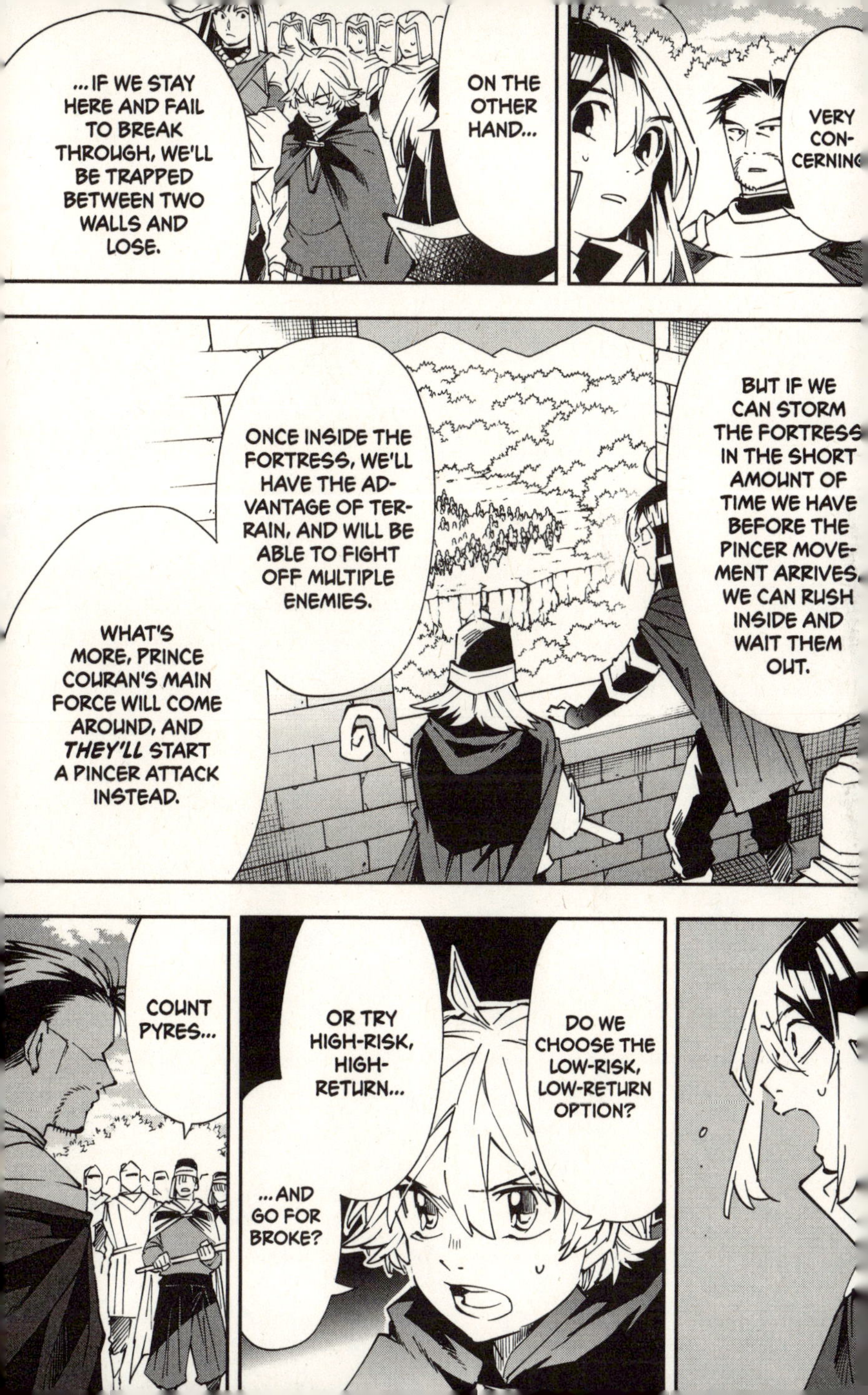
VERY CON-CERNING
ON THE OTHER HAND...
...IF WE STAY HERE AND FAIL TO BREAK THROUGH, WE'LL BE TRAPPED BETWEEN TWO WALLS AND LOSE.
BUT IF WE CAN STORM THE FORTRESS IN THE SHORT AMOUNT OF TIME WE HAVE BEFORE THE PINCER MOVEMENT ARRIVES, WE CAN RUSH INSIDE AND WAIT THEM OUT.
ONCE INSIDE THE FORTRESS, WE'LL HAVE THE ADVANTAGE OF TERRAIN, AND WILL BE ABLE TO FIGHT OFF MULTIPLE ENEMIES.
WHAT'S MORE, PRINCE COURAN'S MAIN FORCE WILL COME AROUND, AND *THEY'LL* START A PINCER ATTACK INSTEAD.
DO WE CHOOSE THE LOW-RISK, LOW-RETURN OPTION?
OR TRY HIGH-RISK, HIGH-RETURN...
...AND GO FOR BROKE?
COUNT PYRES...

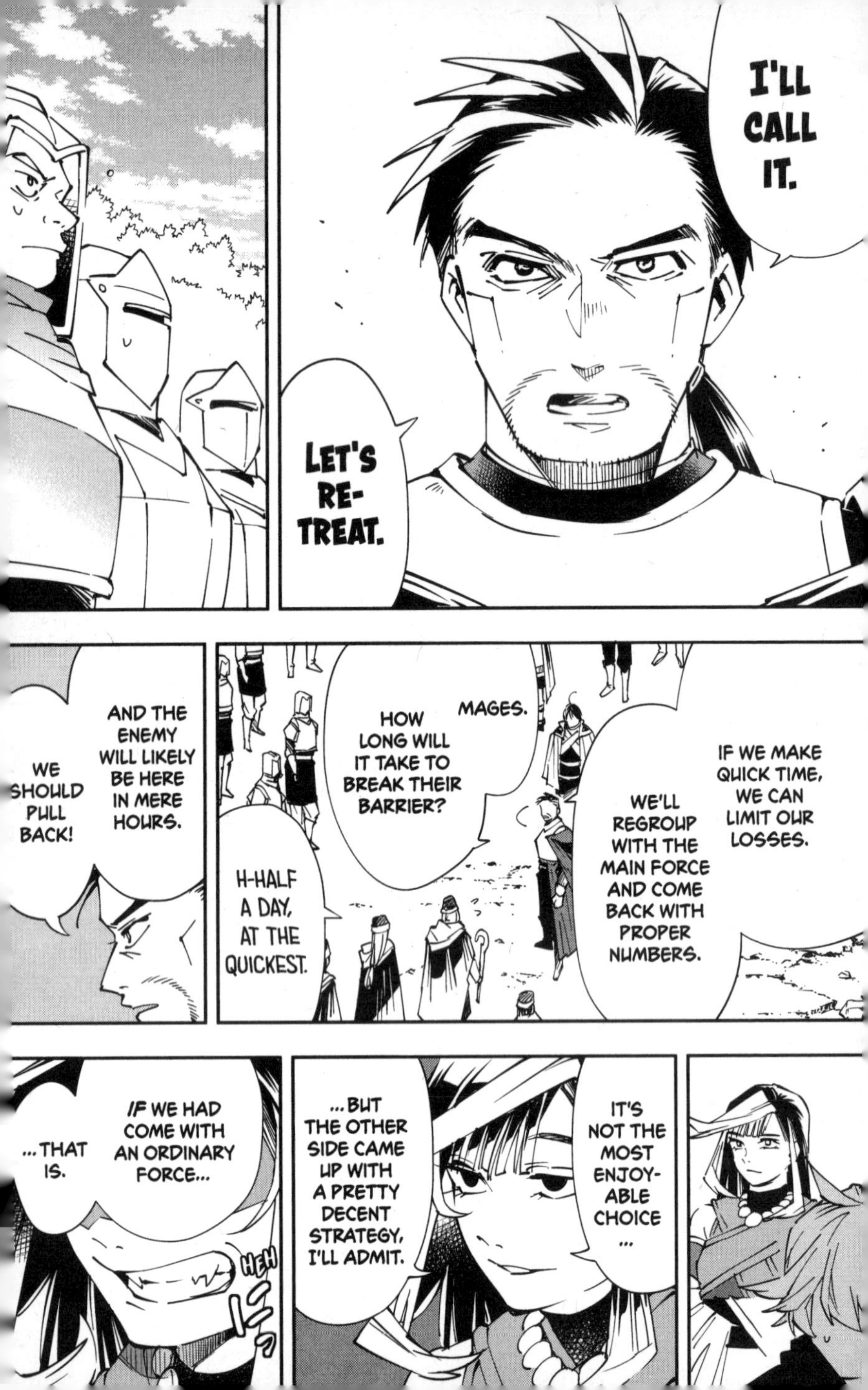
I'LL CALL IT.
LET'S RE-TREAT.
IF WE MAKE QUICK TIME, WE CAN LIMIT OUR LOSSES.
WE'LL REGROUP WITH THE MAIN FORCE AND COME BACK WITH PROPER NUMBERS.
MAGES.
HOW LONG WILL IT TAKE TO BREAK THEIR BARRIER?
H-HALF A DAY, AT THE QUICKEST.
AND THE ENEMY WILL LIKELY BE HERE IN MERE HOURS.
WE SHOULD PULL BACK!
IT'S NOT THE MOST ENJOY-ABLE CHOICE ...
...BUT THE OTHER SIDE CAME UP WITH A PRETTY DECENT STRATEGY, I'LL ADMIT.
IF WE HAD COME WITH AN ORDINARY FORCE...
...THAT IS.
HEH

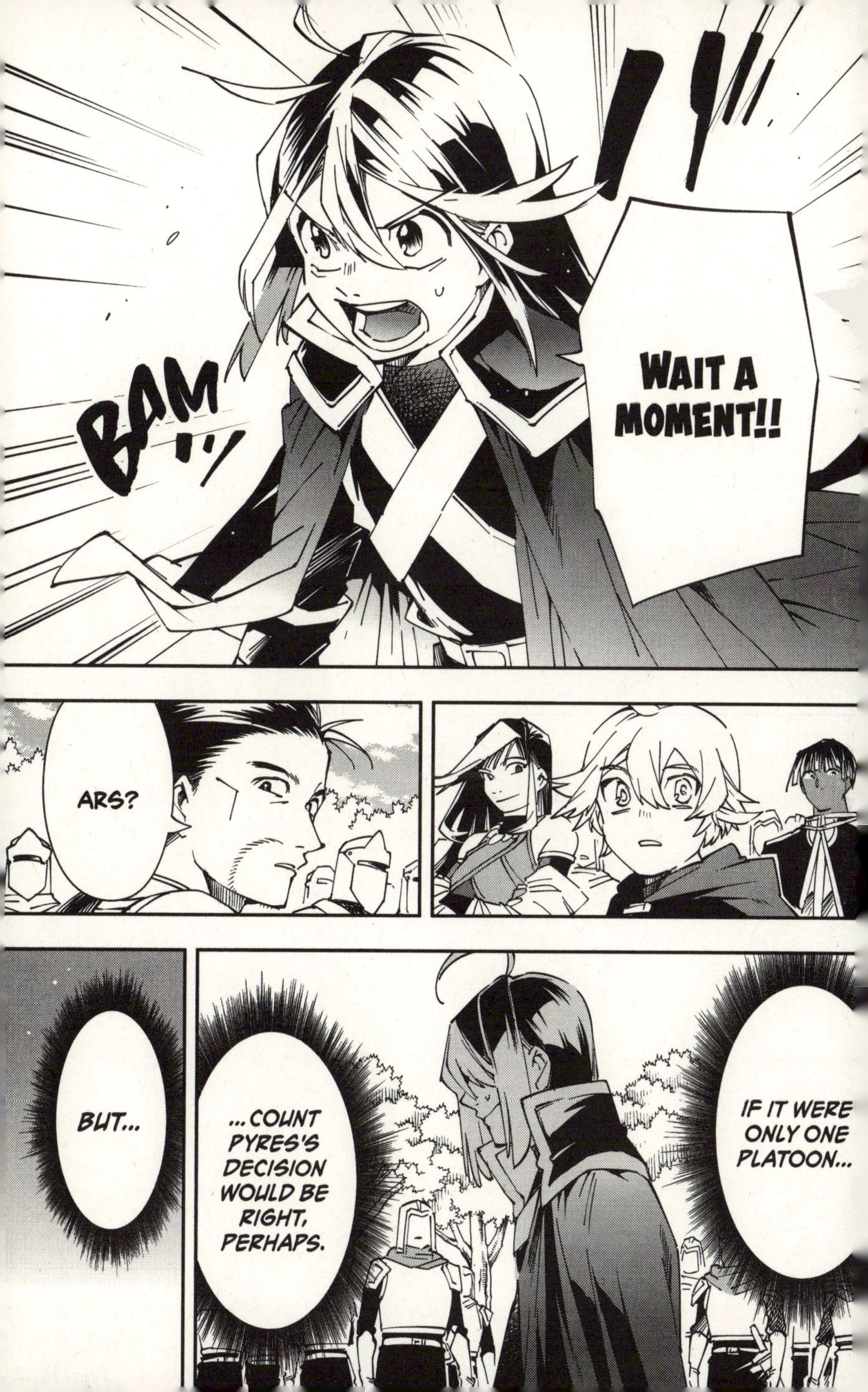
WAIT A MOMENT!!
BAM
ARS?
IF IT WERE ONLY ONE PLATOON...
...COUNT PYRES'S DECISION WOULD BE RIGHT, PERHAPS.
BUT...

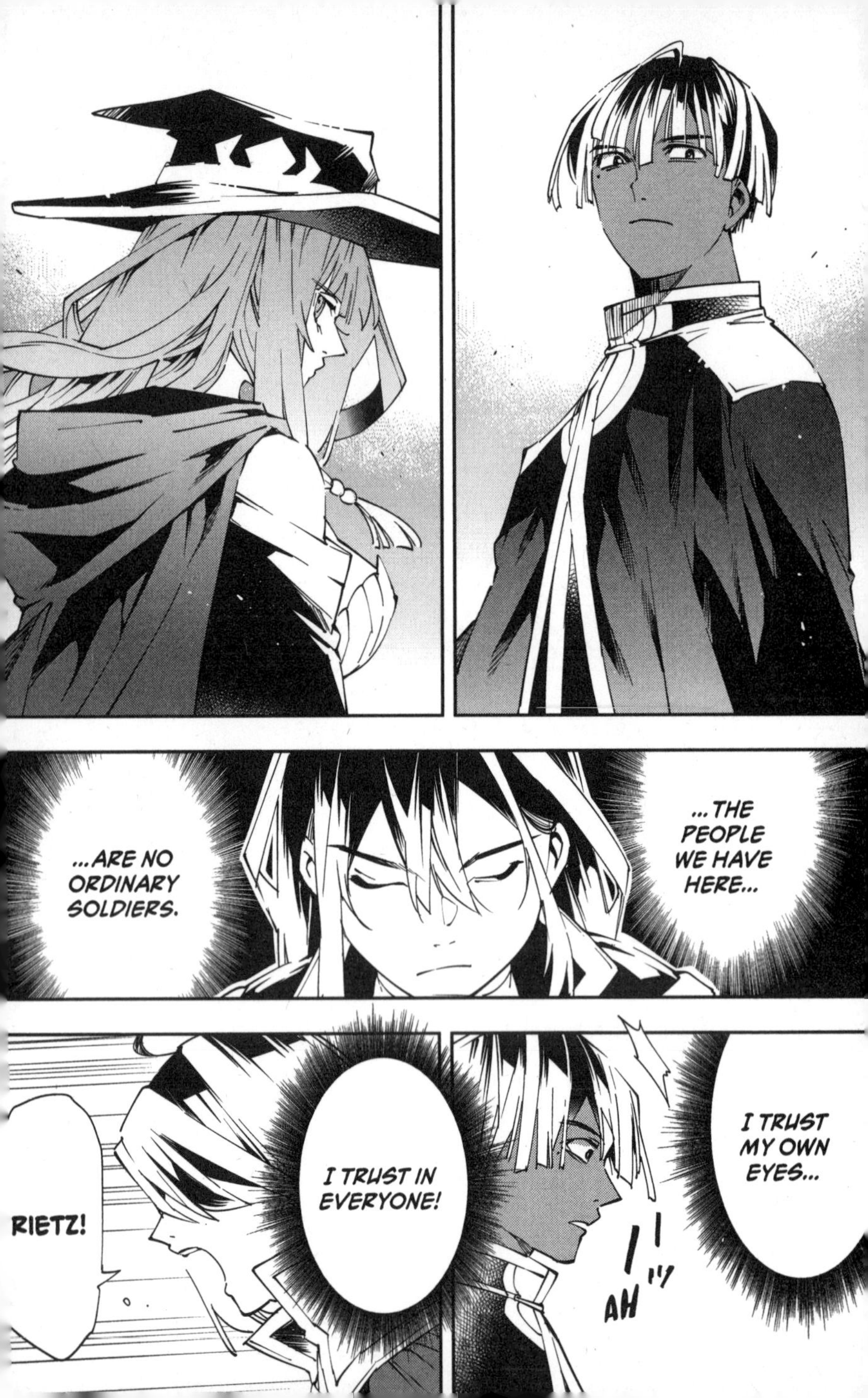
...THE PEOPLE WE HAVE HERE...
...ARE NO ORDINARY SOLDIERS.
I TRUST MY OWN EYES...
AH
I TRUST IN EVERYONE!
RIETZ!

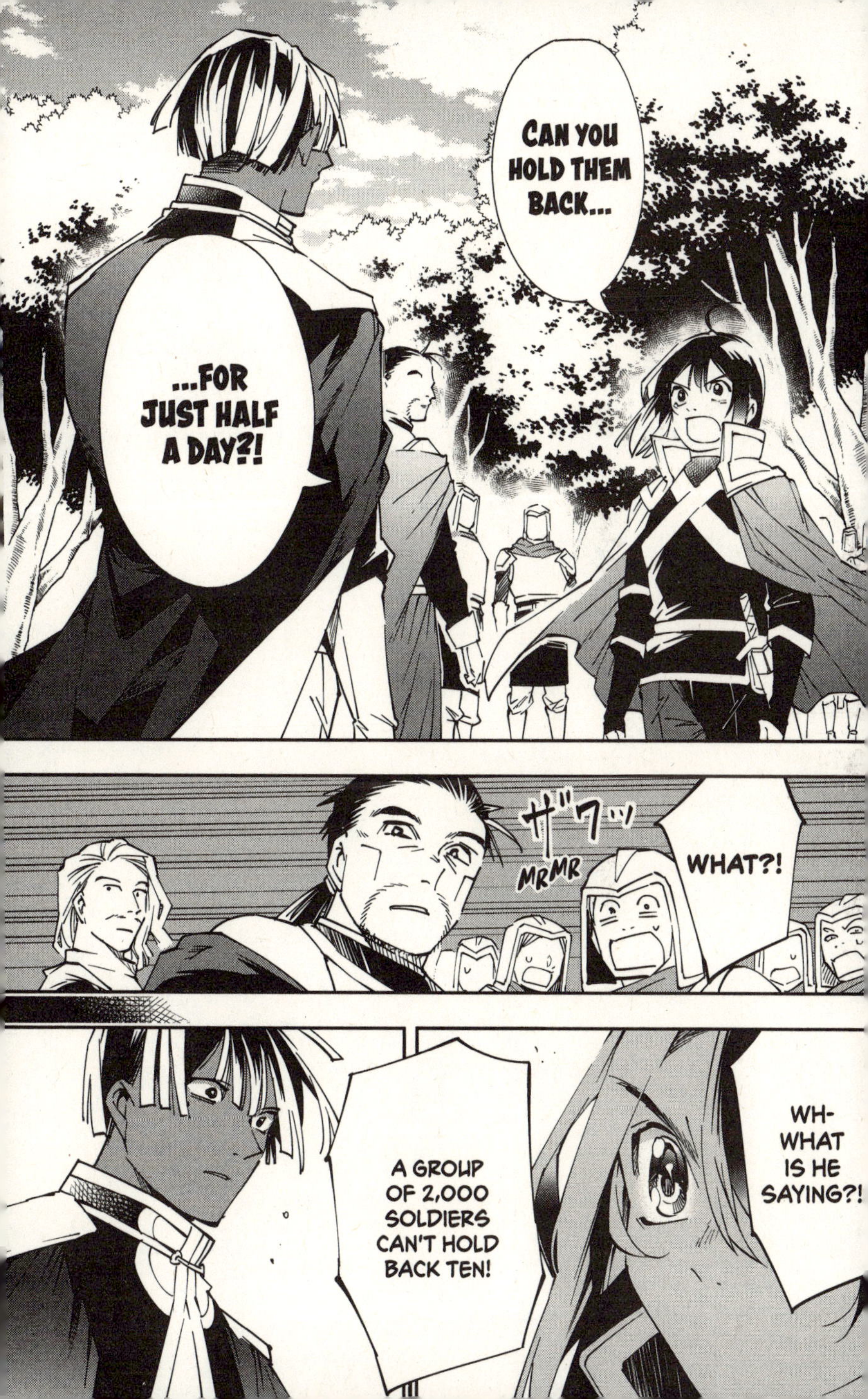

CAN YOU HOLD THEM BACK...
...FOR JUST HALF A DAY?!
WHAT?!
ザワッ
MRMR
WH- WHAT IS HE SAYING?!
A GROUP OF 2,000 SOLDIERS CAN'T HOLD BACK TEN!

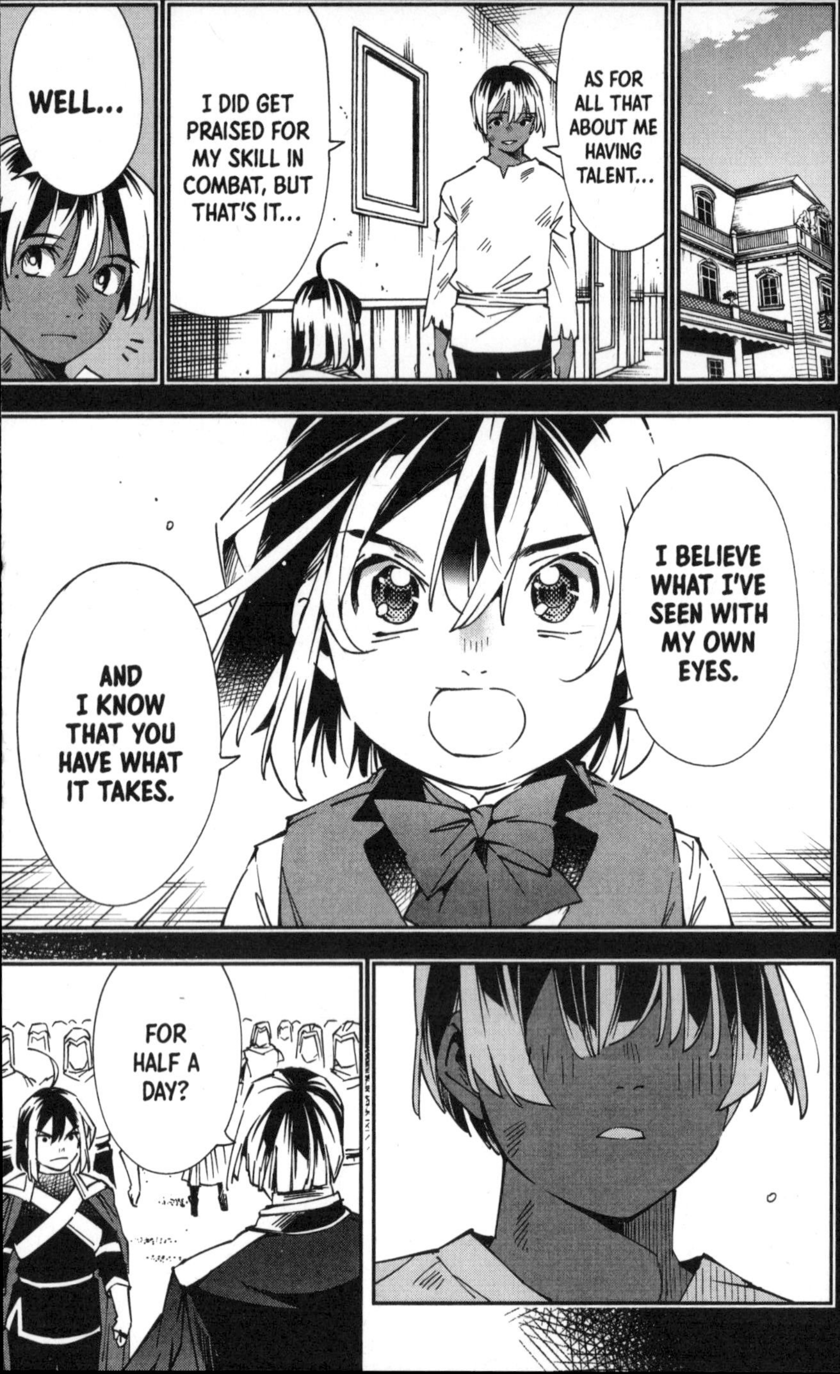
AS FOR ALL THAT ABOUT ME HAVING TALENT...
I DID GET PRAISED FOR MY SKILL IN COMBAT, BUT THAT'S IT...
WELL...
I BELIEVE WHAT I'VE SEEN WITH MY OWN EYES.
AND I KNOW THAT YOU HAVE WHAT IT TAKES.
FOR HALF A DAY?

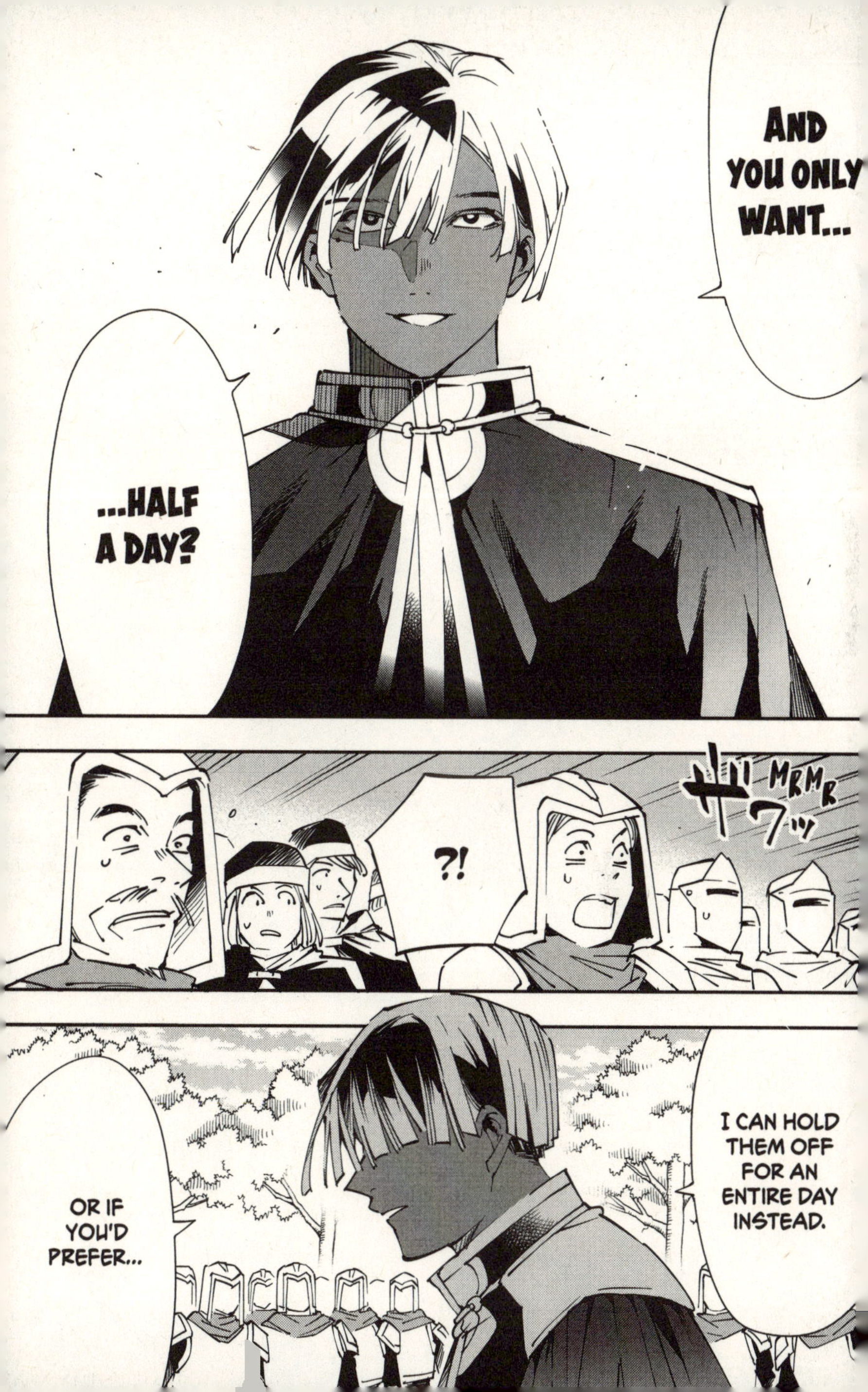

AND YOU ONLY WANT...
...HALF A DAY?
MRMR
?!
I CAN HOLD THEM OFF FOR AN ENTIRE DAY INSTEAD.
OR IF YOU'D PREFER...

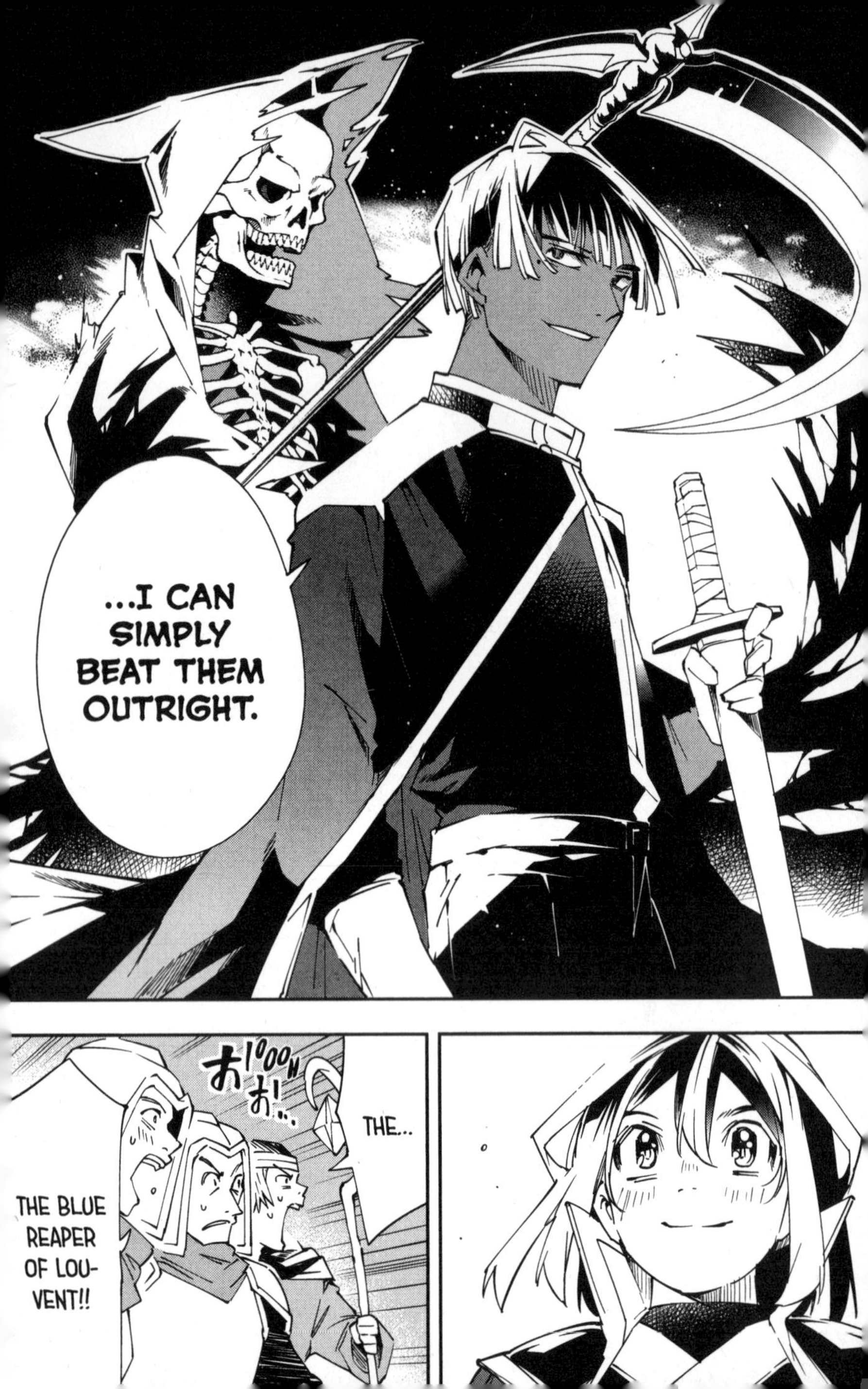
...I CAN SIMPLY BEAT THEM OUTRIGHT.
おOOOHお!...
THE...
THE BLUE REAPER OF LOU-VENT!!

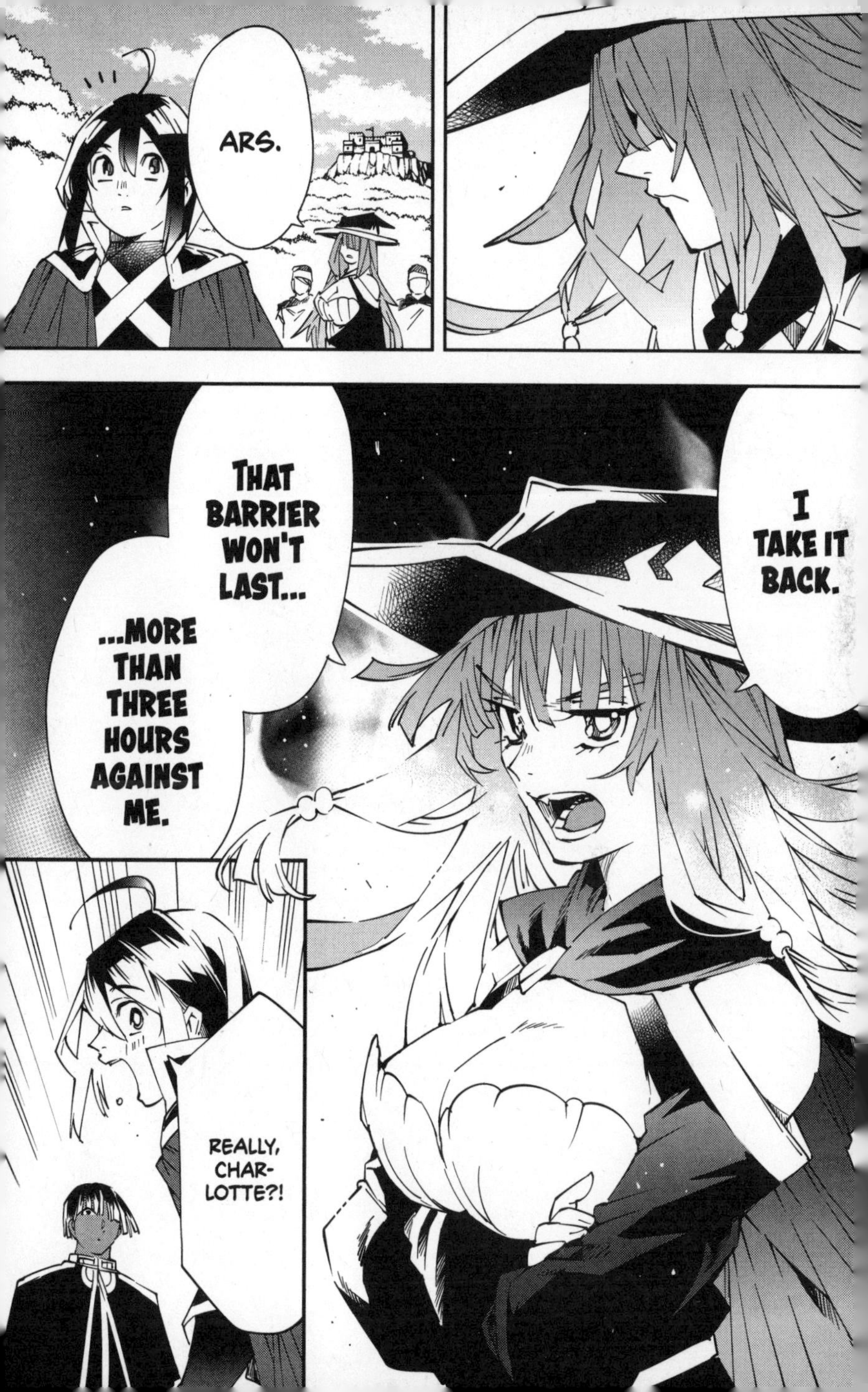
ARS.
I TAKE IT BACK.
THAT BARRIER WON'T LAST...
...MORE THAN THREE HOURS AGAINST ME.
REALLY, CHARLOTTE?!

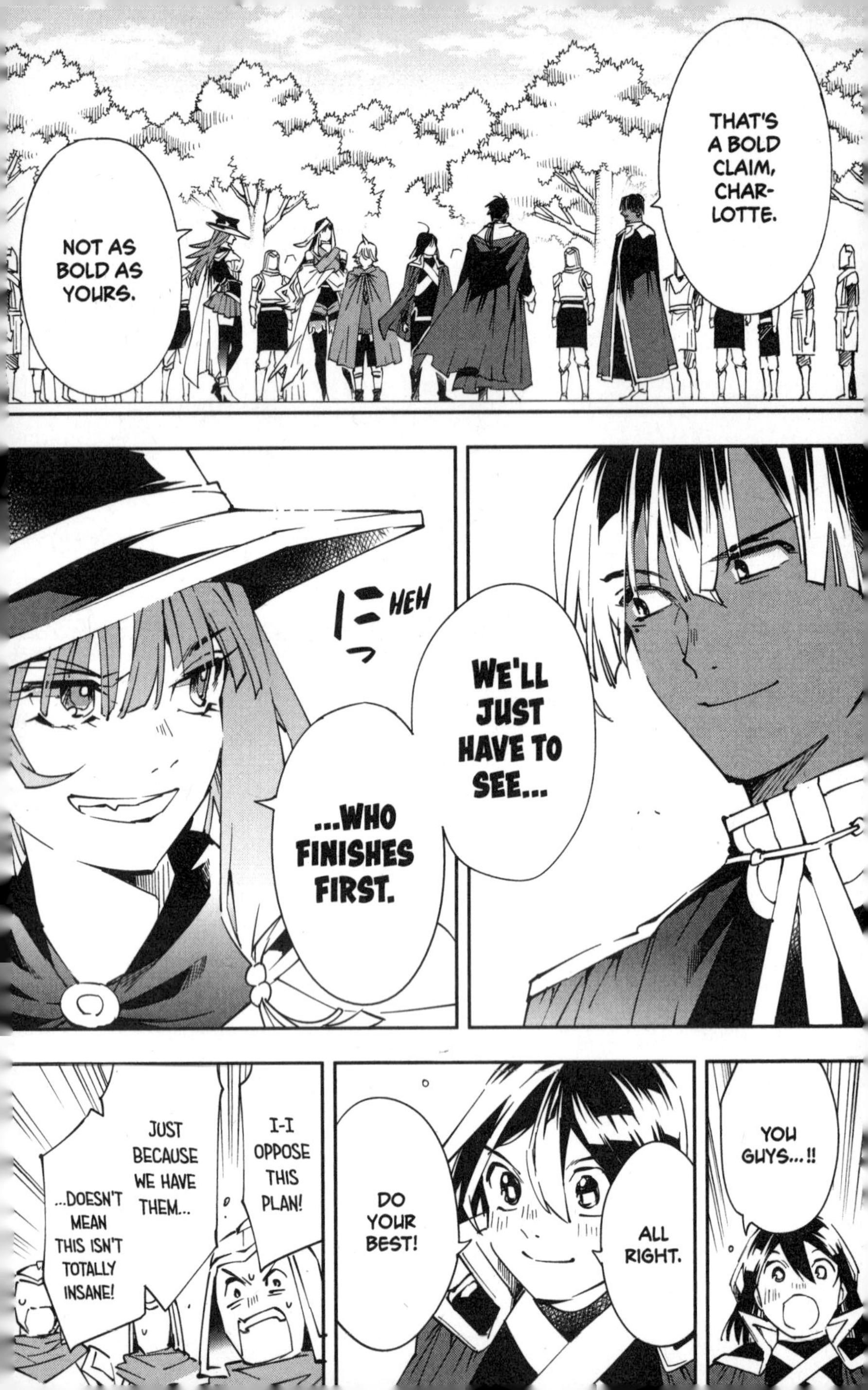
THAT'S A BOLD CLAIM, CHAR-LOTTE.
NOT AS BOLD AS YOURS.
WE'LL JUST HAVE TO SEE...
...WHO FINISHES FIRST.
HEH
YOU GUYS...!!
ALL RIGHT.
DO YOUR BEST!
I-I OPPOSE THIS PLAN!
JUST BECAUSE WE HAVE THEM...
...DOESN'T MEAN THIS ISN'T TOTALLY INSANE!

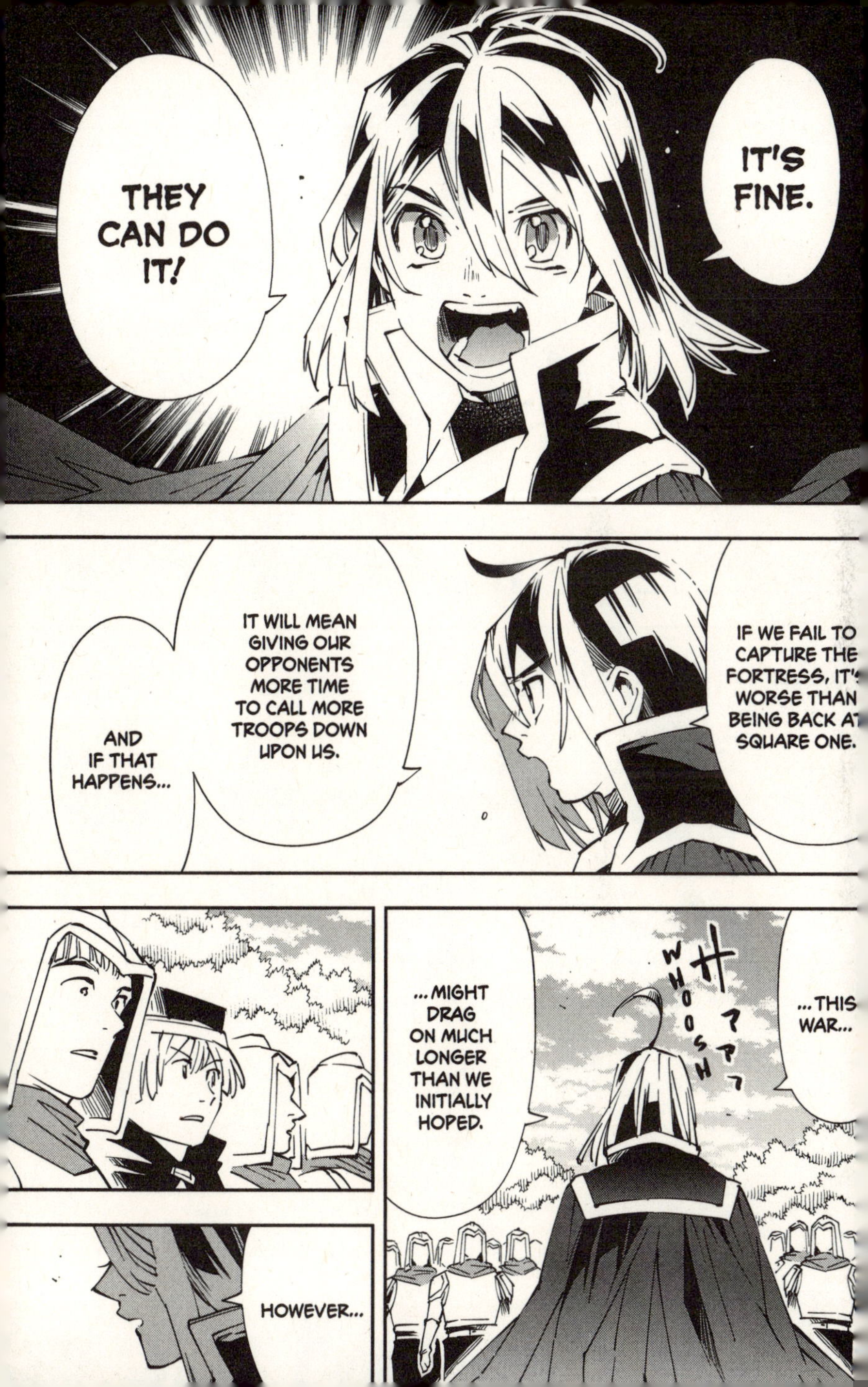
IT'S FINE.
THEY CAN DO IT!
IF WE FAIL TO CAPTURE THE FORTRESS, IT' WORSE THAN BEING BACK AT SQUARE ONE.
IT WILL MEAN GIVING OUR OPPONENTS MORE TIME TO CALL MORE TROOPS DOWN UPON US.
AND IF THAT HAPPENS...
...THIS WAR...
WHOOSH
...MIGHT DRAG ON MUCH LONGER THAN WE INITIALLY HOPED.
HOWEVER...

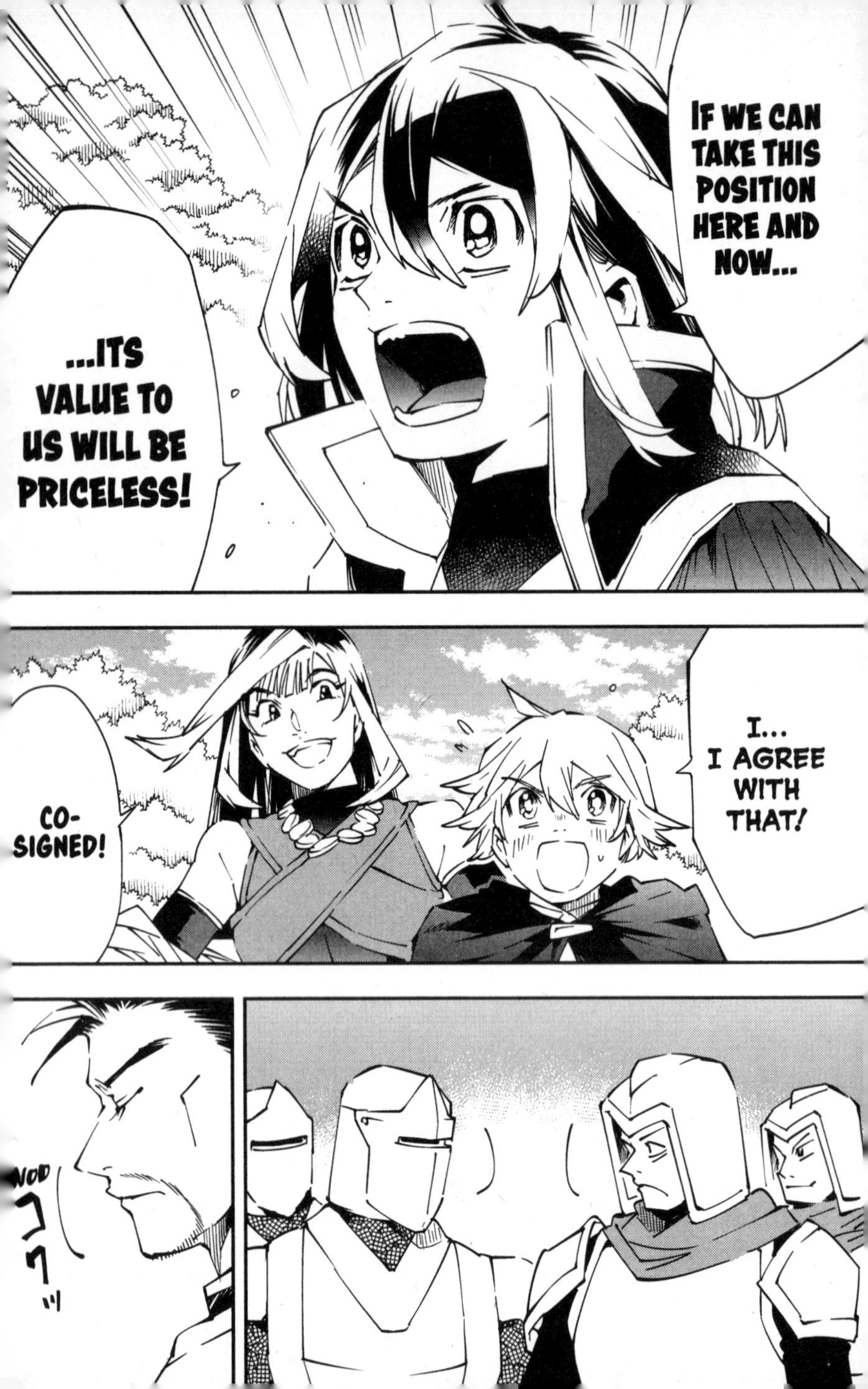
IF WE CAN TAKE THIS POSITION HERE AND NOW...
...ITS VALUE TO US WILL BE PRICELESS!
I... I AGREE WITH THAT!
CO-SIGNED!
NOD
コクッ

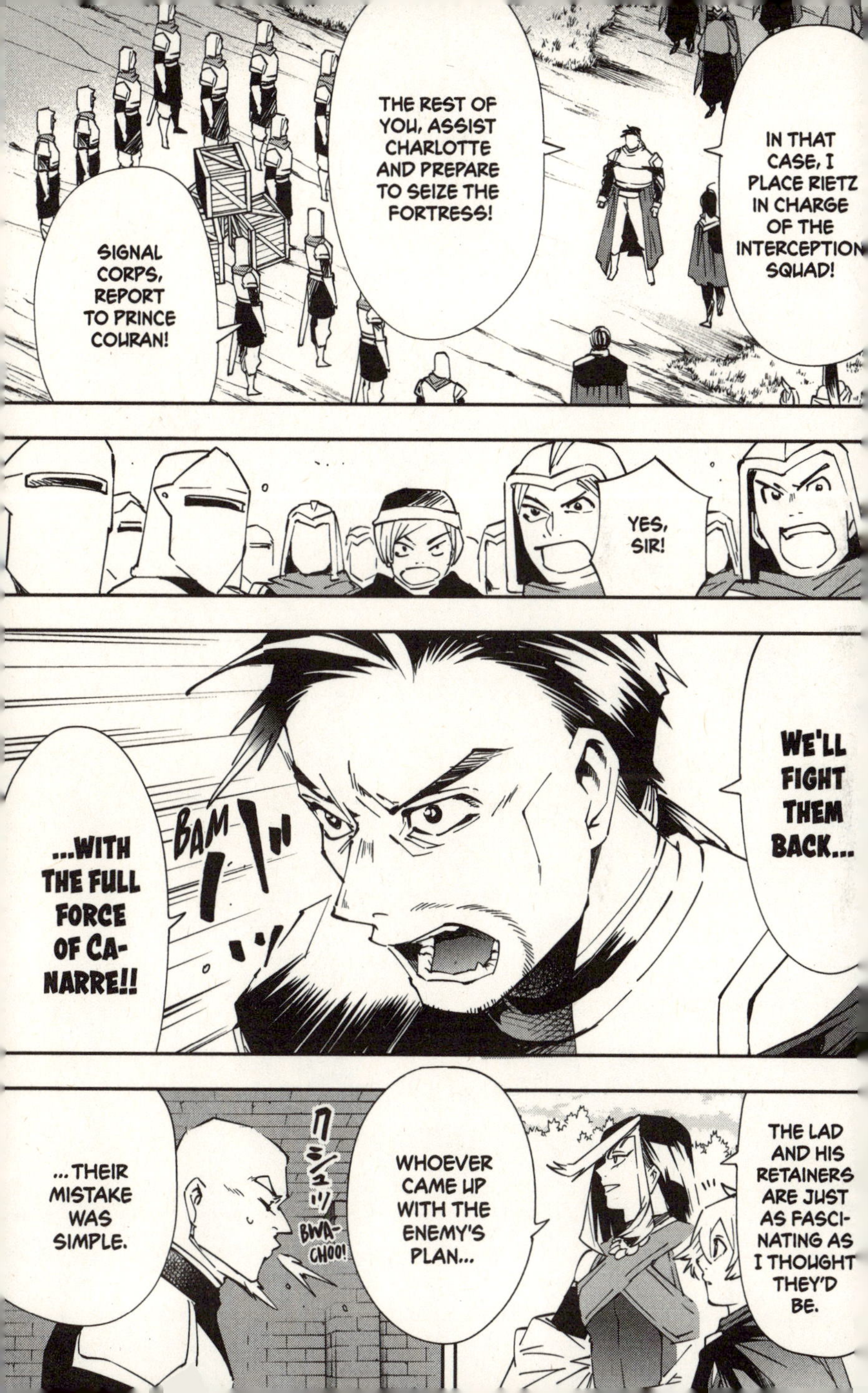
IN THAT CASE, I PLACE RIETZ IN CHARGE OF THE INTERCEPTION SQUAD!
THE REST OF YOU, ASSIST CHARLOTTE AND PREPARE TO SEIZE THE FORTRESS!
SIGNAL CORPS, REPORT TO PRINCE COURAN!
YES, SIR!
WE'LL FIGHT THEM BACK...
BAM
...WITH THE FULL FORCE OF CA-NARRE!!
THE LAD AND HIS RETAINERS ARE JUST AS FASCI-NATING AS I THOUGHT THEY'D BE.
WHOEVER CAME UP WITH THE ENEMY'S PLAN...
クシュッ
BWA-CHOO!
...THEIR MISTAKE WAS SIMPLE.

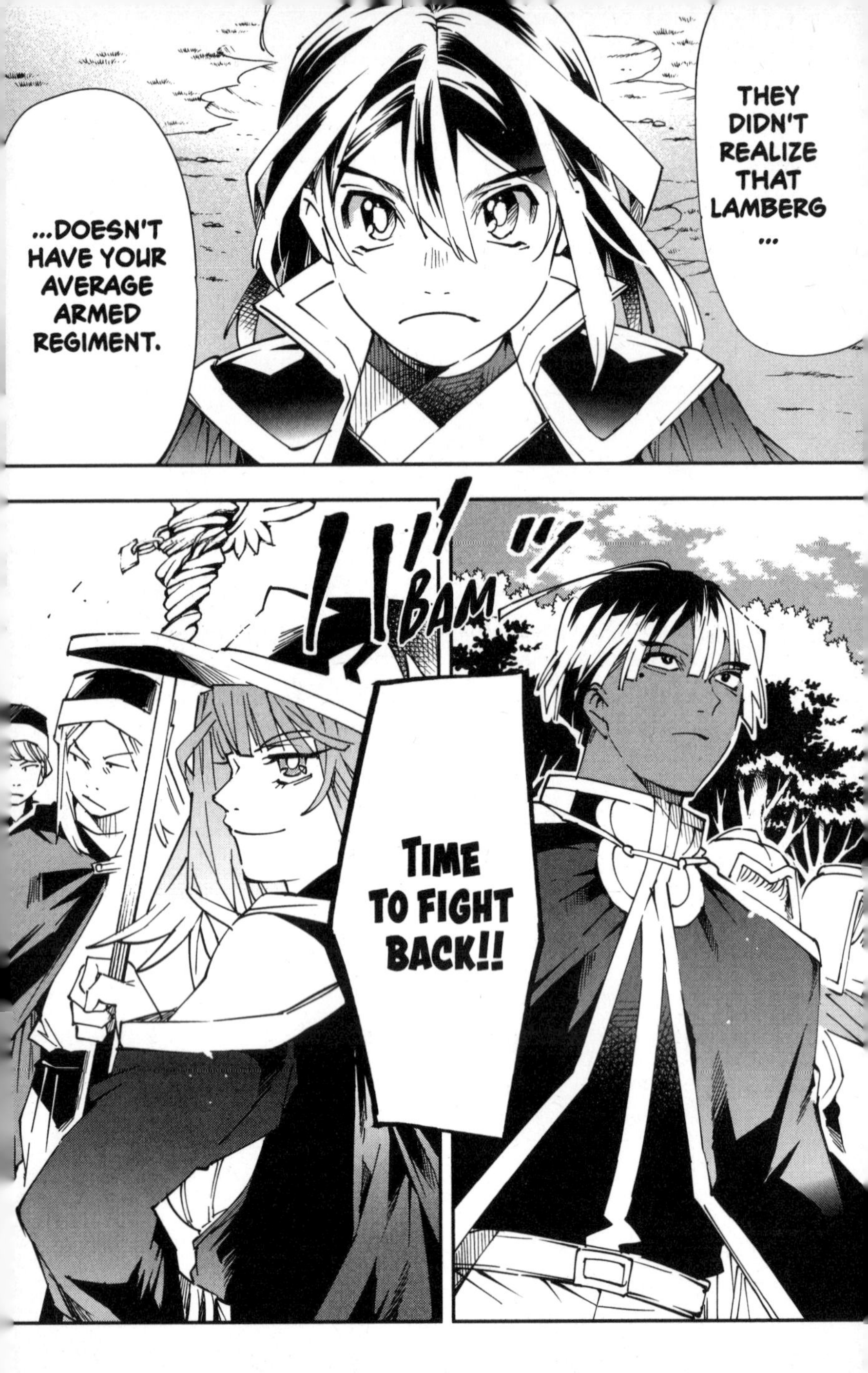
THEY DIDN'T REALIZE THAT LAMBERG ...
...DOESN'T HAVE YOUR AVERAGE ARMED REGIMENT.
BAM
TIME TO FIGHT BACK!!

Chapter 69: Ars's Right Hand

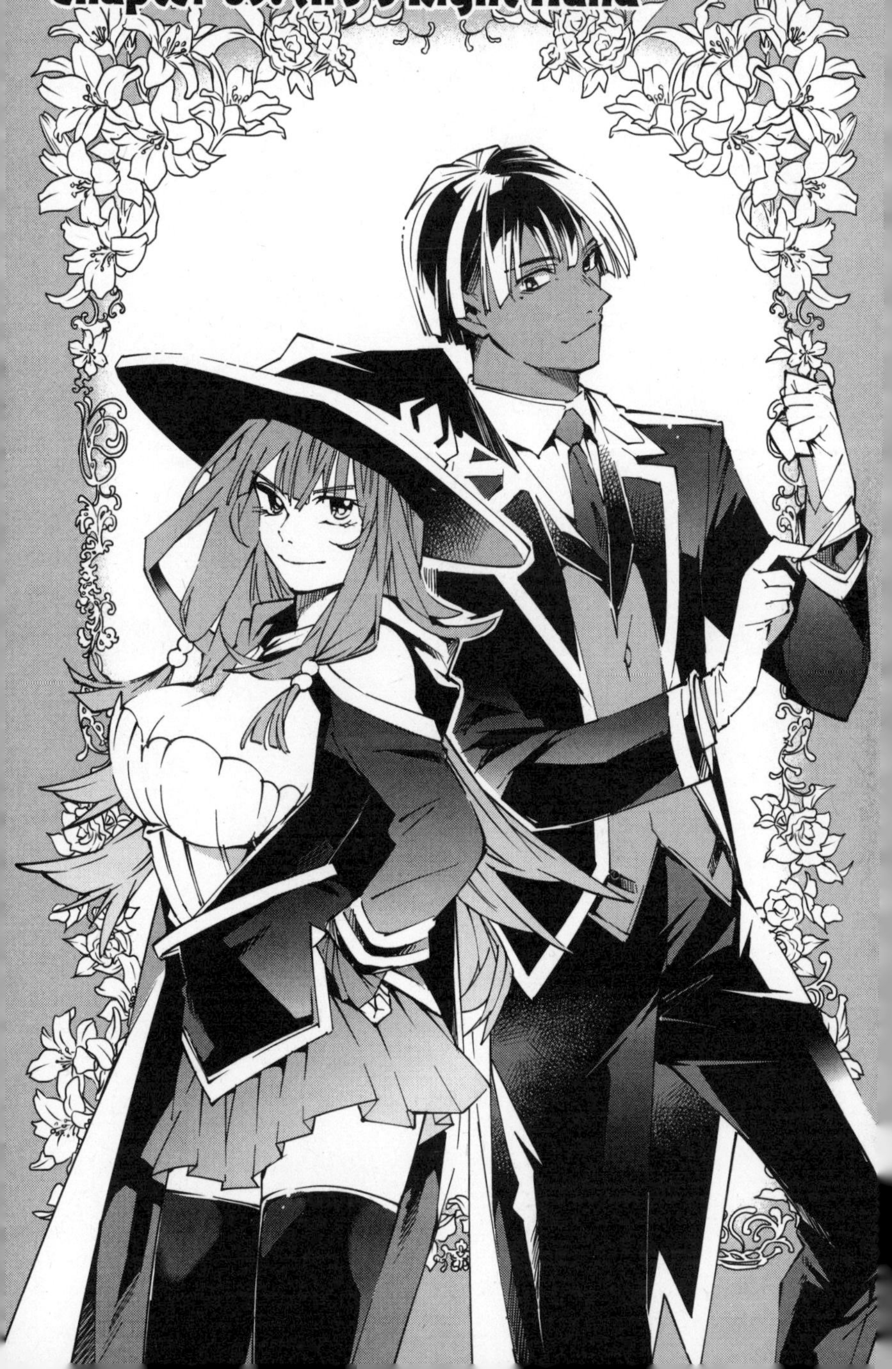

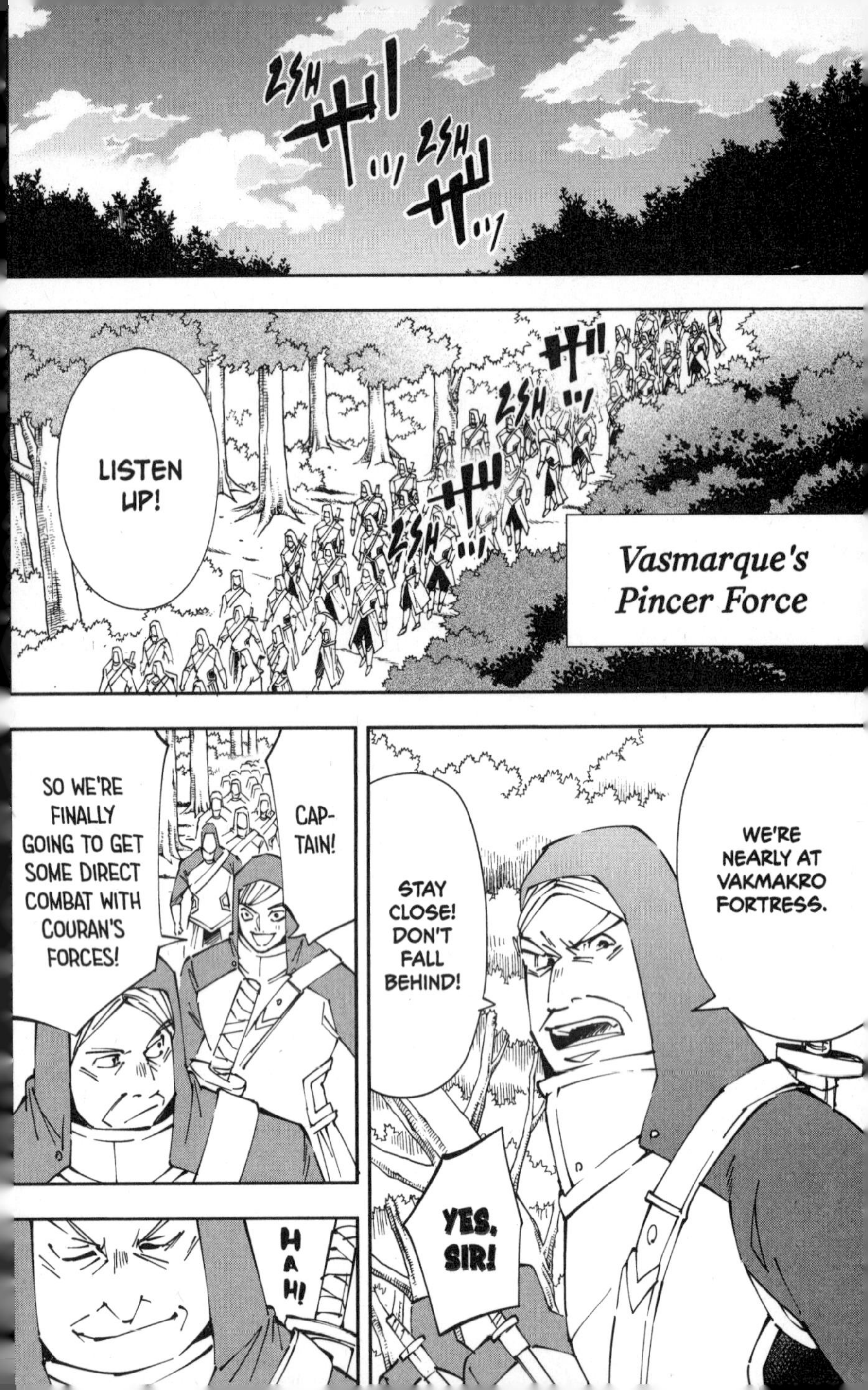
ZSH
ZSH
Vasmarque's Pincer Force
ZSH
ZSH
LISTEN UP!
WE'RE NEARLY AT VAKMAKRO FORTRESS.
STAY CLOSE! DON'T FALL BEHIND!
YES, SIR!
CAP-TAIN!
SO WE'RE FINALLY GOING TO GET SOME DIRECT COMBAT WITH COURAN'S FORCES!
HAH!

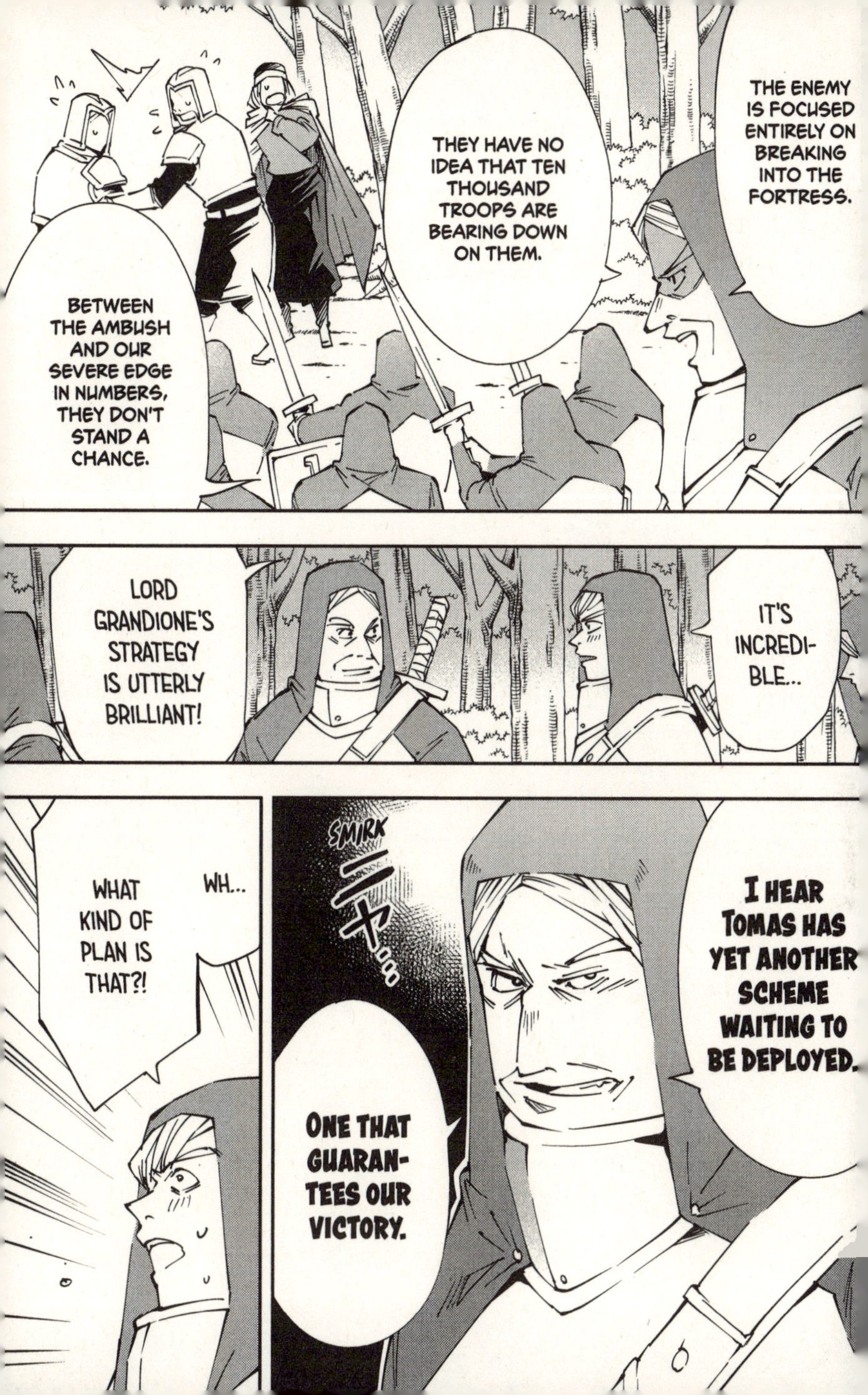
THE ENEMY IS FOCUSED ENTIRELY ON BREAKING INTO THE FORTRESS.
THEY HAVE NO IDEA THAT TEN THOUSAND TROOPS ARE BEARING DOWN ON THEM.
BETWEEN THE AMBUSH AND OUR SEVERE EDGE IN NUMBERS, THEY DON'T STAND A CHANCE.
IT'S INCREDI-BLE...
LORD GRANDIONE'S STRATEGY IS UTTERLY BRILLIANT!
I HEAR TOMAS HAS YET ANOTHER SCHEME WAITING TO BE DEPLOYED.
SMIRK
ONE THAT GUARAN-TEES OUR VICTORY.
WH...
WHAT KIND OF PLAN IS THAT?!

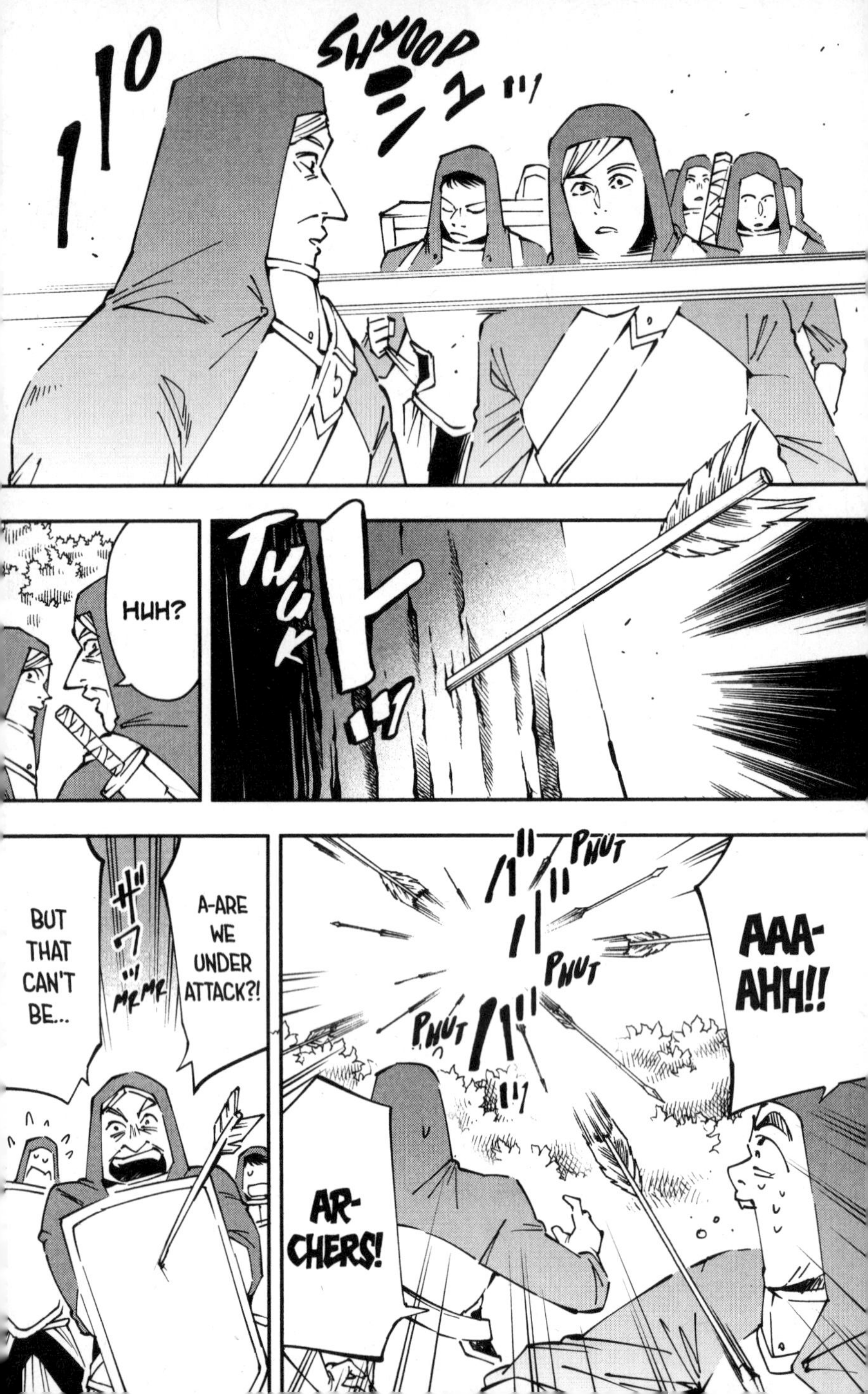
SHYOOP
THUK
HUH?
PHUT
PHUT
PHUT
AAA-AHH!!
AR-CHERS!
A-ARE WE UNDER ATTACK?!
MRMR
BUT THAT CAN'T BE...

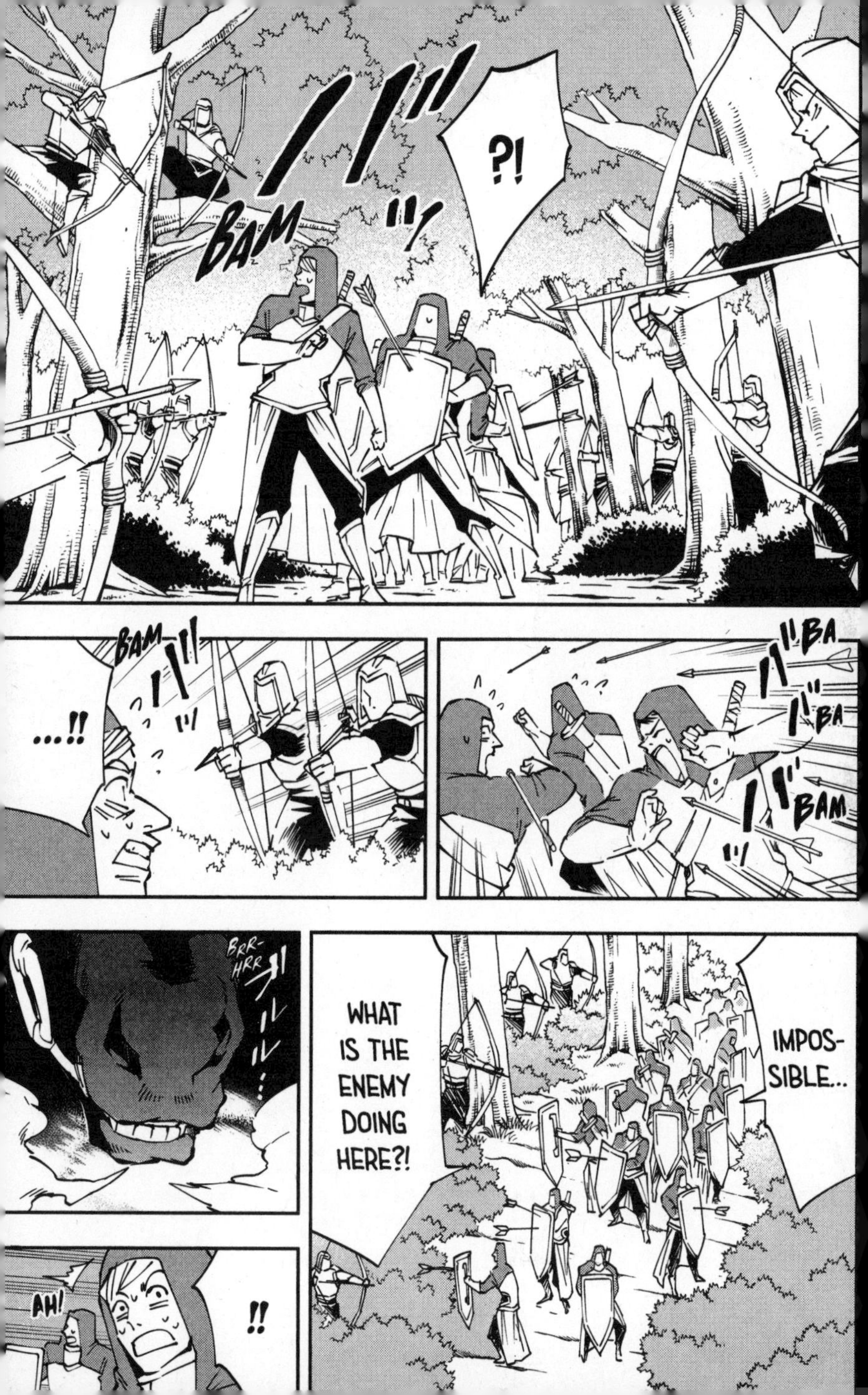
?!
BAM
BA
BA
BAM
BAM
...!!
IMPOS-
SIBLE...
WHAT
IS THE
ENEMY
DOING
HERE?!
BRR-
HRR
!!
AH!

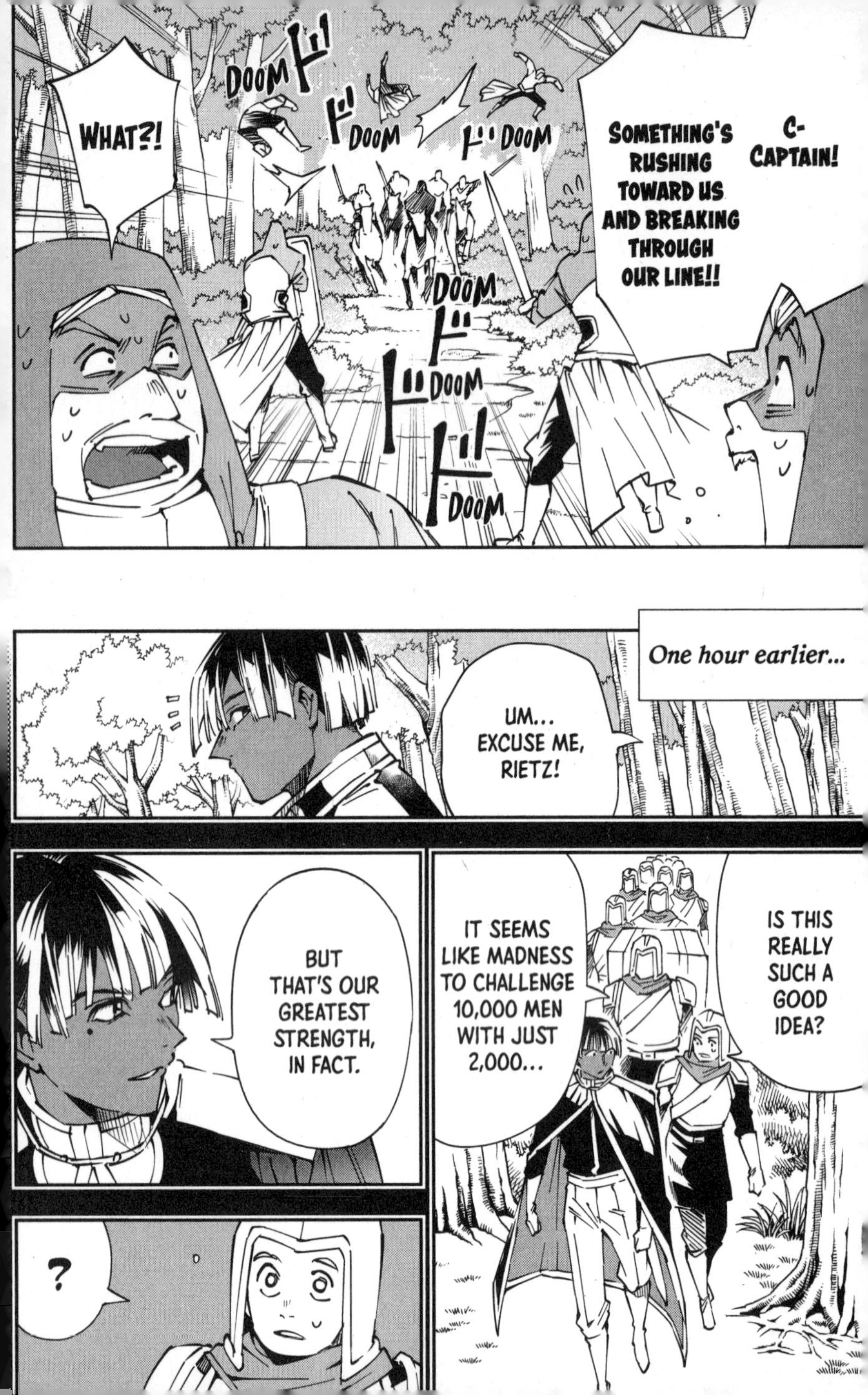
C-CAPTAIN!
SOMETHING'S RUSHING TOWARD US AND BREAKING THROUGH OUR LINE!!
DOOM
DOOM
DOOM
DOOM
DOOM
DOOM
WHAT?!
One hour earlier...
UM... EXCUSE ME, RIETZ!
IS THIS REALLY SUCH A GOOD IDEA?
IT SEEMS LIKE MADNESS TO CHALLENGE 10,000 MEN WITH JUST 2,000...
BUT THAT'S OUR GREATEST STRENGTH, IN FACT.
?

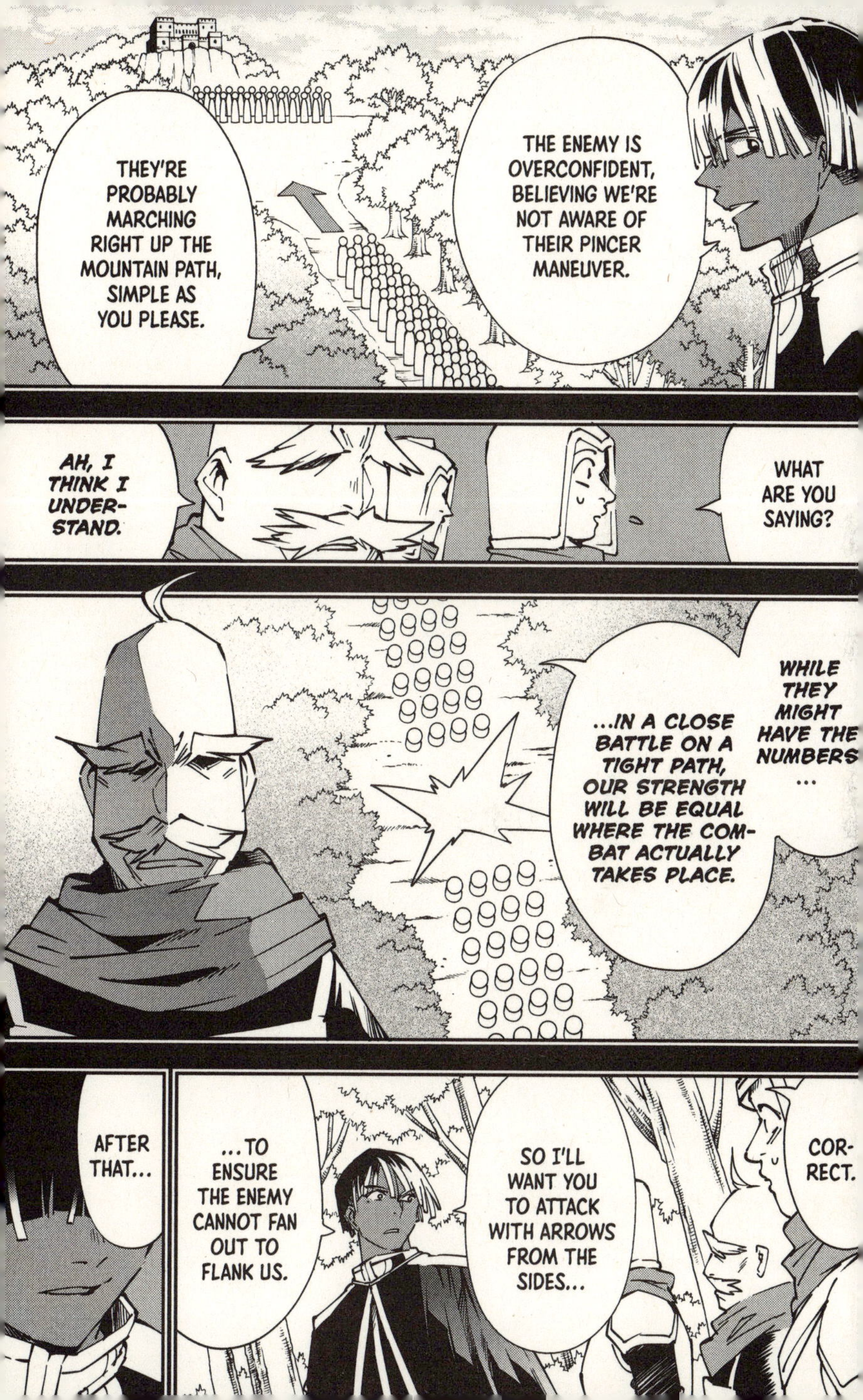
THE ENEMY IS OVERCONFIDENT, BELIEVING WE'RE NOT AWARE OF THEIR PINCER MANEUVER.
THEY'RE PROBABLY MARCHING RIGHT UP THE MOUNTAIN PATH, SIMPLE AS YOU PLEASE.
WHAT ARE YOU SAYING?
AH, I THINK I UNDER-STAND.
WHILE THEY MIGHT HAVE THE NUMBERS...
...IN A CLOSE BATTLE ON A TIGHT PATH, OUR STRENGTH WILL BE EQUAL WHERE THE COM-BAT ACTUALLY TAKES PLACE.
COR-RECT.
SO I'LL WANT YOU TO ATTACK WITH ARROWS FROM THE SIDES...
...TO ENSURE THE ENEMY CANNOT FAN OUT TO FLANK US.
AFTER THAT...

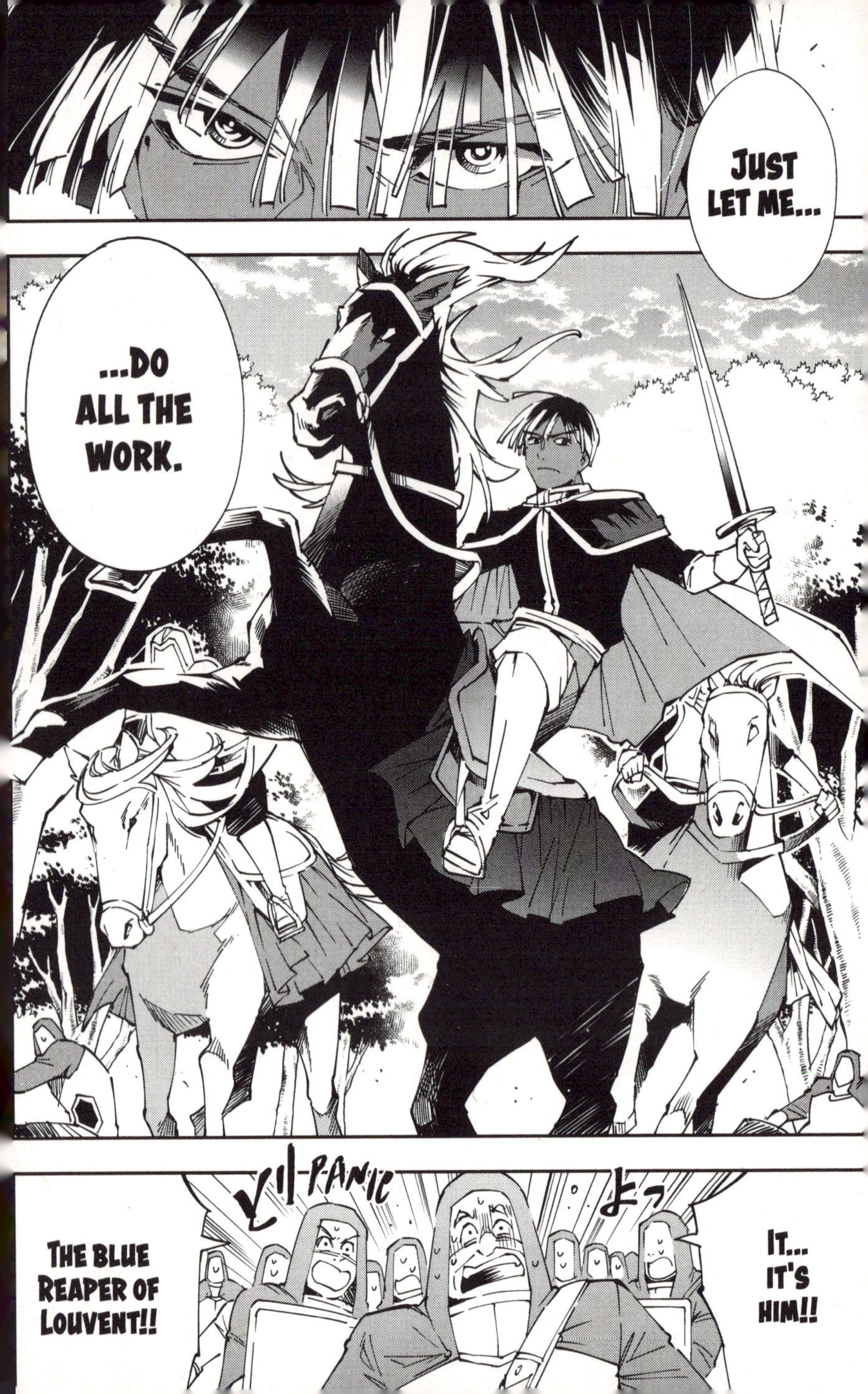
JUST LET ME...
...DO ALL THE WORK.
PANIC
IT... IT'S HIM!!
THE BLUE REAPER OF LOUVENT!!

シュク ウゥゥゥ
FSSS

ド！
''/BOOM

At that moment,
Vakmakro Fortress...

W ゴ H オ A ォ R

オ R

オ R

R オ R

オ R

DAMMIT!

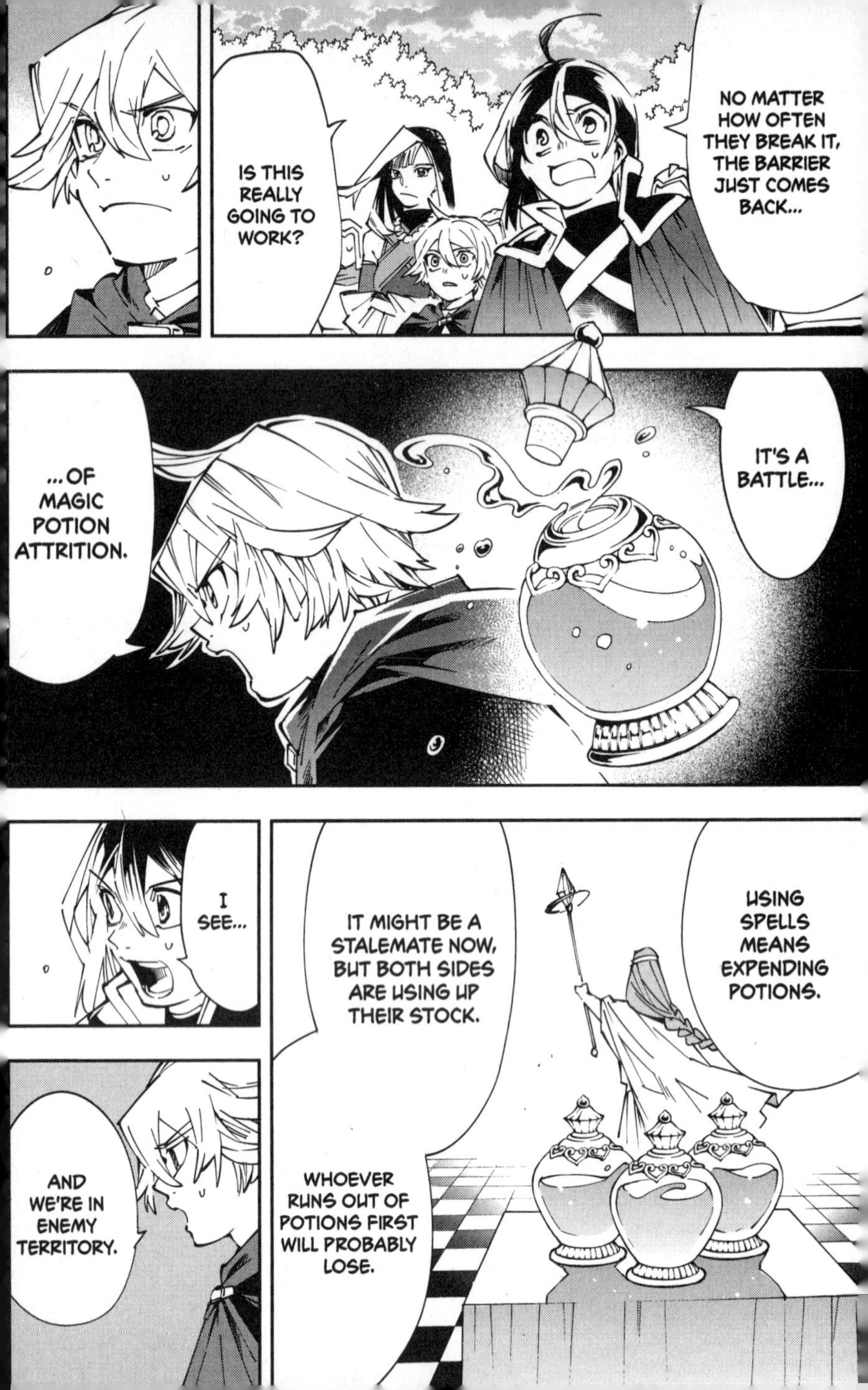
NO MATTER HOW OFTEN THEY BREAK IT, THE BARRIER JUST COMES BACK...
IS THIS REALLY GOING TO WORK?
IT'S A BATTLE...
...OF MAGIC POTION ATTRITION.
USING SPELLS MEANS EXPENDING POTIONS.
IT MIGHT BE A STALEMATE NOW, BUT BOTH SIDES ARE USING UP THEIR STOCK.
WHOEVER RUNS OUT OF POTIONS FIRST WILL PROBABLY LOSE.
I SEE...
AND WE'RE IN ENEMY TERRITORY.

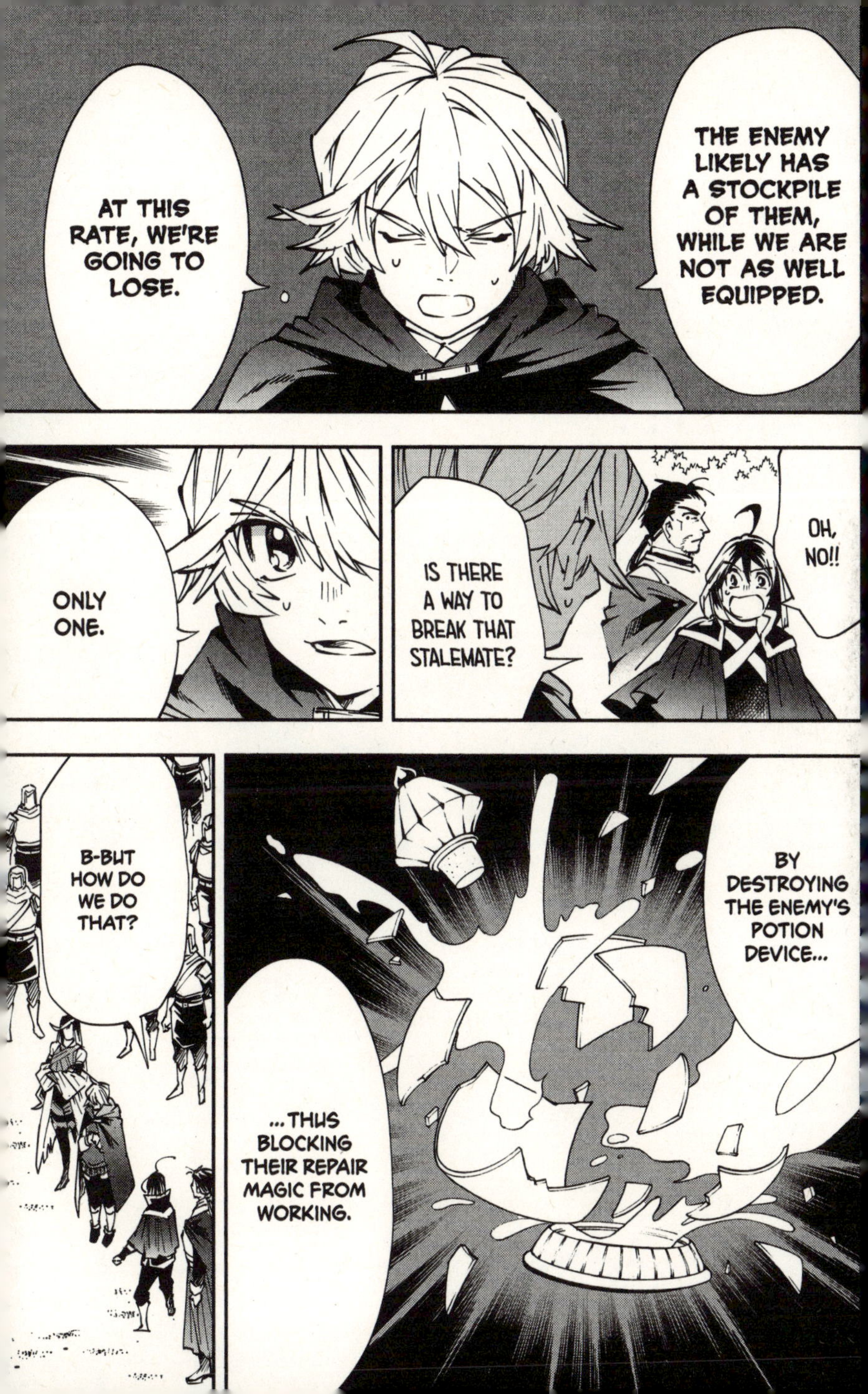
THE ENEMY LIKELY HAS A STOCKPILE OF THEM, WHILE WE ARE NOT AS WELL EQUIPPED.
AT THIS RATE, WE'RE GOING TO LOSE.
OH, NO!!
IS THERE A WAY TO BREAK THAT STALEMATE?
ONLY ONE.
BY DESTROYING THE ENEMY'S POTION DEVICE...
...THUS BLOCKING THEIR REPAIR MAGIC FROM WORKING.
B-BUT HOW DO WE DO THAT?

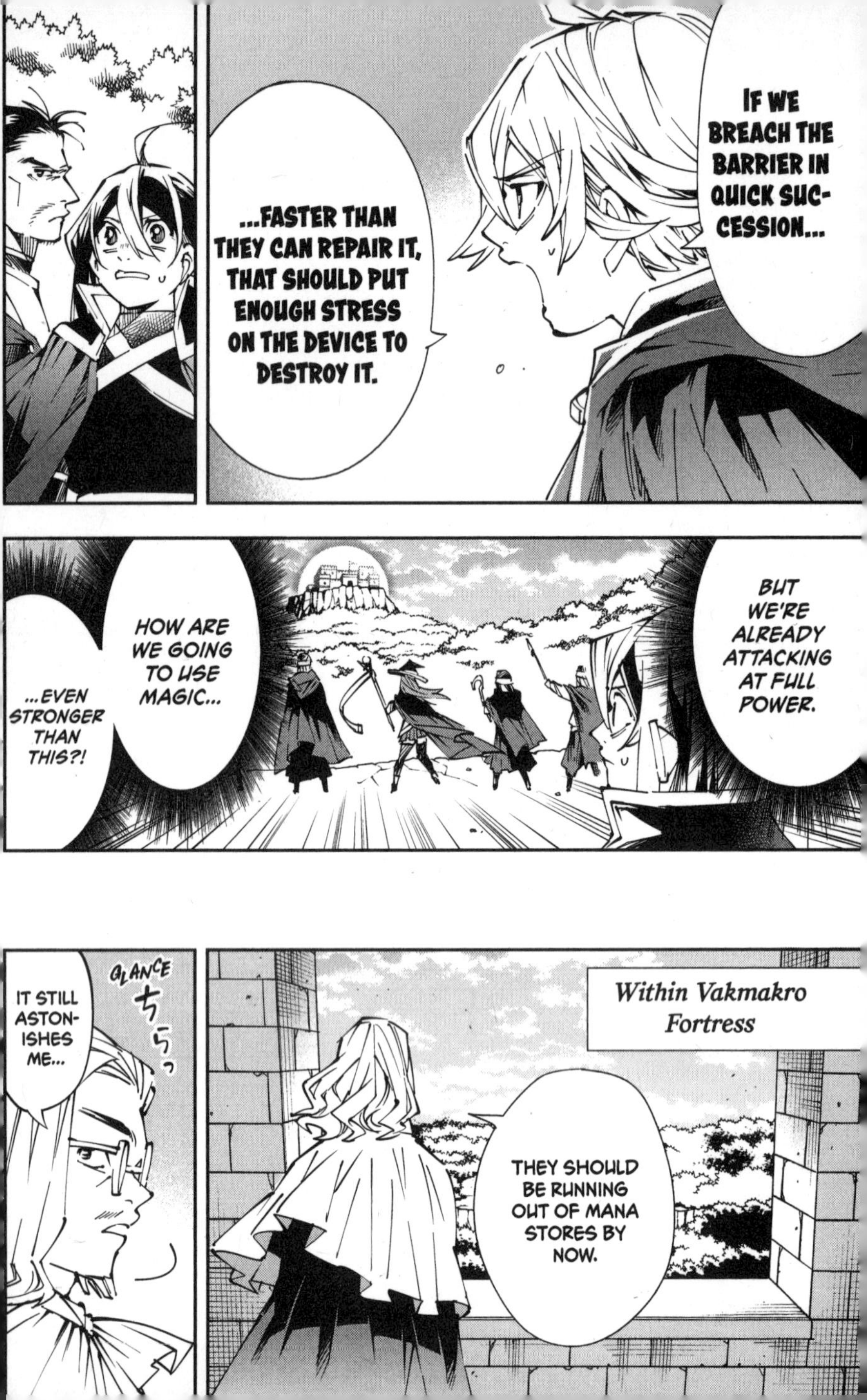
IF WE BREACH THE BARRIER IN QUICK SUC-CESSION...
...FASTER THAN THEY CAN REPAIR IT, THAT SHOULD PUT ENOUGH STRESS ON THE DEVICE TO DESTROY IT.
BUT WE'RE ALREADY ATTACKING AT FULL POWER.
HOW ARE WE GOING TO USE MAGIC...
...EVEN STRONGER THAN THIS?!
Within Vakmakro Fortress
THEY SHOULD BE RUNNING OUT OF MANA STORES BY NOW.
GLANCE
ちらっ
IT STILL ASTON-ISHES ME...

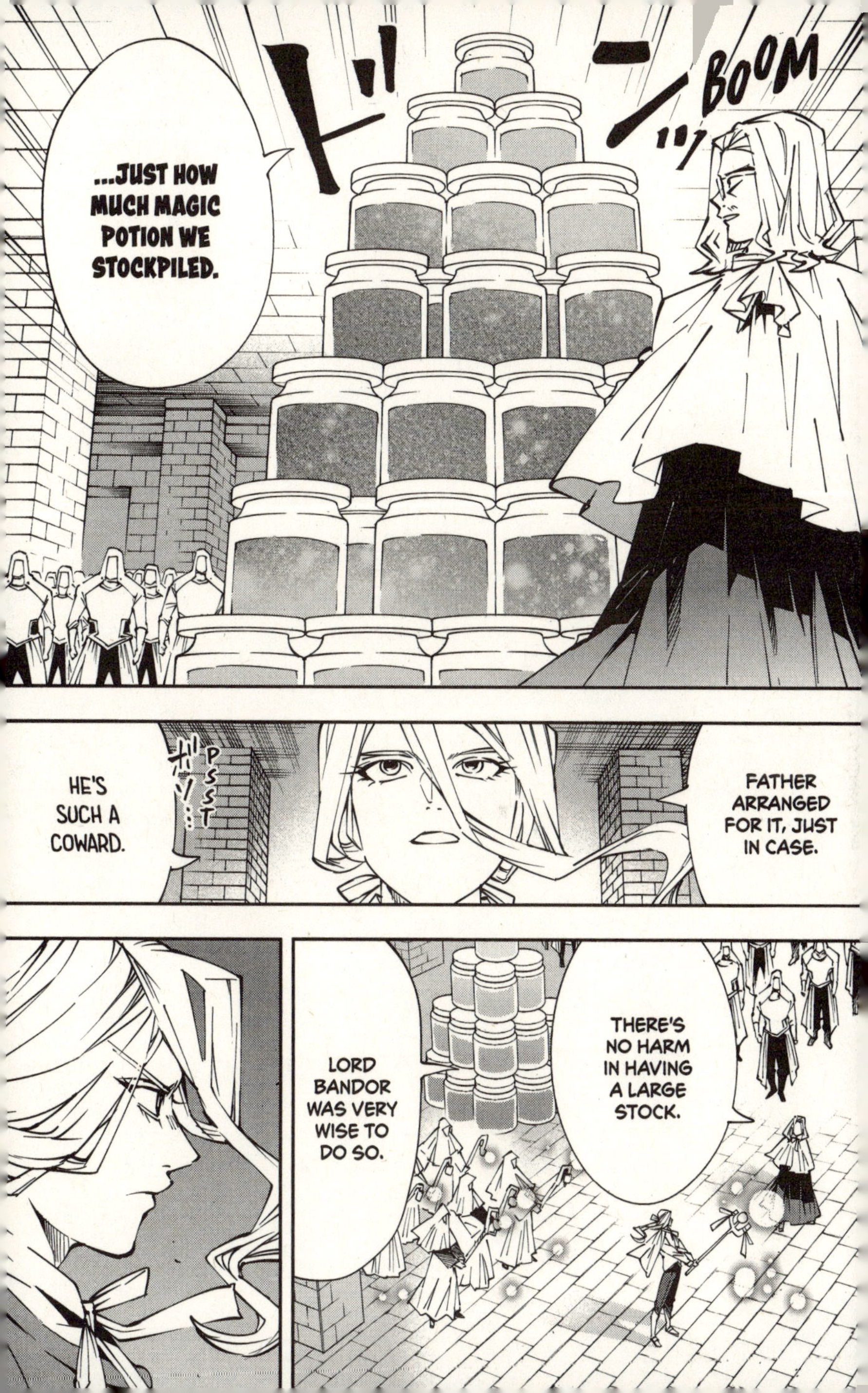
BOOM
...JUST HOW MUCH MAGIC POTION WE STOCKPILED.
FATHER ARRANGED FOR IT, JUST IN CASE.
PSST
HE'S SUCH A COWARD.
THERE'S NO HARM IN HAVING A LARGE STOCK.
LORD BANDOR WAS VERY WISE TO DO SO.

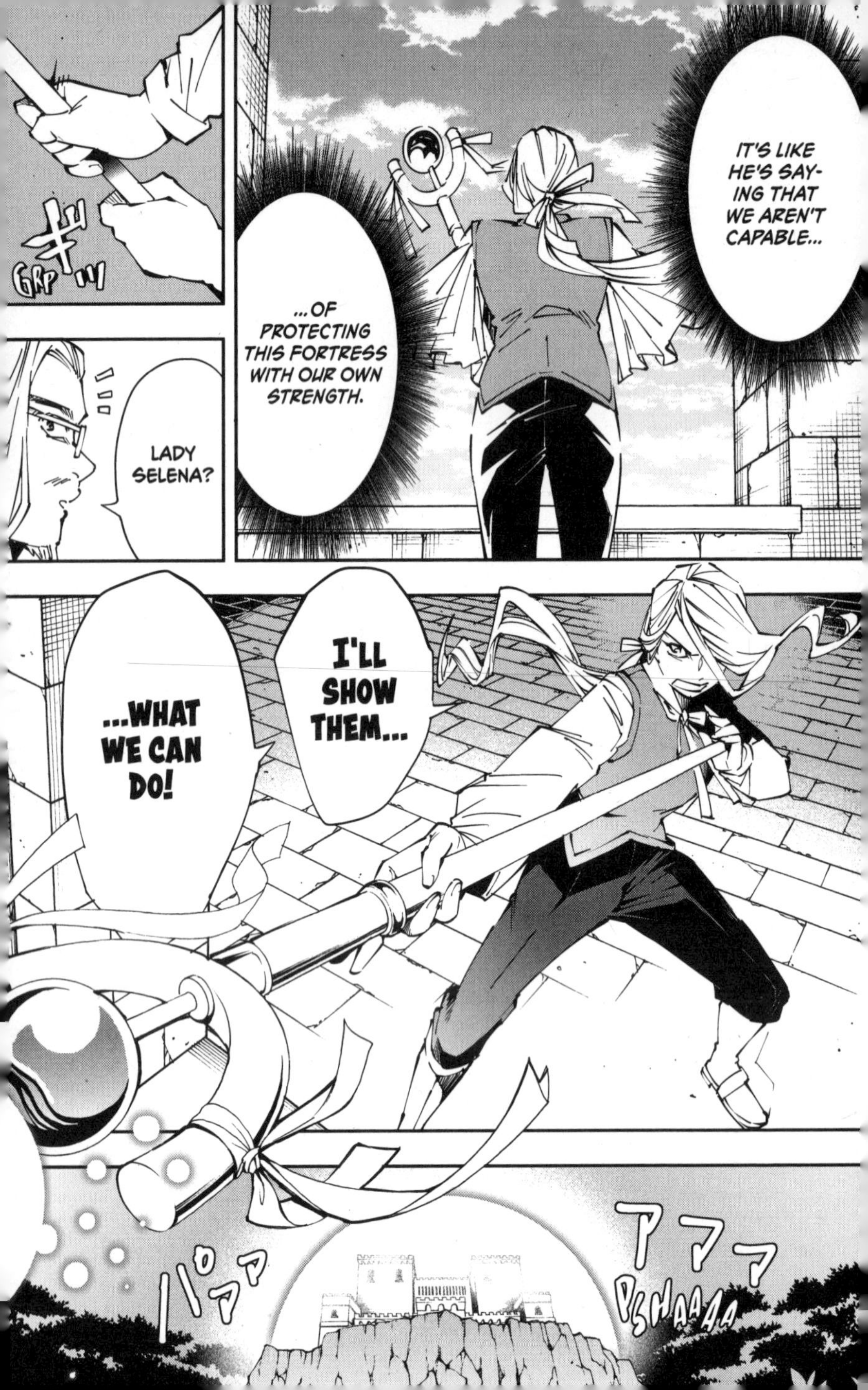
IT'S LIKE HE'S SAYING THAT WE AREN'T CAPABLE...
...OF PROTECTING THIS FORTRESS WITH OUR OWN STRENGTH.
GRP
LADY SELENA?
I'LL SHOW THEM...
...WHAT WE CAN DO!
PSHAAAA

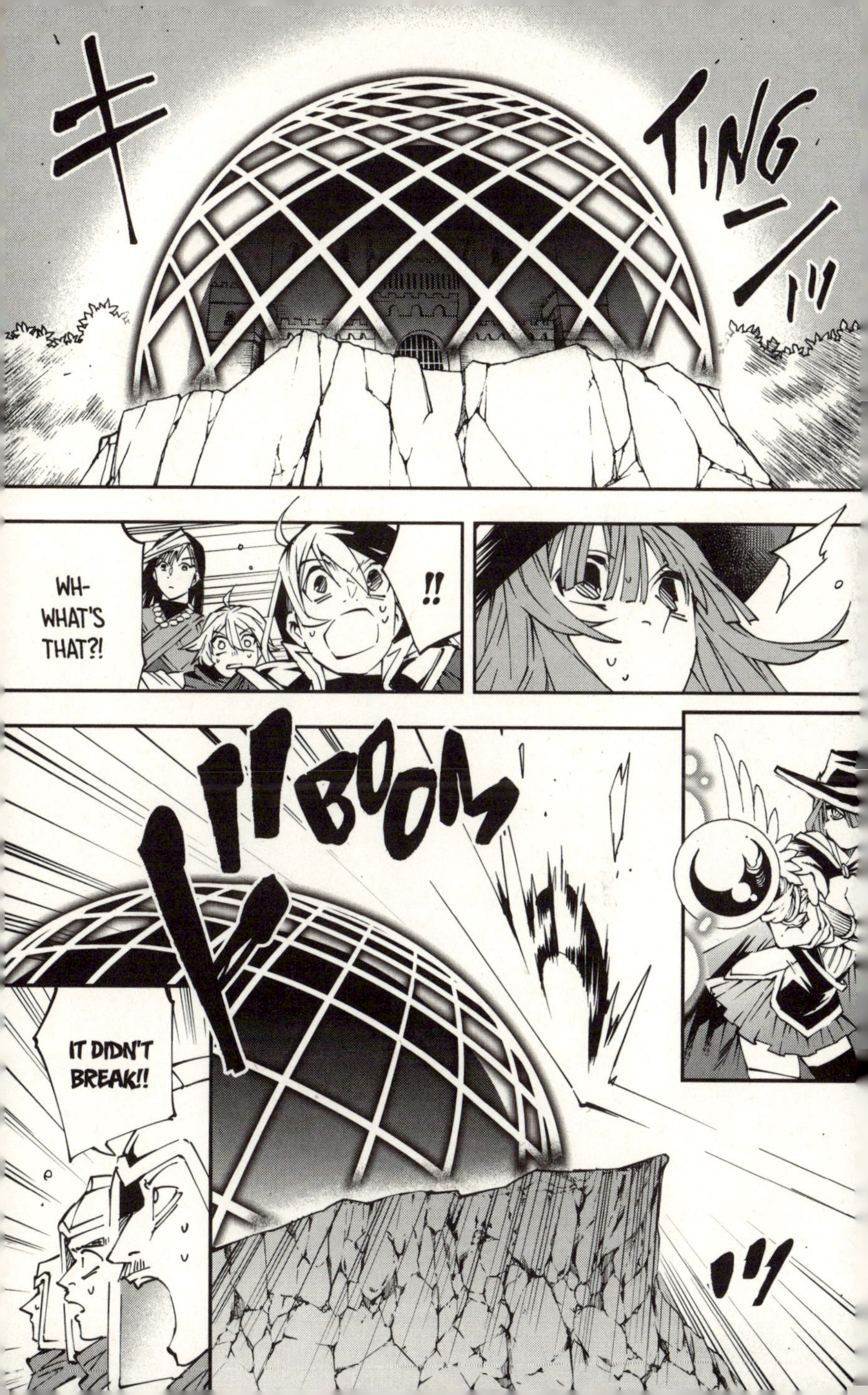

TING
!!
WH-
WHAT'S
THAT?!
BOOM
IT DIDN'T
BREAK!!

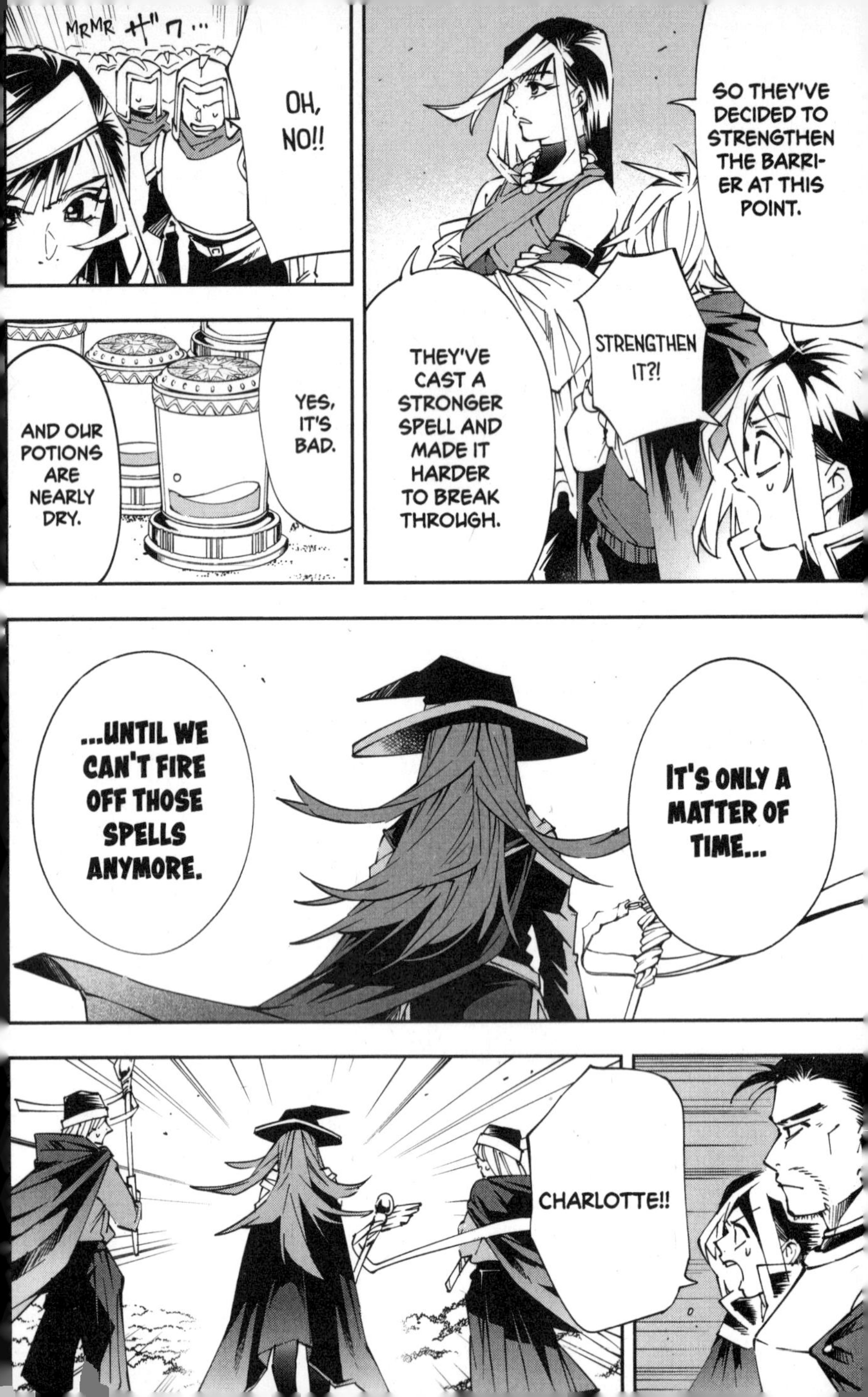
SO THEY'VE DECIDED TO STRENGTHEN THE BARRIER AT THIS POINT.
STRENGTHEN IT?!
THEY'VE CAST A STRONGER SPELL AND MADE IT HARDER TO BREAK THROUGH.
MRMR ザワ...
OH, NO!!
YES, IT'S BAD.
AND OUR POTIONS ARE NEARLY DRY.
IT'S ONLY A MATTER OF TIME...
...UNTIL WE CAN'T FIRE OFF THOSE SPELLS ANYMORE.
CHARLOTTE!!

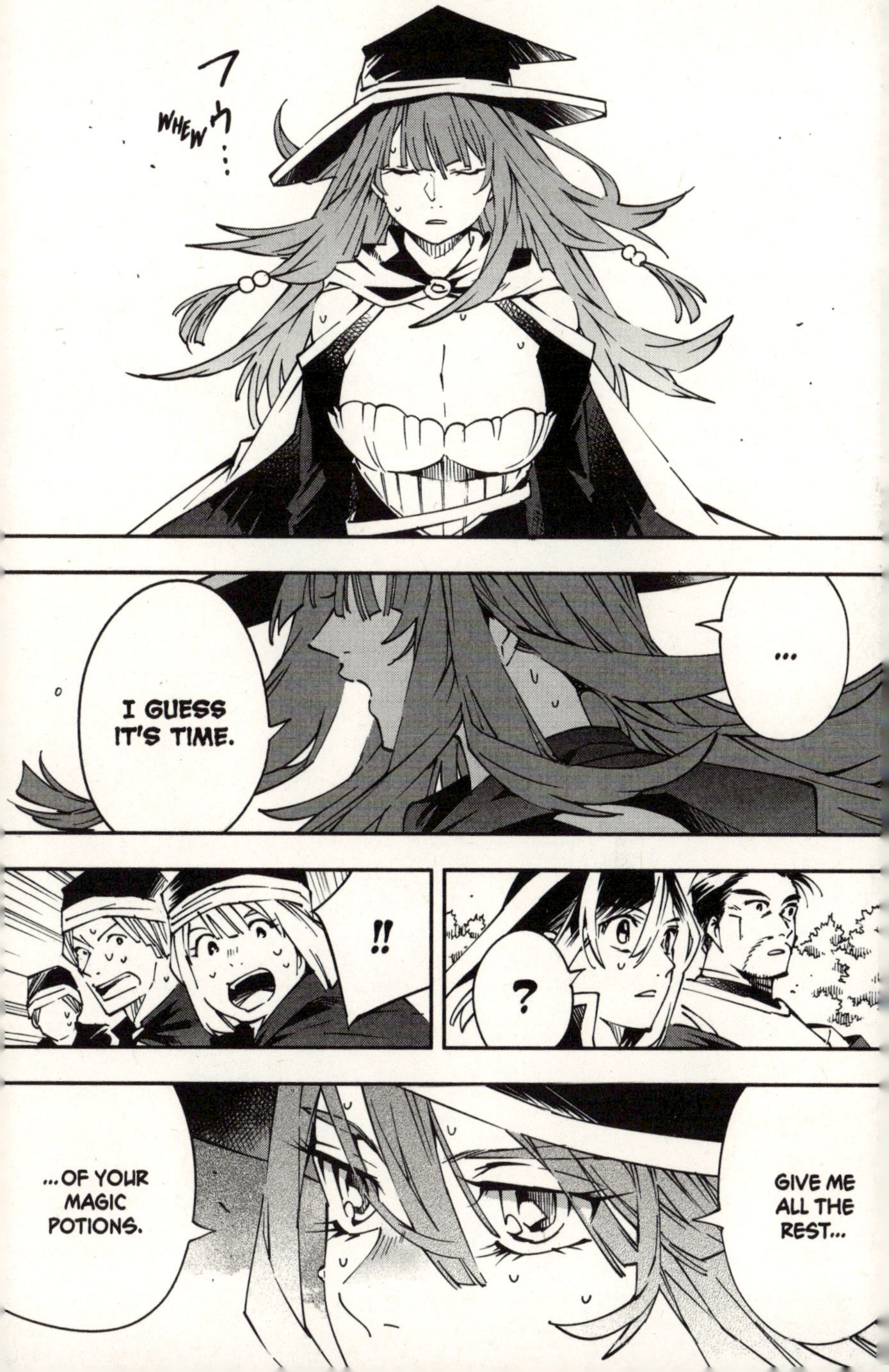
WHEW
...
I GUESS IT'S TIME.
?
!!
GIVE ME ALL THE REST...
...OF YOUR MAGIC POTIONS.

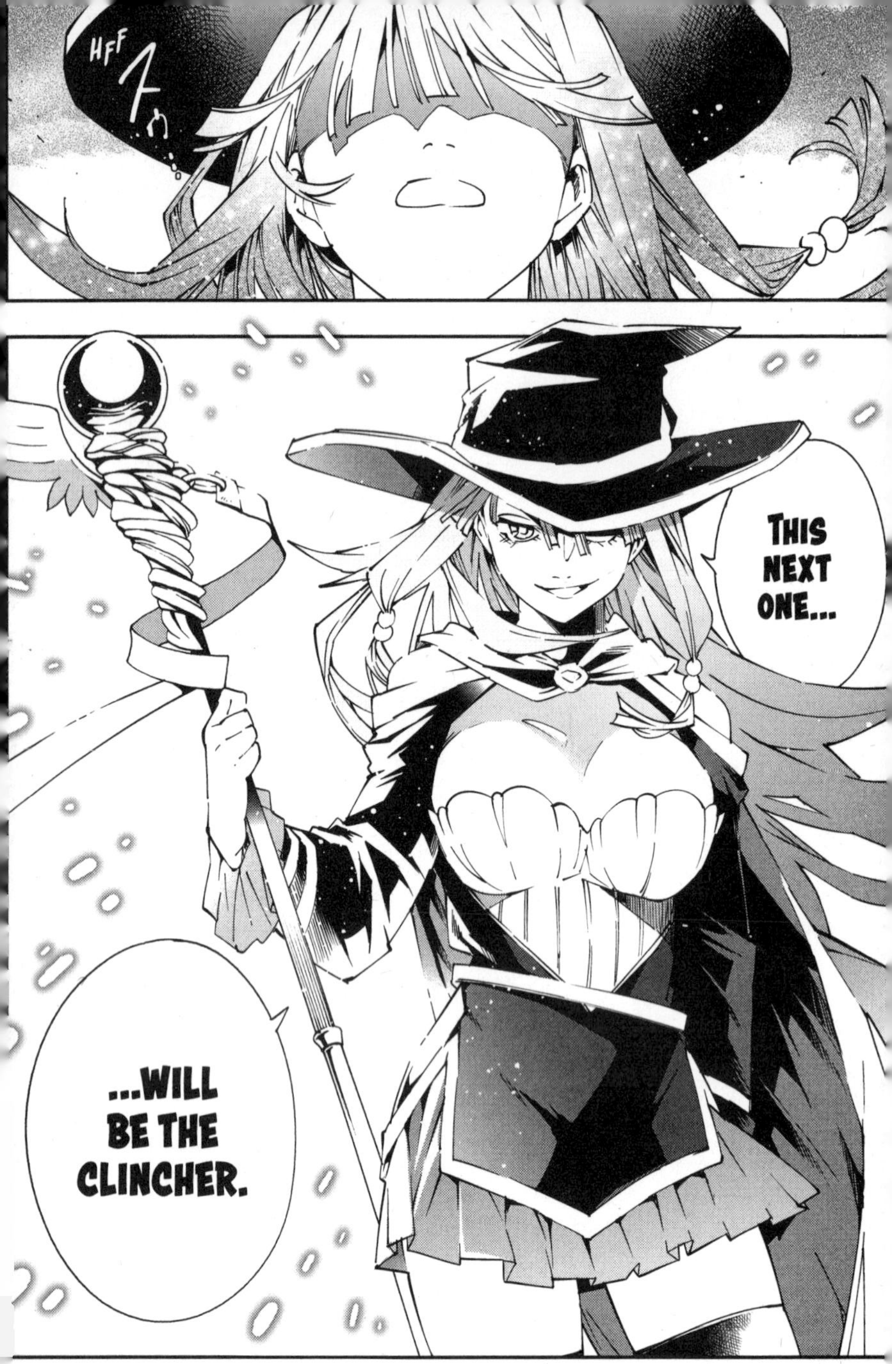
HFF
THIS NEXT ONE...
...WILL BE THE CLINCHER.

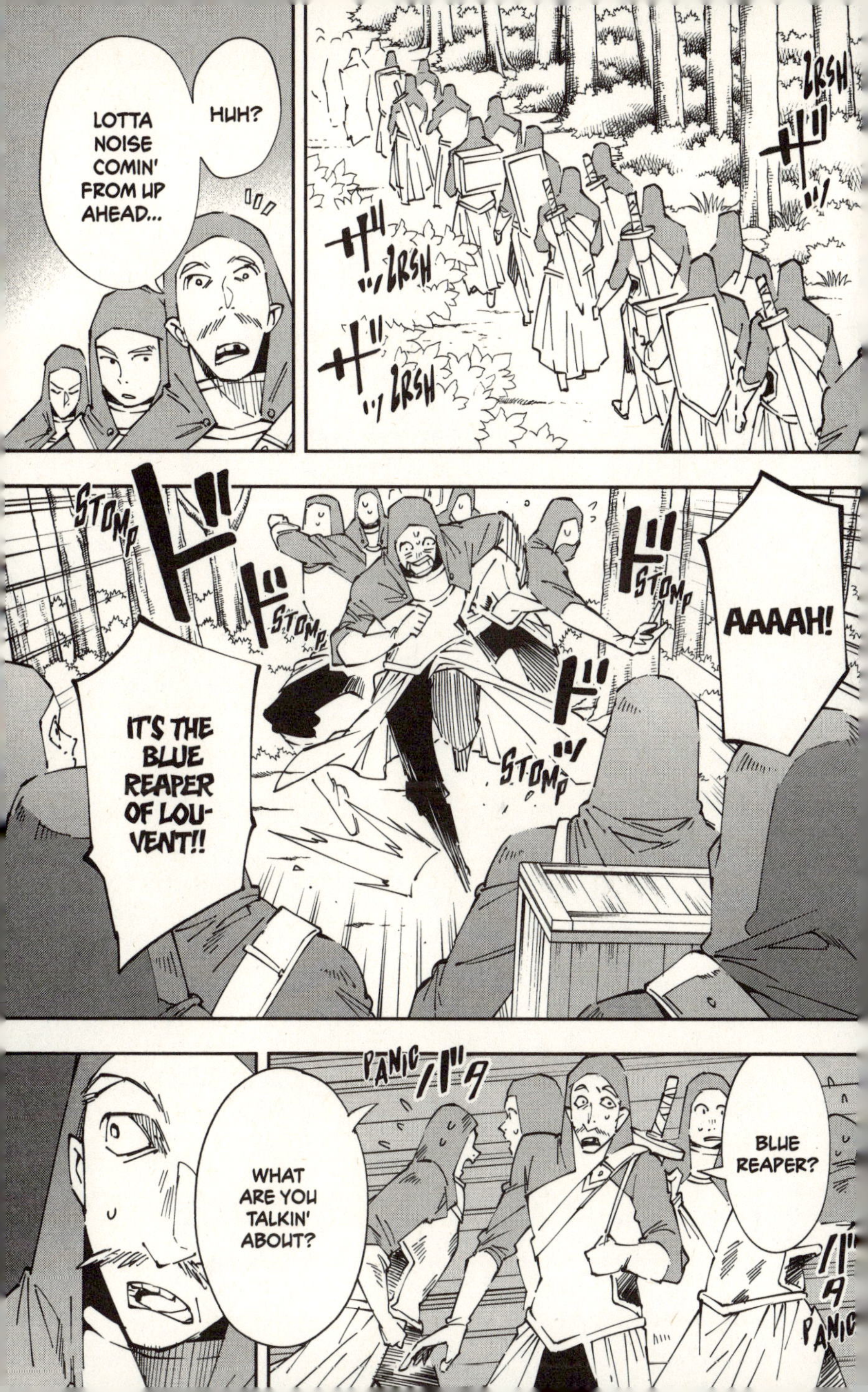
ZRSH
ZRSH
ZRSH
HUH?
LOTTA NOISE COMIN' FROM UP AHEAD...
AAAAH!
STOMP
STOMP
STOMP
STOMP
IT'S THE BLUE REAPER OF LOU-VENT!!
PANIC
BLUE REAPER?
PANIC
WHAT ARE YOU TALKIN' ABOUT?

Chapter 70: A Critical Blow

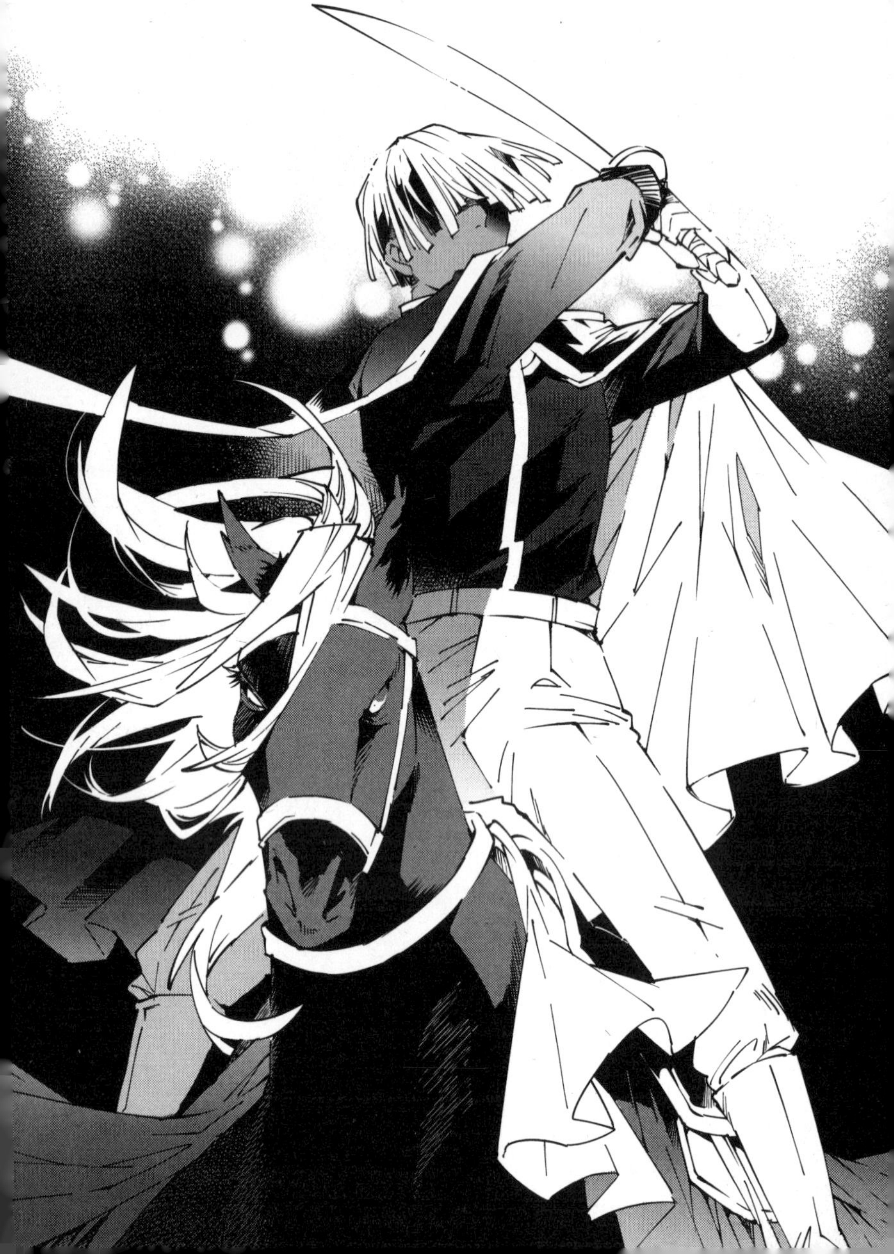

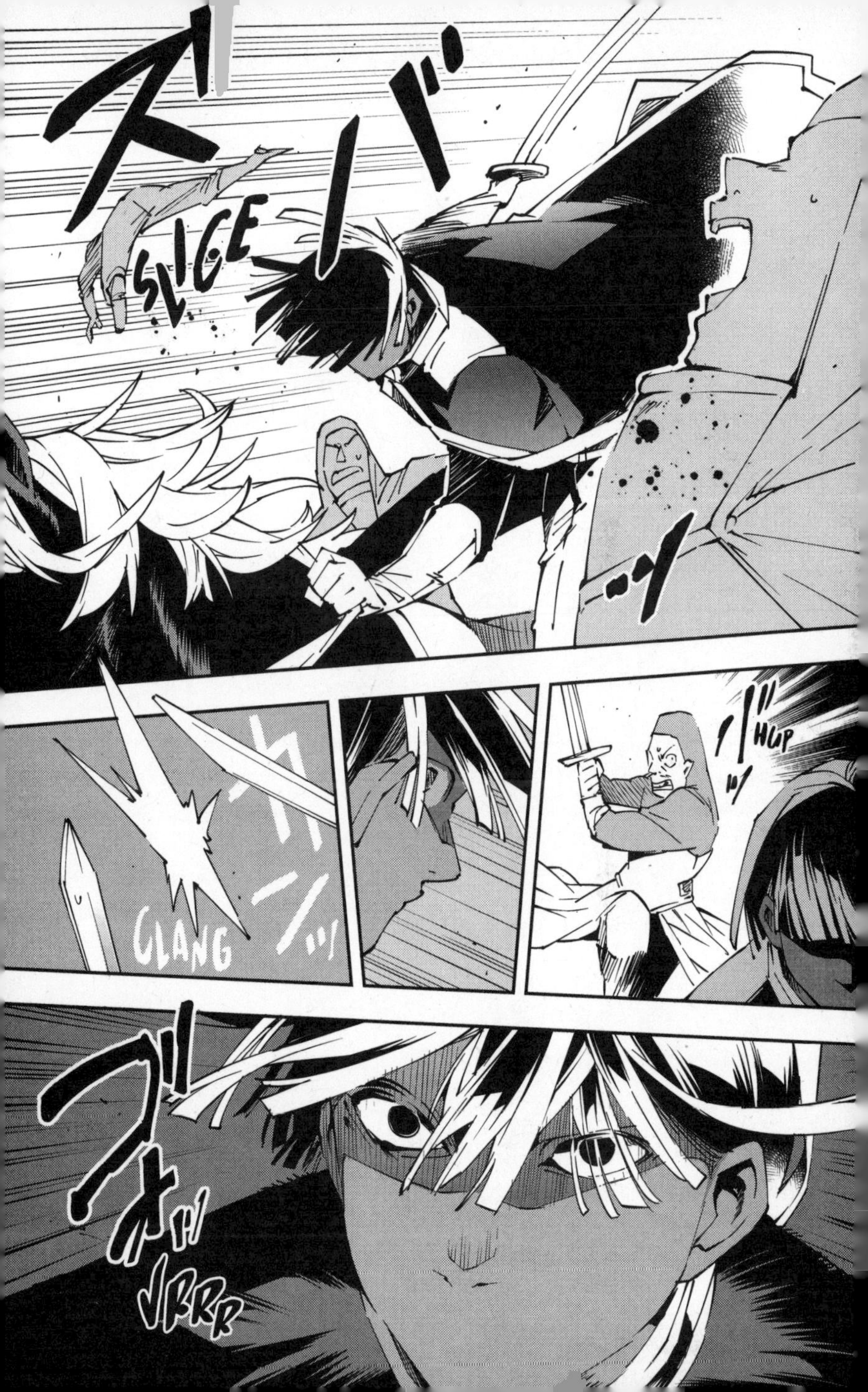
SLICE
HUP
CLANG
VRRR

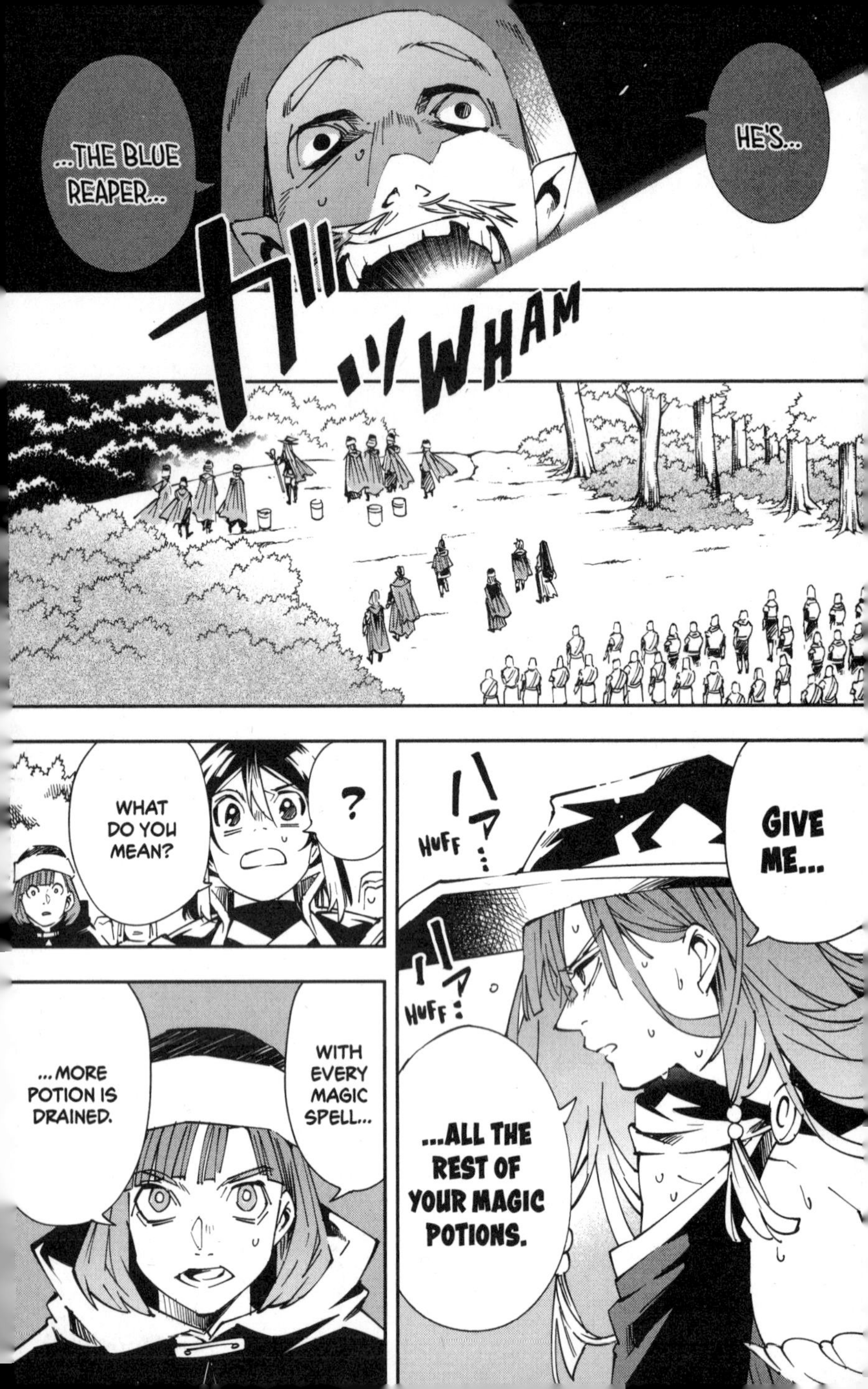
HE'S...
...THE BLUE REAPER...
WHAM
HUFF
GIVE ME...
HUFF
...ALL THE REST OF YOUR MAGIC POTIONS.
?
WHAT DO YOU MEAN?
WITH EVERY MAGIC SPELL...
...MORE POTION IS DRAINED.

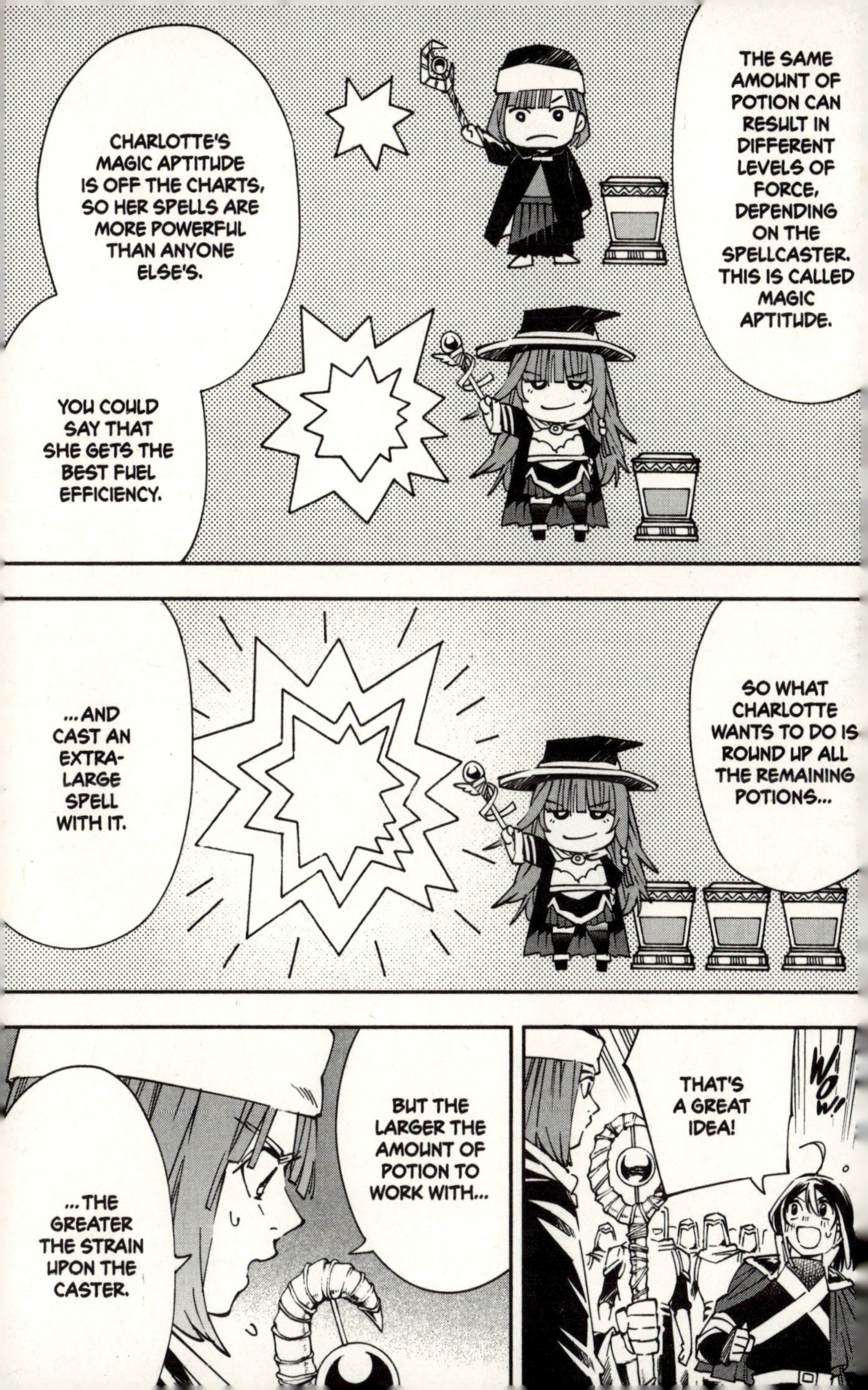
THE SAME AMOUNT OF POTION CAN RESULT IN DIFFERENT LEVELS OF FORCE, DEPENDING ON THE SPELLCASTER. THIS IS CALLED MAGIC APTITUDE.
CHARLOTTE'S MAGIC APTITUDE IS OFF THE CHARTS, SO HER SPELLS ARE MORE POWERFUL THAN ANYONE ELSE'S.
YOU COULD SAY THAT SHE GETS THE BEST FUEL EFFICIENCY.
SO WHAT CHARLOTTE WANTS TO DO IS ROUND UP ALL THE REMAINING POTIONS...
...AND CAST AN EXTRA-LARGE SPELL WITH IT.
WOW!!
THAT'S A GREAT IDEA!
BUT THE LARGER THE AMOUNT OF POTION TO WORK WITH...
...THE GREATER THE STRAIN UPON THE CASTER.

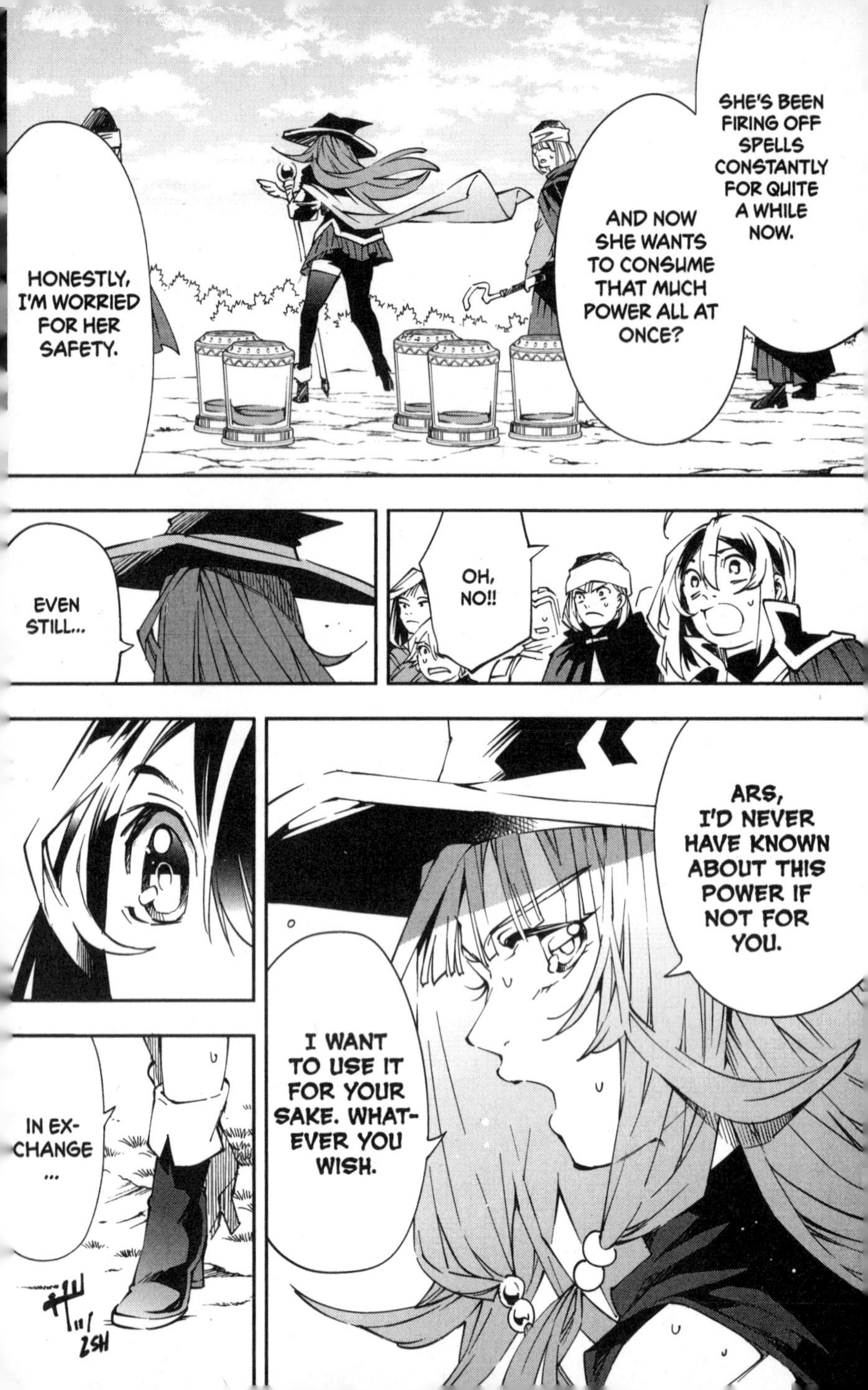
SHE'S BEEN FIRING OFF SPELLS CONSTANTLY FOR QUITE A WHILE NOW.
AND NOW SHE WANTS TO CONSUME THAT MUCH POWER ALL AT ONCE?
HONESTLY, I'M WORRIED FOR HER SAFETY.
OH, NO!!
EVEN STILL...
ARS, I'D NEVER HAVE KNOWN ABOUT THIS POWER IF NOT FOR YOU.
I WANT TO USE IT FOR YOUR SAKE. WHAT-EVER YOU WISH.
IN EX-CHANGE...
ZSH

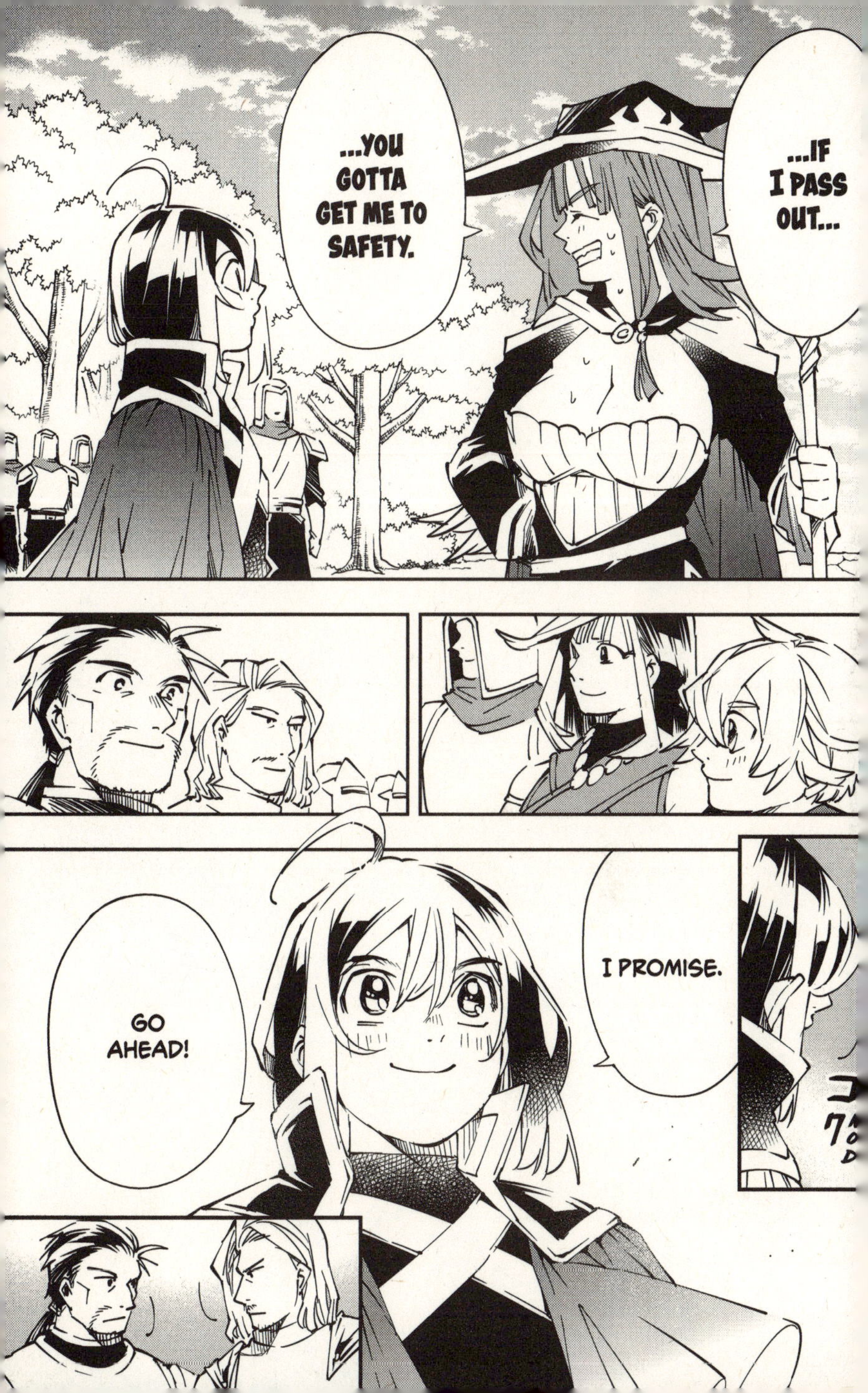

...IF I PASS OUT...
...YOU GOTTA GET ME TO SAFETY.
コク
NOD
I PROMISE.
GO AHEAD!

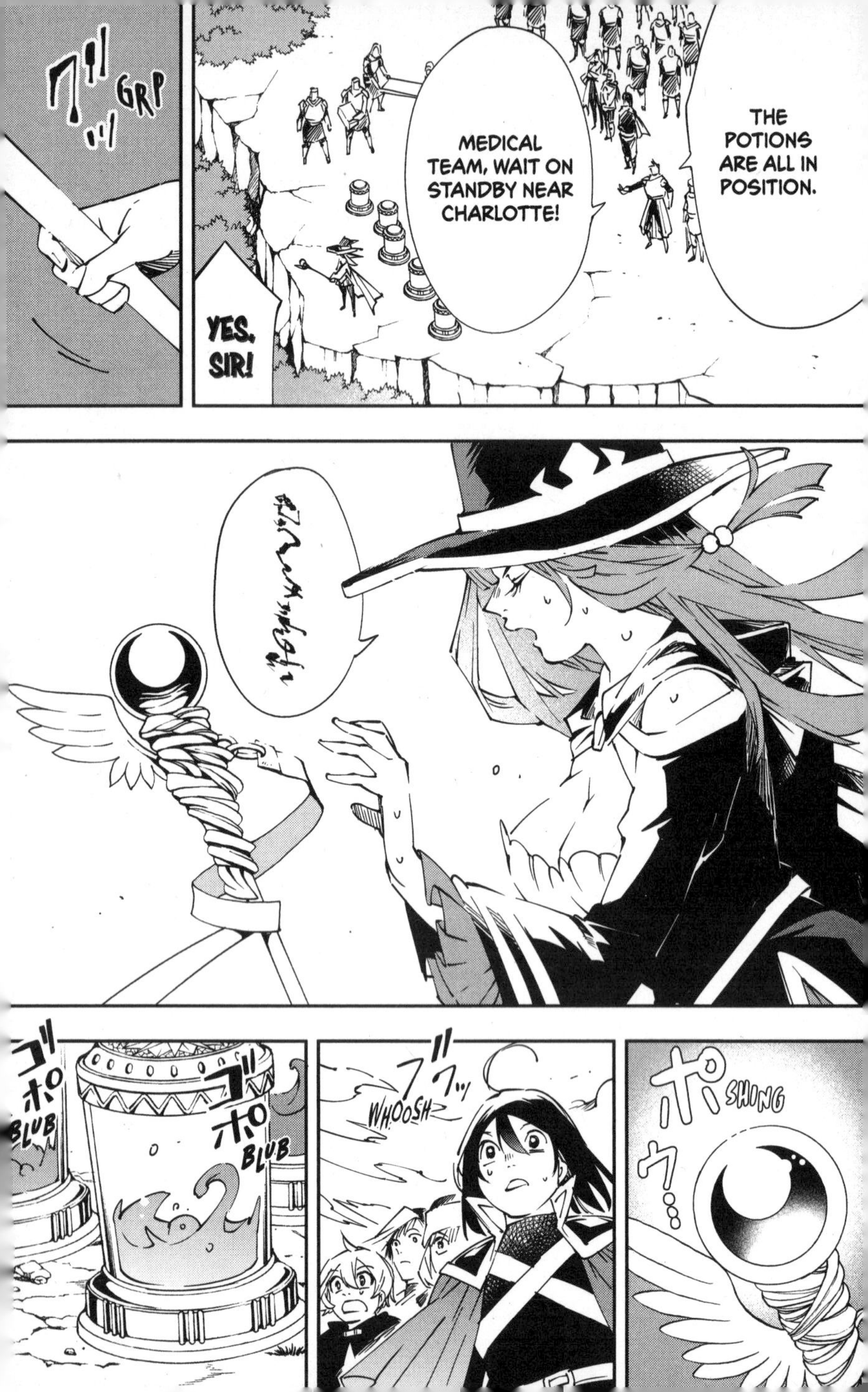
THE POTIONS ARE ALL IN POSITION.
MEDICAL TEAM, WAIT ON STANDBY NEAR CHARLOTTE!
YES, SIR!
GRP
SHING
WHOOSH
BLUB
BLUB

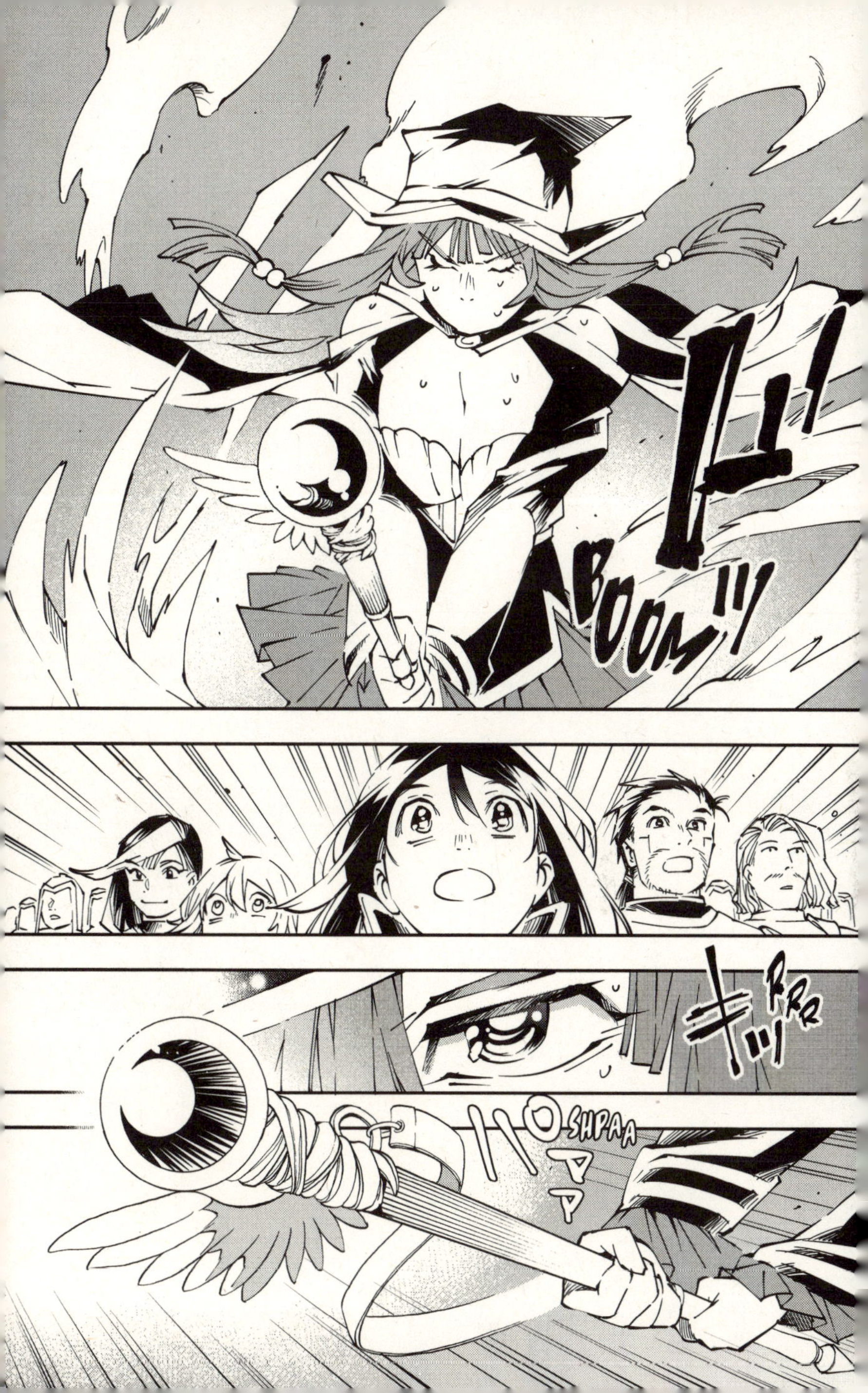
BOOM!!
RRR
SHPAA

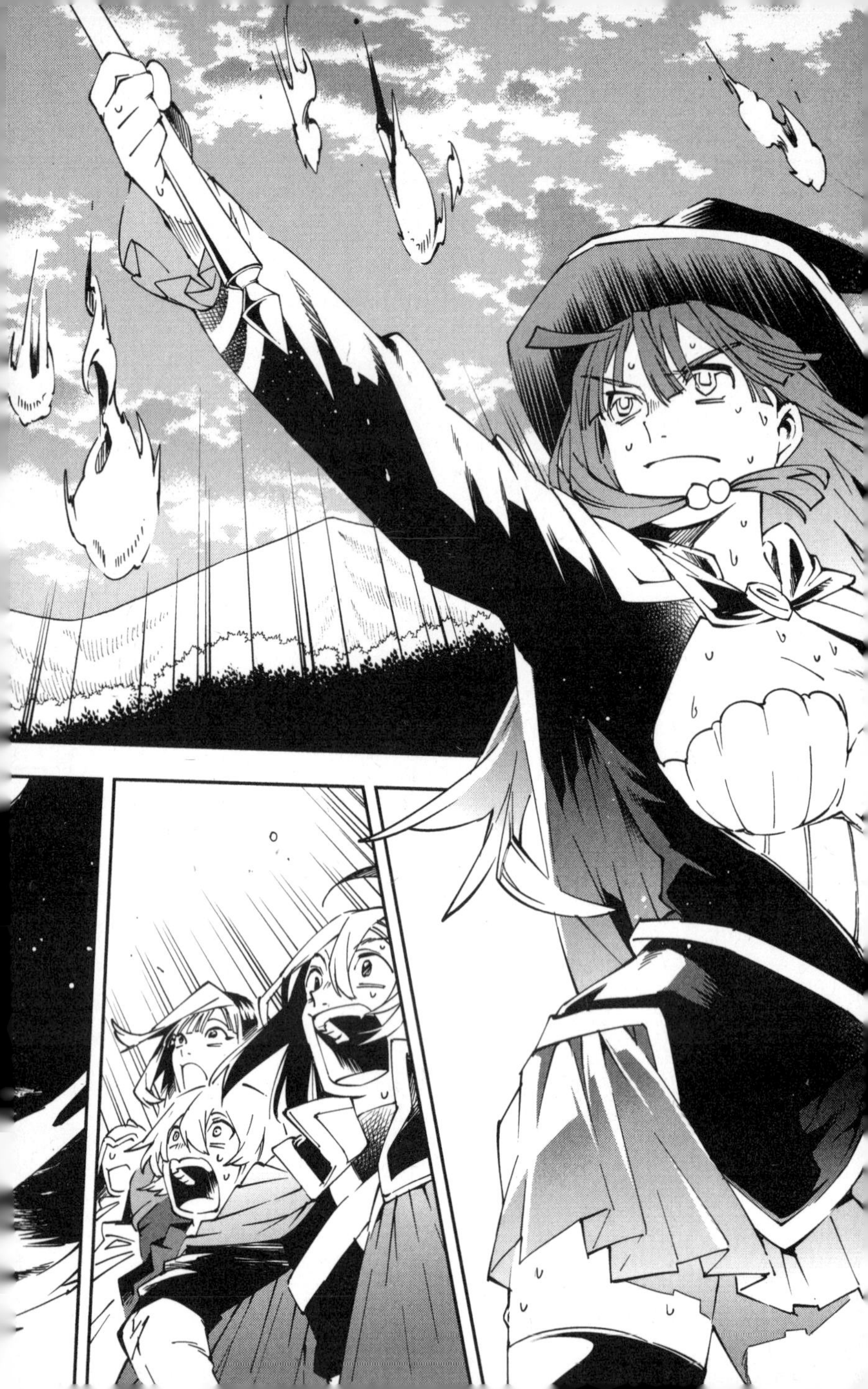

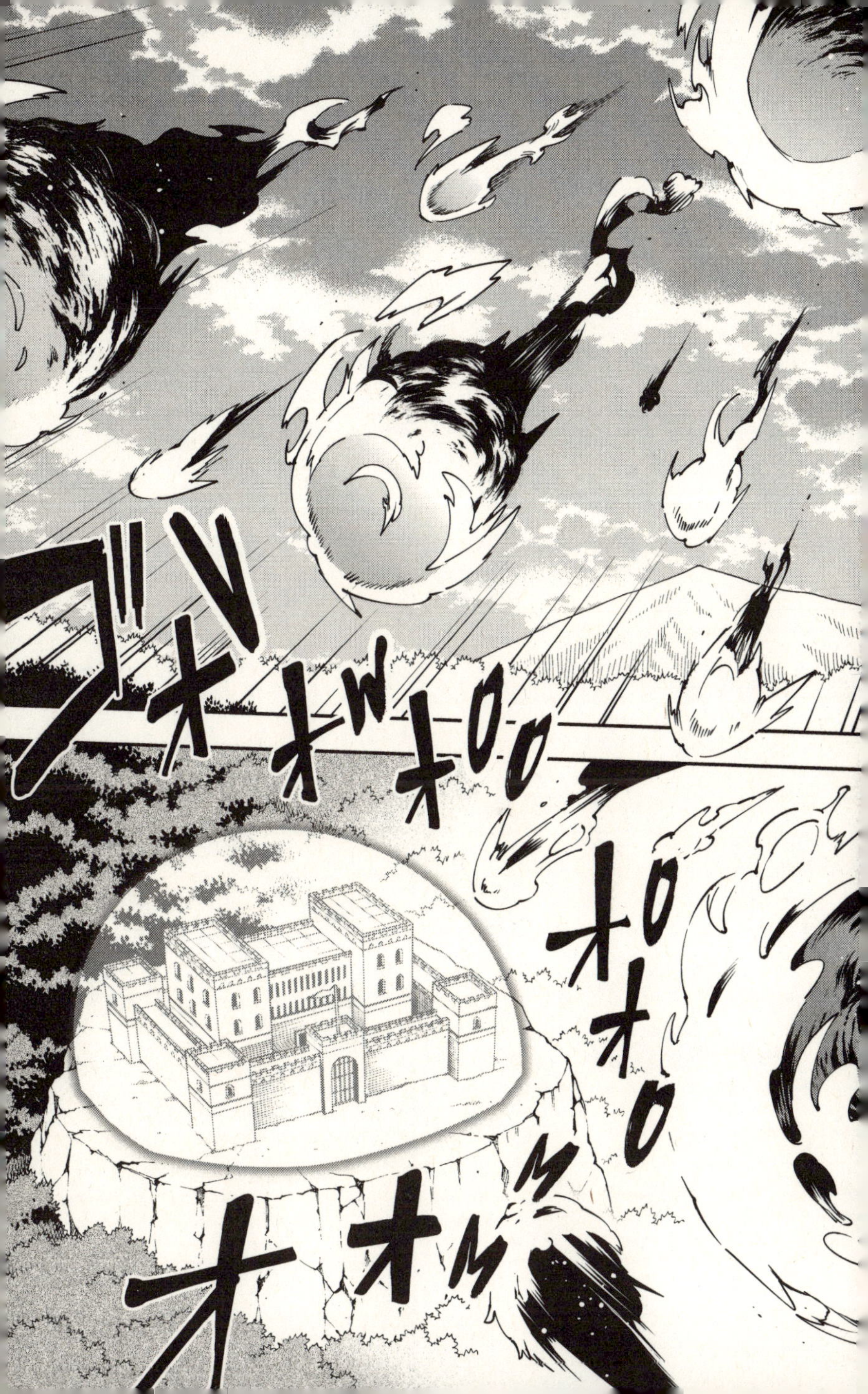
ゴオオオオオオオ

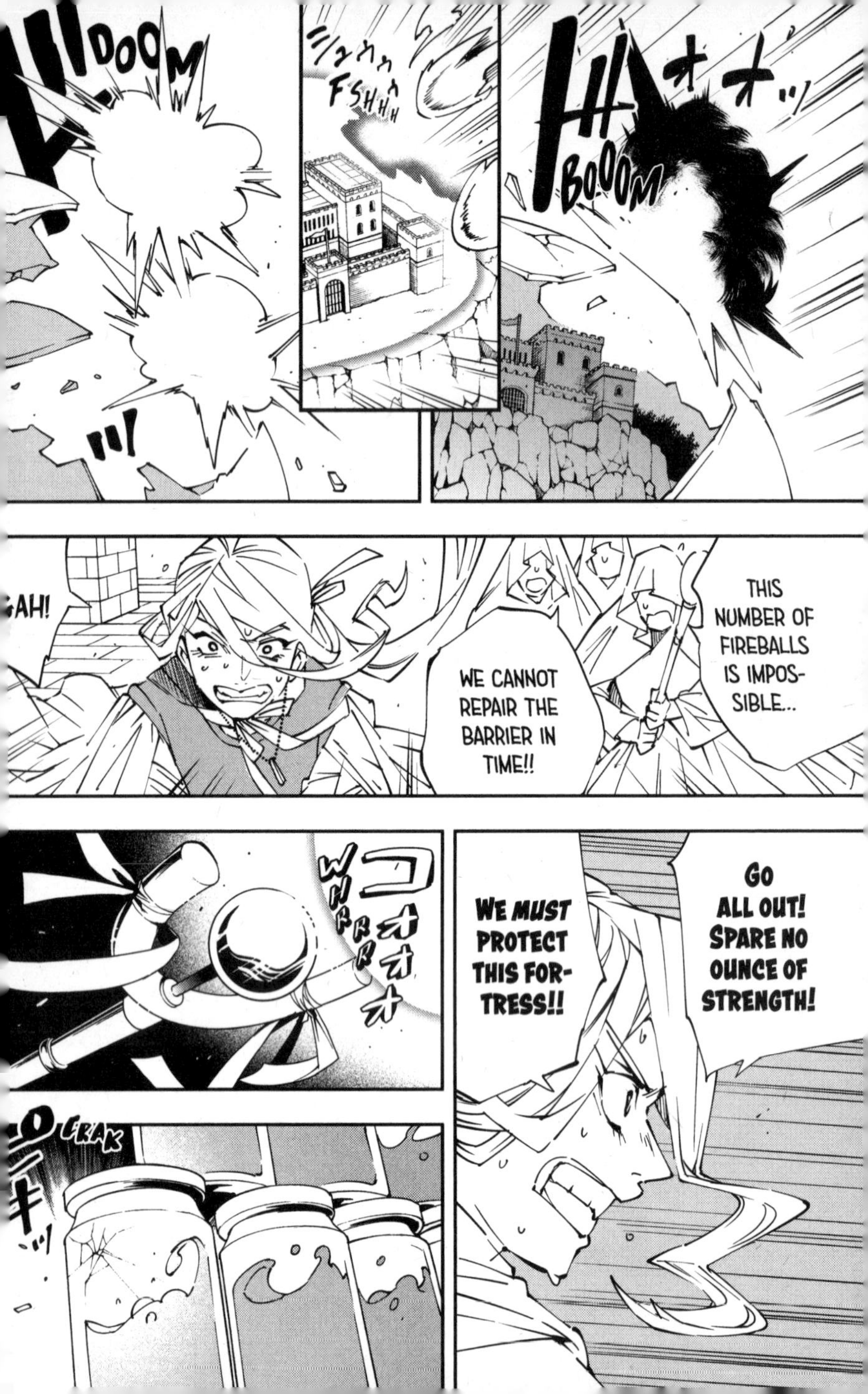
BOOOM
FSHHHH
DOOM
THIS NUMBER OF FIREBALLS IS IMPOSSIBLE...
WE CANNOT REPAIR THE BARRIER IN TIME!!
GAH!
GO ALL OUT! SPARE NO OUNCE OF STRENGTH!
WE MUST PROTECT THIS FORTRESS!!
WHRRRR
CRAK

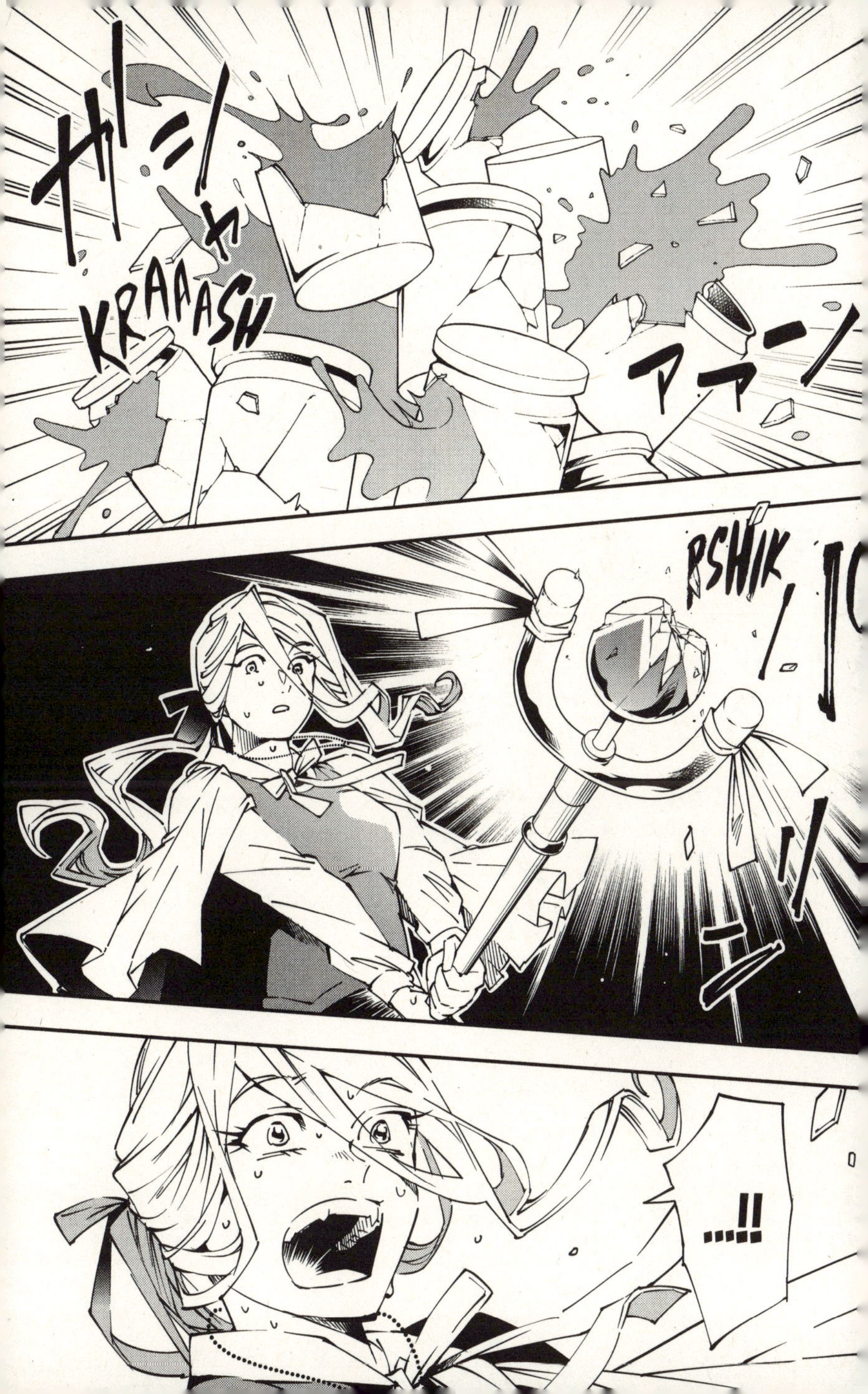
KRAAASH
RSHIK
...!!

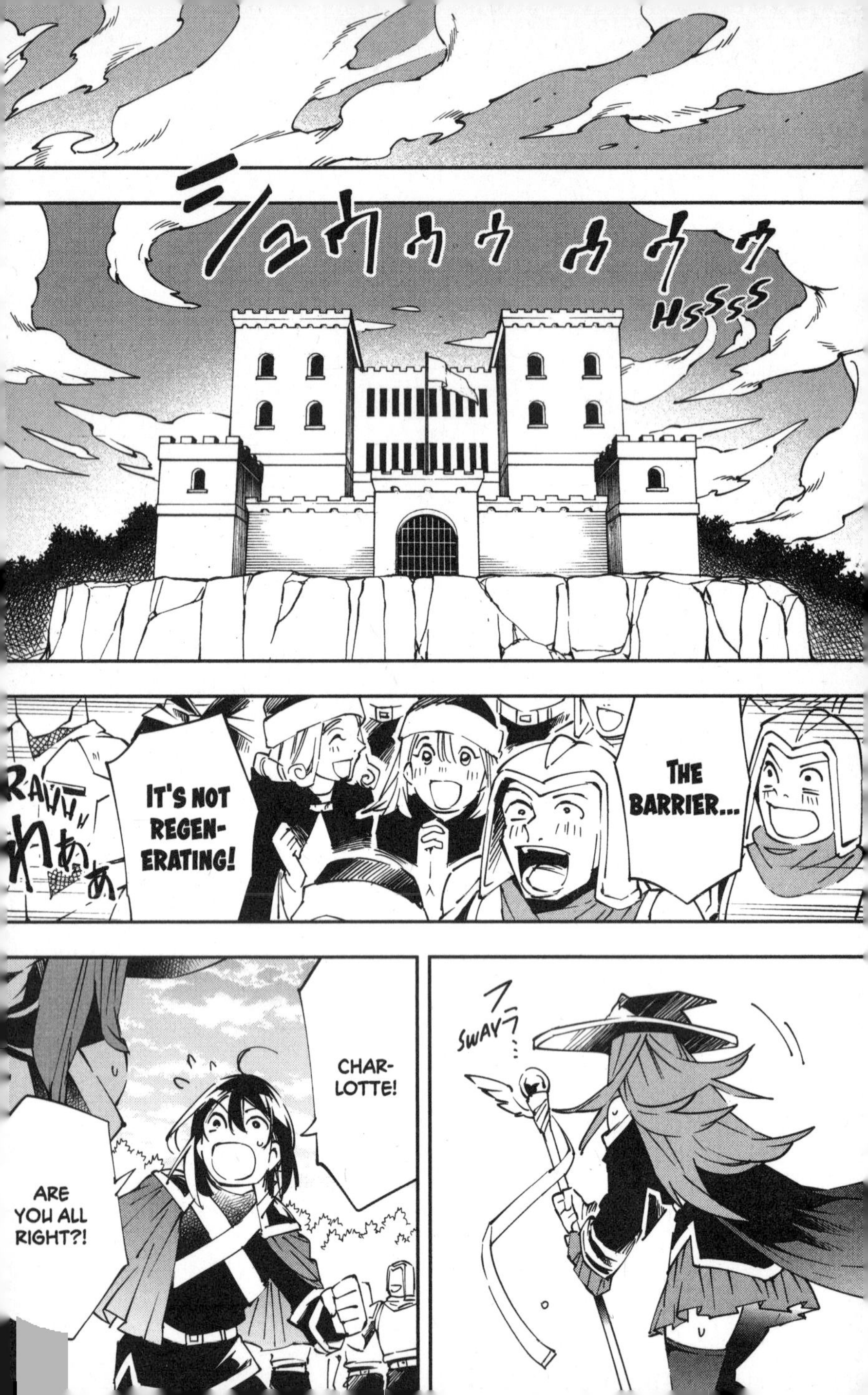

HSSSS
THE BARRIER...
IT'S NOT REGENERATING!
RAWHH
SWAY
CHARLOTTE!
ARE YOU ALL RIGHT?!

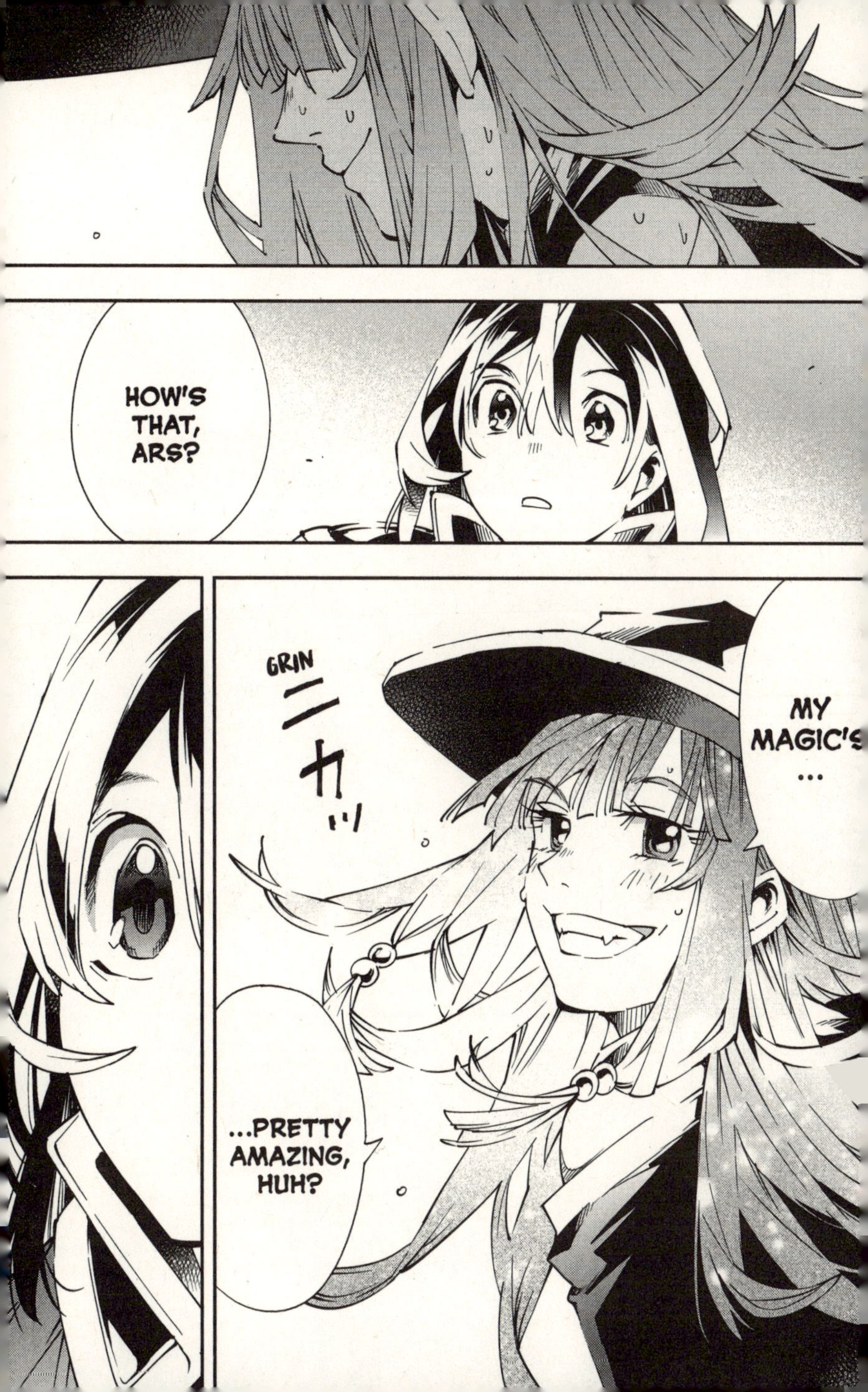
HOW'S THAT, ARS?
MY MAGIC'S ...
GRIN
ニカッ
...PRETTY AMAZING, HUH?

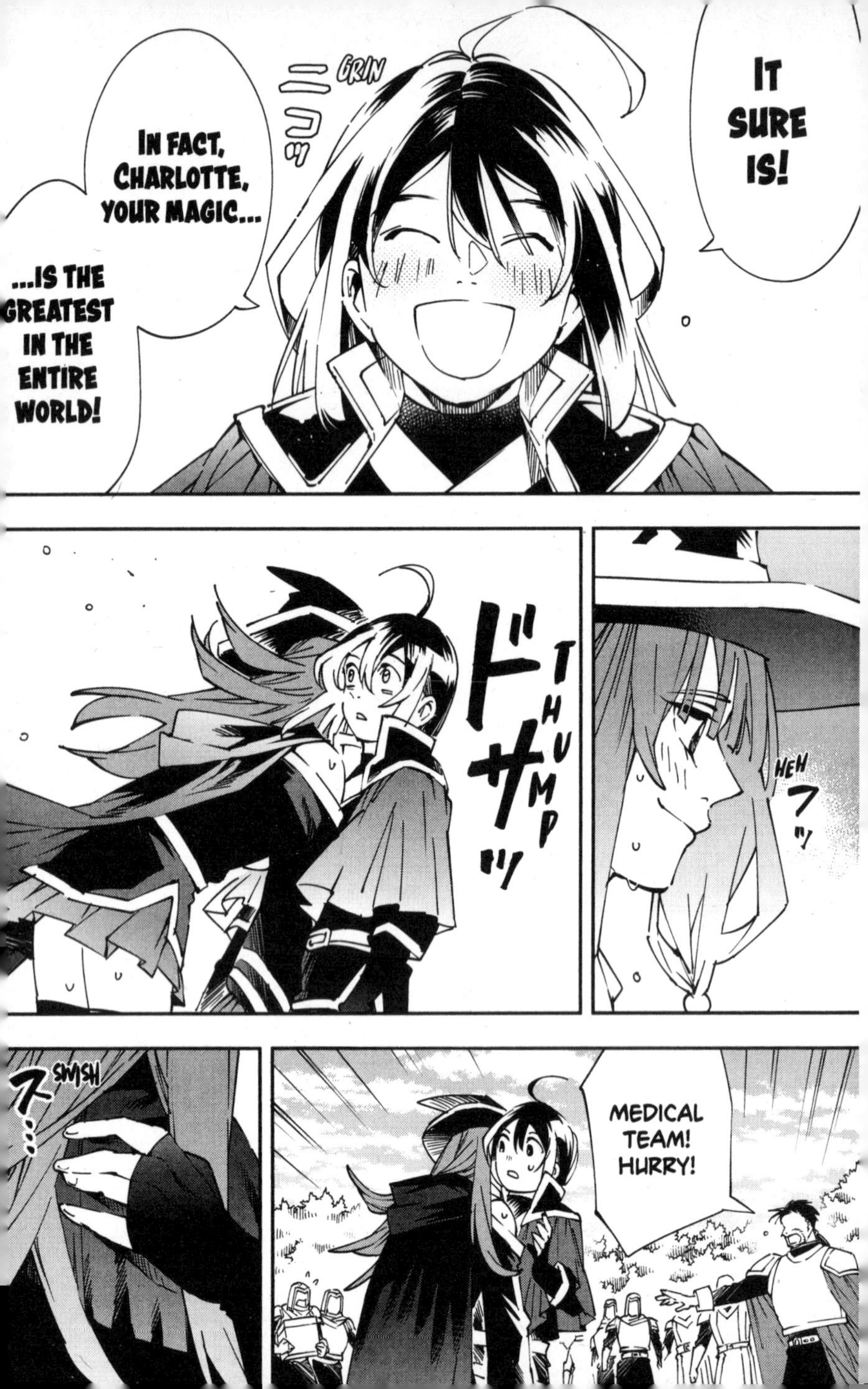
IT SURE IS!
GRIN
ニコッ
IN FACT, CHARLOTTE, YOUR MAGIC...
...IS THE GREATEST IN THE ENTIRE WORLD!
HEH
フッ
ドサッ
THUMP
MEDICAL TEAM! HURRY!
ス…
SWISH

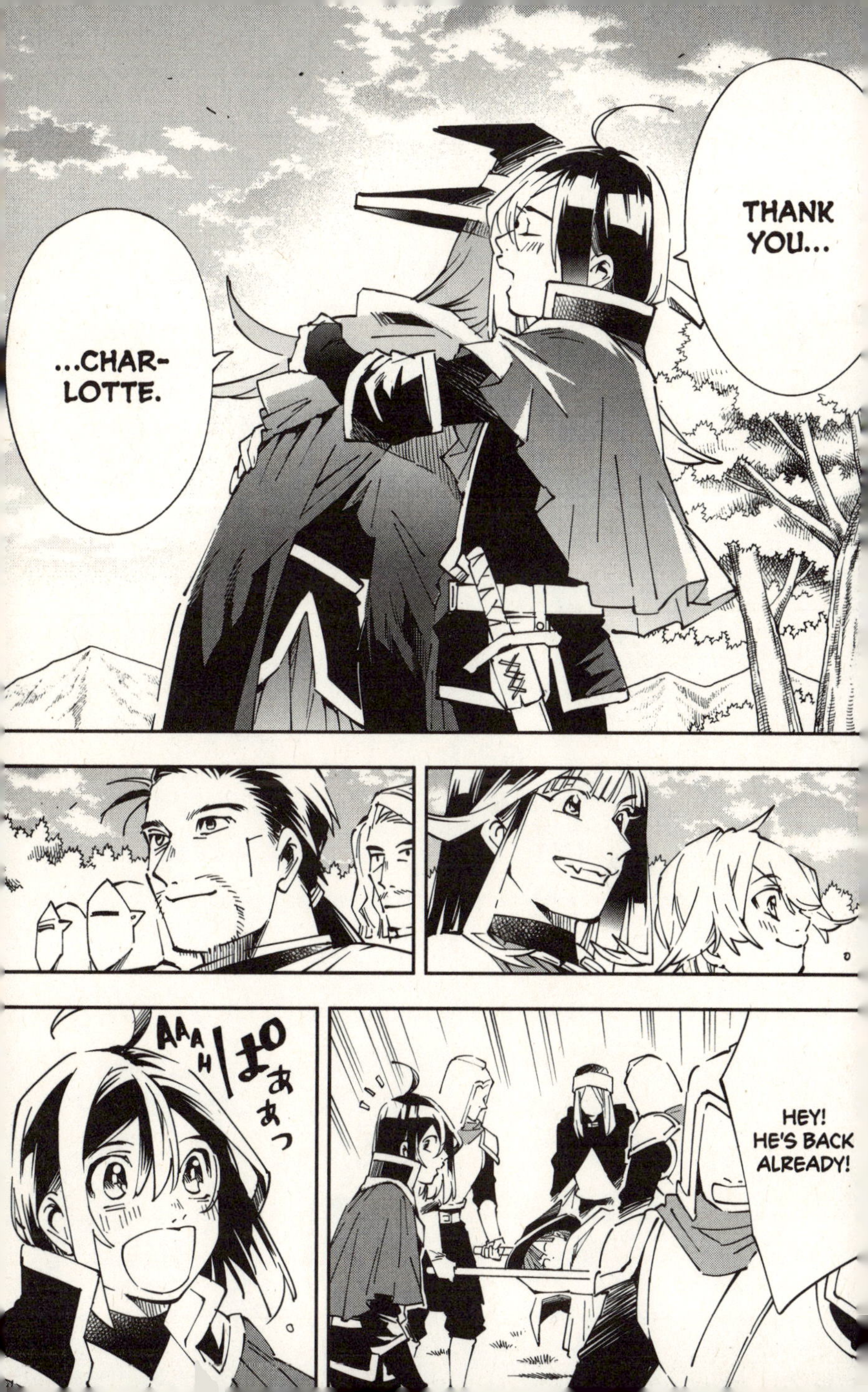
THANK YOU...
...CHAR-LOTTE.
HEY! HE'S BACK ALREADY!
AAAH
ぱああっ

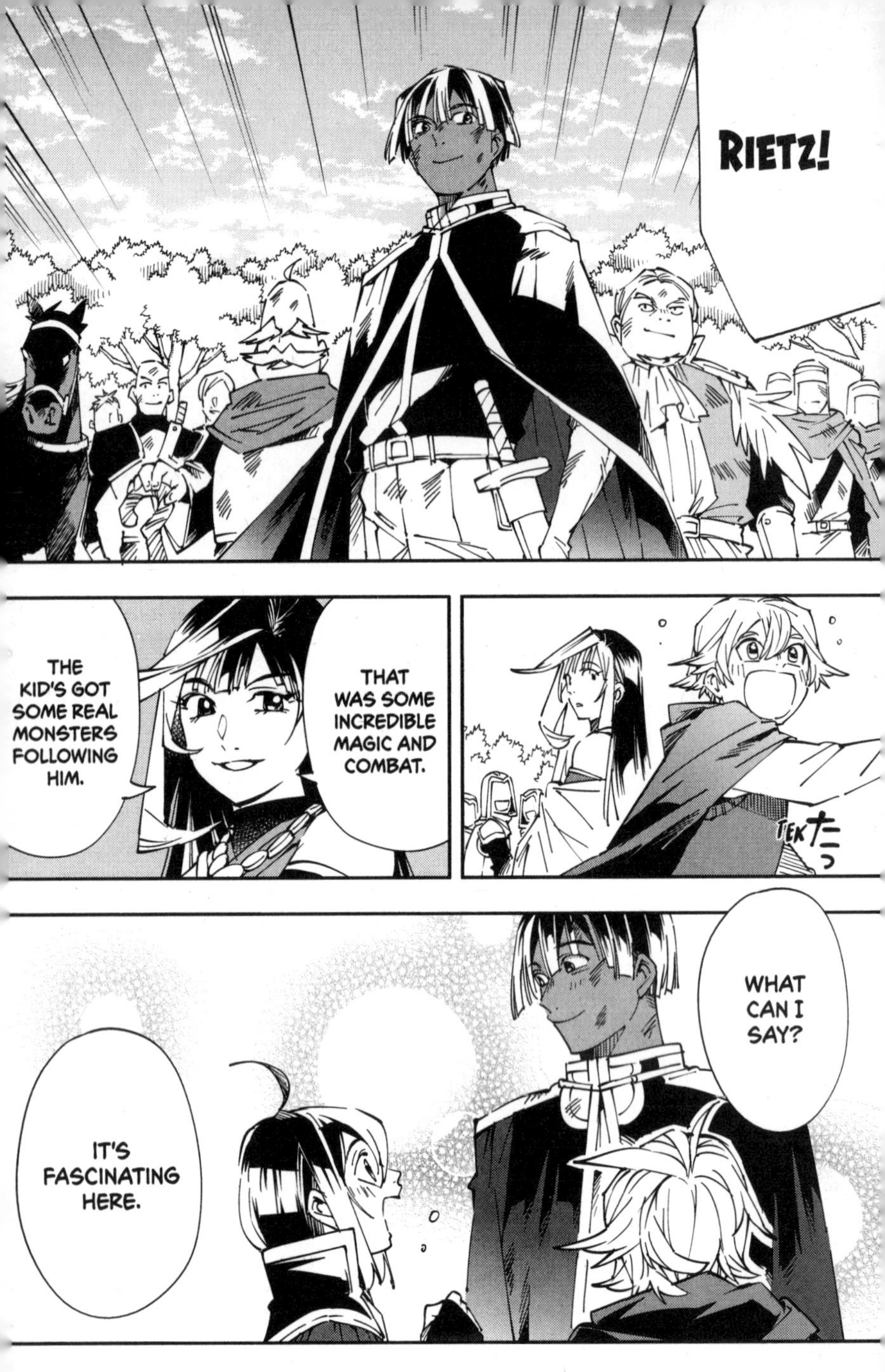
RIETZ!
TEK たっ
THAT WAS SOME INCREDIBLE MAGIC AND COMBAT.
THE KID'S GOT SOME REAL MONSTERS FOLLOWING HIM.
WHAT CAN I SAY?
IT'S FASCINATING HERE.

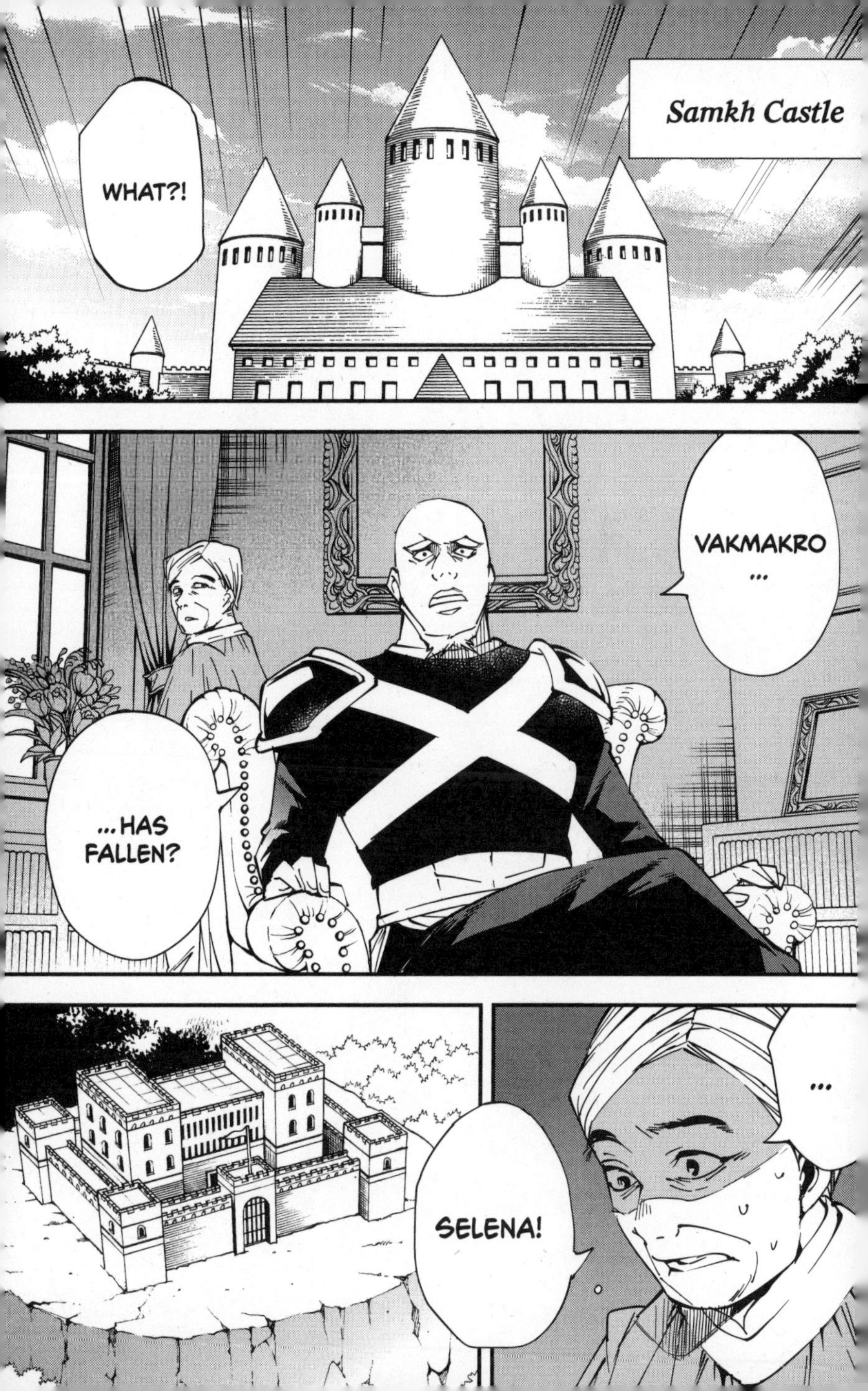
Samkh Castle
WHAT?!
VAKMAKRO ...
...HAS FALLEN?
...
SELENA!

Chapter 71: The Meaning of War

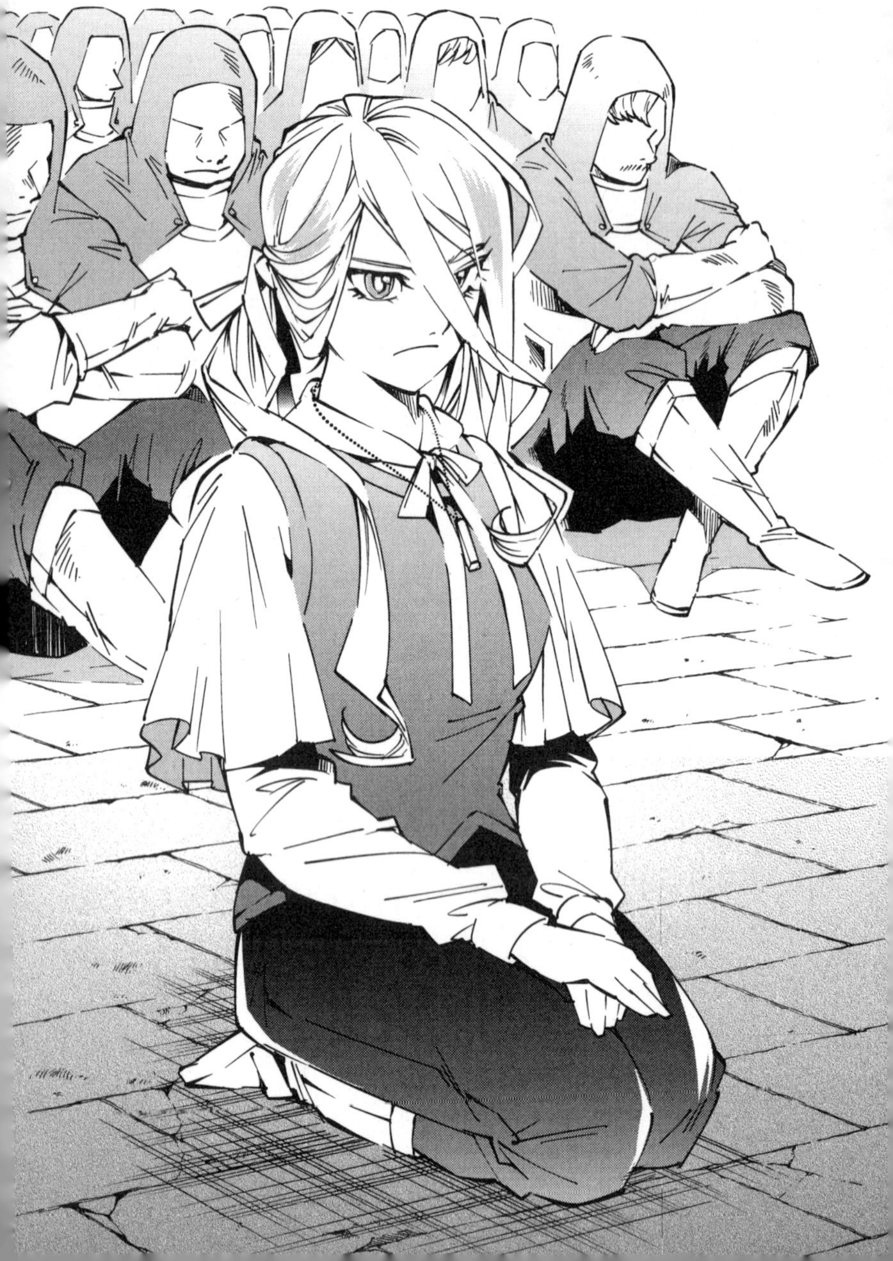

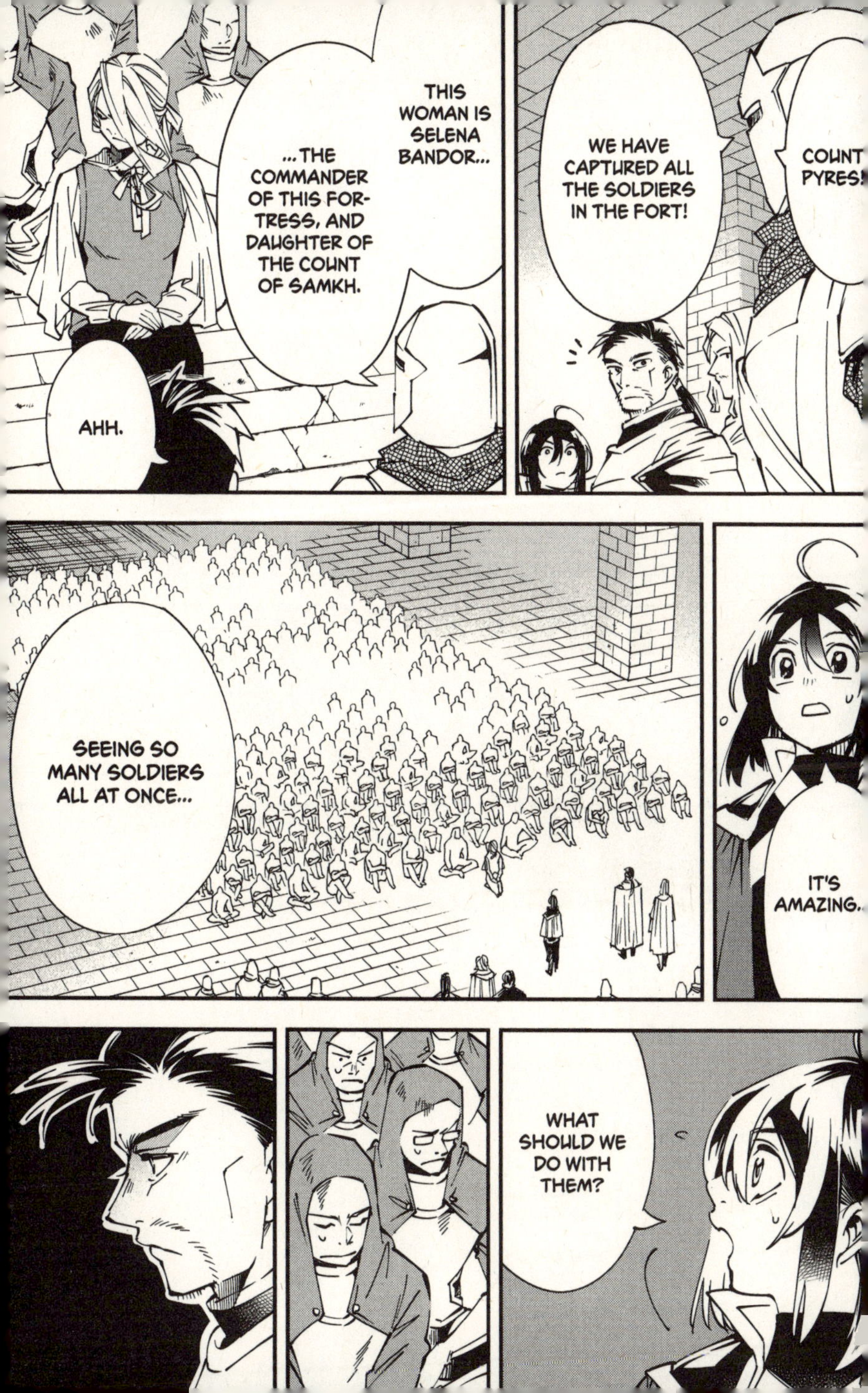
COUNT PYRES!
WE HAVE CAPTURED ALL THE SOLDIERS IN THE FORT!
THIS WOMAN IS SELENA BANDOR...
...THE COMMANDER OF THIS FOR-TRESS, AND DAUGHTER OF THE COUNT OF SAMKH.
AHH.
IT'S AMAZING..
SEEING SO MANY SOLDIERS ALL AT ONCE...
WHAT SHOULD WE DO WITH THEM?

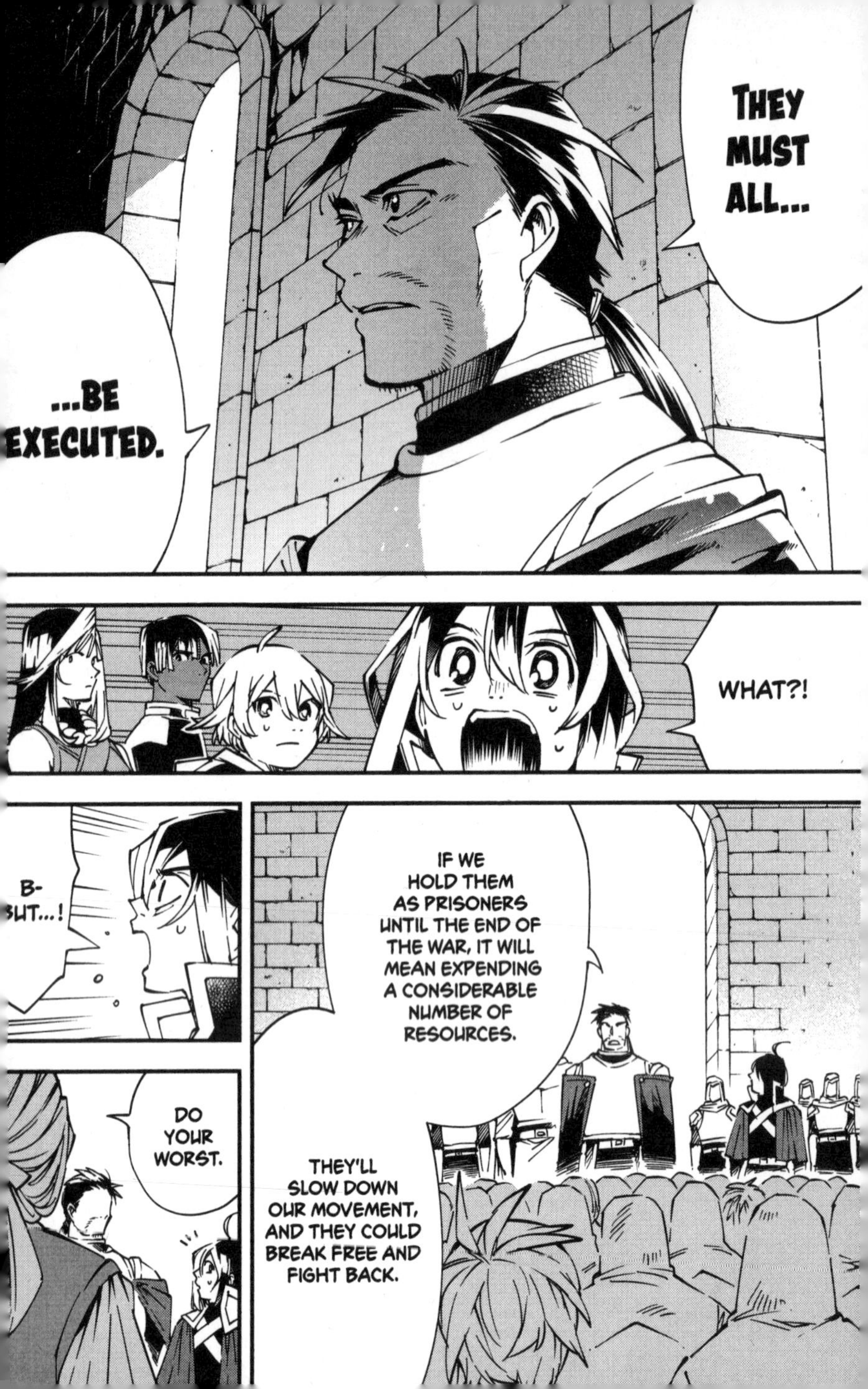
THEY MUST ALL...
...BE EXECUTED.
WHAT?!
IF WE HOLD THEM AS PRISONERS UNTIL THE END OF THE WAR, IT WILL MEAN EXPENDING A CONSIDERABLE NUMBER OF RESOURCES.
THEY'LL SLOW DOWN OUR MOVEMENT, AND THEY COULD BREAK FREE AND FIGHT BACK.
B-BUT...!
DO YOUR WORST.

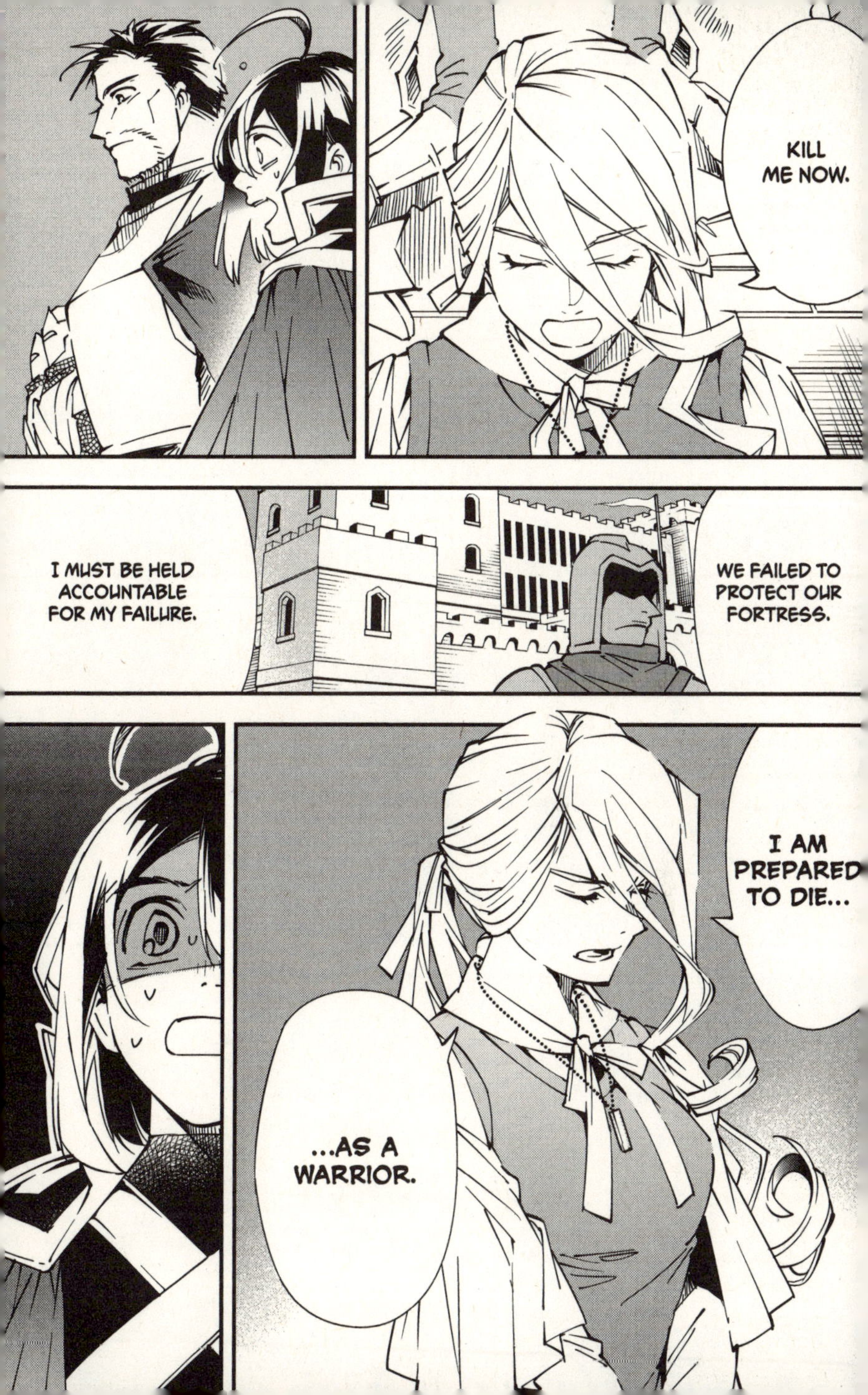
KILL ME NOW.
WE FAILED TO PROTECT OUR FORTRESS.
I MUST BE HELD ACCOUNTABLE FOR MY FAILURE.
I AM PREPARED TO DIE...
...AS A WARRIOR.

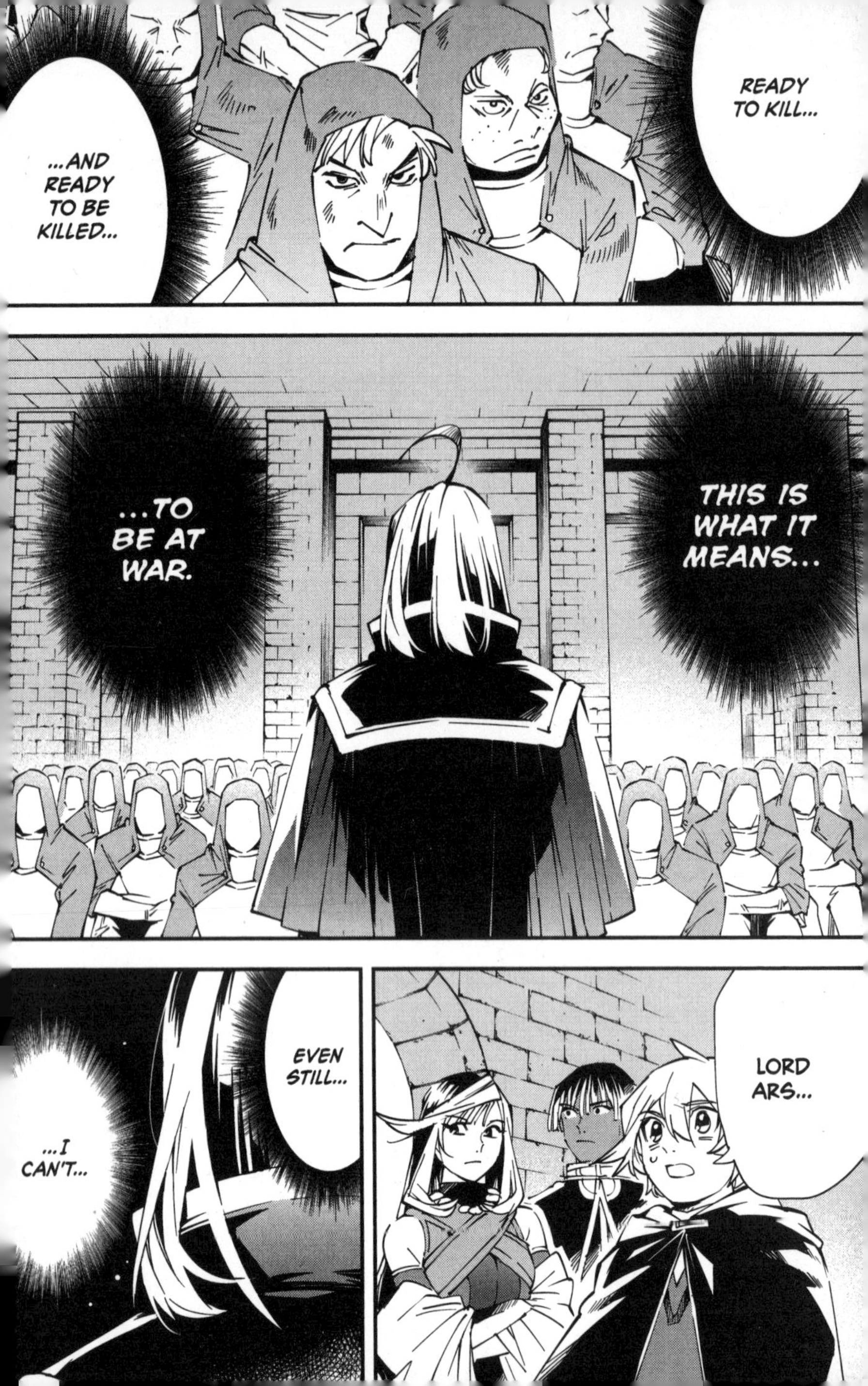
READY TO KILL...
...AND READY TO BE KILLED...
THIS IS WHAT IT MEANS...
...TO BE AT WAR.
LORD ARS...
EVEN STILL...
...I CAN'T...

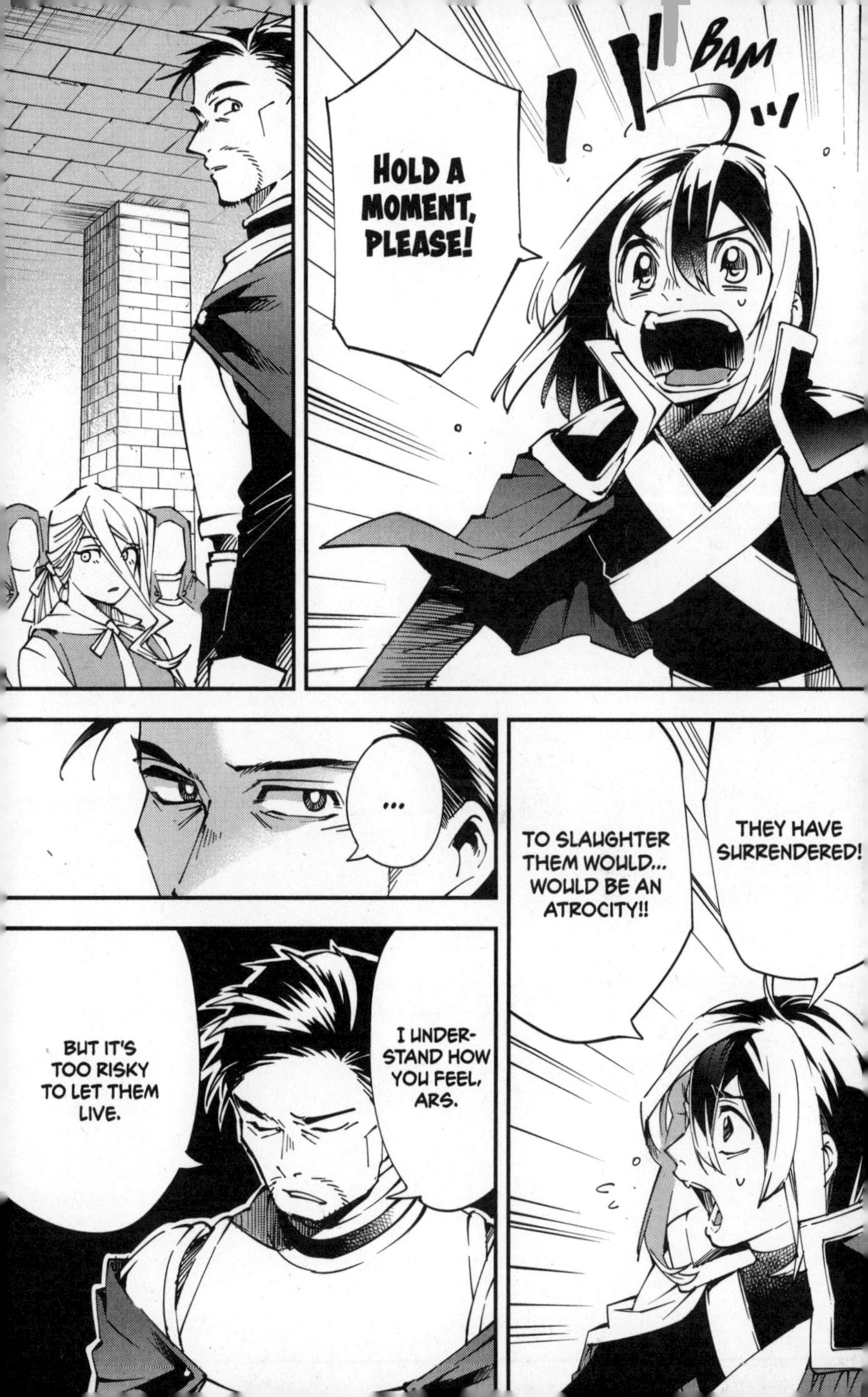
BAM
HOLD A MOMENT, PLEASE!
THEY HAVE SURRENDERED!
TO SLAUGHTER THEM WOULD... WOULD BE AN ATROCITY!!
...
I UNDER-STAND HOW YOU FEEL, ARS.
BUT IT'S TOO RISKY TO LET THEM LIVE.

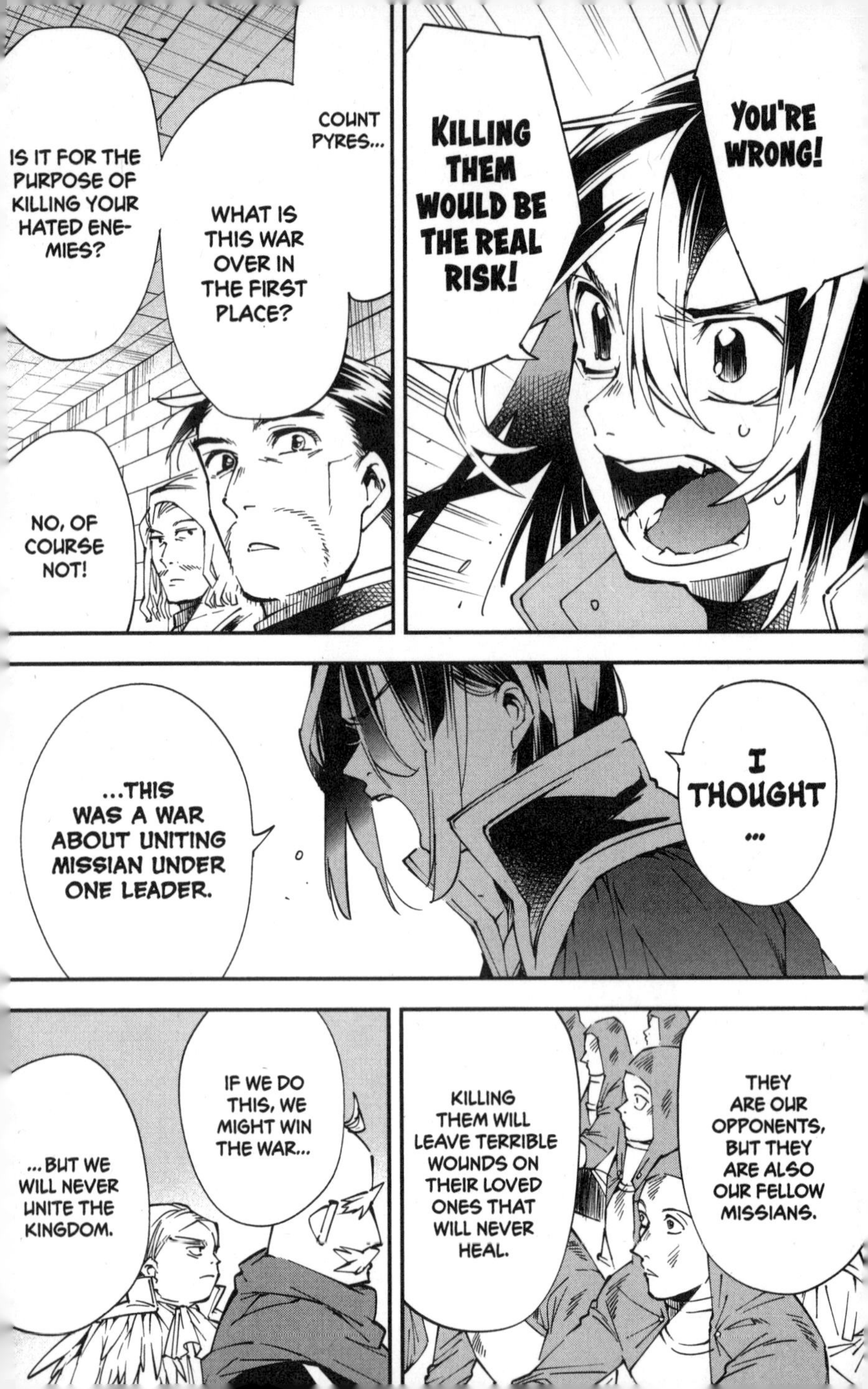
YOU'RE WRONG!
KILLING THEM WOULD BE THE REAL RISK!
COUNT PYRES...
WHAT IS THIS WAR OVER IN THE FIRST PLACE?
IS IT FOR THE PURPOSE OF KILLING YOUR HATED ENEMIES?
NO, OF COURSE NOT!
I THOUGHT...
...THIS WAS A WAR ABOUT UNITING MISSIAN UNDER ONE LEADER.
THEY ARE OUR OPPONENTS, BUT THEY ARE ALSO OUR FELLOW MISSIANS.
KILLING THEM WILL LEAVE TERRIBLE WOUNDS ON THEIR LOVED ONES THAT WILL NEVER HEAL.
IF WE DO THIS, WE MIGHT WIN THE WAR...
...BUT WE WILL NEVER UNITE THE KINGDOM.

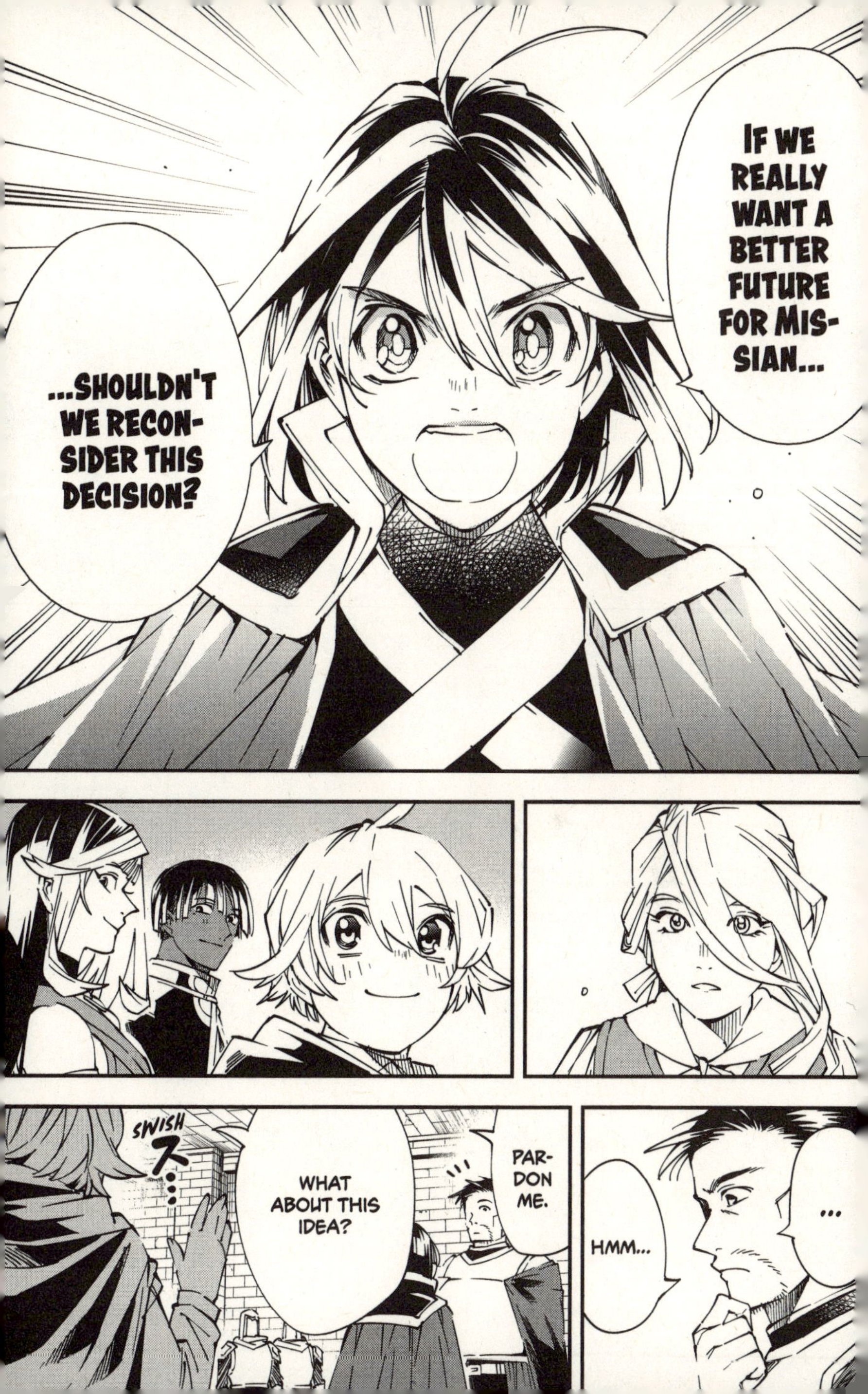
IF WE REALLY WANT A BETTER FUTURE FOR MIS-SIAN...
...SHOULDN'T WE RECON-SIDER THIS DECISION?
...
HMM...
PAR-DON ME.
WHAT ABOUT THIS IDEA?
SWISH
ス

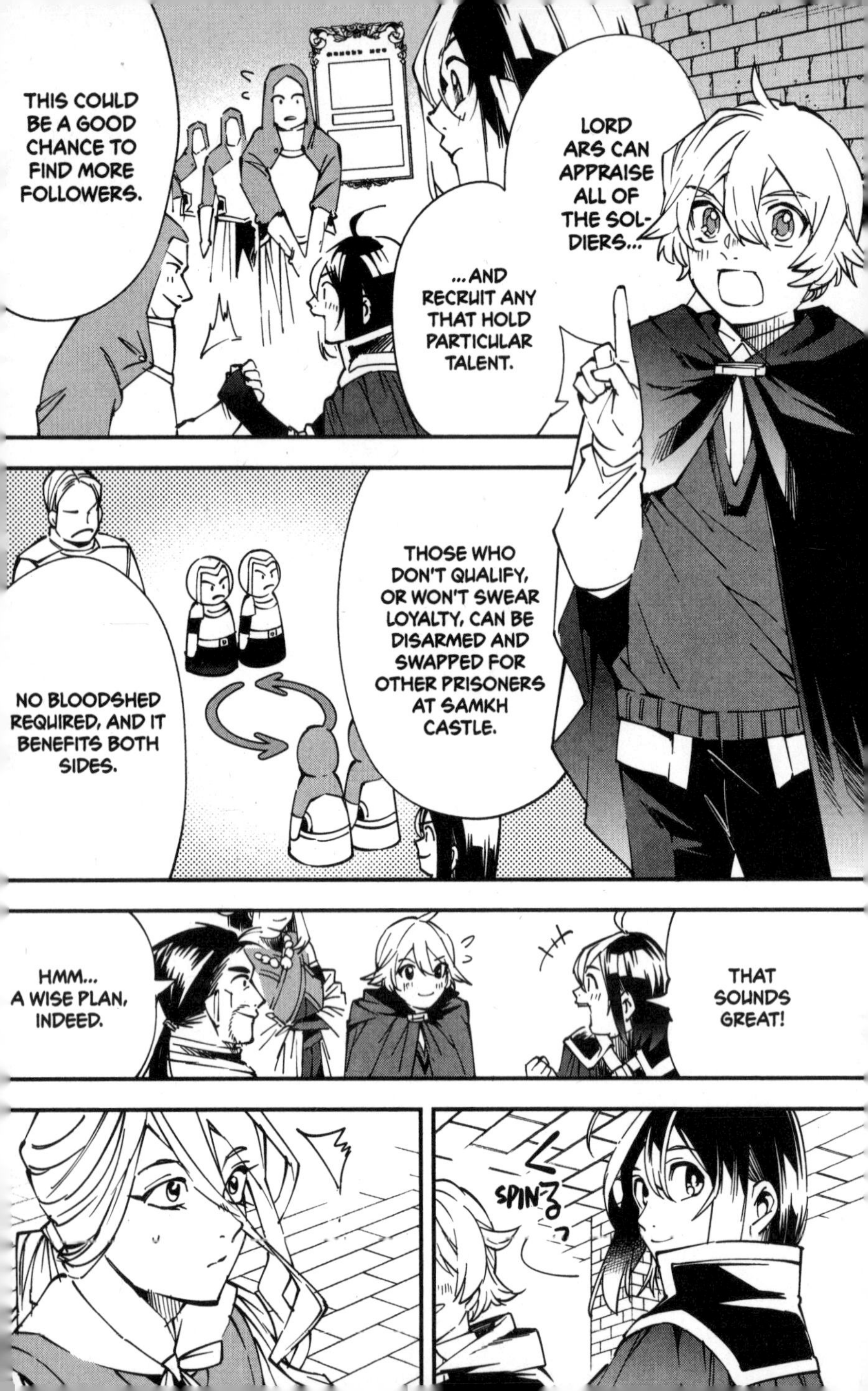
LORD ARS CAN APPRAISE ALL OF THE SOL-DIERS...
...AND RECRUIT ANY THAT HOLD PARTICULAR TALENT.
THIS COULD BE A GOOD CHANCE TO FIND MORE FOLLOWERS.
THOSE WHO DON'T QUALIFY, OR WON'T SWEAR LOYALTY, CAN BE DISARMED AND SWAPPED FOR OTHER PRISONERS AT SAMKH CASTLE.
NO BLOODSHED REQUIRED, AND IT BENEFITS BOTH SIDES.
THAT SOUNDS GREAT!
HMM... A WISE PLAN, INDEED.
SPIN

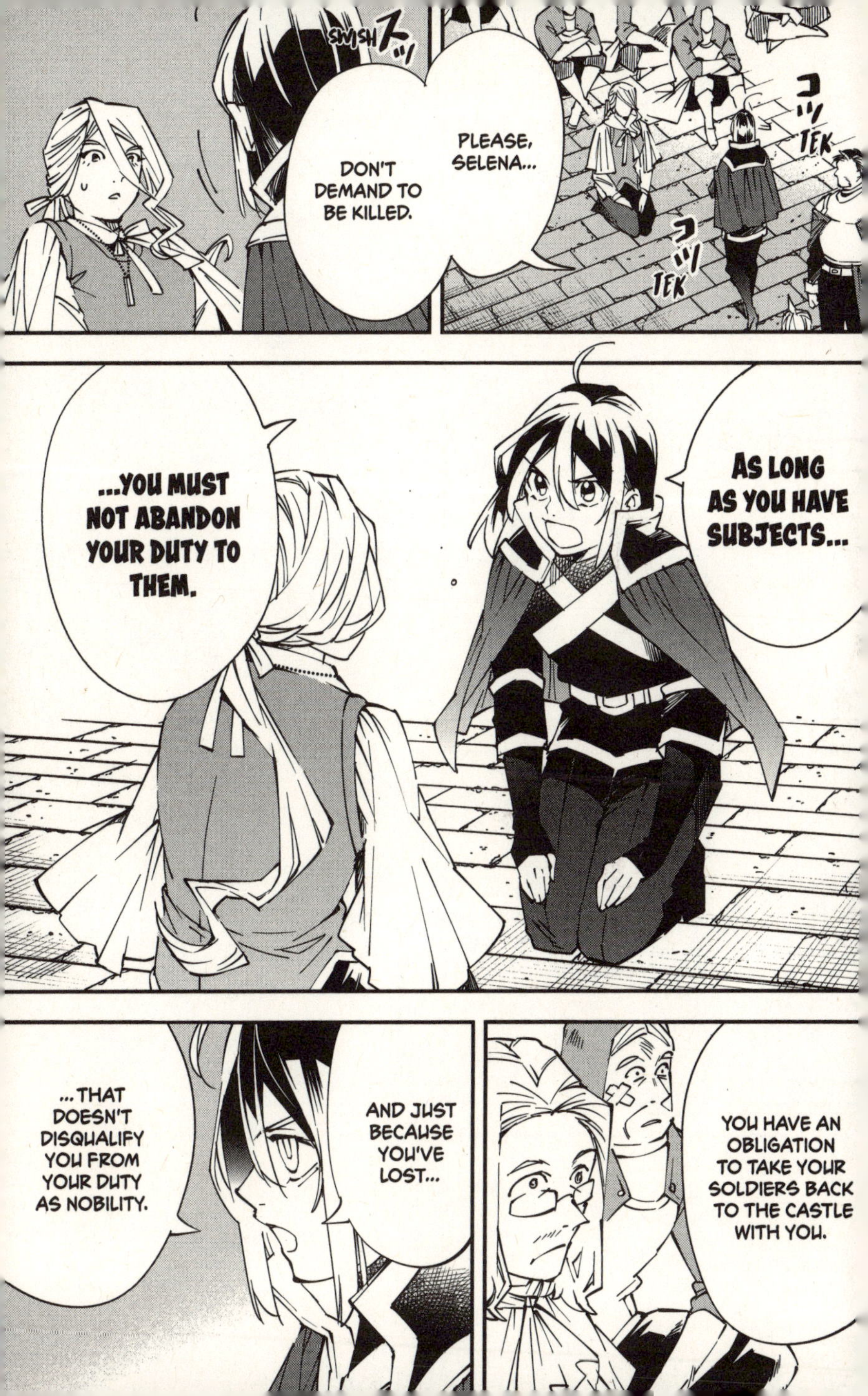
コッ TEK
コッ TEK
SWISH スッ
PLEASE, SELENA...
DON'T DEMAND TO BE KILLED.
AS LONG AS YOU HAVE SUBJECTS...
...YOU MUST NOT ABANDON YOUR DUTY TO THEM.
YOU HAVE AN OBLIGATION TO TAKE YOUR SOLDIERS BACK TO THE CASTLE WITH YOU.
AND JUST BECAUSE YOU'VE LOST...
...THAT DOESN'T DISQUALIFY YOU FROM YOUR DUTY AS NOBILITY.

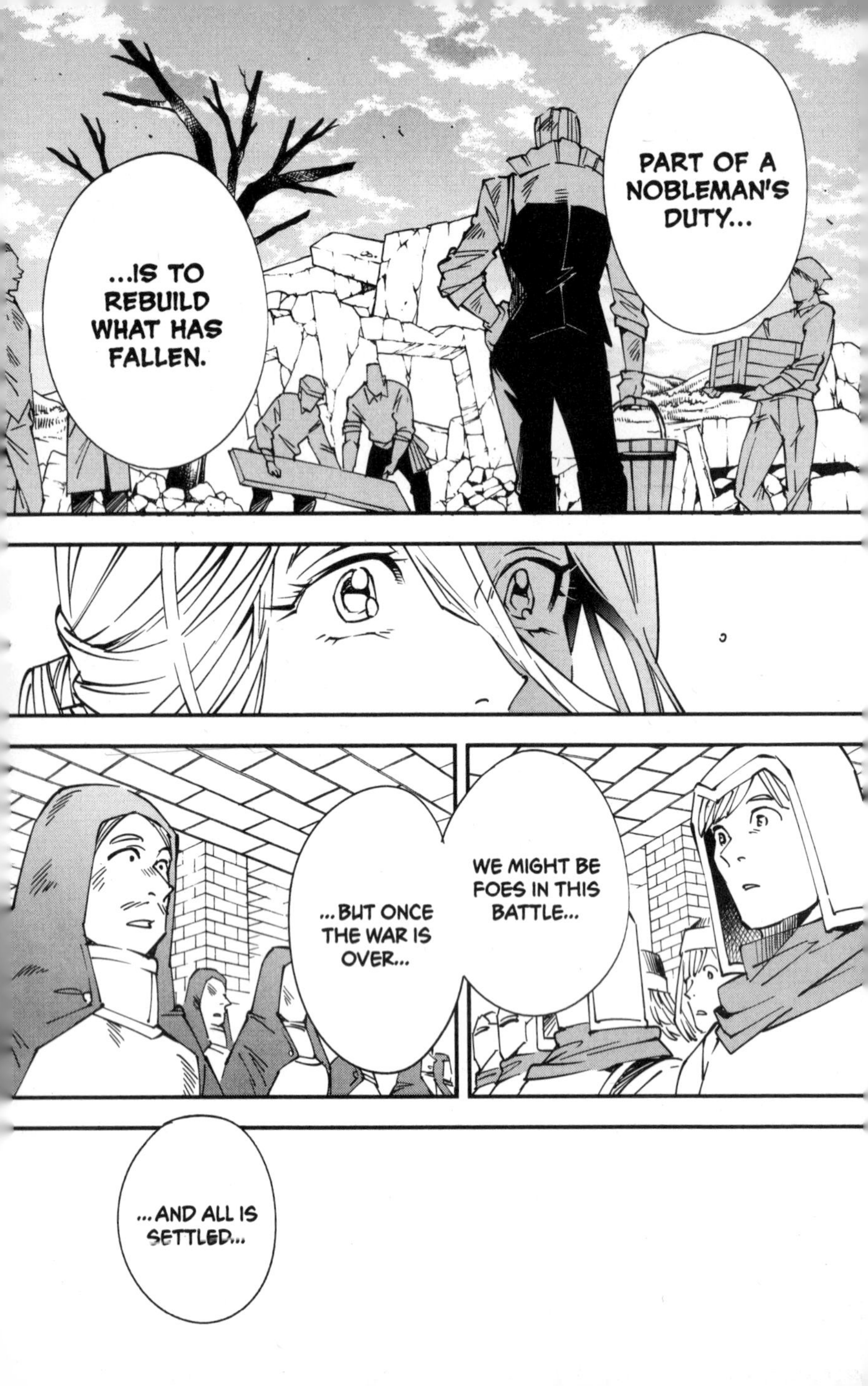
PART OF A NOBLEMAN'S DUTY...
...IS TO REBUILD WHAT HAS FALLEN.
WE MIGHT BE FOES IN THIS BATTLE...
...BUT ONCE THE WAR IS OVER...
...AND ALL IS SETTLED...

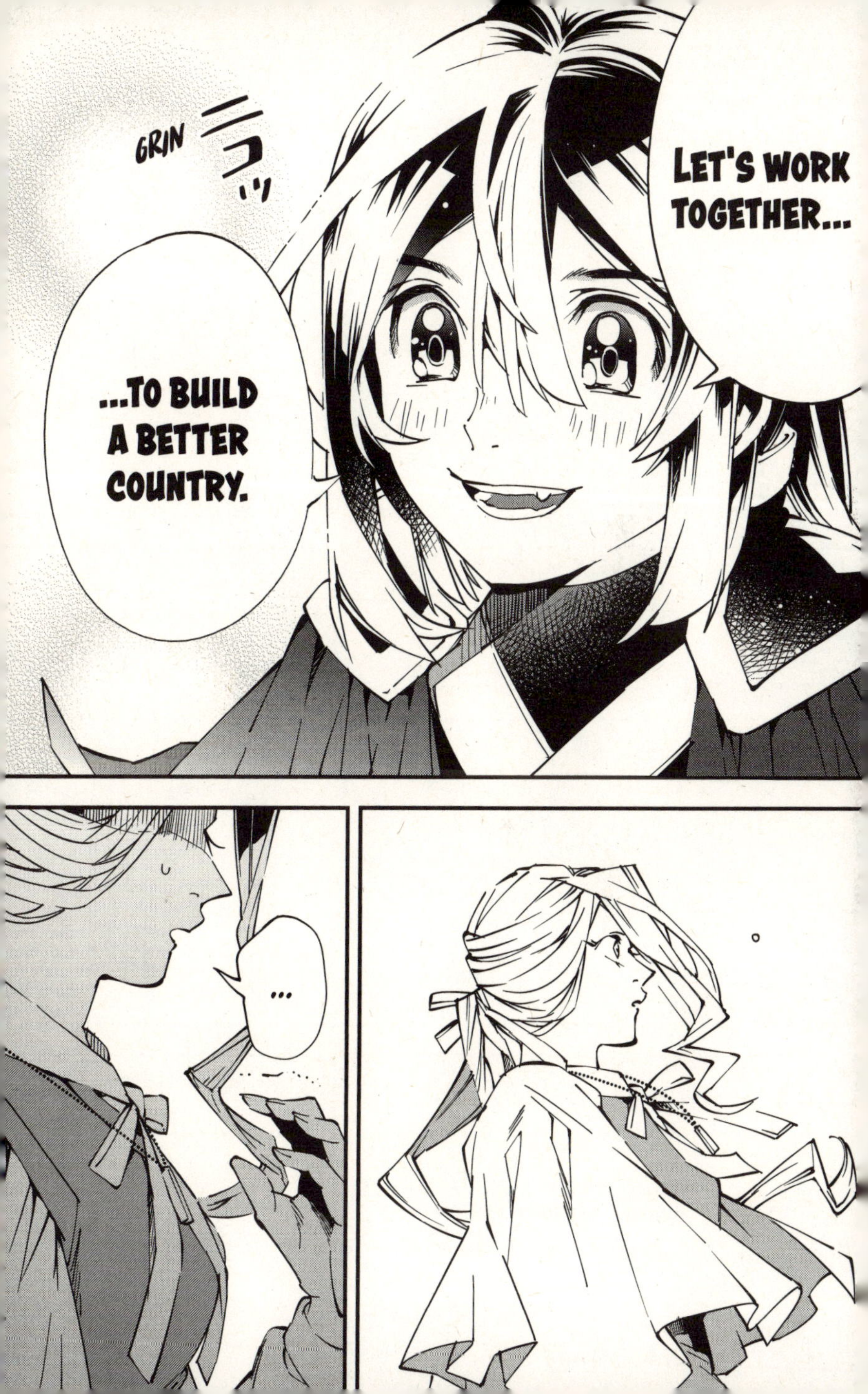
LET'S WORK TOGETHER...
GRIN
...TO BUILD A BETTER COUNTRY.
...

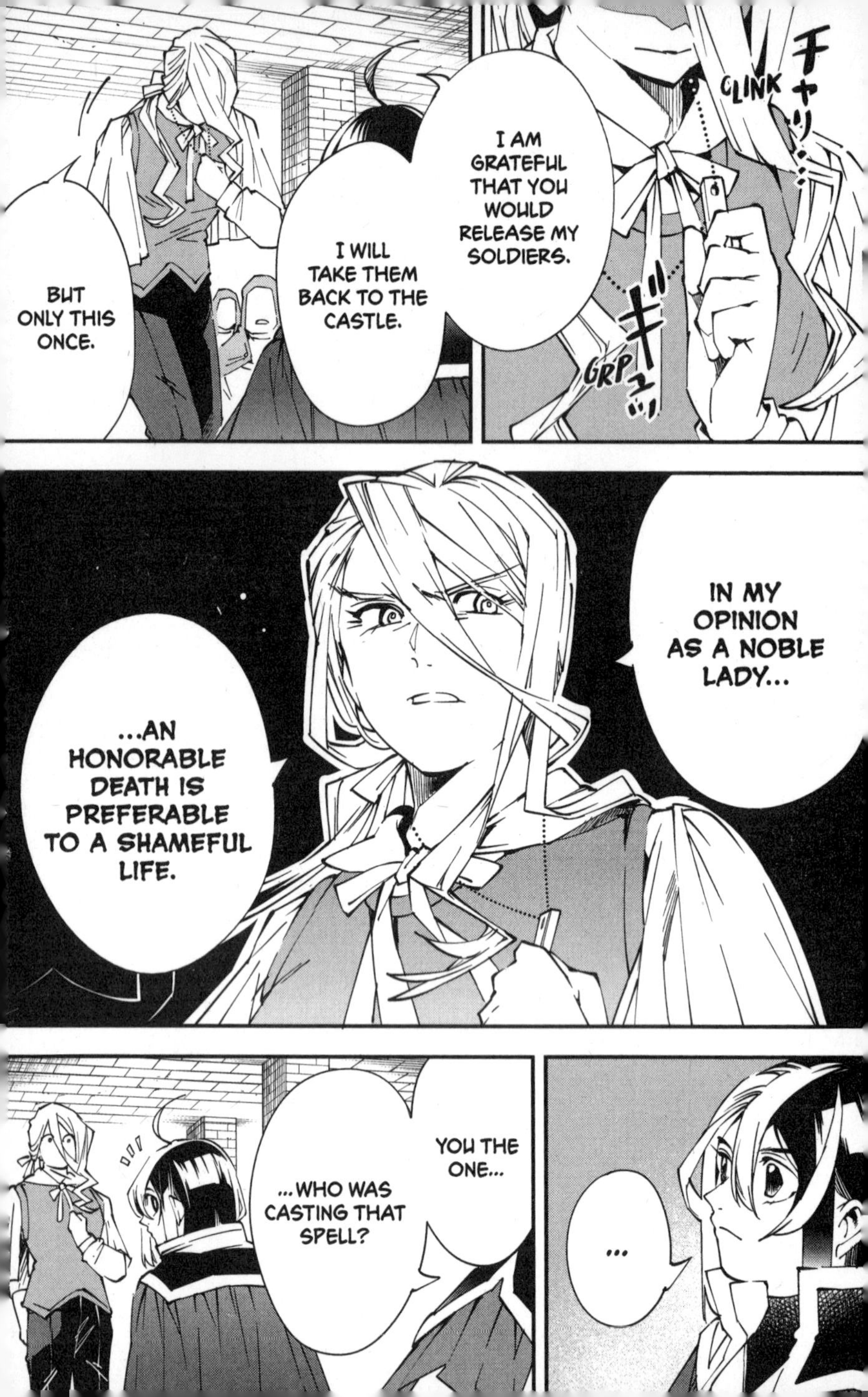
CLINK
チャリ…
GRP
ギュッ
I AM GRATEFUL THAT YOU WOULD RELEASE MY SOLDIERS.
I WILL TAKE THEM BACK TO THE CASTLE.
BUT ONLY THIS ONCE.
IN MY OPINION AS A NOBLE LADY...
...AN HONORABLE DEATH IS PREFERABLE TO A SHAMEFUL LIFE.
...
YOU THE ONE...
...WHO WAS CASTING THAT SPELL?

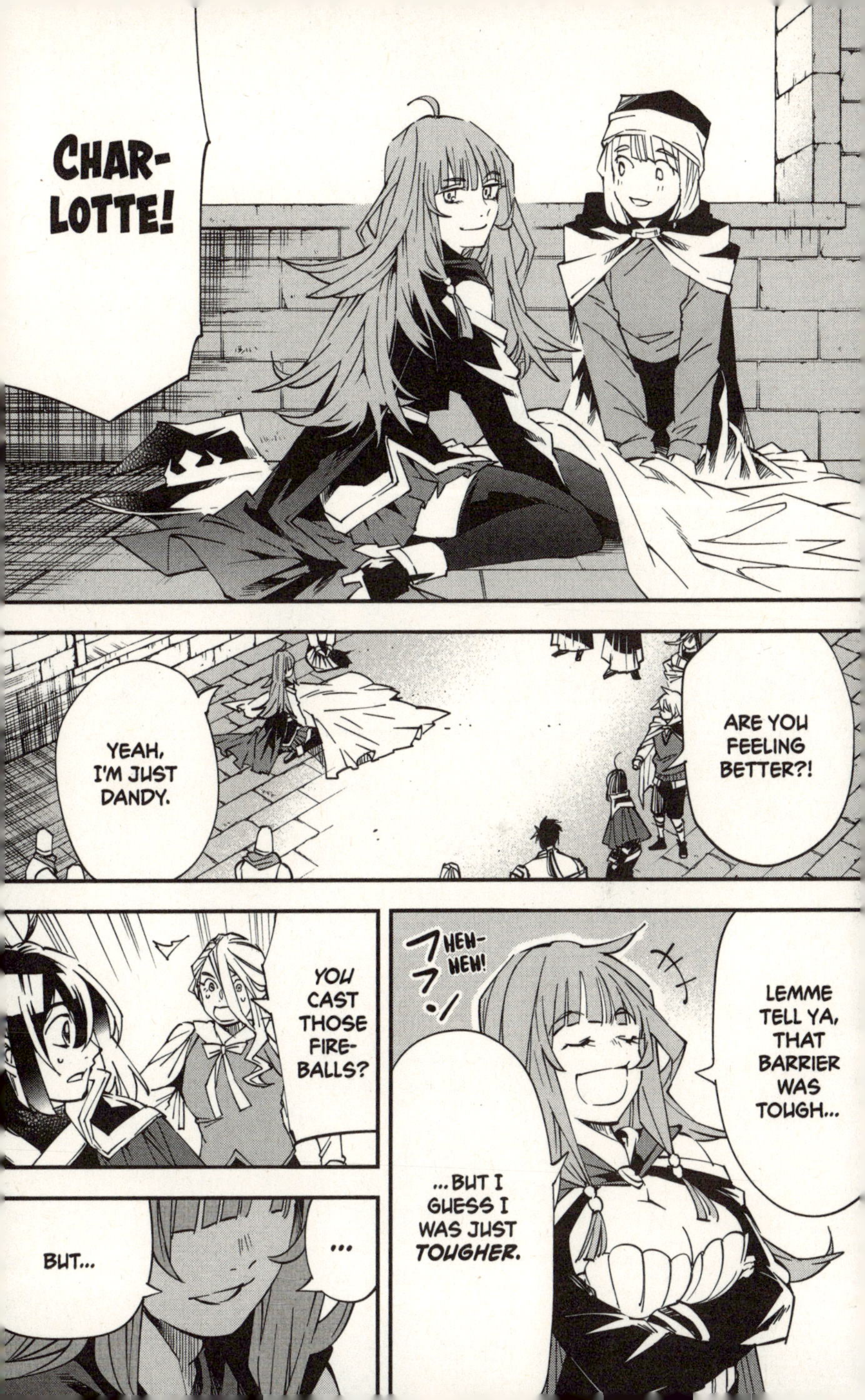
CHAR-LOTTE!
ARE YOU FEELING BETTER?!
YEAH, I'M JUST DANDY.
LEMME TELL YA, THAT BARRIER WAS TOUGH...
HEH-HEH!
...BUT I GUESS I WAS JUST TOUGHER.
YOU CAST THOSE FIRE-BALLS?
...
BUT...

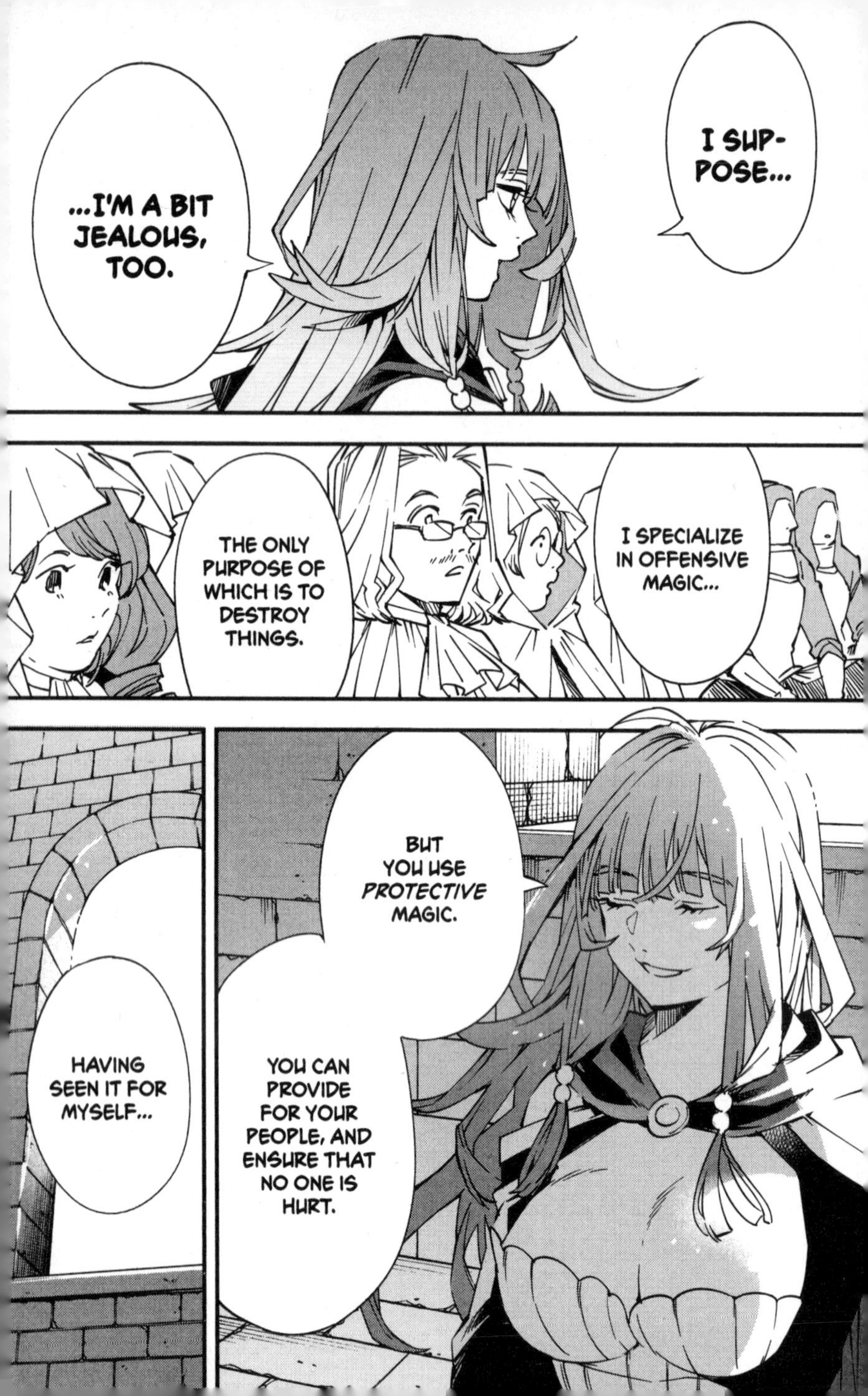
I SUP-POSE...
...I'M A BIT JEALOUS, TOO.
I SPECIALIZE IN OFFENSIVE MAGIC...
THE ONLY PURPOSE OF WHICH IS TO DESTROY THINGS.
BUT YOU USE *PROTECTIVE* MAGIC.
YOU CAN PROVIDE FOR YOUR PEOPLE, AND ENSURE THAT NO ONE IS HURT.
HAVING SEEN IT FOR MYSELF...

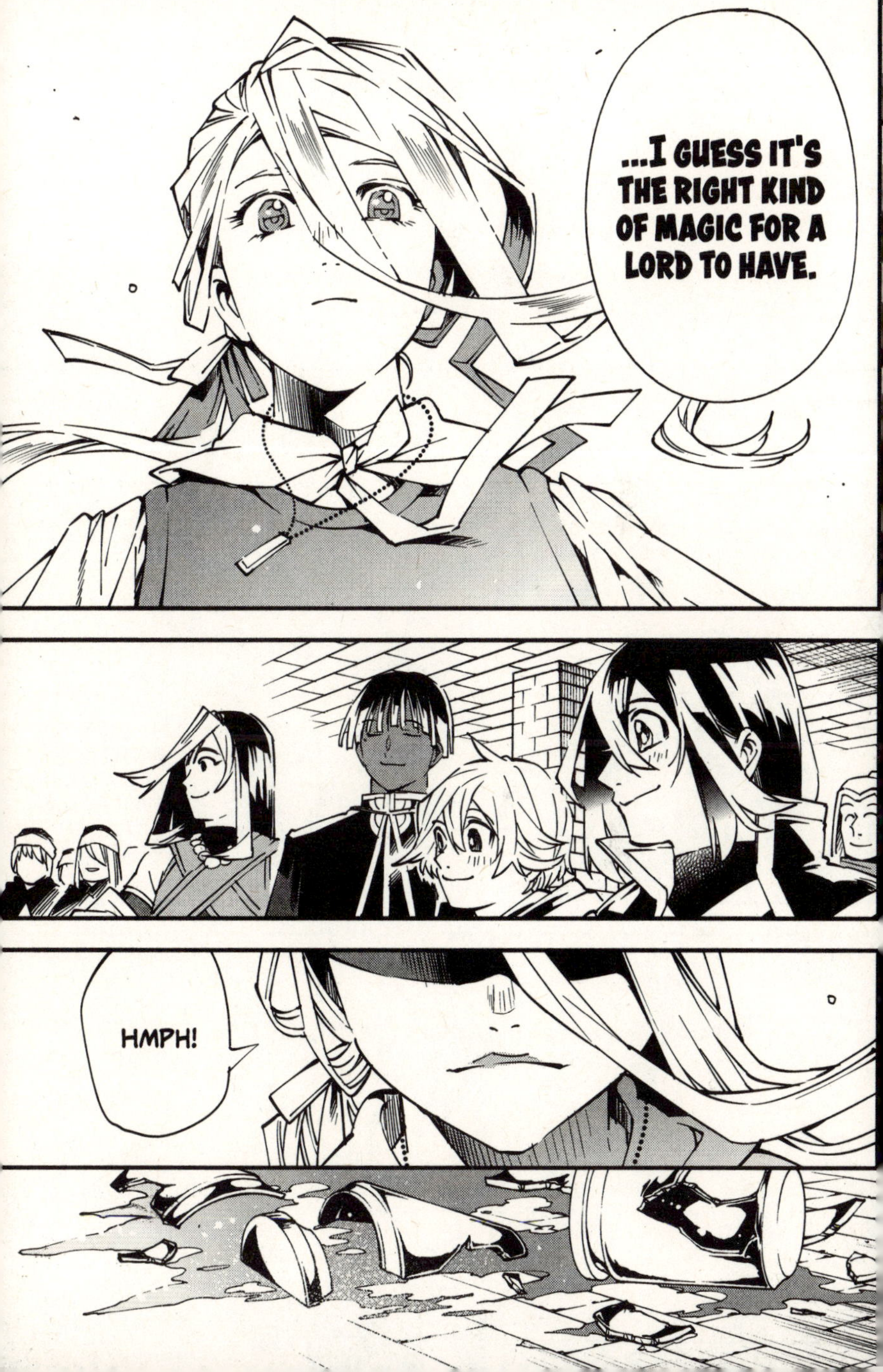
...I GUESS IT'S THE RIGHT KIND OF MAGIC FOR A LORD TO HAVE.
HMPH!

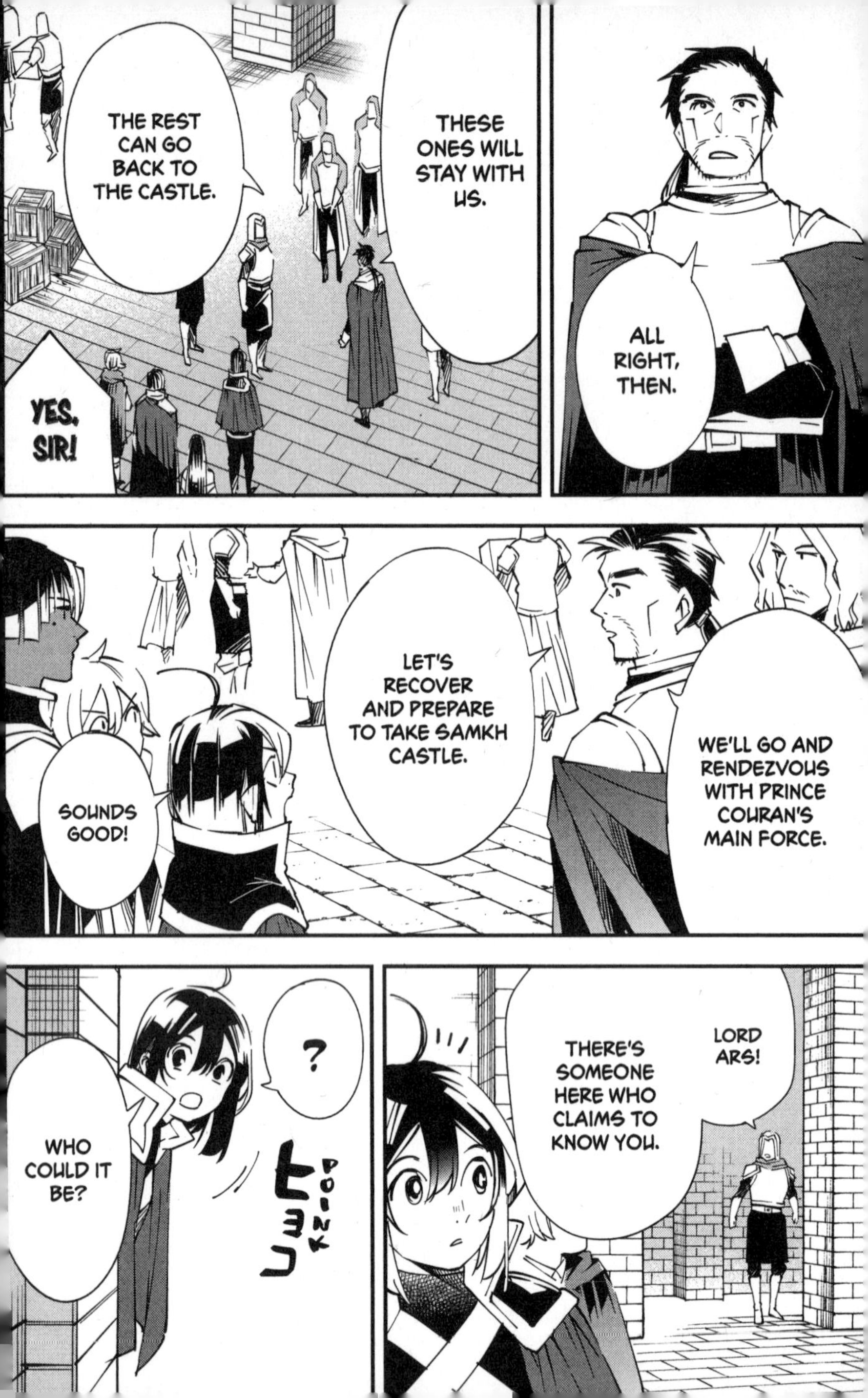
ALL RIGHT, THEN.
THESE ONES WILL STAY WITH US.
THE REST CAN GO BACK TO THE CASTLE.
YES, SIR!
WE'LL GO AND RENDEZVOUS WITH PRINCE COURAN'S MAIN FORCE.
LET'S RECOVER AND PREPARE TO TAKE SAMKH CASTLE.
SOUNDS GOOD!
LORD ARS!
THERE'S SOMEONE HERE WHO CLAIMS TO KNOW YOU.
?
ヒョコ
POINK
WHO COULD IT BE?

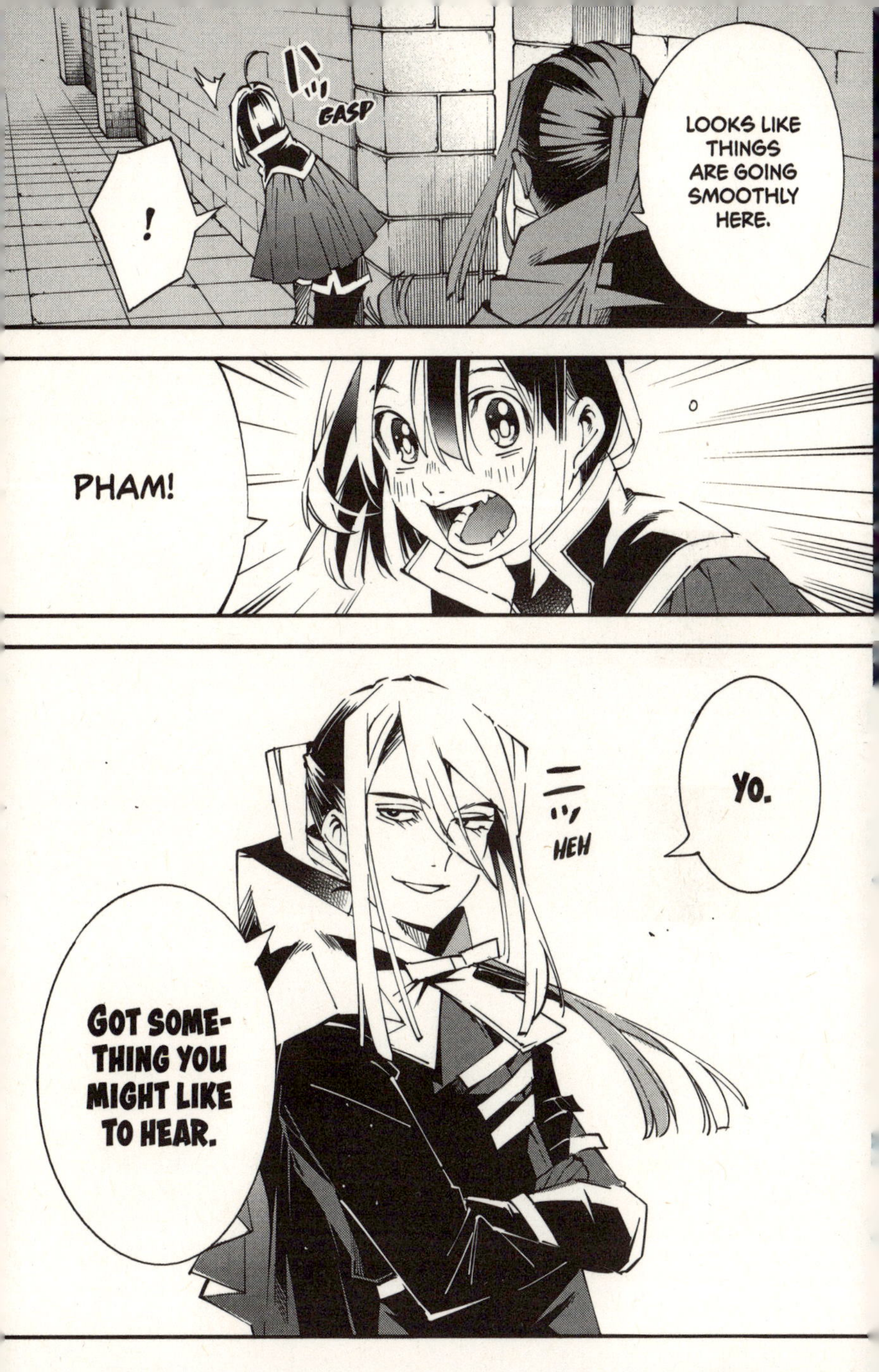
LOOKS LIKE THINGS ARE GOING SMOOTHLY HERE.
GASP
!
PHAM!
YO.
HEH
GOT SOME-THING YOU MIGHT LIKE TO HEAR.

As a Reincarnated
ARISTOCRAT,
I'll Use My Appraisal Skill to
Rise in the World

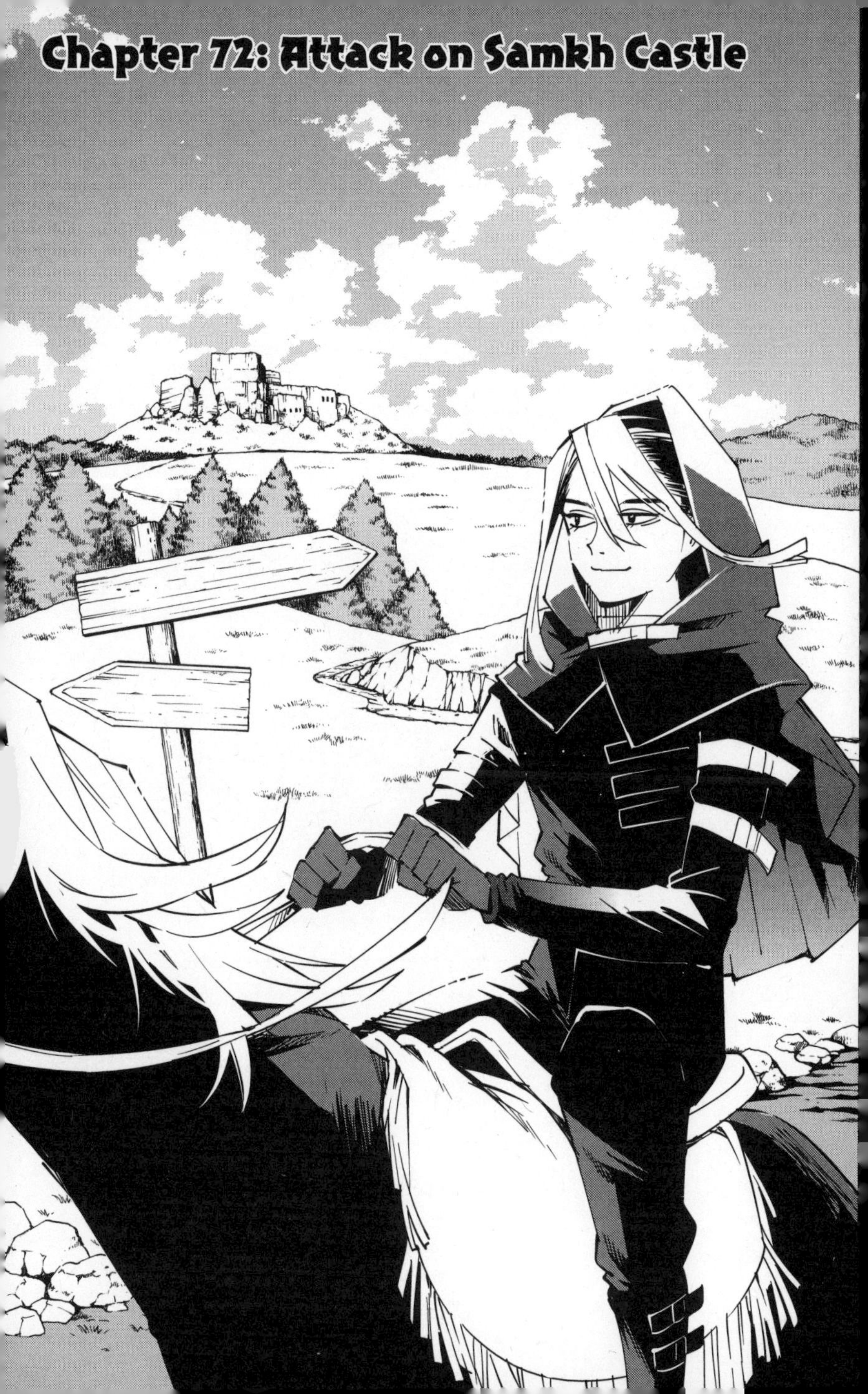
Chapter 72: Attack on Samkh Castle

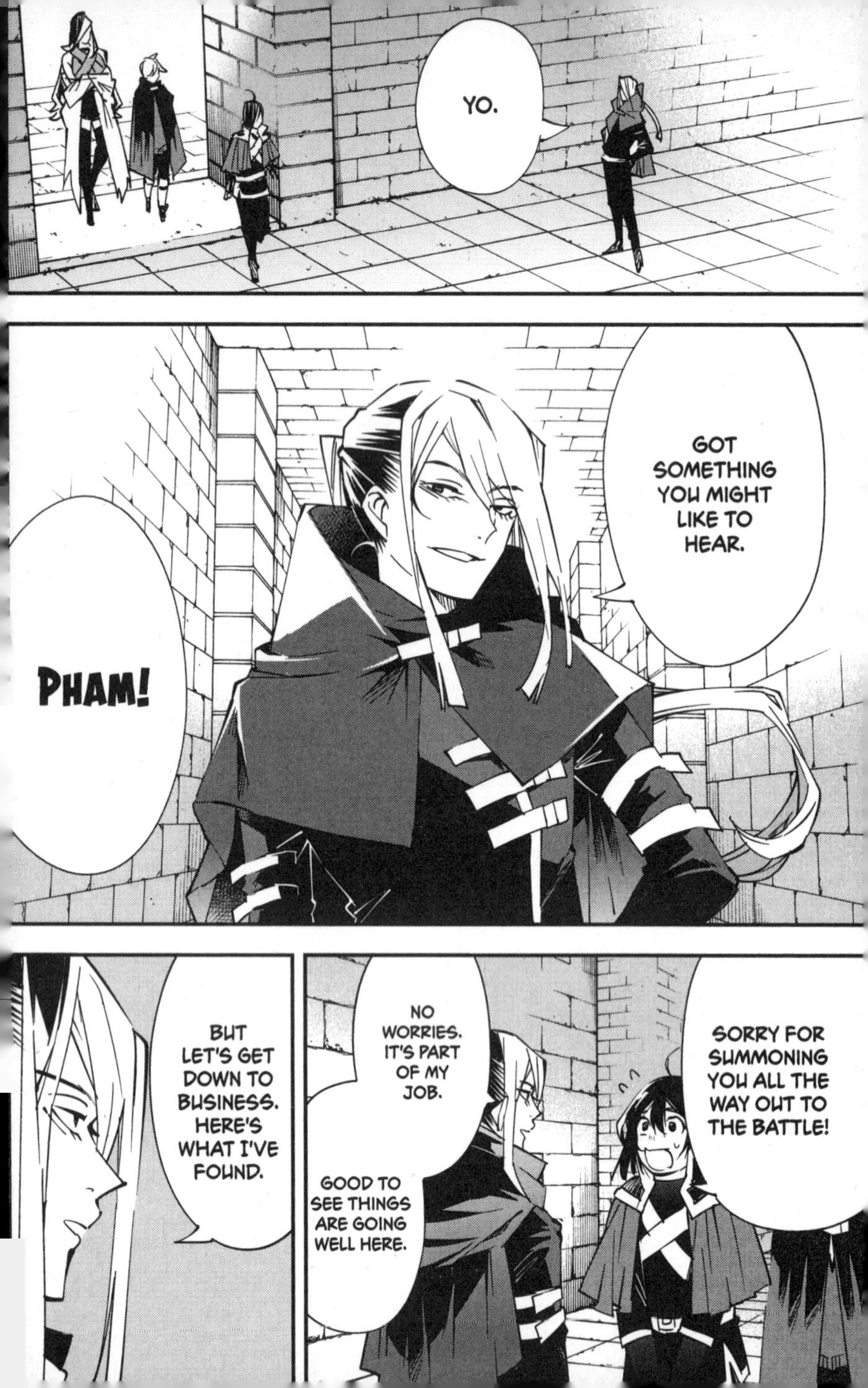
YO.
GOT SOMETHING YOU MIGHT LIKE TO HEAR.
PHAM!
SORRY FOR SUMMONING YOU ALL THE WAY OUT TO THE BATTLE!
NO WORRIES. IT'S PART OF MY JOB.
GOOD TO SEE THINGS ARE GOING WELL HERE.
BUT LET'S GET DOWN TO BUSINESS. HERE'S WHAT I'VE FOUND.

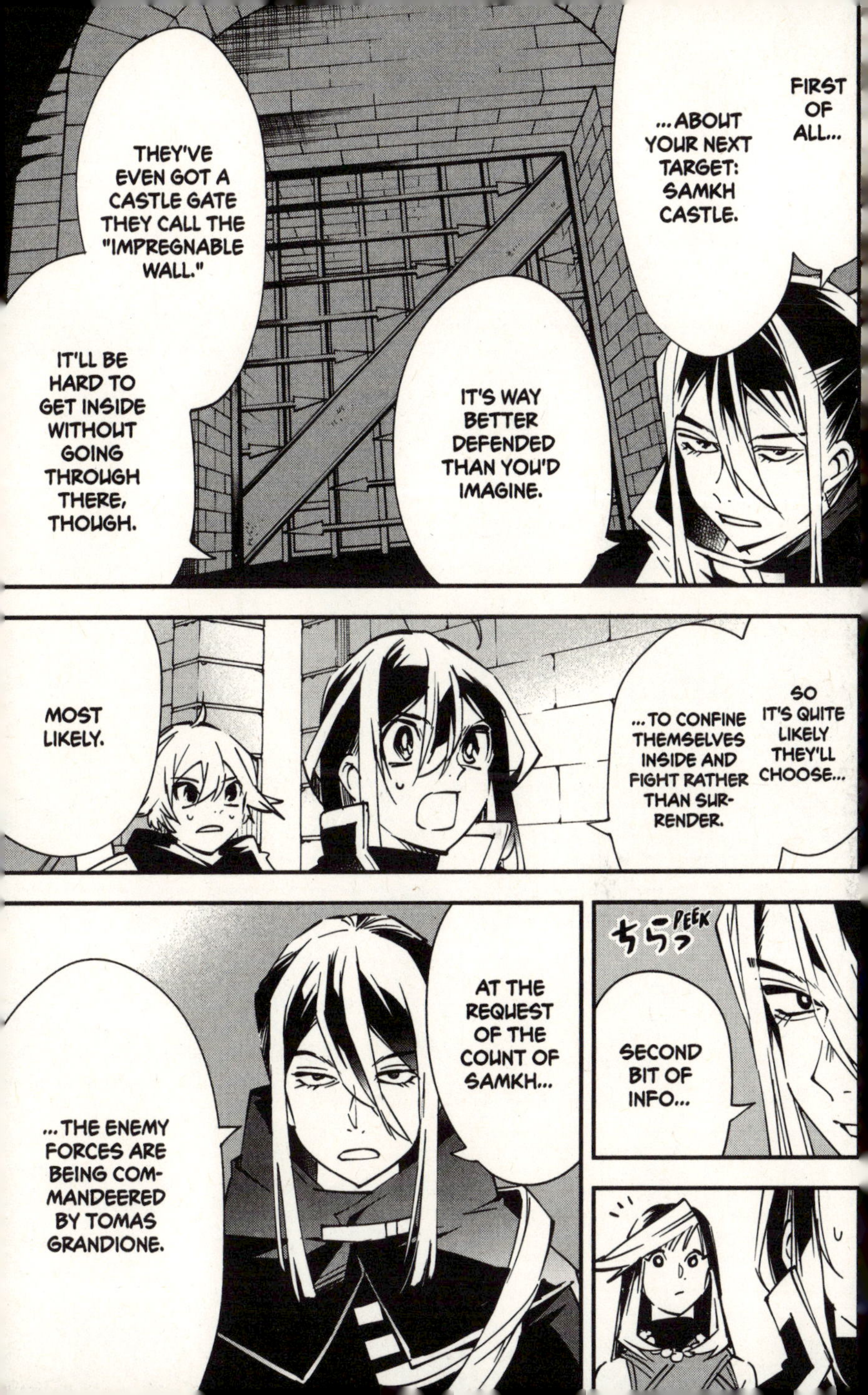
FIRST OF ALL...
...ABOUT YOUR NEXT TARGET: SAMKH CASTLE.
IT'S WAY BETTER DEFENDED THAN YOU'D IMAGINE.
THEY'VE EVEN GOT A CASTLE GATE THEY CALL THE "IMPREGNABLE WALL."
IT'LL BE HARD TO GET INSIDE WITHOUT GOING THROUGH THERE, THOUGH.
SO IT'S QUITE LIKELY THEY'LL CHOOSE...
...TO CONFINE THEMSELVES INSIDE AND FIGHT RATHER THAN SUR-RENDER.
MOST LIKELY.
ちらっ
PEEK
SECOND BIT OF INFO...
AT THE REQUEST OF THE COUNT OF SAMKH...
...THE ENEMY FORCES ARE BEING COM-MANDEERED BY TOMAS GRANDIONE.

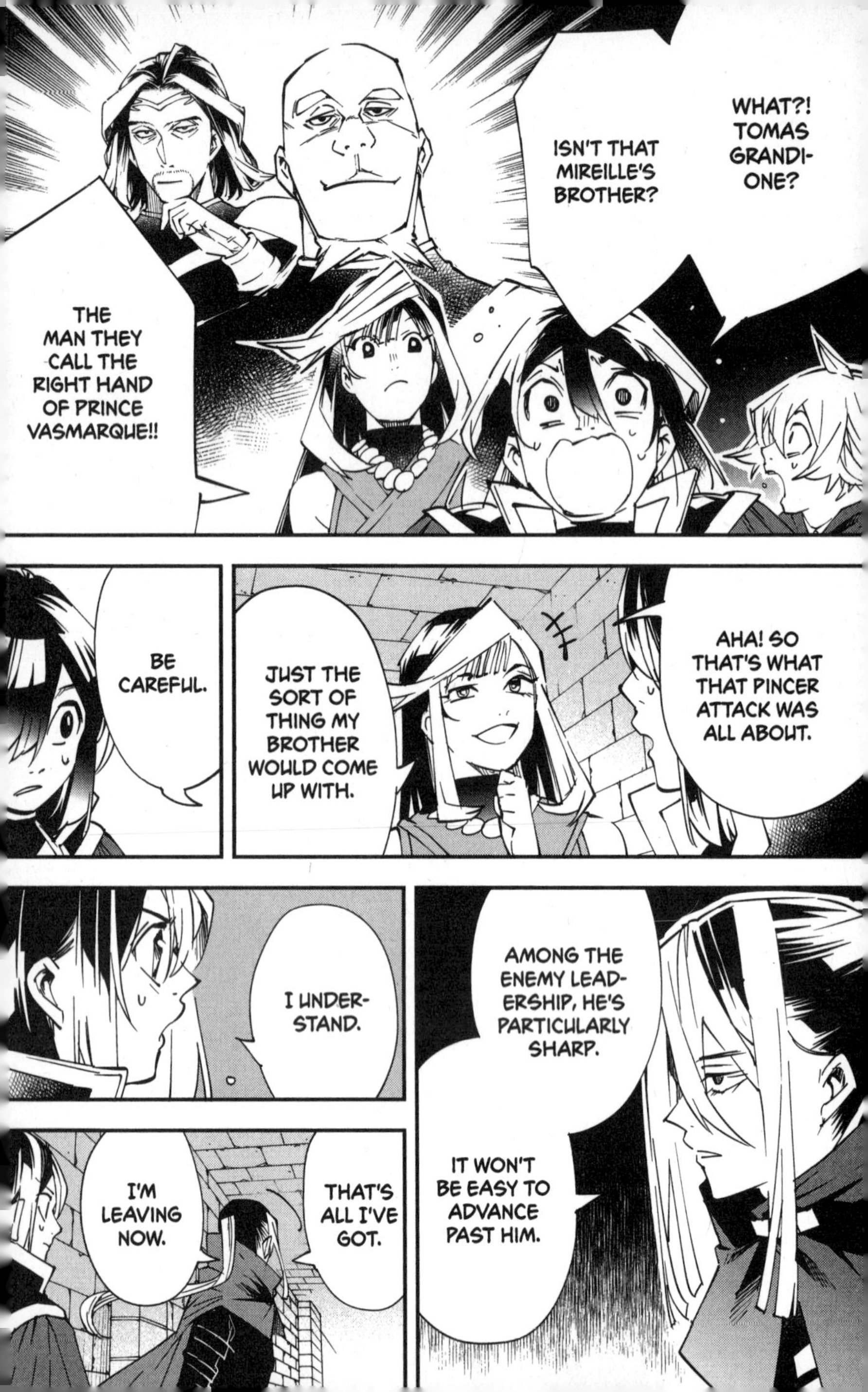
WHAT?! TOMAS GRANDIONE?
ISN'T THAT MIREILLE'S BROTHER?
THE MAN THEY CALL THE RIGHT HAND OF PRINCE VASMARQUE!!
AHA! SO THAT'S WHAT THAT PINCER ATTACK WAS ALL ABOUT.
JUST THE SORT OF THING MY BROTHER WOULD COME UP WITH.
BE CAREFUL.
AMONG THE ENEMY LEADERSHIP, HE'S PARTICULARLY SHARP.
IT WON'T BE EASY TO ADVANCE PAST HIM.
I UNDERSTAND.
THAT'S ALL I'VE GOT.
I'M LEAVING NOW.

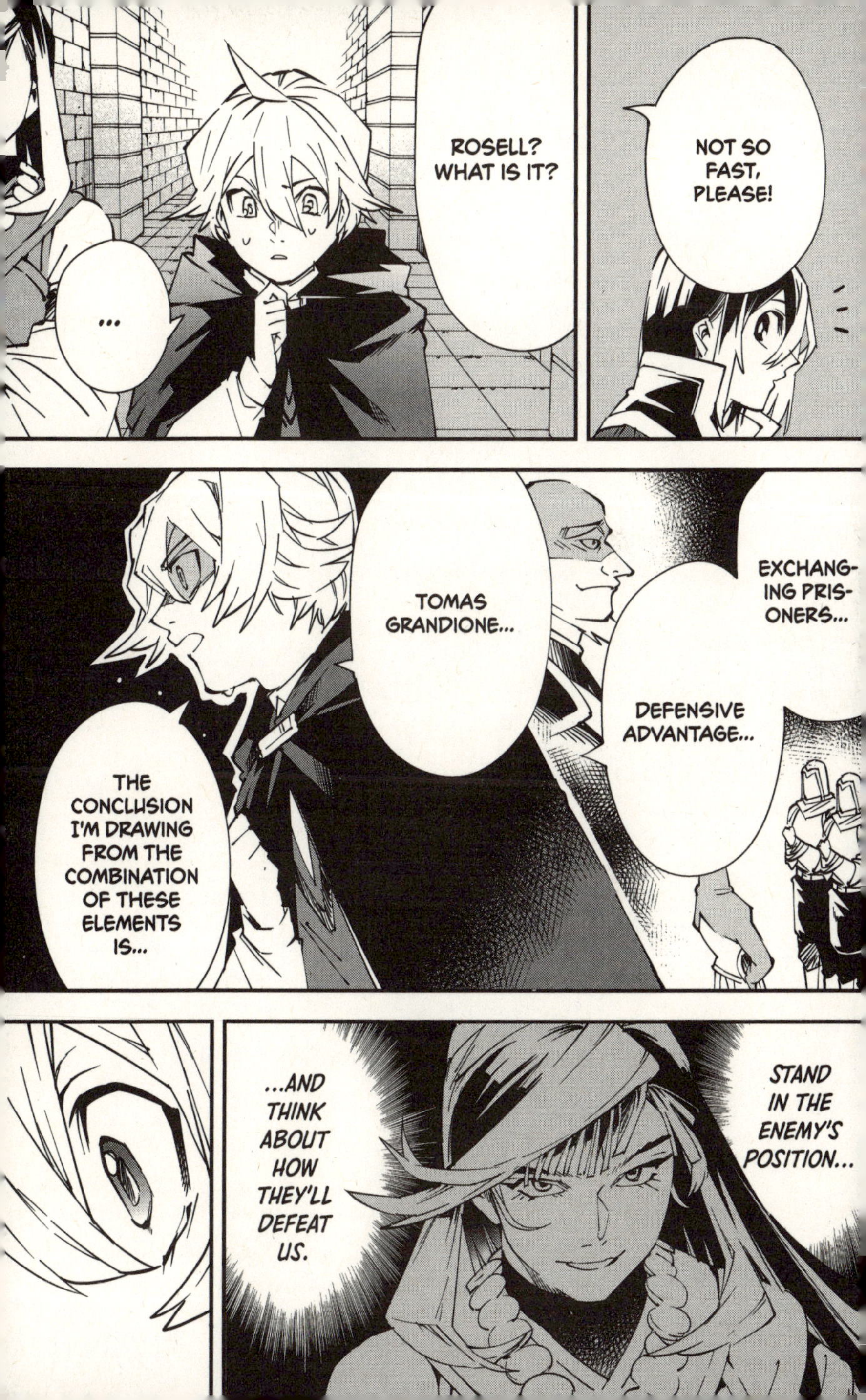
NOT SO FAST, PLEASE!
ROSELL? WHAT IS IT?
...
EXCHANGING PRISONERS...
TOMAS GRANDIONE...
DEFENSIVE ADVANTAGE...
THE CONCLUSION I'M DRAWING FROM THE COMBINATION OF THESE ELEMENTS IS...
STAND IN THE ENEMY'S POSITION...
...AND THINK ABOUT HOW THEY'LL DEFEAT US.

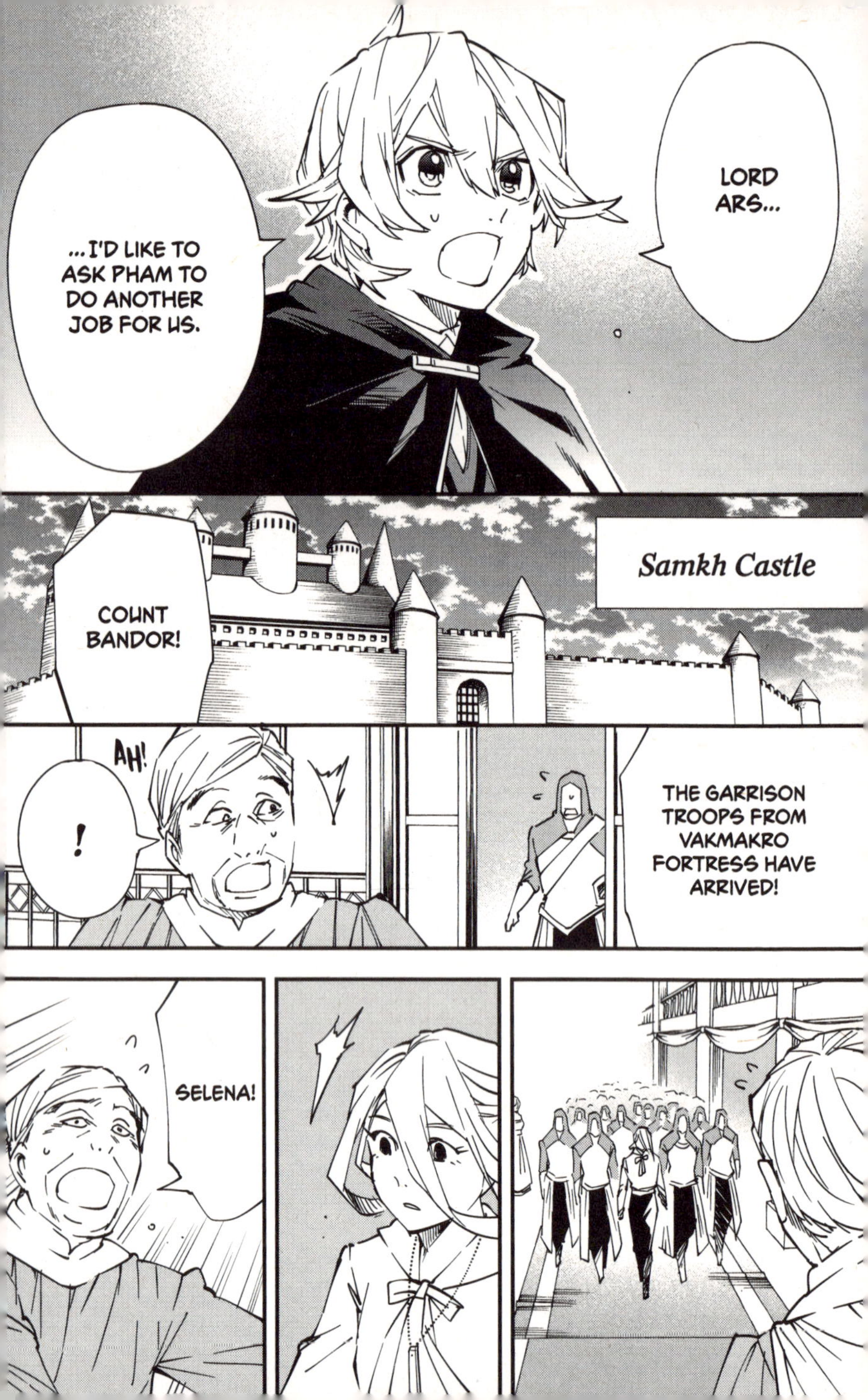
LORD ARS...
...I'D LIKE TO ASK PHAM TO DO ANOTHER JOB FOR US.
Samkh Castle
COUNT BANDOR!
THE GARRISON TROOPS FROM VAKMAKRO FORTRESS HAVE ARRIVED!
AH!
!
SELENA!

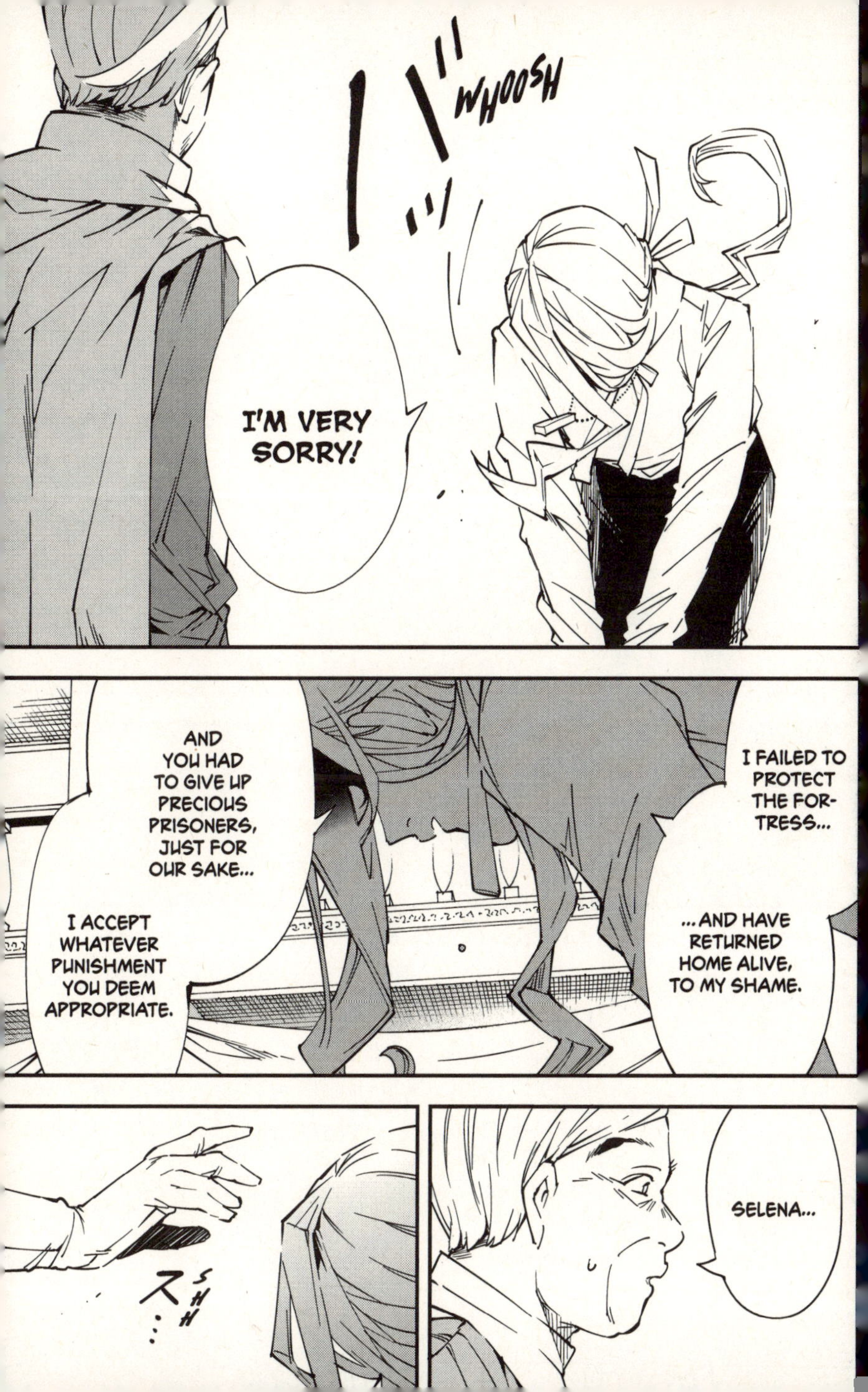
WHOOSH
I'M VERY SORRY!
I FAILED TO PROTECT THE FOR-TRESS...
...AND HAVE RETURNED HOME ALIVE, TO MY SHAME.
AND YOU HAD TO GIVE UP PRECIOUS PRISONERS, JUST FOR OUR SAKE...
I ACCEPT WHATEVER PUNISHMENT YOU DEEM APPROPRIATE.
SELENA...
SHH

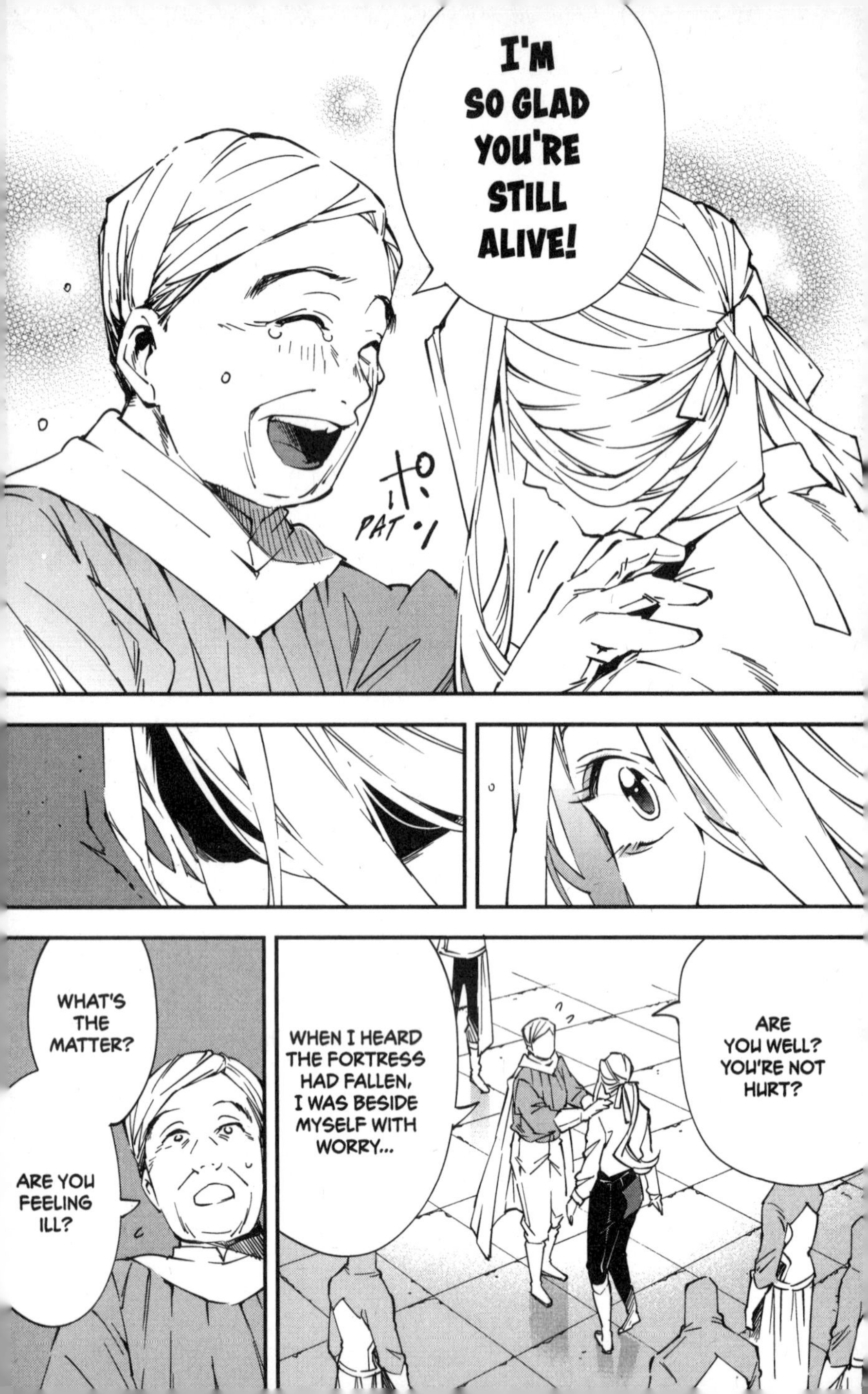
I'M SO GLAD YOU'RE STILL ALIVE!
PAT
ARE YOU WELL? YOU'RE NOT HURT?
WHEN I HEARD THE FORTRESS HAD FALLEN, I WAS BESIDE MYSELF WITH WORRY...
WHAT'S THE MATTER?
ARE YOU FEELING ILL?

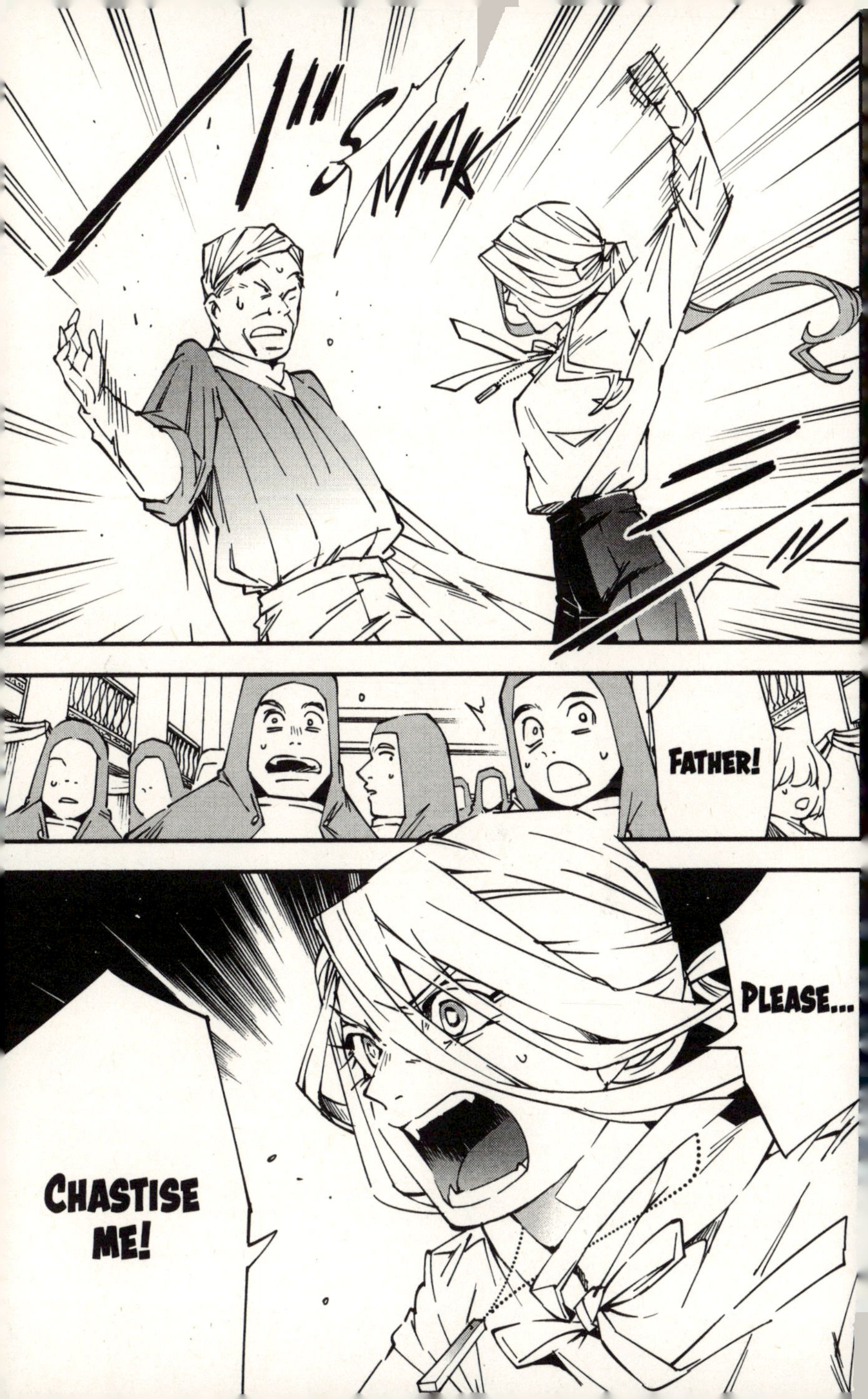
SMAK
FATHER!
PLEASE...
CHASTISE ME!

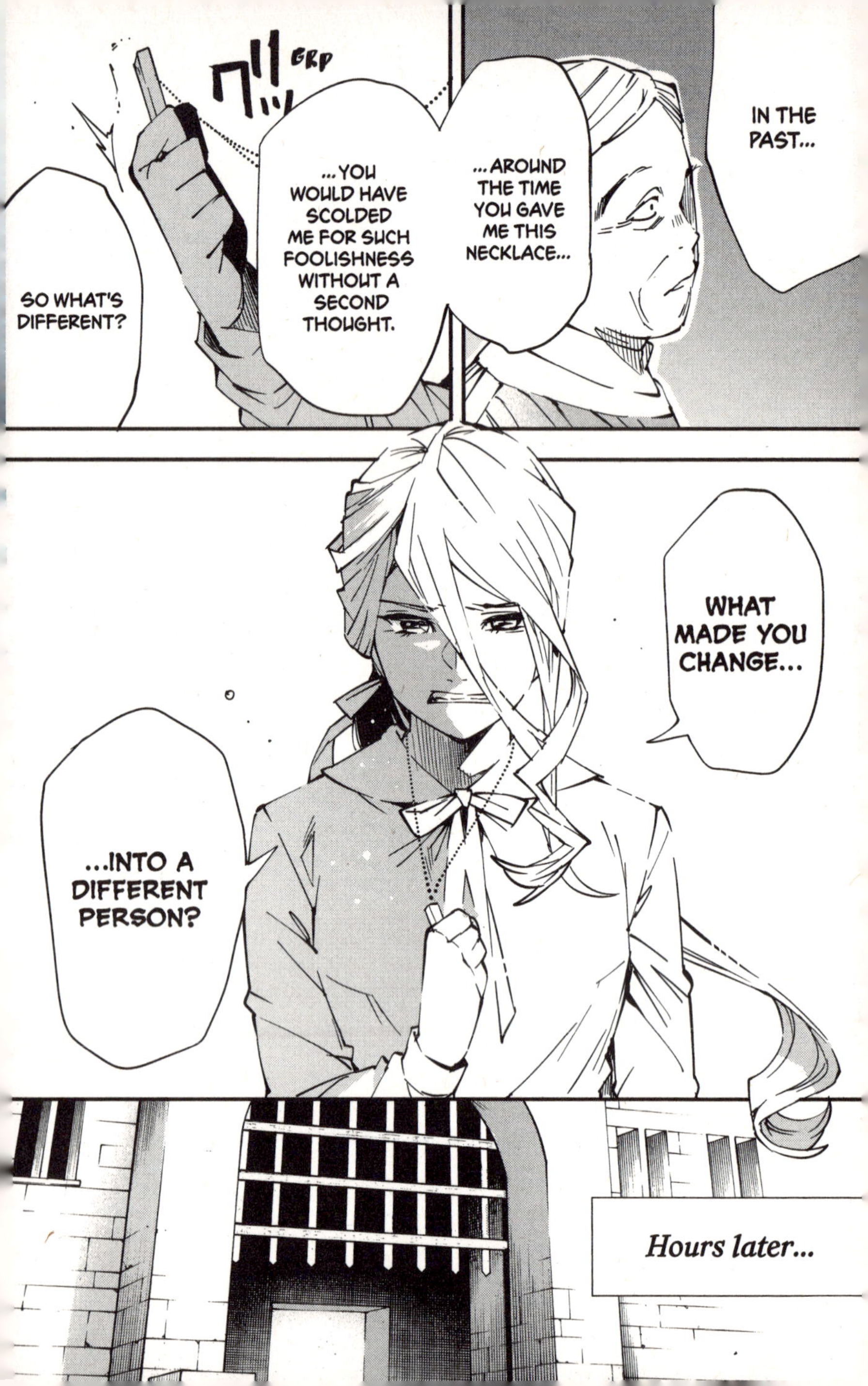
IN THE PAST...
...AROUND THE TIME YOU GAVE ME THIS NECKLACE...
...YOU WOULD HAVE SCOLDED ME FOR SUCH FOOLISHNESS WITHOUT A SECOND THOUGHT.
GRP
SO WHAT'S DIFFERENT?
WHAT MADE YOU CHANGE...
...INTO A DIFFERENT PERSON?
Hours later...

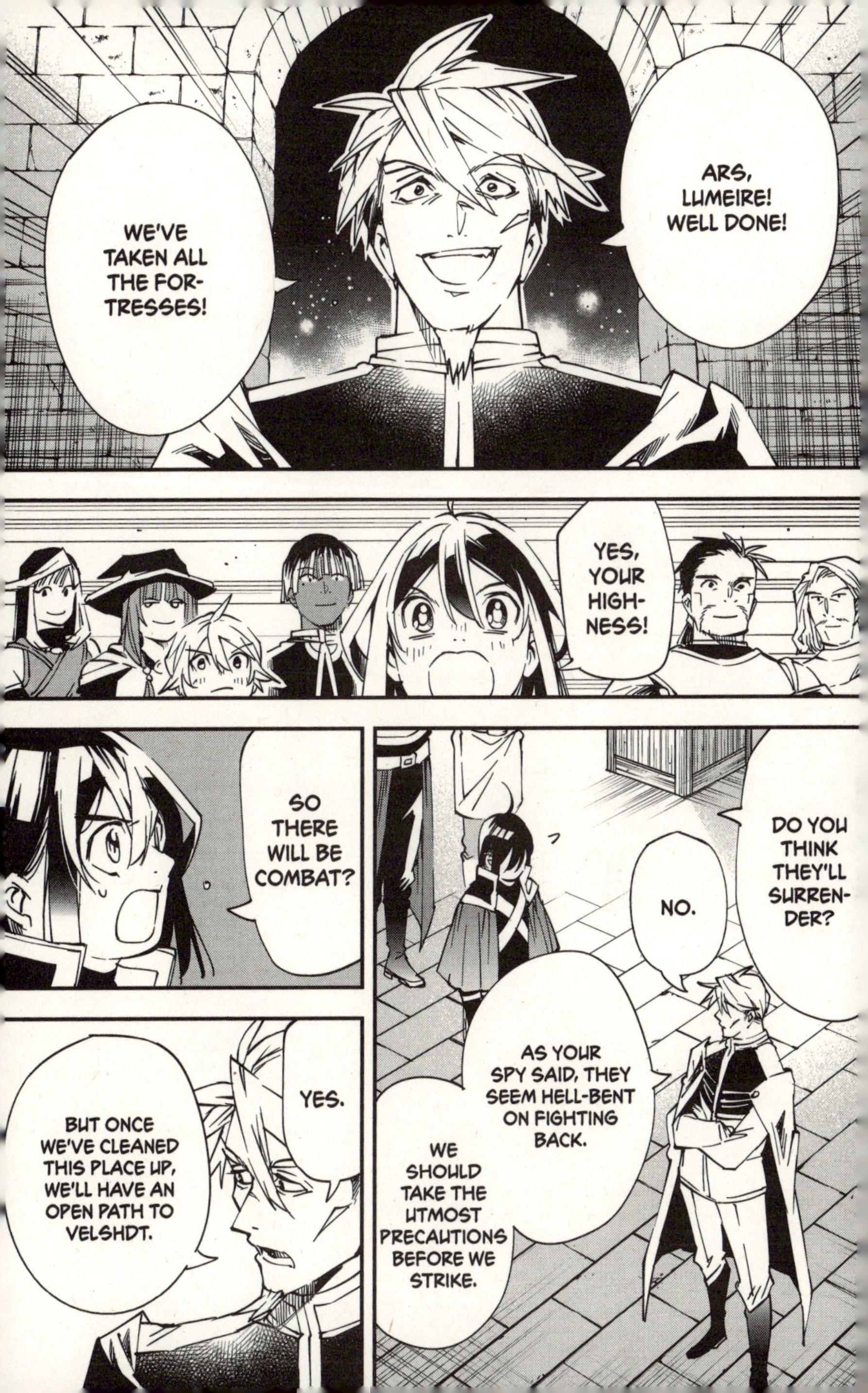
ARS, LUMEIRE! WELL DONE!
WE'VE TAKEN ALL THE FORTRESSES!
YES, YOUR HIGHNESS!
DO YOU THINK THEY'LL SURRENDER?
NO.
AS YOUR SPY SAID, THEY SEEM HELL-BENT ON FIGHTING BACK.
WE SHOULD TAKE THE UTMOST PRECAUTIONS BEFORE WE STRIKE.
SO THERE WILL BE COMBAT?
YES.
BUT ONCE WE'VE CLEANED THIS PLACE UP, WE'LL HAVE AN OPEN PATH TO VELSHDT.

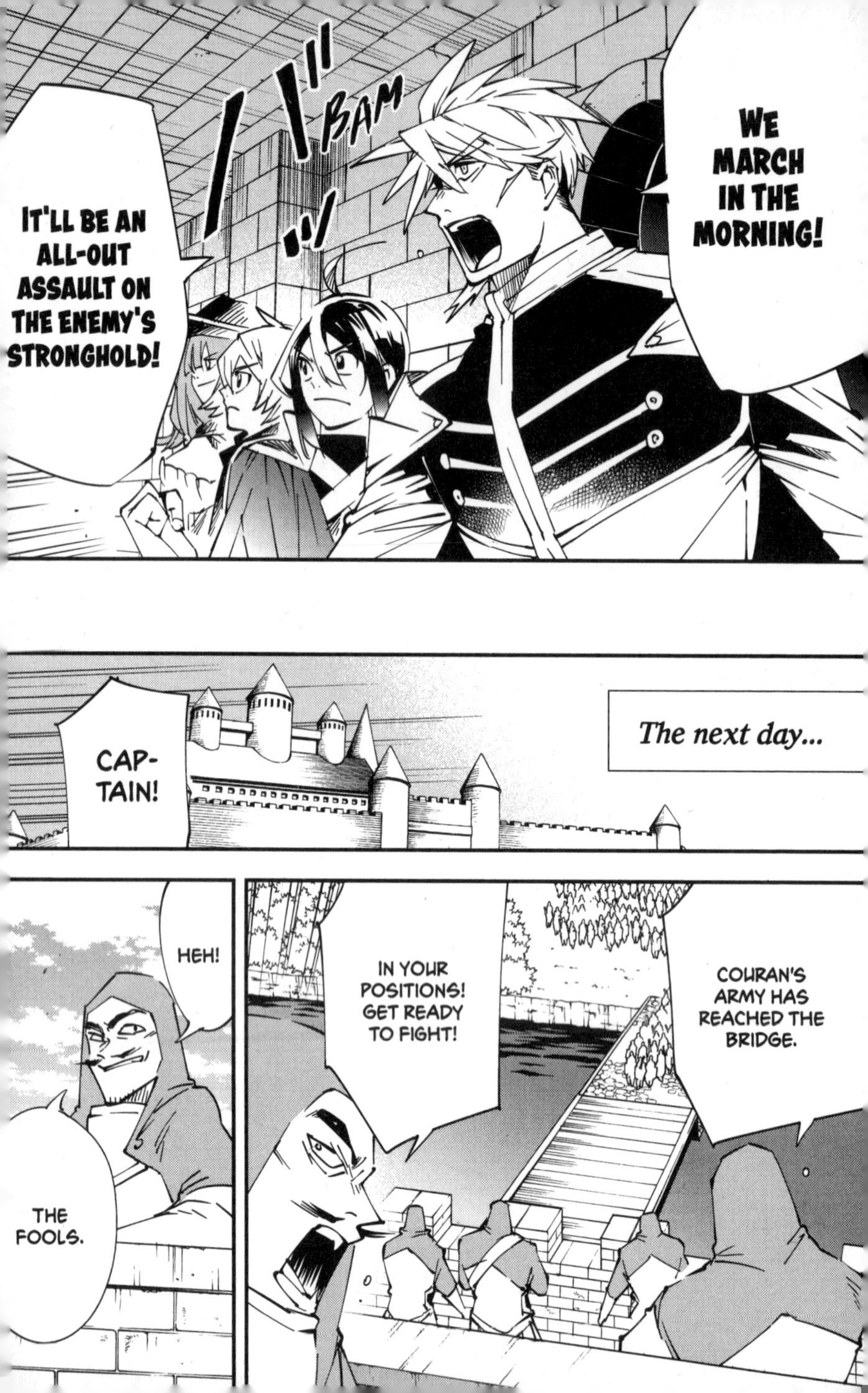
WE MARCH IN THE MORNING!
BAM
IT'LL BE AN ALL-OUT ASSAULT ON THE ENEMY'S STRONGHOLD!
The next day...
CAP-TAIN!
COURAN'S ARMY HAS REACHED THE BRIDGE.
IN YOUR POSITIONS! GET READY TO FIGHT!
HEH!
THE FOOLS.

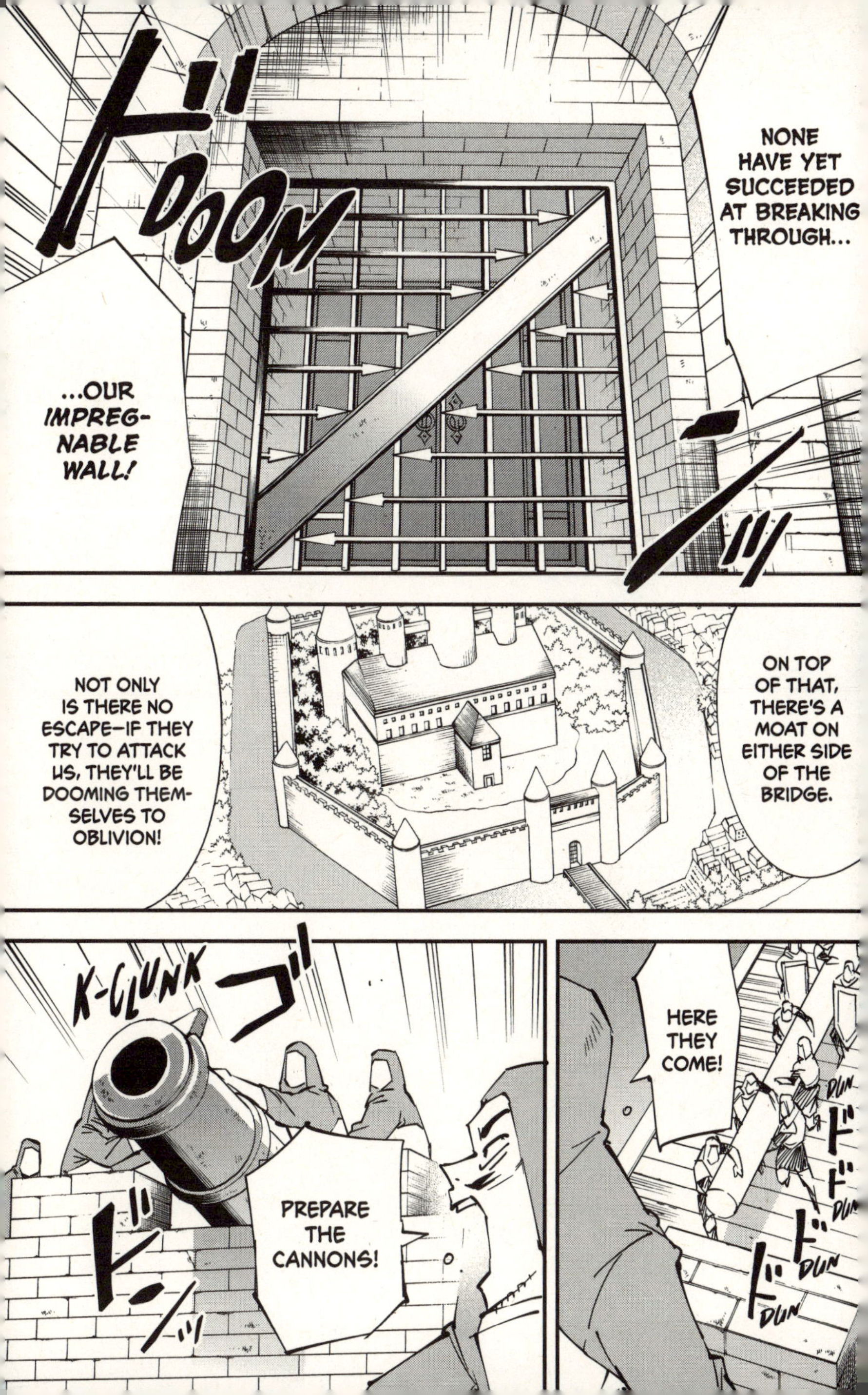
DOOM
NONE HAVE YET SUCCEEDED AT BREAKING THROUGH...
...OUR IMPREG-NABLE WALL!
ON TOP OF THAT, THERE'S A MOAT ON EITHER SIDE OF THE BRIDGE.
NOT ONLY IS THERE NO ESCAPE—IF THEY TRY TO ATTACK US, THEY'LL BE DOOMING THEM-SELVES TO OBLIVION!
HERE THEY COME!
DUN DUN DUN DUN
K-CLUNK
PREPARE THE CANNONS!

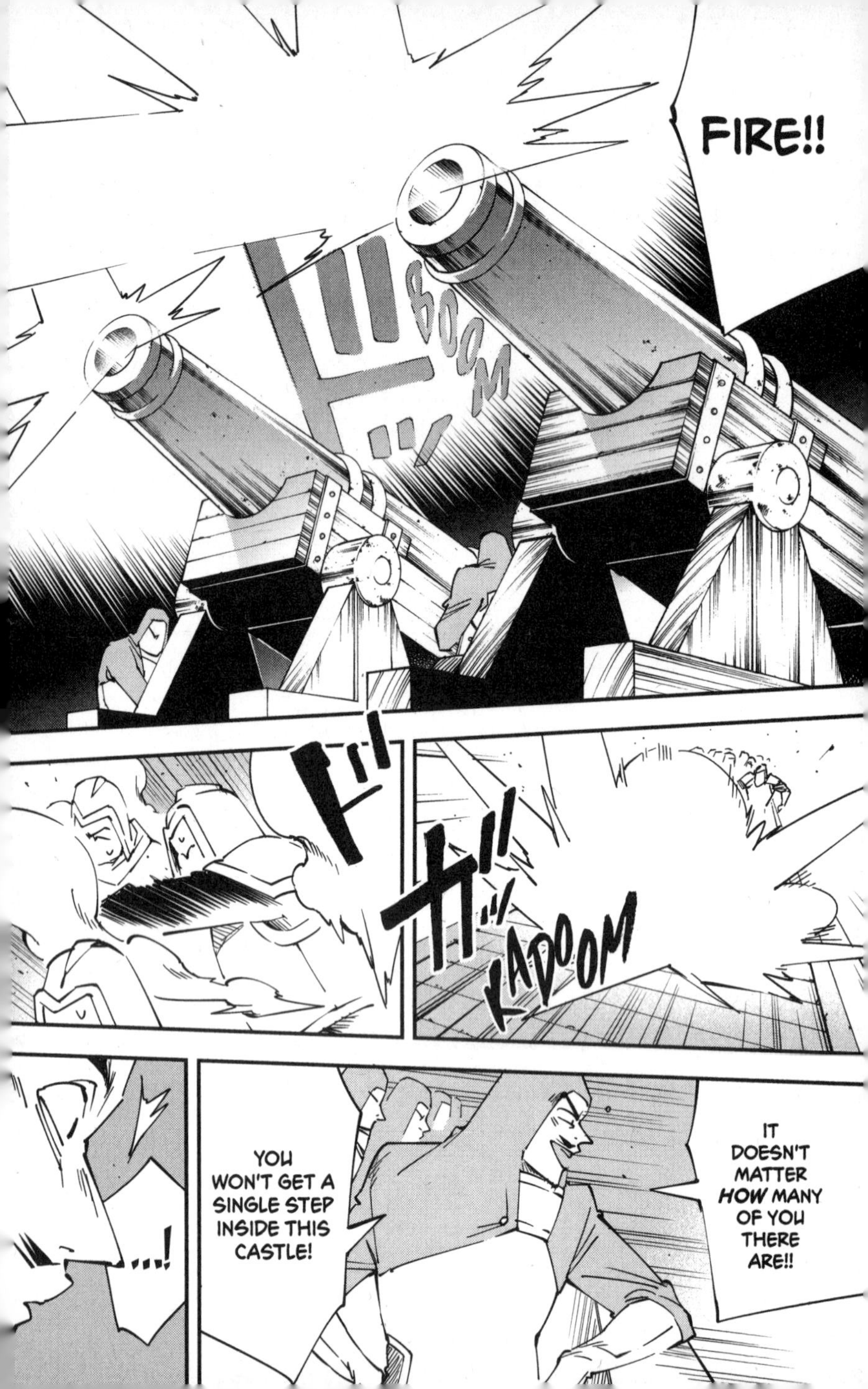
FIRE!!
BOOM
KADOOM
IT DOESN'T MATTER *HOW* MANY OF YOU THERE ARE!!
YOU WON'T GET A SINGLE STEP INSIDE THIS CASTLE!
...!

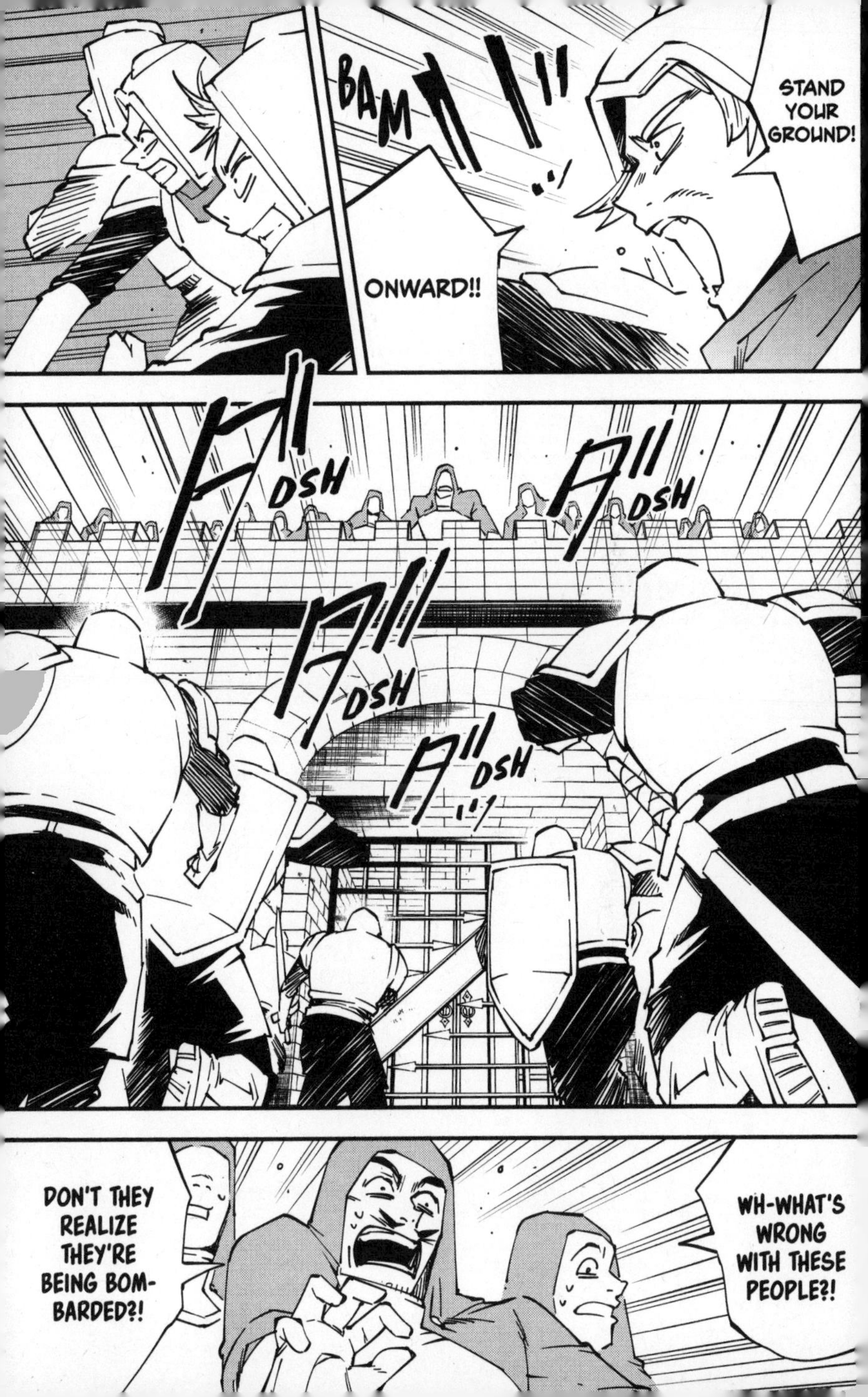
STAND YOUR GROUND!
BAM
ONWARD!!
DSH
DSH
DSH
DSH
WH-WHAT'S WRONG WITH THESE PEOPLE?!
DON'T THEY REALIZE THEY'RE BEING BOM-BARDED?!

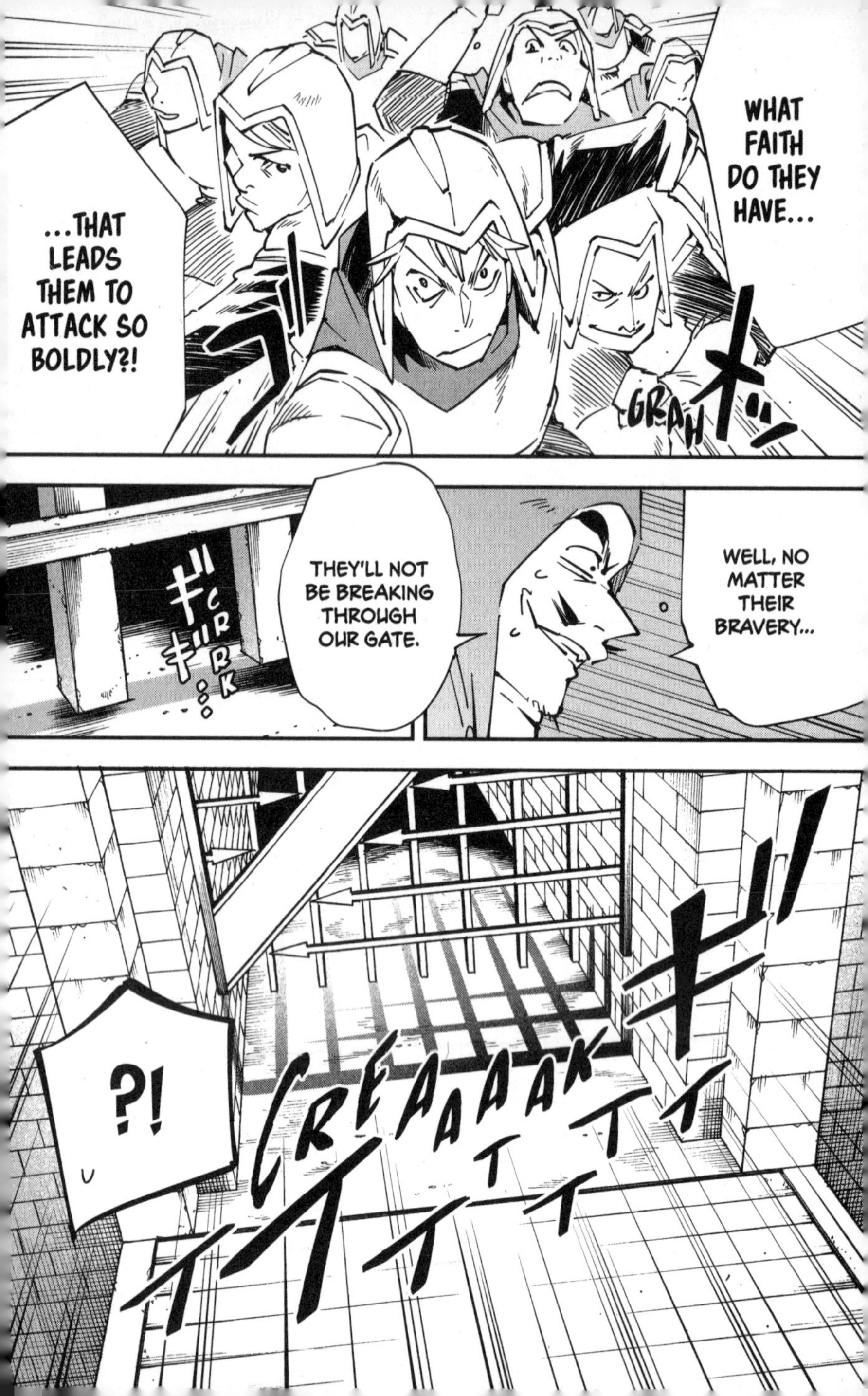
WHAT FAITH DO THEY HAVE...
...THAT LEADS THEM TO ATTACK SO BOLDLY?!
GRAH
WELL, NO MATTER THEIR BRAVERY...
THEY'LL NOT BE BREAKING THROUGH OUR GATE.
CRRK
CREAAAAK
?!

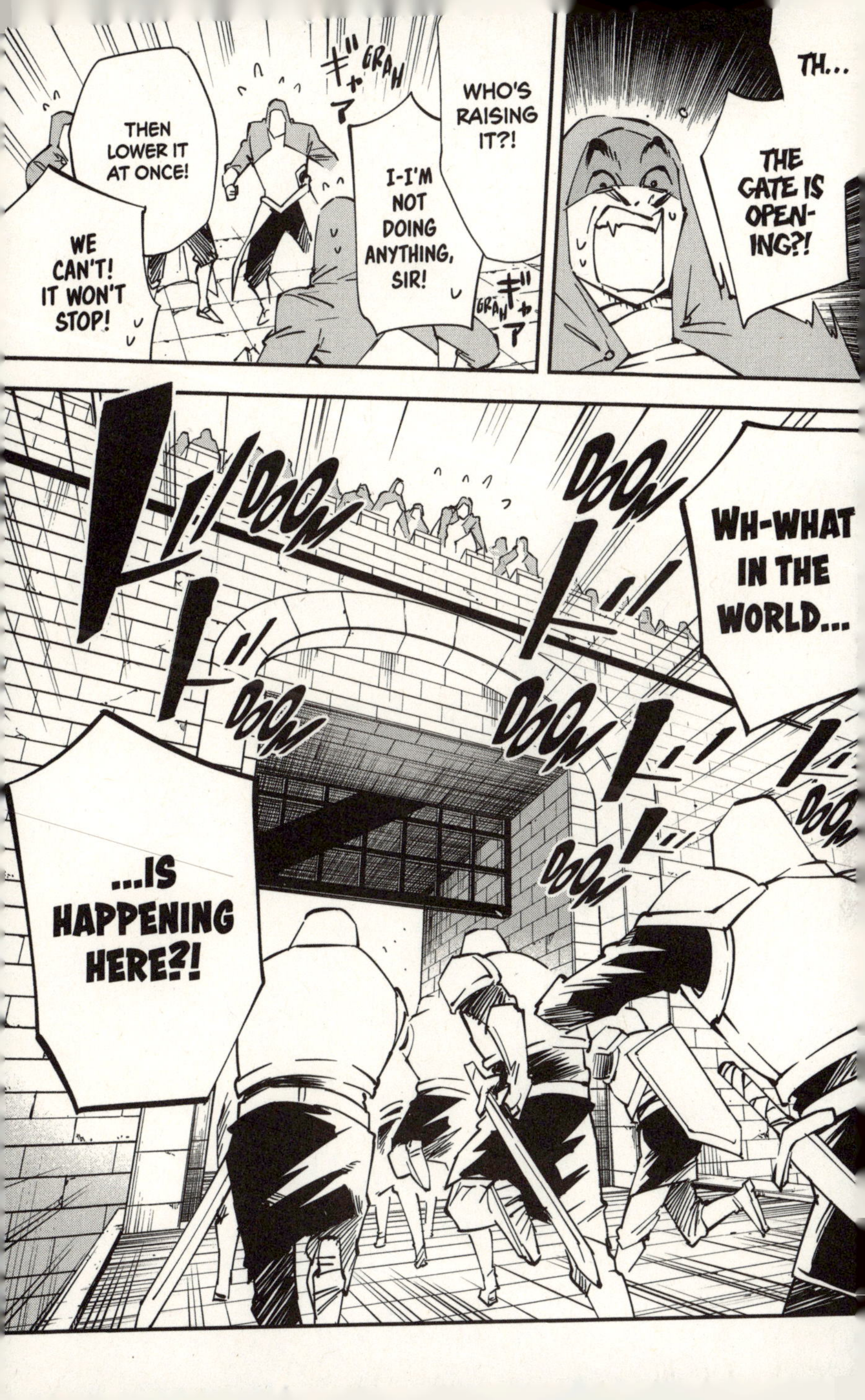
TH...
THE GATE IS OPEN-ING?!
WHO'S RAISING IT?!
ギャア GRAH
I-I'M NOT DOING ANYTHING, SIR!
ギャア GRAH
THEN LOWER IT AT ONCE!
WE CAN'T! IT WON'T STOP!
WH-WHAT IN THE WORLD...
DOOM
DOOM
DOOM
DOOM
DOOM
DOOM
...IS HAPPENING HERE?!

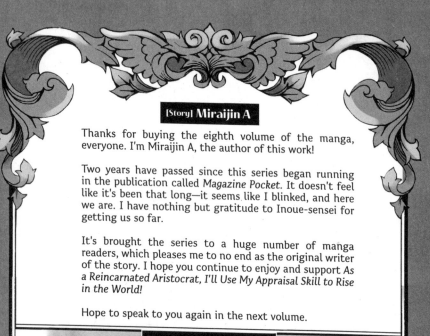

[Story] Miraijin A

Thanks for buying the eighth volume of the manga, everyone. I'm Miraijin A, the author of this work!

Two years have passed since this series began running in the publication called *Magazine Pocket*. It doesn't feel like it's been that long—it seems like I blinked, and here we are. I have nothing but gratitude to Inoue-sensei for getting us so far.

It's brought the series to a huge number of manga readers, which pleases me to no end as the original writer of the story. I hope you continue to enjoy and support *As a Reincarnated Aristocrat, I'll Use My Appraisal Skill to Rise in the World!*

Hope to speak to you again in the next volume.

[Character Design] jimmy

Congratulations on volume eight of the manga!

The master/apprentice duo! They're the best...

jimmy

Rosell Kischa - Age 8 ♂

Stats

	CURRENT	MAX
Command	40	88
Prowess	15	32
Intellect	88	109
Diplomacy	50	95

Ambition	21

Aptitude

Fighter	D	Cavalier	D	Archer	C
Mage	C	Engineer	A	Armorer	A
Mariner	C	Pilot	A	Tactician	S

A Kodansha Trade Paperback Original

As a Reincarnated Aristocrat, I'll Use My Appraisal Skill to Rise in the World 8 copyright © 2022 Miraijin A/Natsumi Inoue/jimmy
English translation copyright © 2023 Miraijin A/Natsumi Inoue/jimmy

Published in the United States by
Kodansha USA Publishing, LLC, New York.

Publication rights for this English edition arranged through
Kodansha Ltd., Tokyo.

First published in Japan in 2022 by Kodansha Ltd., Tokyo
as *Tensei kizoku, kantei sukiru de nariagaru*, volume 8.

ISBN 978-1-64651-832-6

Printed in the United States of America.

9 8 7 6 5 4 3 2 1

Translation: Stephen Paul
Lettering: Nicole Roderick
Editing: Michal Zuckerman
Kodansha USA Publishing edition cover design by Pekka Luhtala

Publisher: Kiichiro Sugawara

Director of Publishing Services: Ben Applegate
Director of Publishing Operations: Dave Barrett
Publishing Services Managing Editorial Assistant: Grace Chen
Production Manager: Claire Kerker

KODANSHA.US

KODANSHA